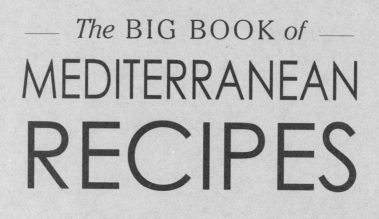

The BIG BOOK *of*

MEDITERRANEAN
RECIPES

The BIG BOOK of
MEDITERRANEAN
RECIPES

More Than 500 Recipes for Healthy and Flavorful Meals

Peter Minaki

Adamsmedia
Avon, Massachusetts

Published by
Adams Media, a division of F+W Media, Inc.
57 Littlefield Street, Avon, MA 02322. U.S.A.
www.adamsmedia.com

Contains material adapted and abridged from *The Everything® Mediterranean Cookbook, 2nd Edition* by Peter
Minaki, copyright © 2013, 2003 by F+W Media, Inc., ISBN 10: 1-4405-6855-3, ISBN 13: 978-1-4405-6855-8; *The
Everything® Mediterranean Diet Book* by Connie Diekman, MEd, RD, LD, FADA and Sam Sotiropoulos,
copyright © 2010 by F+W Media, Inc., ISBN 10: 1-4405-0674-4, ISBN 13: 978-1-4405-0674-1; *The Everything®
Mediterranean Cookbook, 1st Edition* by Dawn Altomari-Rathjen, LPN, BPS and Jennifer M. Bendelius, MS, RD,
copyright © 2003 by F+W Media, Inc., ISBN 10: 1-58062-869-9, ISBN 13: 978-1-58062-869-3.

ISBN 10: 1-4405-7950-4
ISBN 13: 978-1-4405-7950-9
eISBN 10: 1-4405-7951-2
eISBN 13: 978-1-4405-7951-6

Printed in the United States of America.

10 9 8 7 6 5 4 3 2 1

Many of the designations used by manufacturers and sellers to distinguish their product are claimed as
trademarks. Where those designations appear in this book and F+W Media, Inc. was aware of a trademark
claim, the designations have been printed with initial capital letters.

Always follow safety and commonsense cooking protocol while using kitchen utensils, operating ovens and
stoves, and handling uncooked food. If children are assisting in the preparation of any recipe, they should
always be supervised by an adult.

Cover design by Stephanie Hannus.
Cover image © 123RF/Angel Luis Simon Martin.

This book is available at quantity discounts for bulk purchases.
For information, please call 1-800-289-0963.

CONTENTS

4 Appetizers and Sides 111

7 Vegetable and Legume Entrées 299

8 Lamb, Beef, and Pork Entrées 337

9 Poultry Entrées 373

10 Fish and Seafood Entrées 407

11 Desserts and Drinks 447

INTRODUCTION

SPANAKOTYROPITA. LAMB EXOHIKO. BAKLAVA.

Delicious, healthy Mediterranean dishes like these have been served for generations and continue to delight those who want to eat well *and* live well, today. Focused mostly on the consumption of fruits, vegetables, legumes, and grains along with healthy lean proteins such as fish and seafood, the Mediterranean diet has its origins in ancient Greece, but has grown to include dishes from southern Italy, Provence, Spain, Portugal, Turkey, Cyprus, the Middle East, and North Africa. All these cuisines share seasonal, locally grown foods that are prepared simply and are full of flavor.

Whether you're looking to expand your repertoire of these amazing dishes or are just starting to try the Mediterranean diet, in *The Big Book of Mediterranean Recipes* you'll find more than 500 recipes—ranging from Olive Bread to Sage-Ricotta Chicken Breasts to Octopus Stifado—that represent many regions of the Mediterranean. These recipes will take you from breakfast and brunch to lunch and dinner with snacks, sides, and appetizers in between. You'll find many healthy vegetarian, vegan, dairy-free, and gluten-free recipes as well as recipes for fish, seafood, and meat dishes. You'll also find slow-cooked recipes that are perfect when you and your family have a busy week. Whether you're looking for a quick snack, an easy weeknight meal, a decadent dessert, or a special occasion dinner, this book has something for you, your family, and your friends.

People in the Mediterranean have eaten like this for generations and do not see it as a fad or trend; it is a way of life. And these recipes aren't just good, they're good for you, too. Many of the healthy recipes included in this book use olive oil, the cornerstone of the Mediterranean diet. Olive oil should be your preferred oil in the kitchen; use it in salads, cooking, and even frying. Studies have shown that cooking with olive oil can deter heart disease, diabetes, Alzheimer's, and some cancers. In addition to being good for you, olive oil helps make cooked dishes and salads more flavorful, especially when mixed in with citrus juices and an array of herbs.

The health benefits of following this diet aren't just from *what* you eat, but *how* you eat. In the Mediterranean, the main meal of day is lunch; dinner is usually a light meal. Eating one's main meal during the day allows the body time to properly digest the food and burn calories more efficiently for the rest of the day. This allows you to indulge a little without worrying about putting on extra pounds. And once you begin to make these amazing recipes, you won't be able to stop indulging!

To keep mealtime interesting, feel free to experiment with these recipes. Try adding your favorite herbs and spices to your food. If you prefer one kind of cheese to another, try it in the recipe. You'll see that many recipes have specific measurements for salt and pepper, but again, experiment and add as much or as little as you want or need. In addition, you won't find many cream sauces in this book—but if you wish to add some richness to a dish, just add a dollop or two of strained Homemade Greek Yogurt in place of cream. Whatever you do, have fun with your food and make it your own. And don't worry about finding the ingredients used throughout this book—most can be found in your local supermarket or in Mediterranean specialty stores.

The Mediterranean diet is one of the oldest ways of eating and living. How could it not be, with its reliance on local, seasonal ingredients that are prepared so simply—and with such a focus on extraordinary taste? Get ready to try the more than 500 recipes in this book and experience the Mediterranean diet in a way you never have before. Enjoy.

CHAPTER 1

BREAKFAST AND BRUNCH

MUSHROOM STRAPATSATHA WITH HALLOUMI AND CRISPY BACON

There are so many mushroom varieties. Be creative and mix them up in this recipe.

Serves 4

¼ cup plus 2 tablespoons extra-virgin olive oil, divided

⅓ cup chopped onions or scallions

1 clove garlic, peeled and minced

1 cup sliced cremini mushrooms

1 teaspoon salt, divided

½ teaspoon pepper, divided

1 cup sliced oyster mushrooms

4 (¼-inch) slices halloumi cheese, roughly chopped

8 large eggs, beaten

¼ cup heavy cream or evaporated milk

1 teaspoon fresh thyme leaves

1 teaspoon chopped fresh tarragon

4 strips crispy cooked bacon, crumbled and divided

2 tablespoons chopped fresh chives

1 cup jarred or homemade salsa

1. In a large skillet over medium heat, add ¼ cup oil and heat for 30 seconds. Add onions and garlic and cook for 5 minutes or until onions are softened. Add cremini mushrooms and season with ½ teaspoon salt and ¼ teaspoon pepper. Cook for 5 minutes or until the mushrooms are lightly browned. Add the oyster mushrooms and cook for 2 minutes. Stir in the halloumi and cook for 1 more minute.

2. In a medium bowl, whisk together eggs, cream or milk, thyme, tarragon, and the remaining salt and pepper. Add the eggs to the mushrooms and stir until the eggs are scrambled. Stir in bacon.

3. Serve topped with chives and salsa. Drizzle with remaining oil and serve immediately.

Mushrooms

Mushrooms are a great immune system booster. Not only are they high in vitamin B and low in calories, they taste meaty and nutty and are a staple in vegetarian and Mediterranean kitchens.

BREAKFAST BAKLAVA FRENCH TOAST

Use day-old bread like challah or Tsoureki (Greek Easter Bread) (see recipe in Chapter 3) to make this French toast.

Serves 2

3 large eggs

2 tablespoons orange juice

1 teaspoon grated orange zest

⅛ teaspoon vanilla extract

¼ cup plus 1 tablespoon honey, divided

2 tablespoons whole milk

1¼ teaspoons ground cinnamon, divided

¼ cup walnuts

¼ cup blanched almonds

¼ teaspoon ground cloves

1 tablespoon sugar

2 tablespoons white bread crumbs or ground melba toast

4 slices bread

2 tablespoons unsalted butter

1 teaspoon confectioners' sugar

1. In a large bowl, whisk together eggs, orange juice, zest, vanilla, ¼ cup honey, milk, and ½ teaspoon cinnamon. Reserve.

2. Put the walnuts and almonds into a food processor, and pulse until they are finely crumbled. Transfer the nuts to a bowl and add the cloves, ½ teaspoon cinnamon, sugar, and bread crumbs. Stir to combine.

3. Sandwich half of the walnut-and-almond mixture between 2 slices of bread. Repeat with the remaining 2 slices. Carefully dunk both sides of the sandwiches into the egg mixture. Make sure the egg mixture soaks into the bread.

4. Add the butter to a large skillet over medium heat, and heat for 30 seconds. Add the sandwiches and fry for 2 minutes per side or until golden.

5. Carefully cut the French toasts diagonally and serve them dusted with confectioners' sugar.

6. Drizzle the tops with the remaining honey and sprinkle with ¼ teaspoon cinnamon. Serve immediately.

TIGANITES

Tiganites is the Greek equivalent of pancakes. Instead of maple syrup, drizzle with honey or petimezi, a grape molasses found in Greek, Turkish, and Middle Eastern shops.

Serves 4

2 cups all-purpose flour

2 tablespoons sugar

2 teaspoons baking powder

¾ teaspoon salt

2 large eggs

2 cups whole milk

¼ cup vegetable oil

4 tablespoons unsalted butter, divided

¼ cup honey or petimezi (grape molasses)

1. In a medium bowl, combine flour, sugar, baking powder, and salt.

2. In another medium bowl, whisk together eggs, milk, and oil.

3. Add the dry ingredients to the wet ingredients and stir to combine.

4. In a large skillet over medium heat, add 2 tablespoons butter and heat for 30 seconds. To make a pancake, pour ¼ cup of batter into the pan. Cook until you see bubbles forming on the top side of the pancake (about 2 minutes), then flip the pancake over and cook for another 2 minutes. Remove the pancake from the pan and keep warm. Repeat with the remaining batter.

5. Serve hot topped with remaining butter and honey.

Petimezi

Petimezi is an ancient Greek grape molasses made by reducing grape must into thick syrup. It can be found in all Greek, Turkish, or Middle Eastern grocers. Try it on toast or as a topping for ice cream.

BEET AND WALNUT MUFFINS

Greeks use beets in both savory and sweet dishes. This quirky muffin recipe will have your guests guessing!

Serves 12

2 cups plus ¼ cup all-purpose flour, divided

1 tablespoon baking powder

¾ cup sugar

½ teaspoon salt

2 teaspoons ground cinnamon

2 large eggs, beaten

1 cup whole milk

¼ cup extra-virgin olive oil

2 cups grated beets, peeled

¾ cup chopped walnuts

1. In a medium bowl, combine 2 cups flour, baking powder, sugar, salt, and cinnamon. In another medium bowl, whisk together eggs, milk, and oil.

2. In another medium bowl, combine beets, walnuts, and the remaining flour. Toss to combine the ingredients, and to coat the beets and walnuts in flour.

3. Preheat the oven to 375°F. Add the wet ingredients to the dry ingredients, and stir to combine. Stir in the walnuts and beets. Don't overmix the batter or the muffins will be tough.

4. Line a 12-muffin tin with paper cups and divide the batter evenly among the 12 cups. Bake on the middle rack 15–20 minutes. Stick a toothpick into a muffin; if the toothpick comes out clean, the muffins are done.

5. Transfer the muffins to a cooling rack. Allow them to cool before removing them from the pan and serving.

Sinking Feeling

Tossing solid ingredients (chocolate chips, fruits, or nuts) in a little flour before adding them to a batter ensures they do not sink to the bottom of the muffins while baking. Try this trick with your next batch.

FIG JAM

If you're lucky enough to find ripe figs, try this easy recipe and make some delicious fig jam. Preserving this summer fruit makes the cold months bearable.

Makes 6 cups

65–70 medium ripe figs, stems removed and halved

2 cups granulated sugar

1 cup water

2 teaspoons vanilla extract

5 fresh basil leaves

1½ teaspoons grated lemon zest

1 tablespoon fresh lemon juice

1. In a large pot over medium-high heat, add figs, sugar, water, and vanilla. Bring the water to a boil, then reduce the heat to medium-low and cook for 45 minutes. Remove the pot from the heat and allow the jam to cool completely (about 4 hours). Mash the figs to the desired consistency—chunky or smooth.

2. Return the pot to the stove over low heat for 5 minutes. Add basil leaves and simmer 5–6 minutes. Add the lemon zest and juice and simmer another 5–6 minutes. Take the pot off the heat and remove the basil leaves. Again, let the jam cool completely.

3. Pour the jam into sterilized jars and seal them according to standard jarring procedures.

HOMEMADE GREEK YOGURT

Greeks have been making and consuming yogurt for thousands of years. Ignore all the yogurts in the grocery store and make your own.

Makes 16 cups

16 cups whole milk

½ cup plain full-fat yogurt (containing active live cultures)

1. Preheat the oven to 200°F. In a large pot over medium-high heat, add the milk and bring it to a boil. Reduce the heat to medium-low and simmer for 15 minutes, and then take the pot off the heat. Do not cover the pot.

2. Using a candy thermometer, allow the milk to cool to 110°F–115°F. When you have reached the desired temperature, combine ½ cup of warm milk with yogurt in a small bowl. Stir to combine. Add the milk and yogurt back to the pot and stir to combine.

3. Turn off the oven. Ladle the milk-yogurt mixture into storage containers (plastic containers are okay because the oven is at a low temperature) and place on a baking tray in the oven. The yogurt will set in 8–12 hours (check it after 8 hours).

4. Refrigerate the yogurt for at least 4 hours, but preferably overnight. This yogurt will keep in the refrigerator for up to 2 weeks.

Why You Should Eat More Yogurt

Yogurt is easier to digest than milk, and it contributes to good colon health. This immunity booster is high in protein and rich in calcium, and aids in the absorption of B vitamins. Eat yogurt every day!

STRAPATSATHA

Strapatsatha is a dish brought to Greece by the Sephardic Jews from Spain. It's a loose omelet of tomatoes and feta. There are many variations of this classic dish.

Serves 4

¼ cup extra-virgin olive oil

⅔ cup sliced chorizo sausage

4 large ripe tomatoes, passed through a box grater

½ cup diced sweet banana pepper

3 scallions, ends trimmed and sliced

1 cup crumbled feta cheese

8 large eggs, beaten

½ teaspoon pepper

1. Add oil to a large skillet over medium-high heat, and heat for 30 seconds. Add sausage and cook for 2 minutes or until it browns. With a slotted spoon, remove the sausage from the skillet and reserve. Take the skillet off the heat and let it cool for 5 minutes.

2. Return the skillet to a medium heat and add the tomatoes. Cook for 5 minutes or until most of the water is evaporated. Add the peppers and scallions, and cook for 2 more minutes. Add the feta and cook for 1 minute.

3. Add the eggs, pepper, and cooked sausage. Stir the eggs to scramble them, cooking them until they form a loose omelet. Serve immediately or warm.

CHEESE PIES IN YOGURT PASTRY

These crescent-shaped pies are ideal for family members who are rushed in the morning. They can grab a couple of pies and eat on the go!

Serves 10

2 large eggs, divided

½ cup extra-virgin olive oil

¾ cup plain yogurt

1 teaspoon salt

3½ cups self-rising flour, sifted

1 cup crumbled feta cheese

1 cup ricotta cheese

¼ cup grated Graviera (or Gruyère) cheese

½ teaspoon grated fresh nutmeg

¼ teaspoon pepper

1 tablespoon finely chopped fresh mint

1 large egg yolk

1 tablespoon cream

½ cup sesame seeds

1. In a large bowl, whisk together 1 egg, the oil, and yogurt. Combine the salt and flour in another bowl. Using a wooden spoon, stir the dry ingredients into the wet ingredients to form dough. Transfer the dough onto a work surface and knead it until all the flour is incorporated. The dough should be smooth, pliable, and only slightly sticky. Wrap dough in plastic wrap and set it aside.

2. Preheat the oven to 350°F. In a large bowl, combine the remaining egg, the cheeses, nutmeg, pepper, and mint. Mash and mix together with a wooden spoon.

3. Place the dough on a lightly floured work surface and roll it out into a long thin log. Cut the dough into egg-size pieces (you should get twenty). Roll a dough piece into a ball and then flatten it with the palm of your hand into a 3-inch-thin disc. Add 1 tablespoon cheese filling in the middle of the dough. Fold half of the dough over the filling to create a crescent shape. Pinch the ends to seal the cheese into the dough. Place the pie on a parchment-lined baking sheet, and repeat the process with the remaining dough and cheese filling.

4. In a small bowl, whisk together the egg yolk and cream. Brush the top of each pie with the egg-cream mixture. Sprinkle the tops with sesame seeds.

5. Bake the pies on the middle rack for 30 minutes or until they are golden. Serve them warm or at room temperature. You can store pies in a container in the refrigerator for up to 5 days.

PAXIMADIA

Paximadia are twice-baked cookies that are similar to Italian biscotti. They were originally made in ancient Greece for sailors, to last their entire voyage. Serve them with tea or coffee for dunking.

Makes 36

3 large eggs, beaten

1½ cups vegetable oil

1½ cups sugar

2 teaspoons vanilla extract

1 teaspoon almond extract

4 cups all-purpose flour

1 teaspoon baking powder

1 cup chopped almonds

1 cup sesame seeds

1. Preheat the oven to 350°F. In a large bowl, whisk together eggs, oil, sugar, and extracts. Combine the flour, baking powder, and almonds and then stir the mixture into the wet ingredients until it forms a soft dough.

2. Divide the dough and form three equal loaves (9" × 3"). Place equal amounts of the sesame seeds on three pieces of wax paper. Wrap the paper around each loaf so the sesame seeds coat the entire loaf. Repeat with the remaining loaves.

3. Place the loaves on a parchment paper–lined baking sheet. Bake on the middle rack for 20 minutes. Take the baking sheet out of the oven and reduce the temperature to 300°F.

4. Cool the loaves for 2 minutes. Slice each loaf along its width into ¾-inch slices with a serrated knife. Lay the slices flat on the baking sheet and bake them for another 10 minutes. Turn off the oven, but leave the paximadia in the oven for another 30 minutes.

5. Store in a sealed container for up to 6 months.

LENTEN PAXIMADIA

These paximadia are perfect for fasting during Lent because there are no eggs in this recipe.

Makes 36

½ cup fresh orange juice

1 tablespoon grated orange zest

¾ cup vegetable oil

½ cup dry white wine

1½ teaspoons ground cinnamon

¼ teaspoon ground cloves

¾ cup sugar

¼ teaspoon baking soda

1½ tablespoons baking powder

1 cup chopped almonds

3 cups all-purpose flour

1 cup sesame seeds

1. Preheat the oven to 350°F. Add the orange juice, zest, oil, wine, cinnamon, cloves, sugar, baking soda, and baking powder to a food processor and process until the ingredients are well incorporated. In a large bowl, stir together the almonds and flour. Pour the orange juice mixture into the flour mixture and, using a wooden spoon, combine until it forms a soft dough.

2. Divide the dough and form three equal loaves (9" × 3"). Place equal amounts of sesame seeds on three pieces of wax paper. Wrap the paper around each loaf so the sesame seeds coat the entire loaf. Repeat with the remaining loaves.

3. Place the loaves on a parchment paper–lined baking sheet. Bake on the middle rack for 20 minutes. Take the baking sheet out of the oven and reduce the oven to 300°F.

4. Cool the loaves for 2 minutes. Slice each loaf along its width into ¾-inch slices with a serrated knife. Lay the slices flat on the baking sheet, and bake them for another 10 minutes. Turn off the oven, but leave the paximadia in the oven for another 30 minutes.

5. Store them in a sealed container for up to 6 months.

Orthodox Lenten Fasting

During the Christian Orthodox fasting period (Lent), no meat or meat products are to be eaten; that means no animals with blood, and no dairy or eggs. However, olive oil, legumes, vegetables, fruits, grains, and shellfish and seafood are allowed.

PAXIMADIA WITH FIGS, STAR ANISE, AND WALNUTS

Star anise is a spice that is similar to anise, but it has a more floral scent and taste.

Serves 36

1 cup extra-virgin olive oil

2 teaspoons vanilla extract

4 tablespoons ground star anise

1 ounce ouzo

1 cup sugar

3 large eggs

4 cups all-purpose flour

1 tablespoon baking powder

1 cup chopped dry figs

1 cup chopped walnuts

2 tablespoons petimezi (grape molasses)
    diluted in 2 tablespoons warm water

1 cup sesame seeds

1. In a large bowl, whisk together oil, vanilla, star anise, ouzo, sugar, and eggs. In another bowl, combine the flour, baking powder, figs, and walnuts. Add the dry ingredients to the wet ingredients. Use a wooden spoon to combine the mixture until you form a soft dough.

2. Divide the dough and form three equal loaves (9" × 3"). Brush the tops of the loaves with the petimezi mixture. Place equal amounts of sesame seeds on three pieces of wax paper. Wrap a sheet of paper around each loaf so the sesame seeds coat the entire loaf. Repeat with the remaining loaves.

3. Place the loaves on a parchment paper–lined baking sheet. Bake them on the middle rack for 20 minutes. Take the baking sheet out of the oven and reduce the oven to 300°F.

4. Cool the loaves for 2 minutes. Slice each loaf along its width into ¾-inch slices with a serrated knife. Lay the slices flat on the baking sheet and bake for another 10 minutes. Turn off the oven, but leave the paximadia in the oven for another 30 minutes.

5. Store in a sealed container for up to 6 months.

BOUGATSA WITH CUSTARD FILLING

This is a special treat for breakfast. The delicious custard and crispy phyllo are best enjoyed with a Greek coffee.

Serves 12

2 cups melted unsalted butter, divided

¾ cup fine semolina flour

½ cup granulated sugar

1 teaspoon vanilla extract

2¾ cups whole milk

24 sheets phyllo (1 package)

½ cup confectioners' sugar

2 teaspoons ground cinnamon

1. In a deep, medium pot over medium heat, add ¼ cup butter, semolina, sugar, and vanilla. Stir and cook for 2 minutes or until the butter is absorbed and the semolina is golden but not browned.

2. Whisk in milk in a slow, steady stream until all the liquid is absorbed. Stir and cook for 3–4 minutes or until the custard has the texture of loose cream. Transfer the custard to a bowl and allow it to cool completely.

3. Preheat oven to 350°F. Take phyllo sheets out of the box and lay them flat. Cover with a lightly damp kitchen towel to keep them from drying out. You will work with one sheet at a time. Keep the remaining sheets covered. Take one phyllo sheet and lay it on a clean work surface; brush the phyllo with melted butter and cover it with another phyllo sheet. Brush the top of the second phyllo sheet with butter as well.

4. Place 3 tablespoons of custard in the center bottom third of the buttered phyllo sheets (about 2 inches from the edge). Fold the bottom 2 inches over the custard, and then fold the sides in toward the custard. Fold the phyllo up to form a package. Repeat with the remaining phyllo and custard.

5. Bake the phyllo packages on a baking sheet for 15–20 minutes or until golden. Allow them to cool. Dust them with confectioners' sugar and cinnamon before serving.

FRITTATA

This is the Italian version of quiche without a crust. You can also use leftover roasted potatoes in this dish (just omit the first roasting).

Serves 6

1 pound Idaho potatoes, peeled and sliced into large pieces

2 medium yellow peppers, stemmed, seeded, and sliced

2 medium red peppers, stemmed, seeded, and sliced

2 medium green peppers, stemmed, seeded, and sliced

1 large red onion, peeled and sliced

2 teaspoons extra-virgin olive oil

1 teaspoon salt, divided

½ teaspoon pepper, divided

3 large eggs

6 large egg whites

1 cup plain yogurt

1 cup whole milk

3 ounces fontina or Gouda cheese, grated

1 tablespoon chopped fresh oregano leaves

1. Preheat the oven to 375°F. Toss the potatoes, peppers, and onion in oil and place on a baking sheet. Season with ½ teaspoon salt and ¼ teaspoon pepper. Roast in the oven for 10 minutes.

2. In a medium baking dish, add roasted vegetables in one layer.

3. In a medium bowl, whisk eggs, egg whites, yogurt, milk, cheese, and remaining salt and pepper. Pour the egg mixture into the baking dish over the vegetables.

4. Bake until the eggs are completely set, approximately 30–45 minutes. Sprinkle with oregano and serve.

For the Meat Lover

If you think a breakfast just isn't breakfast without pork, consider adding chopped bacon, sausage, or ham to this recipe.

FIG, APRICOT, AND ALMOND GRANOLA

Cardamom is a wonderful earthy spice that lends a citrusy note to this granola.

Serves 16

Nonstick vegetable oil spray

⅓ cup vegetable oil

⅓ cup honey

2 tablespoons white sugar

1 teaspoon vanilla extract

4 cups old-fashioned oats

1¼ cups sliced almonds

½ cup chopped dried apricots

½ cup chopped dried figs

½ cup (packed) brown sugar

½ teaspoon salt

½ teaspoon ground cardamom

1. Preheat the oven to 300°F. Lightly spray two large baking sheets with nonstick spray.

2. In a small pot over medium heat, add oil, honey, sugar, and vanilla. Cook for 5 minutes or until the sugar is dissolved. Remove the pot from the heat and let it cool for 2 minutes.

3. In a large bowl, combine oats, almonds, apricots, figs, brown sugar, salt, and cardamom. Mix with your hands to combine.

4. Pour the hot liquid over the dry ingredients. Using your hands (if it is too hot, use a wooden spoon), toss the ingredients together to make sure everything is well coated. Spread the granola evenly over two baking sheets. Bake for 30 minutes (stirring every 10 minutes).

5. Let the granola cool completely on the baking sheets. This will allow the granola to harden before breaking it up into pieces. Store in an airtight container for up to 3 weeks.

GREEK YOGURT SMOOTHIE

Add whatever fruit you'd like to this smoothie. Use what is fresh and in season. Try blueberries, peaches, or kiwi.

Serves 4

2 cups Homemade Greek Yogurt (see recipe in this chapter)

2 cups orange or apple juice

2 large ripe bananas, peeled and chopped

1 cup fresh or frozen mango slices

½ cup fresh or frozen sliced strawberries

½ cup pineapple chunks

⅓ cup honey

1. Put all the ingredients into the food processor.

2. Process until smooth and all ingredients are well incorporated. Serve cool.

GREEK YOGURT WITH HONEY AND GRANOLA

Use store-bought granola in this recipe or try Fig, Apricot, and Almond Granola (see recipe in this chapter).

Serves 4

1⅓ cups Homemade Greek Yogurt (see recipe in this chapter)

1 cup granola

1 cup fresh berries (raspberries, blueberries, or strawberries)

½ cup honey

1. Divide the yogurt into four small bowls and top with granola and berries.

2. Drizzle honey over each bowl and serve.

GYPSY'S BREAKFAST

Like traveling Gypsies, this dish is very adaptable. Use your favorite sausage, vegetables, and cheese. This hearty breakfast goes well with a smoky Spanish chorizo.

Serves 8

1 cup diced cured sausage

¼ cup water

3 large potatoes, peeled and diced

1 large onion, peeled and sliced

1 large green bell pepper, stemmed, seeded, and sliced

1 large red bell pepper, stemmed, seeded, and sliced

1 teaspoon smoked paprika

¾ teaspoon salt, divided

½ teaspoon pepper

½ teaspoon fresh thyme leaves

1 cup grated Graviera or Gruyère cheese

4 tablespoons extra-virgin olive oil, divided

8 large eggs

1. In a large skillet over medium-high heat, add the sausage and water. Cook for 3 minutes or until the water evaporates and the sausage is crispy. Add the potatoes and stir to coat them in the sausage drippings. Reduce heat to medium and cook for another 5 minutes.

2. Add onions, peppers, and smoked paprika. Cook for 3 more minutes. Season with ½ teaspoon salt, pepper, and thyme. Reduce heat to medium-low and cook for 10–15 minutes or until the potatoes are fork-tender. Sprinkle them with cheese and take the pan off the heat. The residual heat will melt the cheese.

3. In another skillet, add 2 tablespoons oil and fry each egg to your liking (sunny-side up or over-easy). Season the eggs with the remaining salt.

4. To serve, place a scoop of the vegetables onto each plate and a fried egg on top. Drizzle with remaining oil. Serve hot.

BREAKFAST BRUSCHETTA

You will notice that it is not unusual for a Mediterranean breakfast dish to be dominated by vegetables.

Serves 4

½ loaf of Italian or French bread

½ cup extra-virgin olive oil

¼ cup pesto (see recipes in Chapter 2)

1 medium tomato

2 egg whites

2 whole eggs

¼ cup mozzarella cheese

1 Roasted Red Pepper (see recipe in Chapter 4)

1. Slice the bread into four ¾-inch lengthwise pieces. Brush one side of each with a bit of the oil; toast on grill. When that side is toasted, brush oil on the other side, flip, and toast that side.

2. Place the toasted bread on a sheet pan and spread with pesto. Peel and chop the tomato; combine it with the eggs. Dice the pepper and shred the cheese.

3. Heat the remaining oil in a sauté pan over medium heat; add the egg mixture and cook omelet style. Cut the omelet and place on the bread; top with cheese and pepper.

ROASTED POTATOES WITH VEGETABLES

This dish serves double duty as a treat for breakfast or as a side dish at dinner.

Serves 6

3 Idaho baking potatoes

1 sweet potato

3 carrots

1 yellow onion

½ pound button mushrooms

2 tablespoons olive oil

Kosher salt, to taste

Fresh-cracked black pepper, to taste

1. Preheat the oven to 400°F.

2. Large-dice the potatoes and carrots. Large-dice the onion. Trim off any discolored ends from the mushroom stems.

3. In a large bowl, mix together the olive oil, potatoes, onions, carrots, and mushrooms. Place them evenly in a roasting pan, and sprinkle with salt and pepper.

4. Roast the vegetables for 30–45 minutes, until tender. Serve warm.

RYE-PUMPERNICKEL STRATA WITH BLEU CHEESE

Savory breakfast is traditional in the Mediterranean. This dish is perfect to serve at brunch as well.

Serves 6

3 (1½-inch) slices seedless rye bread

3 (1½-inch) slices pumpernickel bread

½ teaspoon extra-virgin olive oil

2 whole eggs

6 egg whites

¼ cup skim milk

¼ cup plain nonfat yogurt

2 ounces bleu cheese

Fresh-cracked black pepper, to taste

1. Preheat the oven to 375°F.

2. Tear the bread into large pieces. Grease a 2-quart casserole pan with the oil.

3. In a large mixing bowl, beat the eggs and egg whites; add the milk, yogurt, and cheese. Place the bread pieces in the prepared casserole pan, then pour in the egg mixture. Bake for 40–50 minutes, until the mixture is set and the top is golden brown. To serve, cut into squares and season with pepper.

POLENTA

Polenta lends itself well to the incorporation of all of your favorite ingredients. Experiment!

Serves 6

1 cup skim milk

2 cups favorite stock (see recipes in Chapter 2)

½ cup cornmeal

¼ cup grated cheese (optional)

Fresh-cracked black pepper, to taste

Bring the milk and stock to a boil over medium heat in a saucepan. Slowly whisk in the cornmeal a bit at a time; stir frequently until cooked, approximately 15 minutes until mixture is the consistency of mashed potatoes. Remove from heat, add the cheese, and season with pepper.

FRUIT-STUFFED FRENCH TOAST

The rich eggy flavor of challah creates the rich profile of this dish.

Serves 6

½ teaspoon olive oil

3 small to medium loaves challah bread

1 pint seasonal fresh fruit

2 whole eggs

4 egg whites

¼ cup skim milk

1 cup orange juice

¼ cup nonfat plain yogurt

¼ cup confectioners' sugar

1. Preheat the oven to 375°F. Grease a baking sheet with the oil.

2. Slice the bread into thick (2½- to 3-inch) slices with a serrated knife at a severe angle to form long bias slices (a medium-large loaf of challah will yield three thick bias slices). Cut a slit into the bottom crust to form a pocket.

3. Peel the fruit if necessary, then dice into large pieces and fill the pockets in the bread. Press the pocket closed.

4. In a large mixing bowl, beat the eggs and egg whites, then add the milk. Dip the bread into the egg mixture, letting it fully absorb the mixture. Place the bread on the prepared baking sheet. Bake for 10 minutes on one side, flip, and bake 10 minutes more.

5. While the bread is baking, pour the orange juice in a small saucepan; boil until reduced by half and the mixture becomes syrupy. Remove the French toast from the oven, and cut in half diagonally. Serve each with dollop of yogurt, a drizzle of juice, and a sprinkling of sugar.

PASTINA AND EGG

Pasta for breakfast? Why not—this hearty breakfast is great on a cold morning to fortify you for the day.

Serves 6

1 whole egg

2 egg whites

3 cups chicken broth (fat removed)

1½ cups pastina

1 ounce fresh Parmesan cheese, grated

Fresh-cracked black pepper

¼ bunch fresh parsley, chopped

1. Beat the egg and egg whites. Bring the broth to a slow boil in a medium-size saucepot, then add the pastina; stir frequently until almost al dente.

2. Whisk in the eggs, stirring constantly until the eggs are completely cooked and the pasta is al dente. Remove from heat and ladle into bowls. Sprinkle in cheese, pepper, and parsley.

MEDITERRANEAN OMELET

Omelets in the Mediterranean are light and fluffy.

Serves 6

2 whole eggs

6 egg whites

¼ cup plain nonfat yogurt

½ teaspoon extra-virgin olive oil

2 ounces pancetta (sliced paper-thin) or lean ham

3 ounces cheese (Swiss or any other), shredded

¼ bunch fresh parsley, chopped

Fresh-cracked black pepper, to taste

1. In a medium-size bowl, beat the eggs and egg whites, then whisk in the yogurt. Heat half of the oil to medium temperature in a sauté pan. Quickly sauté the pancetta, then remove and drain on paper towel.

2. Heat the remaining oil to medium temperature in a large sauté pan. Pour in the egg mixture, then sprinkle in the pancetta and cheese. Stir once only. Continuously move the pan over the heat, using a spatula to push the edges inward slightly to allow the egg mixture to pour outward and solidify. When the mixture is mostly solidified, use a spatula to fold it in half.

3. Cover and finish cooking on the stovetop on low heat or uncovered in a 350°F oven for approximately 5 minutes. Sprinkle with parsley and black pepper and serve.

Season the Pan

When making omelets, always make sure your pan is properly seasoned. A properly seasoned pan is worth its weight in gold. To season, coat the pan with oil and put it in a warm oven or cover the surface generously with salt and then wipe clean.

STOVETOP-POACHED FRESH COD

A great example of a savory breakfast that provides you with protein early in the day. Great for that fresh-caught fish!

Serves 6

3 celery stalks

½ bunch fresh parsley stems

1½ pounds fresh cod (cut into 4-ounce portions)

1 bay leaf

2 cups Fish Stock (see recipe in Chapter 2)

1 tablespoon freshly squeezed lemon juice

Fresh black pepper, to taste

Kosher salt, to taste

1. Roughly chop the celery and parsley. Place the celery and parsley in the bottom of a sauté pan and arrange the cod pieces on top. Add the bay leaf, stock, and lemon juice, and place over medium-high heat. Cover with parchment paper or a loose-fitting lid.

2. Bring to a simmer and cook covered until the fish flakes, approximately 15–20 minutes, depending on thickness of the fish. Remove from heat and season with pepper and salt; remove the bay leaf. Serve with or without poaching liquid.

SWEETENED BROWN RICE

This recipe is perfect for a cold winter day, providing a great alternative to cold cereal.

Serves 6

1½ cups soy milk

1½ cups water

1 cup brown rice

1 tablespoon honey

¼ teaspoon nutmeg

Fresh fruit (optional)

Place all the ingredients except the fresh fruit in a medium-size saucepan; bring the mixture to a slow simmer and cover with a tight-fitting lid. Simmer for 45–60 minutes, until the rice is tender and done. Serve in bowls, topped with your favorite fresh fruit, if desired.

CREAMY SWEET RISOTTO

This sweet version of the classic risotto can also be used for a dessert.

Serves 6

1 teaspoon clarified butter

1 teaspoon olive oil

1 cup Arborio rice

¼ cup white grape juice

2 cups skim milk

⅓ cup shredded coconut

½ cup raisins or dried currants

3 teaspoons honey

1. Heat a large sauté pan over medium heat, then add the butter and oil. Using a wooden spoon, stir in the rice. Add the juice, stirring until completely incorporated. Add the skim milk ¼ cup at a time, stirring constantly. Make certain that each ¼ cup is fully incorporated before adding the next.

2. When the rice is completely cooked, add the coconut. Serve in bowls or on plates, sprinkled with raisins and drizzled with honey.

EGGS IN CRUSTY ITALIAN BREAD

Using crusty Italian bread is so much better than the more familiar version with empty-calorie white bread.

Serves 6

6 (2-inch) slices Italian bread

1 teaspoon virgin olive oil

2 red peppers, thinly sliced

½ shallot, minced

6 eggs

Fresh-cracked black pepper, to taste

Kosher salt, to taste

1. Cut out large circles from the center of the bread slices; discard the center pieces and set the hollowed-out bread slices aside. Heat half of the oil over medium heat in a sauté pan. Sauté the peppers and shallots until tender. Remove from heat and drain on paper towel; keep warm.

2. Heat the remaining oil over medium-high heat in a large sauté pan. Place the bread slices in the pan. Crack 1 egg into the hollowed-out center of each bread slice. When the eggs solidify, flip them together with the bread (being careful to keep the egg in place), and cook to desired doneness.

3. To serve, top with pepper-shallot mixture, and add pepper and salt.

FRESH TUNA WITH SWEET LEMON LEEK SALSA

The tuna can be prepared the night before, refrigerated, then either reheated or served at room temperature.

Serves 6

Tuna

1½ pounds fresh tuna steaks (cut into 4-ounce portions)

¼–½ teaspoon extra-virgin olive oil

Fresh-cracked black pepper, to taste

Kosher salt, to taste

Salsa

1 teaspoon extra-virgin olive oil

3 fresh leeks (light green and white parts only), thinly sliced

1 tablespoon fresh lemon juice

1 tablespoon honey

1. Preheat grill to medium-high temperature.

2. Brush each portion of the tuna with the oil and drain on a rack. Season the tuna with pepper and salt, then place the tuna on the grill; cook for 3 minutes. Shift the tuna steaks on the grill to form an *X* grill pattern; cook 3 more minutes.

3. Turn the steaks over and grill 3 more minutes, then change position again to create an *X* grill pattern. Cook to desired doneness.

4. For the salsa: Heat the oil in a medium-size sauté pan over medium heat, then add the leeks. When the leeks are wilted, add the lemon juice and honey. Plate each tuna portion with a spoonful of salsa.

YOGURT CHEESE AND FRUIT

This breakfast is worth the extra effort of making the yogurt cheese. If you do not have the time or inclination, use farmer cheese instead.

Serves 6

3 cups plain nonfat yogurt

1 teaspoon fresh lemon juice

½ cup orange juice

½ cup water

1 fresh Golden Delicious apple

1 fresh pear

¼ cup honey

¼ cup dried cranberries or raisins

1. Prepare the yogurt cheese the day before by lining a colander or strainer with cheesecloth. Spoon the yogurt into the cheesecloth and place the strainer over a pot or bowl to catch the whey; refrigerate for at least 8 hours before serving.

2. In a large mixing bowl, mix together the juices and water. Cut the apple and pear into wedges, and place the wedges in the juice mixture; let sit for at least 5 minutes. Strain off the liquid.

3. When the yogurt is firm, remove from refrigerator, slice, and place on plates. Arrange the fruit wedges around the yogurt. Drizzle with honey and sprinkle with cranberries just before serving.

Fruit for Breakfast

Proponents of proper food-combining say that fruit makes the best breakfast. Always eat fruit on an empty stomach, and wait 2 hours before eating any other food. This ensures proper digestion.

PANCETTA ON BAGUETTE

This Mediterranean version of "bacon and cheese" is incredibly delicious!

Serves 6

1 loaf baguette

½–1 teaspoon extra-virgin olive oil

6 ounces pancetta (ham, prosciutto, or Canadian bacon can be substituted)

¼ cantaloupe, medium-diced

¼ honeydew melon, medium-diced

3 ounces goat cheese

Fresh-cracked black pepper, to taste

1. Preheat the broiler on medium-high heat.

2. Slice the baguette on the bias and place on baking sheet. Brush each slice with oil, then toast lightly on each side.

3. Slice the pancetta paper-thin and into thin strips, then place on top of each baguette slice; place under broiler. Cook quickly, paying close attention so as not to burn (approximately 1 minute).

4. While the baguette cooks, mix the cantaloupe and melon in a small bowl. When baguettes are done, remove them from the oven and place on a plate. To serve, sprinkle with cheese and black pepper. Garnish with a spoonful of melon mix.

Pancetta a Must

The salty spice of the pancetta is a perfect foil for the sweet fruit. Using pancetta or prosciutto is a must for a full appreciation of this recipe.

VEGETABLE PITA WITH FETA CHEESE

Let your imagination go wild with seasonal veggies. This simple-to-prepare pita delight is delicious, and good for you, too.

Serves 6

1 eggplant, sliced into ½-inch pieces, lengthwise

1 zucchini, sliced into ½-inch pieces, lengthwise

1 yellow squash, sliced

1 red onion, cut into ⅓-inch rings

1 teaspoon virgin olive oil

Fresh-cracked black pepper

6 whole-wheat pita bread

3 ounces feta cheese

1. Preheat the oven to 375°F.

2. Brush the sliced vegetables with oil and place on a racked baking sheet. Sprinkle with black pepper. Roast until tender. (The vegetables can be prepared the night before, refrigerated, then reheated or brought to room temperature before roasting.)

3. Slice a 3-inch opening in the pitas to gain access to the pockets. Toast the pitas if desired. Fill the pitas with the cooked vegetables. Add cheese to each and serve.

ISRAELI COUSCOUS WITH DRIED-FRUIT CHUTNEY

Quick and easy to prepare, this sweet version can also be used as a side dish for a spicy entrée.

Serves 6

Chutney

¼ cup medium-diced dried dates

¼ cup medium-diced dried figs

¼ cup medium-diced dried currants

¼ cup slivered almonds

Couscous

2¼ cups fresh orange juice

2¼ cups water

4½ cups couscous

1 teaspoon grated orange rind

2 tablespoons nonfat plain yogurt

1. Mix together all the chutney ingredients; set aside.

2. Bring the orange juice and water to a boil in a medium-size pot. Stir in the couscous, then add the orange rind. Remove from heat immediately, cover, and let stand for 5 minutes. Fluff the mixture with a fork.

3. Serve in bowls with a spoonful of chutney and a dollop of yogurt.

ALMOND MASCARPONE DUMPLINGS

Mascarpone is Italy's answer to cream cheese, with much more flavor.

Serves 6

1 cup whole-wheat flour

1 cup all-purpose unbleached flour

¼ cup ground almonds

4 egg whites

3 ounces mascarpone cheese

1 teaspoon extra-virgin olive oil

2 teaspoons apple juice

1 tablespoon butter

¼ cup honey

1. Sift together both types of flour in a large bowl. Mix in the almonds. In a separate bowl, cream together the egg whites, cheese, oil, and juice on medium speed with an electric mixer.

2. Combine the flour and egg white mixture with a dough hook on medium speed or by hand until a dough forms.

3. Boil 1 gallon water in a medium-size saucepot. Take a spoonful of the dough and use a second spoon to push it into the boiling water. Cook until the dumpling floats to the top, about 5–10 minutes. You can cook several dumplings at once, just take care not to crowd the pot. Remove with a slotted spoon and drain on paper towels.

4. Heat a medium-size sauté pan over medium-high heat. Add the butter, then place the dumplings in the pan and cook until light brown. Place on serving plates and drizzle with honey.

MULTIGRAIN TOAST WITH GRILLED VEGETABLES

Grilling vegetables brings out the sweet flavor. Use any seasonal vegetables.

Serves 6

½ eggplant

½ zucchini

½ yellow squash

½ red pepper

½ yellow pepper

½ green pepper

1 teaspoon extra-virgin olive oil

6 multigrain bread slices

3 ounces goat cheese

¼ bunch fresh marjoram

Fresh-cracked black pepper, to taste

1. Slice the eggplant, zucchini, and squash in 3-inch lengths, ¼- to ½-inch thick, and cut the peppers in half. Preheat a grill to medium heat. Brush the vegetables with the oil and grill all until fork-tender. Cut all the vegetables into large dice. (Vegetables can be prepared the night before; refrigerate and reheat or bring to room temperature before serving.)

2. Grill the bread until lightly toasted, then remove from heat and top with vegetables. Sprinkle with cheese, chopped marjoram, and black pepper.

Grilled Vegetables

As you can see, many of the recipes in this book use grilled vegetables. When preparing roasted or grilled vegetables for dinner or any meal, always make double the quantity. Refrigerate the extra portion and use it the next day in your breakfast or lunch meal.

CHAPTER 2

SAUCES, STOCKS, AND SPREADS

GREEK MEAT SAUCE

Serve over cooked pasta and grate lots of kefalotyri or Romano cheese on top.

Serves 10

⅓ cup extra-virgin olive oil

3 medium onions, peeled and diced

6 cloves garlic, peeled and minced

1 medium carrot, peeled and grated

2 pounds lean ground beef

3 bay leaves

6 allspice berries

¼ cup dry white wine

1 (28-ounce) can puréed tomatoes

2½ teaspoons salt

1 teaspoon pepper

1 tablespoon dried oregano

⅛ teaspoon cinnamon

1. Heat the oil in a large skillet over medium heat for 30 seconds. Add the onions, garlic, and carrots, and cook for 10 minutes or until the vegetables are softened.

2. Increase the heat to medium-high, and add the ground beef, bay leaves, and allspice. Break the beef up with a wooden spoon; brown the beef for 5–6 minutes. Add the wine, and cook for 2 minutes or until most of the liquid has evaporated.

3. Add the tomatoes, and season with the salt and pepper. Bring the sauce to a boil, reduce the heat to medium-low, and cook the sauce for 30–40 minutes or until it thickens.

4. Take the sauce off the heat, remove the bay leaf, and add the oregano and cinnamon.

Always Remove the Bay Leaves

Bay leaves have sharp edges that can cut the inside of your throat, and they can also cause intestinal problems. While they are excellent for flavoring the dish, always remove them before serving it.

BÉCHAMEL SAUCE

This sauce is a master recipe that can be used for Pastitsio (see recipe in Chapter 6) and Moussaka (see recipe in Chapter 8).

Makes 4 cups

3 tablespoons unsalted butter

¼ cup all-purpose flour

3 cups warm whole milk

½ teaspoon salt

¼ cup kefalotyri or Romano cheese

⅛ teaspoon grated nutmeg

2 large eggs, beaten

1. Melt the butter in a medium pan over medium heat. Stir in the flour and keep stirring for 2 minutes.

2. Stir in the milk, one ladle at a time. Continue stirring until the sauce thickens. Add the salt, cheese, and nutmeg. Take the pan off the heat and let the sauce cool for 10 minutes.

3. Slowly stir the eggs into the sauce, mixing well to combine the ingredients.

4. The béchamel should be used when hot or warm. If the sauce is cold, slowly reheat it over medium-low heat.

Cooling Béchamel Sauce

When cooling a béchamel, place a tea towel between the pot and the lid. The tea towel will absorb any condensation and prevent the sauce from becoming watery.

LADOLEMONO

Ladolemono is a compound word in Greek that means "oil-lemon." Heavy cream sauces are scarce in the Mediterranean region, because olive oil does lots of the heavy lifting in sauces and dressings. This basic recipe is great on grilled meats like steak, souvlaki, and fish. Try adding different herbs to this versatile sauce.

Makes about ½ cup

3 tablespoons fresh lemon juice

½ cup extra-virgin olive oil

1 teaspoon salt

2 teaspoons dried oregano

1. Whisk all the ingredients in a small bowl until they are well combined.

2. Adjust the seasoning with salt, if necessary. Serve the sauce at room temperature.

ROMESCO SAUCE

This sauce from Spain is delicious served on grilled or toasted bread, spread on chicken or fish, or offered with grilled vegetables.

Makes 2 cups

1 small Roasted Red Pepper (see recipe in Chapter 4)

1 small chili pepper, stemmed

¼ cup chopped roasted almonds

3 cloves garlic, peeled and smashed

1 slice stale white bread

3 ripe plum tomatoes, peeled, seeded, and roughly chopped

1 tablespoon balsamic vinegar

½ teaspoon salt

¼ teaspoon pepper

⅔ cup extra-virgin olive oil

1. Combine all the ingredients, except the oil, in a food processor. Process the ingredients until they are puréed into a paste.

2. With the processor running, slowly add the oil until it is well incorporated.

3. Season the sauce with more salt and pepper, if necessary. Serve at room temperature.

TARTAR SAUCE

This tartar sauce is a little more healthful than a traditional recipe because the amount of mayonnaise is reduced and Greek yogurt is added. Serve this sauce with fried fish or other seafood.

Makes 1 cup

¼ cup mayonnaise

3 tablespoons Homemade Greek Yogurt (see recipe in Chapter 1)

¼ cup finely chopped red onion

2 tablespoons minced dill pickles

2 tablespoons chopped chives

2 tablespoons chopped fresh parsley

2 tablespoons chopped fresh dill

2 tablespoons capers, drained and finely chopped

1–2 tablespoons lemon juice

¼ teaspoon pepper

1. Combine all the ingredients in a small bowl.

2. Cover the sauce and refrigerate it until needed. Serve it cold.

FETA-YOGURT SAUCE

Try this sauce on stuffed zucchini blossoms, a salad, fries, or nachos.

Makes about 2 cups

½ cup crumbled feta cheese

½ cup plain yogurt

1 clove garlic, peeled and minced

½ cup warm Basic Vegetable Stock (see recipe in this chapter)

¼ cup chopped fresh chives

1. Combine the feta, yogurt, and garlic in a medium bowl. Mash the ingredients with a fork.

2. Add the stock and stir until it is well combined. Stir in the chives. The sauce may be served warm by reheating over a low heat or served at room temperature.

SHORTCUT SOUR CHERRY SPOON SWEET

This is a shortcut recipe for making a sour cherry sauce, ideal for topping a cheesecake, serving on top of strained Greek yogurt, or to spike a sauce for pork or game meat.

Makes about 2½ cups

1½ cups jarred sour cherries, plus 1 cup of the liquid

1 cup sugar

1 teaspoon vanilla extract

1. Bring the cherries, the cherry liquid, and the sugar to a boil in a medium pot over medium-high heat. Reduce the heat to medium-low, and cook the sauce for 15–20 minutes to break down the cherries a little and to thicken the sauce to a consistency like syrup.

2. Remove from the heat and add the vanilla. Allow the sauce to cool; store it in the refrigerator until needed. Bring the sauce to room temperature before serving.

GREEK-STYLE CHIMICHURRI

Chimichurri is a specialty of Argentina and is often served with grilled meats. This Greek-style recipe highlights Greek oregano. You may use fresh or dried oregano in this sauce.

Makes 2 cups

1 cup fresh parsley leaves

2 tablespoons dried oregano

3 or 4 scallions, ends trimmed and chopped

3 cloves garlic, peeled and smashed

½ large carrot, peeled and grated

½ cup extra-virgin olive oil

2 tablespoons red wine vinegar

½ teaspoon salt

¼ teaspoon pepper

1. Combine all the ingredients in a food processor, and process until the mixture is creamy.

2. If the sauce is too thick, add some cold water until it's the consistency you like.

3. Store the sauce in the refrigerator until needed, but let it come to room temperature before serving.

ALMOND-POTATO SKORDALIA

Skordalia is a garlicky Greek condiment that is often paired with fried salted cod, but it also goes well with roast beets.

Makes 2 cups

2 large Yukon gold potatoes, unpeeled

1 teaspoon salt, divided

5 or 6 cloves garlic, peeled and minced

½ cup chopped blanched almonds

2 tablespoons red wine vinegar

1. Place the potatoes, ½ teaspoon of salt, and enough water to cover the potatoes by 1 inch in a medium pot over high heat. Cover the pot, and bring the water to a boil. Reduce the heat to medium, and cook the potatoes for 15 minutes or until they are fork-tender. Drain the potatoes. Let them cool. As soon as the potatoes are cool enough to handle, peel the skins off with the back of a knife. Cut the potatoes into quarters, and set them aside.

2. Put the garlic, almonds, remaining salt, and vinegar in a mortar. Using the pestle, mash the ingredients into a paste. Add the potatoes to the mortar. Mash the potatoes into the mixture. Stir the remaining oil into the potato mash in small increments.

3. Adjust the seasoning with the salt and vinegar, if necessary. Serve at room temperature.

FIG-OUZO SAUCE

This sauce makes a wonderful topping for ice cream. You can also top Homemade Greek Yogurt (Chapter 1), soft cheeses, or grilled halloumi.

Makes 2 cups

1 cup boiling water

15 dried figs, halved

¼ cup honey

¼ cup ouzo

1. Combine the hot water and figs in a medium bowl. Cover the bowl and allow the figs to steep in the water for 10 minutes.

2. Put the figs and the soaking water into a food processor, and process until the sauce is puréed.

3. Transfer half the fig mixture from the processor to a small saucepan over medium heat. Add the honey, and cook for 5 minutes. Add the remaining fig mixture, and cook for 5 more minutes.

4. Stir in the ouzo, increase the heat to medium-high, and cook for 2–3 minutes.

5. Allow the sauce to cool to room temperature before using.

BASIL AND PINE NUT PESTO

Mix in the cheese, salt, and pepper by hand after you have removed the sauce from the processor or blender.

Yields 1 cup

½ cup pine nuts

8 cloves garlic, peeled and smashed

1 cup basil leaves

¼ cup extra-virgin olive oil

¼ cup Parmesan or Romano cheese

½ teaspoon salt

¼ teaspoon pepper

1. Put the nuts and garlic in a food processor, and process until the nuts are finely chopped and the garlic is minced.

2. Add the basil and pulse until the mixture becomes a paste.

3. With the processor running, slowly add the oil until the mixture is smooth.

4. Empty the sauce into a bowl, and add the cheese, salt, and pepper.

5. Adjust the seasoning with more salt and pepper, if necessary. The sauce may be served warm by reheating over a low heat or served at room temperature.

The Old-Fashioned Way

Although it is easier to use a food processor or blender to prepare this pesto sauce, take a break from modern conveniences by making this pesto the old-fashioned way, using a mortar and pestle. The perfect texture that is achieved using this method cannot be duplicated with a food processor.

CREAMY LEMON SAUCE

This sauce is creamy without the use of eggs or cream, and is an ideal sauce for vegetarians or people who are lactose-intolerant. Try the sauce on baked or poached fish.

Makes about 2 cups

1½ cups Basic Vegetable Stock (see recipe in this chapter)

1 medium white onion, chopped

1 (½-inch) slice of lemon

½ cup extra-virgin olive oil

2 tablespoons Arborio rice

¼ teaspoon salt

⅛ teaspoon pepper

½ teaspoon fresh lemon juice

1. In a small pan over medium-high heat, boil stock, onions, lemon, and oil. Reduce heat to medium-low.

2. Add the rice, cover, and cook for 15 minutes, stirring occasionally. Remove the pot from the heat and remove the lemon slice. Let sauce cool for 5 minutes.

3. Using an immersion blender or a regular blender, purée the sauce until smooth. Season with salt and pepper. Stir in the lemon juice. Serve warm.

PARSLEY AND WALNUT PESTO

Try this variation of a classic pesto sauce on any pasta for a delicious meal. Serve the sauce warm or at room temperature.

Yields 1 cup

½ cup walnuts

8 cloves garlic, peeled and smashed

1 cup parsley leaves

¼ cup extra-virgin olive oil

¼ cup Parmesan or Romano cheese

½ teaspoon salt

¼ teaspoon pepper

1. Pulse the nuts and garlic in a food processor until the nuts are finely chopped and the garlic is minced. Add parsley and pulse until the mixture becomes a paste.

2. With the processor running, slowly add the oil until the mixture is smooth.

3. Empty the sauce into a small bowl and add the cheese, salt, and pepper.

A New Twist on an Old Recipe

Most people are familiar with traditional pesto, which is made with basil and pine nuts, but this variation with parsley and walnuts is very popular.

PAPRIKA SAUCE

This sauce is great with Keftedes (see recipe in Chapter 4) and with French fries as an alternative to ketchup.

Makes 2½ cups

1 tablespoon unsalted butter

2 tablespoons all-purpose flour

1 cup warm whole milk

¼ cup finely diced onion

1 teaspoon sweet paprika

½ cup grated Graviera cheese or Gruyère

⅓ cup Greek yogurt

½ teaspoon salt

¼ teaspoon pepper

¼ cup chopped fresh chives

⅛ teaspoon red pepper flakes

1. Melt the butter in a medium pot over medium heat. Stir in the flour and keep stirring for 2 minutes.

2. Whisk in the milk, onions, and paprika. Once the milk has thickened, add the cheese and cook until the cheese has melted into the sauce. If the sauce is too thick, add a little more milk.

3. Take the sauce off the heat and stir in the yogurt. Season with the salt and pepper.

4. Stir in the chives and red pepper flakes. The sauce may be served warm by reheating over a low heat or served at room temperature.

DEMI-GLACE REDUCTION SAUCE

Demi-glace sauces are a central part of the Mediterranean cuisine. Demi-glace is the French term to define a sauce that is made by slowly simmering stock down to an intensely flavored glaze.

Yields 4 cups

16 cups stock (see recipes in this chapter: Lamb Stock, Fish Stock, Veal Stock, Chicken or Turkey Stock, or Basic Vegetable Stock)

Place the stock in a large, shallow saucepan; boil the stock on high heat until it is reduced to 4 cups.

Demi-Glace Reduction Sauce Variations

You can create different demi-glace sauces just by changing the stock. Try this recipe with a vegetable or seafood stock.

GLACÉ REDUCTION SAUCE

Glacé gives you an incredible flavor profile and a beautiful sauce with no thickening agent.

1 quart Demi-Glace Reduction Sauce (see recipe in this chapter)

Place the sauce in a shallow saucepan; bring to a slow simmer on medium heat and reduce by half. Keep a close eye as to not scorch the cooking liquid.

Glacé Defined

The term *glacé* refers to a reduction of stock to a quarter of its original amount.

MEDITERRANEAN MIGNONETTE SAUCE

Serve with fresh shucked Oysters on the Half Shell (see recipe in Chapter 10).

Makes 1 cup

⅔ cup sparkling rosé wine

2 tablespoons red wine vinegar

½ teaspoon pepper

2 tablespoons finely diced red onions or shallots

1 tablespoon finely diced radishes

1. Bring the wine and vinegar to a boil in a small pot over medium heat. Reduce the heat to medium-low, and cook until the liquid is reduced by half.

2. Remove the pot from the heat, and add the pepper, onions, and radishes.

3. Let the sauce cool to room temperature before serving.

MEDITERRANEAN SALTSA

Use this fresh sauce as a topping for grilled salmon or any other grilled fish.

Makes about 2 cups

16 kalamata olives, pitted and sliced

2 tablespoons capers

¼ cup finely sliced scallions

½ cup diced red peppers, stemmed and seeded

½ cup chopped ripe tomato, seeded

1 clove garlic, peeled and minced

¼ cup chopped fresh parsley

⅓ cup extra-virgin olive oil

1 teaspoon fresh lemon juice

1. Gently mix all the ingredients in a small bowl.

2. Keep the saltsa in the refrigerator until it is needed. Serve it cold or at room temperature.

BASIC VEGETABLE STOCK

If you want an earthier flavor, add mushrooms.

Makes 16 cups

2 pounds yellow onions, peeled and roughly chopped

1 pound carrots, peeled and roughly chopped

1 pound celery (stalks only), trimmed and roughly chopped

24 cups water

½ cup chopped fresh parsley stems

1 teaspoon fresh thyme leaves

2 bay leaves

10–20 peppercorns

1 tablespoon salt

1. Bring the onions, carrots, celery, and water to a boil in a large pot over medium-high heat. Reduce the heat to medium, and cook the stock for 1½ hours.

2. Add the parsley, thyme, bay leaves, and peppercorns, and cook for 45 minutes. Season the stock with the salt.

3. Remove the pot from the heat. Strain and reserve the liquid stock; remove the bay leaf. Allow the stock to cool.

4. Freeze the stock in freezer-safe containers until you are ready to use it.

Homemade Stocks

Homemade stocks are easy to make and add a special touch to dishes that call for them. A homemade stock always tastes better than store-bought, and you control the ingredients that go into it—especially the salt. Always cook stocks uncovered; covering them will cause them to turn cloudy.

LAMB STOCK

If you want stock in a hurry, try using a pressure cooker. You can cut your cooking time in half.

Makes 10 cups

3 pounds lamb shoulder

2 large onions, peeled and quartered

1 large carrot, peeled and chopped

1 stalk celery, trimmed and chopped

12 cups water

2 teaspoons salt

1. Put all the ingredients in a large pot over medium-high heat. Bring the stock to a boil, reduce the heat to medium-low, and cook for 2½ hours.

2. Cool but don't strain stock. Refrigerate overnight. Remove the hardened fat that has collected at the top of the stock and discard it. Strain the stock.

3. Freeze in freezer-safe containers.

FISH STOCK

Whitefish or lighter fish bones and heads are ideal for making a fish stock. Do not use salmon, because it is an oily fish. You can also put in lobster, crab, and shrimp shells to give the stock an additional depth of flavor.

Makes 16 cups

4 pounds fish bones and heads, rinsed in cold water

2 large onions, peeled and roughly chopped

2 white leeks, thoroughly cleaned and roughly chopped

½ pound parsnips, peeled and roughly chopped

2 celery stalks, ends trimmed and roughly chopped

1 cup dry white wine

24 cups water

½ cup chopped fresh parsley stems

1 teaspoon fresh thyme leaves

2 dried bay leaves

10–20 peppercorns

1 tablespoon salt

1. Bring the fish bones and heads, vegetables, wine, and water to a boil in a large pot over medium-high heat. Reduce the heat to medium-low, and cook the stock, uncovered, for 1 hour.

2. Add the parsley, thyme, bay leaves, and peppercorns. Cook for 30 minutes. Season the stock with salt.

3. Remove the stock from the heat and allow it to cool. Strain and reserve the liquid stock; remove the bay leaf.

4. Freeze the stock in freezer-safe containers until you are ready to use it.

VEAL STOCK

The cooked veal from this recipe can be used to make Vrasto (see recipe in Chapter 5) or Giouvetsi with Veal (see recipe in Chapter 6).

Makes 8 cups

2 pounds veal shoulder, cut into chunks

1 teaspoon salt

½ teaspoon pepper, divided

10 cups water

1. Season the veal with the salt and pepper. Put the veal and the water in a pressure cooker, secure the lid, and crank the heat to high. As soon as the seal forms, the cooker will whistle. Turn the heat to medium, and cook the meat for 20–30 minutes.

2. Take the pressure cooker off the heat and release the pressure according to the manufacturer's instructions.

3. If you don't have a pressure cooker, cook the veal and water in a large pot over medium heat, uncovered, for 90 minutes. Allow the stock to cool. Strain the stock and reserve. The meat can be used for other purposes such as sandwiches or pastas.

4. Freeze the stock in freezer-safe containers until you are ready to use it.

CHICKEN OR TURKEY STOCK

Consider buying chicken carcasses from the butcher or using the leftover carcass of a roasted turkey to make this poultry stock.

Makes 12 cups

3 chicken carcasses (or 1 turkey carcass)

1 large onion, peeled and roughly chopped

1 large carrot, roughly chopped

1 stalk celery, roughly chopped

14 cups water

½ cup chopped parsley stems

10 whole peppercorns

1 tablespoon salt

1. Bring the carcasses, onion, carrot, celery, and water to a boil in a large pot over medium-high heat. Reduce the heat to medium-low and cook for 1½ hours.

2. Add the parsley, peppercorns, and salt, and cook for 30 minutes.

3. Allow the stock to cool, but don't strain it. Refrigerate the stock overnight.

4. Remove the hardened fat that has collected at the top of the stock and discard it. Strain the stock.

5. Freeze the stock in freezer-safe containers until you are ready to use it.

PARSLEY SPREAD

A refreshing dip for summertime parties. Best kept refrigerated when not used immediately.

Serves 4

2 bunches of fresh parsley

4 slices stale bread, no crusts

3 green onions, diced

½ cup extra-virgin olive oil

¼ cup fresh lemon juice

1 tablespoon vinegar

1 teaspoon dried oregano

Salt and fresh-ground pepper

1. Wash and drain parsley well; remove all stalks.

2. Moisten the bread; squeeze to drain excess water.

3. In a food processor on low speed, chop parsley and onion to combine well. Slowly and alternately add moistened bread, olive oil, lemon juice, vinegar, oregano, salt, and pepper until smooth. Serve cold.

TZATZIKI (YOGURT-GARLIC SAUCE)

Make sure to drain as much water from the cucumber as possible. The dip should be as thick as possible, so you don't want the cucumber leeching its water in the dip.

Yields approximately 2½ cups

½ seedless cucumber

2 cups Homemade Greek Yogurt (see recipe in Chapter 1)

3–6 cloves garlic, pressed or grated

1 tablespoon fresh dill, finely chopped

1 tablespoon extra-virgin olive oil

Pinch of salt

¼ teaspoon white vinegar

1. Peel cucumber; grate onto clean kitchen towel. Wrap; squeeze towel to remove as much water as possible from cucumber. Set aside to drain on fresh towel.

2. In a mixing bowl, combine yogurt, garlic, cucumber, and dill; mix thoroughly until smooth.

3. Add olive oil, salt, and vinegar; mix well once more. Refrigerate at least 1 hour before serving.

Is Your Refrigerator Running?

Before the advent of some of the cooler modern conveniences, yogurt was the easiest way to preserve milk's freshness in the warm Mediterranean region.

TZATZIKI WITH OUZO

Ouzo is an anise-flavored aperitif that Greeks enjoy drinking with appetizers. It is also the secret ingredient in this Tzatziki.

Serves 4

½ long English cucumber, seeded and grated

1¼ teaspoons salt, divided

18 ounces strained Greek yogurt

2 cloves garlic, peeled and minced

2 tablespoons red wine vinegar

1 ounce ouzo

2 tablespoons chopped fresh dill

¼ cup extra-virgin olive oil

1. In a fine-mesh strainer over a medium bowl, add cucumber and ¼ teaspoon salt. Strain the cucumber for 30 minutes. Hand-squeeze any remaining water from the cucumber.

2. In a large bowl, stir together cucumber, remaining salt, yogurt, garlic, vinegar, ouzo, and dill. Slowly stir in the oil so it is thoroughly combined. Adjust salt, if necessary.

FRESH TOMATO SAUCE

Quick-cooked fresh tomato sauce has a wonderful flavor and many uses.

Yields 1 gallon

2 large yellow onions

1 shallot

8 cloves garlic

20 fresh plum tomatoes

10 large fresh basil leaves

3 sprigs fresh oregano leaves

¼ bunch fresh parsley

1 tablespoon olive oil

½ cup dry red wine

Fresh-cracked black pepper, to taste

2 tablespoons cold unsalted butter (optional)

1. Dice the onions and mince the shallot and garlic. Chop the tomatoes and herbs.

2. Heat the oil over medium heat in a large stockpot. Add the onions, shallots, and garlic. Sauté lightly for approximately 2–3 minutes, then add the tomatoes. Toss the tomatoes in the onion mixture for approximately 3 minutes. Add the wine and let it reduce for approximately 10 minutes.

3. Add the herbs and spices. Add the butter, if desired. Adjust seasonings to taste, then remove from heat and serve.

Wine in Cooking

Do not use cooking wines—they have a high salt content and do not taste good! Use a wonderful full-bodied red wine that you would drink with dinner. You don't have to spend a lot, however—ordinary "house" or "table" wines are usually more than sufficient for cooking purposes.

LONG-COOKING TRADITIONAL TOMATO SAUCE

Tomato sauce is a mainstay of a substantial portion of Mediterranean cuisine.

Yields 1 gallon

2 large yellow onions

2 shallots

½ bulb garlic

30 fresh plum tomatoes or 4 (28-ounce) cans tomatoes

1 tablespoon olive oil

3 pounds pork bones and/or sausage

1 cup dry red wine

½ gallon water

½ teaspoon dried basil

½ teaspoon dried oregano

½ teaspoon dried parsley

½ teaspoon dried marjoram

Fresh-cracked black peppercorns, to taste

¼–½ teaspoon red pepper flakes (optional)

2 ounces fresh grated Parmesan or Romano cheese

1. Dice the onions, shallots, and garlic. Peel and dice the tomatoes.

2. Heat the oil to medium temperature in a large stockpot. Add the pork bones and/or sausage, onions, shallots, and garlic; lightly brown (approximately 5–10 minutes).

3. Add the tomatoes; toss with the pork mixture for approximately 5 minutes.

4. Add the wine, water, herbs, and spices; let simmer for 6–8 hours.

5. Adjust seasonings to taste. Remove from heat and serve as desired, topped with cheese.

LEMON MUSTARD SAUCE

This sauce goes well with grilled fish as well as a dressing for green salads.

Yields approximately ⅔ cup

¼ cup fresh lemon juice

2 cloves garlic, pressed

1 tablespoon lemon rind, grated

1 tablespoon prepared mustard

¼ cup extra-virgin olive oil

1 teaspoon thyme honey

Salt and pepper

Combine all ingredients; mix until smooth. Serve immediately.

ALMOND-ARUGULA PESTO

Arugula will spice up any dish with its peppery taste. It is complemented by any nut or fruit.

Yields 1 cup

¼ cup almonds

6 cloves garlic

1 bunch arugula, roughly chopped

⅓ cup olive oil

Salt, to taste

Fresh-cracked black pepper, to taste

1. Chop the almonds in a food processor or blender. Add the garlic and process to form a paste. Add the arugula; pulse into the almond mixture.

2. While the blender is running, drizzle in the oil until the mixture is smooth. Add salt and pepper to taste.

APPLE CHUTNEY

Try this as a side for pork dishes instead of applesauce. It also is wonderful with hearty winter squash.

Yields 1 pint

2 cups ice water

1 tablespoon fresh lemon juice

3 Granny Smith apples

1 shallot

3 sprigs fresh mint

1 tablespoon fresh-grated lemon zest

¼ cup white raisins

½ teaspoon ground cinnamon

1. Combine the water and lemon juice in a large mixing bowl. Core and dice the unpeeled apples and place them in the lemon water.

2. Thinly slice the shallot and chop the mint.

3. Thoroughly drain the apples, then mix together all the ingredients in a medium-size bowl.

RED PEPPER COULIS

Coulis can be made using any fruit or vegetable. To add variety, experiment with the addition of herbs and spices.

Yields 1 pint

6 red peppers

1 tablespoon olive oil

Fresh-cracked black pepper, to taste

Kosher salt, to taste

1. Preheat the oven to 375°F.

2. Toss the red peppers with the oil in a medium-size bowl. Place the peppers on a racked sheet pan and put in the oven for 15–20 minutes, until the skins begin to blister and the red peppers wilt.

3. Remove from oven and immediately place the red peppers in a plastic bag; let sit for approximately 5 minutes, then peel off the skin from the peppers. Stem, seed, and dice the peppers.

4. Place the red peppers in a blender and purée until smooth. Season with black pepper and salt.

COMPOUND BUTTER

You can use parchment paper instead of plastic wrap or wax paper. Use any herbs and spices that are on hand.

Yields 1 pint

1 bunch parsley, chopped

8 cloves garlic, minced

1 pound unsalted butter

Fresh-cracked black pepper, to taste

Kosher salt, to taste

1. Allow the butter to soften at room temperature.

2. In a medium-size bowl, thoroughly mix together the parsley, garlic, and butter. Season with pepper and salt to taste.

3. Spread onto wax paper or plastic wrap, and wrap tightly. Freeze completely, then slice into small pats.

Uses for Flavored Butters

In addition to serving flavored butter with crusty bread at the table, you can use it in the kitchen while cooking. For example, place a slice on top of the item you are preparing or getting ready to serve and it will melt, imparting its flavor to the dish. Compound butter is also good to serve with light, poached dishes.

BASIC VELOUTÉ

This sauce is the base for many cream sauces.

Yields ½ gallon

1 tablespoon olive oil

1 tablespoon flour

1 gallon stock (vegetable, poultry, fish, or seafood; see recipes in this chapter)

1. Heat the oil slightly over medium heat. Using a wooden spoon, mix in the flour. Whisk in the stock and simmer until reduced by half.

2. Remove from heat and cool in an ice-water bath. Place in freezer-safe containers. Store in freezer.

Using Butter

When making velouté you can use butter in place of oil for a richer flavor. However, keep in mind that using butter is not in keeping with a Mediterranean diet.

BALSAMIC REDUCTION

To get the very best flavor, it is worth purchasing a high-quality vinegar instead of going for the cheaper kinds.

Yields 1 cup

1 quart balsamic vinegar (or other vinegar)

2 tablespoons cold unsalted butter (optional)

Heat the vinegar in a large, shallow pan over medium-high heat. Allow the mixture to boil until reduced to 1 cup. Cut the butter into thin pats and whisk them into the reduced vinegar to aid in thickening.

VINAIGRETTE

Experiment using different types of herbs and vinegars. You may also want to consider adding citrus juices in place of the vinegar.

Yields 1½ cups

½ teaspoon fresh ginger

4 cloves garlic

½ bunch scallions

⅔ cup extra-virgin olive oil

⅓ cup rice vinegar

Mince the ginger and garlic. Trim the scallions and slice thinly. In a medium-size bowl, mix together all the ingredients.

RED WINE REDUCTION

The same method can be used to make a white wine reduction.

Yields 1 cup

1 quart dry red wine

2 tablespoons cold unsalted butter (optional)

Heat the wine in a large, shallow pan over medium-high heat. Allow the mixture to boil until reduced to 1 cup. Cut the butter into thin pats and whisk them into the reduced wine to aid in thickening.

SEASONED OIL

You can omit garlic and substitute dried chili, or go crazy and use any herb.

Yields 1 point

1 pint olive oil

5 cloves garlic (optional)

2 sprigs fresh tarragon

Place all the ingredients in a bottle and store for up to 1 month in the refrigerator.

Alert

Exercise extreme caution in storing seasoned oil in the refrigerator. Make sure to discard it after 1 month to avoid botulism.

SPICY MANGO SAUCE

This sauce gives that extra zing to a dish!

Yields ½ cup

¼ Scotch bonnet pepper

1 unripe mango

¼ teaspoon vinegar

¼ teaspoon honey

Salt, to taste

Stem, seed, devein, and mince the pepper. Chop the mango. Place all the ingredients in a small saucepan and simmer for 5 minutes over medium heat.

RED WINE VEGETABLE STOCK

Use a Merlot, Pinot Noir, or your favorite Mediterranean dry red wine. The richer, more full-bodied the wine, the more flavorful the stock.

Yields 1 gallon

1½ teaspoons olive oil

1½ pounds yellow onions

¼ pound shallots

½ pound carrots

4 cloves garlic

1 pound celery

½ pound tomatoes

½ pound portobello mushrooms

1 cup dry red wine

1½ gallons water

1 bunch fresh parsley stems

4 stems fresh thyme

2 bay leaves (fresh or dried)

10–20 peppercorns

1. Peel and chop all the vegetables.

2. Heat the olive oil over medium heat in a stockpot. Add the onions and shallots; sauté until light brown. Add carrots and sauté for 2 minutes. Add the garlic and celery and sauté an additional 2 minutes. Add the tomatoes and mushrooms, and stir for 1 minute.

3. Pour in the wine and reduce until almost completely evaporated. Add the water and bring to simmer; cook, uncovered, for 1½ hours.

4. Add the herbs and peppercorns; continue to simmer uncovered for 45 minutes.

5. Remove from heat, strain, remove the bay leaves, and cool in an ice-water bath. Place in freezer-safe containers and store in the freezer until ready to use.

HEARTY RED WINE BROWN STOCK

Use beef or veal for this recipe. Lamb and pork can be utilized, but they will definitely give a distinctive flavor to the stock.

Yields 1 gallon

3 large yellow onions

½ pound carrots

3 stalks celery

1 cup chopped tomatoes (fresh or canned)

1 bunch fresh parsley stems

1 tablespoon olive oil

5 pounds bone-in beef

3 gallons water

1 cup dry red wine

4 stems fresh thyme

2 dried bay leaves

10–20 peppercorns

1. Preheat the oven to 400°F.

2. Peel and roughly chop all the vegetables. Chop the parsley stems.

3. Place the oil, beef, and all the vegetables in a large roasting pan; brown in the oven for approximately 45 minutes, stirring frequently to prevent burning.

4. Transfer all the meat and vegetables to a large stockpot with the water.

5. Place the roasting pan on the stovetop over medium heat; pour in the wine to deglaze the pan, gently stirring all the residue from the bottom of the pan. Pour this mixture into the stockpot with the meat and vegetables. Simmer, uncovered, for 8–12 hours.

6. Add the herbs and peppercorns; continue to simmer for 30 minutes.

7. Remove from heat, strain, remove the bay leaves, and cool in an ice-water bath. Remove all fat that solidifies on surface before using or freezing.

SEAFOOD STOCK

Seafood shells such as those from lobster and shrimp are ideal for making a seafood stock. Also, be sure to thoroughly clean the leeks.

Yields 1 gallon

4 pounds seafood shells

3 large yellow onions

¼ pound shallots

1 white leek

½ pound parsnips

2 stalks celery

1 bunch fresh parsley stems

1 cup dry white wine

1½ gallons water

4 stems fresh thyme

2 dried bay leaves

10–20 peppercorns

1. Thoroughly rinse the seafood shells in ice-cold water. Peel and roughly chop all the vegetables. Chop the parsley stems.

2. Place the shells, vegetables, wine, and water in a stockpot over medium heat; bring to a simmer and let cook, uncovered, for 2 hours.

3. Add the thyme and bay leaves, and continue to simmer uncovered for 30 minutes.

4. Remove from heat, strain, remove the bay leaves, and cool in an ice-water bath. Place in freezer-safe containers and store in the freezer until ready to use.

Wine Choice

Use a semidry-to-dry Mediterranean white wine. If you have a specific recipe in mind that would be complemented by a sweeter flavor, try experimenting with a Sauternes or a late-harvest wine.

BEEF STOCK

Always thoroughly cool the stock and remove solidified fat from the top before using or freezing.

Yields 1 gallon

3 large yellow onions

½ pound carrots

3 stalks celery

1 bunch fresh parsley stems

1 tablespoon olive oil

5 pounds bone-in beef

3 gallons water

4 stems fresh thyme

2 dried bay leaves

10–20 peppercorns

1. Preheat oven to 400°F.

2. Peel and roughly chop all the vegetables.

3. Place the oil, beef, and all the vegetables in a large roasting pan; brown in the oven for approximately 30–45 minutes.

4. Transfer all the meat and vegetables to a large stockpot with the water. Gently scrape the bottom of the roasting pan to pick up all food residue and add it to the stockpot. Simmer over medium heat, uncovered, for 8–10 hours.

5. Add the herbs and peppercorns; continue to simmer uncovered for 30 minutes.

6. Remove from heat, strain, remove the bay leaves, and cool in an ice-water bath.

The Fond

The residue left in the bottom of the pan is known as fond. If you find you cannot release it all, return the pan to the stovetop, add a small amount of water or wine, and whisk to remove; then add it to the stock. The fond has a high concentration of flavor and should not be discarded.

CHAPTER 3

PHYLLO AND BREADS

PIZZA DOUGH

There is no need to order takeout—make your own pizza at home! The key to a good pizza is a great crust, and a great crust starts with great dough.

Makes 1 large or 2 medium pizzas

1½ teaspoons active dry yeast

½ teaspoon sugar

1½ cups warm water

½ teaspoon salt

3 tablespoons extra-virgin olive oil, divided

3¾ cups all-purpose flour, divided

1. In a large bowl, add the yeast, sugar, and warm water. Set the mixture aside for 7–10 minutes to allow the yeast to activate (bubble or froth). Stir in the salt and 2 tablespoons of oil.

2. Place ¼ cup of flour on your work surface. Add the remaining 3½ cups of flour, a little at a time, to the yeast mixture; mix the ingredients with your hands. When the mixture comes together as a dough, empty the bowl onto the floured work surface and begin to knead it. Keep kneading until the dough is pliable and no longer sticks to your hands. For a large pizza, roll the dough into one ball. For two medium pizzas, divide the dough in half and roll the halves into balls.

3. To use the dough immediately, place each ball in a bowl and rub the surface of the dough with the remaining oil. Cover the bowl with plastic wrap, and let the dough rise in a warm place until it doubles in size (1½–2 hours).

4. The dough can be frozen to use later. Rub the surface of the dough with the remaining oil and wrap it in plastic. Place the wrapped dough into a plastic bag and freeze it until needed. Then thaw the dough and let it rise before using it.

Active Dry Yeast

Active dry yeast is sometimes referred to as baker's yeast. It is a live culture used to make dough for bread, pizza, and rolls. Unlike fresh yeast, baker's yeast is dried and must have warm water to be activated. Keep active dry yeast sealed in a cool, dark place.

LADENIA

This flatbread comes from the Greek island of Kimolos and is a favorite during Greek Lent. Simplicity rules here: olive oil, onions, tomatoes, and oregano top the dough.

Serves 12

½ cup extra-virgin olive oil, divided

¼ cup semolina flour

Pizza Dough (see recipe in this chapter)

2 large onions, peeled and thinly sliced

2 large tomatoes, cut in half and then cut into half-moon slices

1 teaspoon salt

½ teaspoon pepper

2 tablespoons dry oregano

1. Cover the surface of a large baking pan evenly with ¼ cup of oil. Sprinkle the semolina flour evenly over the oil. Roll out the dough to the dimensions of the baking pan and transfer it to the pan, stretching it to fit.

2. Cover the baking pan with a tea towel and allow the dough to rise for 30 minutes in a warm place. Preheat the oven to 400°F.

3. Pour the remaining oil over the dough and spread it out evenly. Sprinkle the top with the onions followed by the tomatoes. Sprinkle with salt, pepper, and oregano.

4. Bake the ladenia on the middle rack for 40–50 minutes or until the edges have browned and the top is lightly golden.

5. Serve hot or at room temperature.

FETA AND HERB PULL-APARTS

This savory bread makes a great light lunch or snack.

Serves 12

Pizza Dough (see recipe in this chapter)

¼ cup all-purpose flour

3 cloves garlic, peeled and smashed

¼ cup finely chopped scallions, ends trimmed

2 tablespoons chopped fresh parsley

½ teaspoon pepper, divided

1¼ teaspoons dried oregano, divided

½ teaspoon plus ⅛ teaspoon dried rosemary, divided

¼ teaspoon plus ⅛ teaspoon red pepper flakes, divided

⅔ cup crumbled feta cheese

⅔ cup grated kasseri cheese or other sheep's milk cheese

¼ teaspoon sesame seeds

1. Let the dough rise in a warm place for 1½–2 hours. Sprinkle flour on a clean work surface. Punch the dough down and tuck the outer edges inward; then place the dough on a floured work surface. Press your fingers down on the dough and spread it out. Divide the dough into 16–18 equal pieces and roll each piece into a ball. Cover the dough balls with a tea towel and let them rest.

2. Process garlic, scallions, parsley, ¼ teaspoon pepper, 1 teaspoon oregano, ½ teaspoon rosemary, and ¼ teaspoon red pepper flakes in a food processor for 1 minute. Add the cheeses and pulse until smooth.

3. Take one dough ball (keep the others covered) and press it into a 3-inch disc with the palm of your hand. Put 2 teaspoons of the cheese filling in the center and bundle the dough around the filling. Place the dough ball (seam-side down) in a greased, 14-inch round baking pan. Repeat with the remaining dough balls.

4. In a small bowl, combine the remaining pepper, oregano, rosemary, red pepper flakes, and sesame seeds. Brush the tops of the dough with water and sprinkle with the herb mixture. Allow the dough to rise again in a warm place for 30 minutes. Preheat the oven to 400°F.

5. Bake the dough on the middle rack for 30 minutes or until the top is golden. Let the bread cool for 10 minutes before removing it from the pan. Serve warm or at room temperature.

Kasseri

Kasseri, a sheep's milk cheese, is a medium sharp cheese that is not too salty. It is often served as a table cheese in Greece. Enjoy kasseri with toast for breakfast.

PONTIAKA PIROSKI

This recipe is a specialty of the Pontian Greeks who resided for centuries around the Black Sea. The piroski are half moon–shaped fried pieces of dough that have a variety of fillings. This simple potato-and-herb filling is addictive.

Serves 12

1½ teaspoons active dry yeast

1 teaspoon sugar

1½ cups tepid water

¾ cup plus 1 tablespoon extra-virgin olive oil plus extra for frying, divided

2½ teaspoons salt, divided

3½ cups all-purpose flour, divided

2 medium onions, peeled and finely chopped

4 scallions, ends trimmed and thinly sliced

4 large potatoes, cooked, skins peeled, and finely mashed

1 cup finely chopped fresh parsley

¼ cup finely chopped fresh mint

½ teaspoon pepper

1. In a large bowl, combine the yeast, sugar, water, and ¼ cup oil. Set the mixture aside for 5 minutes. Stir in 1½ teaspoons salt. Spread ¼ cup flour on a work surface. Using a large wooden spoon or your hands, gradually stir 3¼ cups of flour into the yeast mixture. When the mixture comes together, empty the bowl onto the floured surface and knead until the dough is pliable and no longer sticks to your hands.

2. Roll the dough into a ball and place it in a bowl. Rub the surface of the dough with 1 tablespoon of oil. Cover the bowl with plastic wrap, and let the dough rise in a warm place until it doubles in size (1½–2 hours).

3. Heat the remaining oil in a skillet over medium heat. Add the onions and scallions. Cook for 12–15 minutes or until the onions are light brown. Cool completely. In a medium bowl, combine onions and scallions, potatoes, parsley, mint, remaining salt, and pepper. Reserve.

4. Pinch off a walnut-size piece of dough. Roll it into a ball and flatten it into a 3-inch disc. Place a tablespoon of filling in the center, and fold the dough over to create a half-moon shape. Pinch the ends to seal the filling into the dough. Repeat with the remaining dough and filling.

5. Heat 3 inches of oil in a deep frying pan over medium-high heat until the oil temperature reaches 365°F. Fry the piroski for 2 minutes per side or until just golden. Transfer to a tray lined with paper towels. Serve them warm or at room temperature.

LAHMACUN

This flatbread is made in the Middle East, Turkey, and Cyprus. Pizza dough works like a charm in this recipe, and Lahmacun is a delicious alternative to pizza. You can find red pepper paste at Middle Eastern grocery stores.

Serves 8

½ large green bell pepper, stemmed, seeded, and chopped

1 medium red onion, peeled and chopped

2 cloves garlic, peeled and smashed

1 tablespoon red pepper paste

1 medium tomato, blanched, peeled, and chopped

½ pound ground lamb or beef

1 teaspoon salt

½ teaspoon pepper

½ teaspoon red pepper flakes

1 teaspoon ground allspice

1 teaspoon dried oregano

¼ cup extra-virgin olive oil

Pizza Dough (see recipe in this chapter)

¼ cup all-purpose flour

1. Preheat the oven to 450°F. Set a pizza stone on the middle rack to preheat as well. If you don't have a pizza stone, use a large greased baking sheet.

2. In a food processor, combine the peppers, onion, garlic, red pepper paste, and tomato. Pulse until the ingredients form a coarse paste. Add the ground lamb or beef, salt, pepper, red pepper flakes, allspice, oregano, and oil.

3. Make sure the Pizza Dough has risen in a warm place for 1½–2 hours. Punch down the dough and divide it into three pieces. Work with one piece of dough at a time. While one is baking, assemble the next one. Stretch and flatten the dough into a long oval shape (about 10" × 4"). Transfer the dough to a well-floured pizza peel (paddle), which is a traditional Italian tool like a wide flat shovel, for moving a pizza so that the dough doesn't stick when you transfer it to the pizza stone (or baking sheet).

4. Spread a third of the lamb filling over the top of the dough. Using your fingers, massage the filling into the dough, getting as near to the edges as possible. Carefully slide the lahmacun onto the pizza stone and bake it for 7–8 minutes or until the crust is browned. Repeat with the remaining dough and filling.

5. Serve this dish hot or at room temperature.

Pizza Stones

If you want pizzeria-grade crusts, you'll need a pizza stone. They are inexpensive and readily available in any cooking store. The stone gets very hot and distributes the heat evenly across the pizza base for a wonderfully crispy crust. The key to a great crust is to preheat the pizza stone in the oven before using it.

EASY HOMEMADE BREAD

Once you've mastered this no-knead recipe, play with the shape of the loaves you create. Try an oval or even a long, lean baguette.

Makes 3 loaves

2 tablespoons active dry yeast

1 teaspoon sugar

3½ cups tepid water

6¾ cups plus 2 tablespoons unbleached all-purpose flour, divided

1½ tablespoons salt

2 tablespoons coarse semolina flour

1. In a large bowl, combine yeast, sugar, and water. Set aside for 7–10 minutes. Gradually stir in 6½ cups flour and salt until a dough starts to form. If the mixture seems a little dry, add up to ½ cup tepid water until the dough comes together. It should feel smooth and not too sticky. Cover the bowl with plastic wrap, leaving a small opening to allow the gases to escape. Let the dough rise a minimum of 2 hours or overnight.

2. Sprinkle ¼ cup flour on a work surface. Divide dough into three pieces and work with one at a time. Stretch the dough outward and then fold under. Repeat this for 2–3 minutes. You should end up with a smooth, round ball (boule) of dough. Repeat with remaining dough.

3. Sprinkle the semolina flour over a piece of parchment paper the same size as a pizza stone or baking sheet. Place the boules on the parchment, leaving room in between to allow the dough to rise. Sprinkle remaining flour over the boules. Let rise for 45 minutes. Use a sharp knife to cut three shallow slices into the top of each boule.

4. Preheat the oven to 500°F. Set a pizza stone or large baking sheet on the middle rack to preheat. Add hot water to a broiler pan and place it on the top rack. Transfer the boules to the pizza stone or baking sheet and bake for 5 minutes. Reduce the temperature to 450°F and bake for 20 minutes or until the boules are golden. Carefully remove them from the oven and allow them to cool to room temperature before serving.

Easy Transfer

Form loaves on a piece of parchment paper that is roughly the size of the pizza stone or baking sheet. Simply slide the parchment paper with the loaves onto the pizza stone for a safe, nonstick transfer.

RAISIN BREAD

The simplicity of toasted raisin bread with butter cannot be beat.

Makes 3 loaves

2 tablespoons active dry yeast

3½ cups tepid water

½ cup honey

1 teaspoon salt

¼ cup extra-virgin olive oil

3 tablespoons powdered milk

6¾ cups plus 2 tablespoons unbleached all-purpose flour, divided

1½ cups raisins

2 tablespoons coarse semolina flour

1. In a large bowl, mix yeast, water, and honey. Set aside for 7–10 minutes. Stir in salt, oil, and powdered milk. Gradually stir in 3 cups flour. Stir in raisins and then gradually stir in another 3½ cups of flour. If the dough seems dry, add up to ½ cup tepid water until it comes together. The dough should feel smooth and not too sticky.

2. Cover the bowl with plastic wrap, but leave a small opening to allow the gases to escape. Let the dough rise in a cool place for a minimum of 6 hours or overnight.

3. When the dough is ready, sprinkle ¼ cup of flour on a work surface. Divide the dough in thirds and work with one piece at a time. Shape the dough into oval loaves.

4. Sprinkle the semolina flour over a piece of parchment paper cut to the same size as a pizza stone or baking sheet. Place the loaves on the parchment, leaving room in between to allow the dough to rise. Sprinkle the remaining flour over the loaves. Let them rise for 1½ hours. When the loaves have risen, use a sharp knife to cut three shallow slices into the top of each loaf.

5. Preheat the oven to 425°F. Set a pizza stone or large baking sheet on the middle rack to preheat. Add hot water to a broiler pan and place it on the top rack. Transfer the loaves to the pizza stone or baking sheet and bake for 30–35 minutes until the bread is golden. Carefully remove the loaves from the oven and allow them to cool to room temperature before serving.

LAGANA

Lagana is a flatbread that originated in ancient Greece. It is still made during the Greek Lent period that precedes Orthodox Easter.

Serves 10

2½ teaspoons active dry yeast

1 teaspoon sugar

1½ cups tepid water

1½ teaspoons salt

3¾ cups all-purpose flour, divided

1 tablespoon vegetable oil

½ cup sesame seeds

1. In a large bowl, combine the yeast, sugar, and water. Set the mixture aside for 7–10 minutes to allow the yeast to activate. Stir in the salt. Using a large wooden spoon or your hands, gradually stir in 3½ cups flour until a dough starts to form. If the mixture seems a little dry, add up to ¼ cup tepid water until the dough comes together. The dough should feel smooth and not too sticky. Cover the bowl with plastic wrap and let the dough rise for 1–1½ hours. It should double in size.

2. Grease two medium baking sheets with oil. Put the remaining flour on a work surface. Punch down the dough and empty the bowl onto the floured surface. Divide the dough in half and place each half on a separate baking sheet. Using your fingers, stretch the dough to fill the baking sheets and form a rectangular shape with rounded ends. Allow the dough to rise another 45–60 minutes.

3. Preheat the oven to 375°F. Deflate the lagana; use your fingertips to poke the dough, leaving behind indentations. Sprinkle each lagana with the sesame seeds.

4. Bake on the middle rack in the oven for 30–35 minutes. Cool completely before serving.

OLIVE BREAD

This olive bread is a celebration of the bounty (olives and mint) of the Halkidiki region of Greece.

Makes 4 loaves

1¾ teaspoons active dry yeast

½ teaspoon sugar

1¾ cups tepid water

1½ tablespoons salt

¾ cup plus 2 tablespoons extra-virgin olive oil, divided

4¼ cups unbleached all-purpose flour, divided

12 medium onions, peeled and diced

¼ cup chopped fresh mint

2 cups black salt-cured olives, pitted and chopped

2 tablespoons fresh rosemary leaves

1. In a large bowl, mix yeast, sugar, and water. Set aside for 7–10 minutes. Stir in salt and ½ cup oil. Gradually stir in 4 cups of flour until it starts to form a dough. If the mixture seems a little dry, add up to ¼ cup tepid water until the dough comes together. Spread the remaining flour on a work surface. Place dough on the surface and knead it for 5–7 minutes or until the dough is pliable and no longer sticky. Place the dough back in the bowl, cover it with plastic wrap, and let it rise in a warm place for 45 minutes.

2. Heat ¼ cup of oil in a large pot over medium heat for 30 seconds. Reduce the heat to medium-low and add onions. Cook onions for 30 minutes or until they soften and most of the water evaporates. Stir in mint and olives. Remove the pot from the heat and allow the onion-olive mixture to cool completely. Reserve.

3. Preheat oven to 375°F. Line two baking sheets with parchment paper. Punch the dough down and knead it for 5 minutes; then divide it into four balls. Using a rolling pin, roll each ball to the size of a large pizza. Spread a quarter of the onion-olive mixture over the dough and roll it. Set the loaf, seam-side down, on a baking sheet. Repeat with the remaining dough and filling.

4. Brush the top of the loaves with the remaining oil and sprinkle with the rosemary. Bake in batches on the middle rack for 30 minutes or until the bread is golden. Allow the bread to cool for 30 minutes before serving.

Wild Rosemary

One thing you will notice near the shorelines of Greece is the growth of wild rosemary. Residents often have hedges of rosemary doubling as fences around their properties.

TSOUREKI (GREEK EASTER BREAD)

This traditional bread is made in large quantities so loaves can be given away as Easter gifts. Mastic and mahlepi can be found at Greek grocery stores. If you can't find mahlepi, you can substitute cardamom.

Makes 5 loaves

½ pound unsalted butter

3 cups plus 1 tablespoon sugar, divided

2½ cups plus 2 tablespoons whole milk, divided

Zest of 1 medium lemon

Zest of 1 medium orange

4 tablespoons fresh orange juice

2 tablespoons plus 1 teaspoon active dry yeast

1 cup warm or tepid water

7 large eggs (6 beaten and 1 unbeaten), divided

12¼ cups all-purpose flour, sifted and divided

1 tablespoon ground mahlepi or ground cardamom

¼ teaspoon ground mastic

1 tablespoon vegetable oil

½ cup sesame seeds

1. In a large pot over medium-low heat, combine the butter, 2½ cups of sugar, and 2½ cups of milk. Cook the mixture for 5 minutes until the butter is melted. Add the lemon zest, orange zest, and orange juice. Set the mixture aside but keep it warm.

2. In a medium bowl, add the yeast, remaining sugar, and water. Set aside for 7–10 minutes to allow the yeast to activate. Whisk the beaten eggs and add them to the reserved milk-butter mixture. Whisk milk-butter mixture into the yeast mixture.

3. In a very large bowl, combine 12 cups of flour, the mahlepi, and the mastic. Add the egg mixture to the dry ingredients. Stir until a dough forms. Spread the remaining flour on a work surface. Knead the dough on the floured surface until it is soft and pliable. Place the dough back in the bowl, rub the surface with the oil, and cover it with plastic wrap. Allow the dough to double in size in a warm place (about 2 hours). Punch the dough down and let it rise a second time (about 2 hours).

4. Divide the dough into fifteen equal balls. Work with three balls at a time. Cover the remaining balls with a tea towel. Roll each ball into a 15-inch-long log. Pinch the top ends of the logs together and then braid the logs. When you get to the end, pinch the bottom ends together. Tuck the top and bottom ends underneath the dough. Braid the dough in batches. Place the braided loaves on baking sheets lined with parchment paper, two braids per baking sheet. Repeat these steps with the remaining dough. Keep the loaves in a warm spot, and allow the dough to rise until braids have doubled in size.

5. Preheat the oven to 350°F. In a small bowl, whisk the remaining egg and milk. Brush the tops of the loaves with the mixture, and then sprinkle them with the sesame seeds. Bake the loaves (in batches) for 25–30 minutes. Allow the bread to cool completely before serving.

GARLIC BREAD

This recipe will have your guests asking for more, so make a lot!

Serves 6

1 cup extra-virgin olive oil

2 cloves garlic, peeled and minced

1 sun-dried tomato, minced

¼ cup chopped fresh chives

2 tablespoons chopped fresh parsley

1 teaspoon dried rosemary

1 teaspoon dried oregano

1 teaspoon salt

¼ teaspoon red pepper flakes

1 (20-inch) baguette

1. Preheat the oven to 300°F. In a small bowl, whisk the oil, garlic, tomato, chives, parsley, rosemary, oregano, salt, and red pepper flakes. Continue whisking until the ingredients are well incorporated.

2. Slice the baguette lengthwise, but leave the back seam intact. Spread the garlic mixture evenly inside both the top and bottom of the baguette. Let it sink into the bread. Fold the bread closed.

3. Wrap the bread in aluminum foil and bake it for 15–20 minutes.

4. Unwrap the garlic bread and serve it warm.

RUFFLED-PHYLLO CHEESE PIE

In the old days, people usually made their phyllo from scratch, until excellent commercial phyllo reached most stores. When time was short or unexpected guests showed up, Greeks used this method to make a lazy phyllo pie.

Serves 12

3 large eggs

½ cup whole milk

2 cups crumbled feta cheese

2 cups ricotta cheese

¼ teaspoon pepper

½ cup unsalted butter, melted

1 package phyllo pastry, thawed, at room temperature

1 (12-ounce) can club soda or sparkling water

1. Preheat the oven to 375°F. In a large bowl, whisk the eggs and milk. Stir in the feta, ricotta, and pepper. Mix well, breaking up the large pieces of feta with your spoon. Reserve the filling.

2. Brush butter on the bottom of a 13" × 9" baking pan. Open the package of phyllo and lay the sheets flat on a work surface. Cover the sheets with a slightly damp tea towel. Phyllo dries quickly so keep the sheets covered.

3. Place a sheet of phyllo on a work surface. Spread 3 tablespoons of the cheese filling over the sheet. Loosely fold about 1 inch of phyllo from the bottom over the filling and lightly pinch the right and left ends. Continue to loosely fold, over and under so it looks like ruffled curtains, and lightly pinch the ends together. Set the folded phyllo sheet in the baking pan with the ruffles facing up, not lying down. Repeat with the remaining phyllo sheets, and set them in the pan leaning against each other until the pan is full.

4. Brush the tops of the phyllo with butter. Pour the club soda or sparkling water over the entire surface. Bake the pie on the middle rack of the oven for 35–45 minutes or until it turns golden brown.

5. Remove the pie from the oven and allow it to cool for 5–10 minutes. Cut the pie into squares and serve.

Thawing Phyllo

Store phyllo in the freezer. When you're ready to use it, it's best to defrost it overnight in the refrigerator. If you can't wait that long, leave the unopened phyllo package at room temperature for at least 2 hours.

FAMILY-STYLE PHYLLO PIE

Before working with phyllo, it's important to be organized and have your filling already prepared.

Serves 12

1 package phyllo pastry, thawed, at room temperature

1 pound unsalted butter, melted

Chicken Pie Filling, Spanakopita Filling, Tyropita Cheese Filling, Smoked Eggplant and Feta Pie Filling, or Leek and Cheese Pie Filling (see recipes in this chapter)

1. Remove the phyllo from the package and count the sheets. Divide the sheets into two equal piles, then take two sheets from one pile and add it to the other pile. The pile with a greater number of sheets will form the bottom layer, and the other pile will form the top layer. Cover each pile with a slightly damp tea towel so the phyllo doesn't dry out. Brush the bottom and sides of a 13" × 9" rectangular or 9" × 9" square pan with the butter.

2. Take one sheet of phyllo from the bottom-layer pile and brush the surface with the butter. Place the sheet in the bottom of the pan with a quarter of the sheet hanging over the side of the pan. Continue buttering and laying the bottom-layer sheets in the pan until the entire bottom and edges are covered with phyllo. Add the filling evenly over the bottom sheets and wrap the overhanging phyllo over the filling (it might not cover all the filling).

3. Take one sheet from the top-layer pile and brush the surface with butter. Place the sheet on top of the filling and repeat the process with the remaining sheets to cover the entire surface of the pan. If excess phyllo hangs from the edges of the pan, gently tuck the excess into the sides of the pan. Chill the pie for 30 minutes. Preheat the oven to 350°F. With a sharp knife, score the top layers of phyllo into serving squares, about ¼-inch deep. The scoring will make the pie easier to cut after it is baked.

4. Bake the pie on the middle rack of the oven for 45 minutes or until the pie is golden. Let the pie cool for 15–20 minutes before serving.

SPIRAL PHYLLO PIES

This spiral phyllo pie is easy to make and always gets rave reviews. Cut it into wedges for a dramatic presentation that reveals the filling.

Serves 12

1 pound unsalted butter, melted

1 package phyllo pastry, thawed, at room temperature

Tyropita Cheese Filling or Spanakopita Filling (see recipes in this chapter)

1. Preheat the oven to 350°F. Brush the melted butter on the bottom and sides of a large round baking pan (about the size of a large pizza). Open the package of phyllo and lay the sheets flat on a work surface. Cover the sheets with a slightly damp tea towel.

2. Place a sheet of phyllo on the work surface with its longest side parallel to you. Brush the sheet with butter and fold the bottom of the sheet upward about 2 inches. Spread about 4 tablespoons of filling along the bottom, but leave 1 inch on the right and left sides empty. Fold the phyllo from the bottom over the filling, and then roll it to form a tight log. Pinch the ends to seal in the filling.

3. Gently lift the log and place it in the center of the baking pan. Twist it to form a coil in the center of the pan. Repeat the process with the remaining phyllo and filling. Wrap each phyllo log snugly around the middle coil to form one large spiral, then tuck the ends of the phyllo logs underneath the other logs to continue forming a continuous large spiral.

4. Brush the top of the spiral with butter and bake it on the middle rack for 45–50 minutes or until golden.

5. Allow the pie to cool for 15–20 minutes before serving.

Oil Versus Butter

Some people prefer to brush phyllo with olive oil instead of butter. You can also try an equal blend of melted butter and olive oil.

PHYLLO TRIANGLES

These flaky triangles of phyllo are popular at parties and easy to make.

Serves 40

1 pound unsalted butter, melted

1 package phyllo pastry, thawed, at room temperature

Tyropita Cheese Filling or Spanakopita Filling (see recipes in this chapter)

1. Preheat the oven to 350°F. Brush the melted butter on the bottom of a large baking tray. Open the package of phyllo and lay the sheets flat on the work surface. Cover the sheets with a slightly damp tea towel.

2. Place a sheet of phyllo on the work surface. Brush the sheet with butter, and then place another sheet on top of it. Brush the top sheet with butter. Place a third sheet on top of the second sheet. Cut the stack of phyllo sheets lengthwise into four equal strips.

3. To form a triangle, place a tablespoon of filling on the phyllo, 1 inch from the bottom of a strip. Fold the end over the filling at a 45-degree angle. Continue folding right to the top to form a triangle that completely encloses the filling. Repeat the process with the remaining three strips. Place the triangles on the baking sheet and brush the tops with butter. Repeat these steps with the remaining phyllo and filling.

4. Bake the phyllo triangles on the middle rack for 30 minutes or until they are golden. Allow them to cool for 10 minutes and serve them warm.

CHICKEN PIE FILLING

This recipe is a great way to use up leftover chicken or turkey. If you don't have time to roast a chicken, buy a rotisserie chicken from the supermarket.

Serves 12

¼ cup extra-virgin olive oil

1 large onion, peeled and diced

3 scallions, ends trimmed and thinly sliced

1 clove garlic, peeled and minced

2 cups quartered button mushrooms

1 teaspoon salt, divided

½ teaspoon pepper, divided

¼ cup brandy

2½ cups roasted or cooked shredded chicken or turkey meat

2 tablespoons chopped fresh sage

1 cup grated smoked Gouda cheese

¾ cup half-and-half cream

3 large eggs

1. Heat the oil in a large skillet over medium heat for 30 seconds. Stir in the onions, scallions, garlic, and mushrooms. Cook for 5–6 minutes, and then season with ½ teaspoon of salt and ¼ teaspoon of pepper.

2. Stir in the brandy and cook for 2 minutes. Add the chicken and cook for 2–3 minutes. Take the skillet off the heat. Stir in the sage, and season with the remaining salt and pepper. Allow the filling to cool for 15 minutes. Stir in the cheese.

3. In a small bowl, whisk the cream and eggs. Add the mixture to the chicken filling and stir to thoroughly combine the ingredients.

4. The filling can be used immediately, or it can be refrigerated. If you refrigerate the filling, bring it to room temperature before using it.

SPANAKOPITA FILLING

This is a spinach-and-ricotta filling that can be used as a filling option for the Family-Style Phyllo Pie (see recipe in this chapter). You can also use it as a filling for Spiral Phyllo Pies or Phyllo Triangles (see recipes in this chapter).

Serves 12

¼ cup extra-virgin olive oil

4 or 5 scallions, ends trimmed and thinly sliced

1½ cups blanched and drained spinach, excess water removed, chopped

1 cup ricotta cheese

1 cup crumbled feta cheese

½ teaspoon pepper

2 large eggs, beaten

½ cup chopped fresh dill

1. Heat the oil in a large skillet over medium heat for 30 seconds. Add the scallions and cook for 5 minutes or until the scallions are soft. Remove the skillet from the heat, and allow the scallions to cool.

2. In a large bowl, combine the cooled scallions, spinach, ricotta, feta, pepper, eggs, and dill. Stir well to combine.

3. The filling can be used immediately, or it can be refrigerated. If you refrigerate the filling, bring it to room temperature before using it.

TYROPITA CHEESE FILLING

For a change, try adding some of your favorite chopped fresh herbs to this cheese filling.

Serves 12

2 cups ricotta cheese

2 cups crumbled feta cheese

3 large eggs, beaten

½ teaspoon pepper

1. Put all the ingredients in a large bowl, and stir well to combine them.

2. The filling can be used immediately, or it can be refrigerated. If you refrigerate the filling, bring it to room temperature before using it.

SMOKED EGGPLANT AND FETA PIE FILLING

Combine any leftover filling with cooked pasta for a quick and tasty dinner.

Serves 12

4 large eggplants, skins pierced several times with a fork

1 teaspoon red wine vinegar

2 cups crumbled feta cheese

4 large eggs, beaten

½ teaspoon pepper

1. Preheat a gas or charcoal grill to medium-high. Grill the eggplants for 20–30 minutes or until the skin is completely charred and the insides are soft. Cool for 10 minutes. Cut them open lengthwise and scoop out the softened flesh, discarding the charred skin.

2. In a large bowl, combine the eggplant and vinegar. Stir in feta, eggs, and pepper. The filling can be used immediately, or it can be refrigerated. If you refrigerate the filling, bring it to room temperature before using it.

LEEK AND CHEESE PIE FILLING

This filling is ideal for the autumn and winter months when leeks are in season.

Serves 12

¼ cup extra-virgin olive oil

4 leeks (white parts only), ends trimmed, thoroughly cleaned, cut lengthwise, and finely chopped

2 medium zucchini, peeled and grated

1 teaspoon salt

1 cup ricotta cheese

1 cup crumbled feta cheese

3 large eggs, beaten

½ cup chopped fresh dill

½ teaspoon pepper

1. Heat the oil in a large skillet over medium heat. Add the leeks and cook for 5 minutes or until they soften. Stir in zucchini and salt. Reduce heat to medium-low and cook for 30 minutes. Take the skillet off the heat and cool the mixture to room temperature.

2. In a large bowl, combine the leek mixture, ricotta, feta, eggs, dill, and pepper. The filling can be used immediately, or it can be refrigerated. If you refrigerate the filling, bring it to room temperature before using it.

PASTOURMA PIE

This phyllo pie features pastourma, an air-cured beef. This unique ingredient can be found at Greek, Turkish, and Middle Eastern shops.

Serves 12

1 package phyllo pastry, thawed and at room temperature

1 cup butter, melted

16 thin slices pastourma

3 medium tomatoes, thinly sliced

1½ cups Béchamel Sauce (see recipe in Chapter 2)

½ pound sliced kasseri or Havarti cheese

1. Divide the phyllo sheets into two equal piles, take two sheets from one pile, and add them to the other pile. The pile with a greater number of sheets will form the bottom layer, and the other pile will form the top layer. Cover each pile with a slightly damp tea towel so the phyllo doesn't dry out. Brush the bottom and sides of a 13" × 9" rectangular or square pan with the butter.

2. Take one sheet of phyllo from the bottom layer pile, and brush the surface with the butter. Place the sheet in the bottom of the pan with a quarter of the sheet hanging over the side of the pan. Continue buttering and laying the bottom-layer sheets in the pan until the entire bottom and edges are covered with phyllo.

3. Add a layer of pastourma over the bottom layer of phyllo. Then add a layer of tomatoes. Spread the Béchamel Sauce over the tomatoes. Top with a layer of cheese.

4. Take one sheet from the top-layer pile and brush the surface with butter. Place the sheet on top of the filling (butter side up) and repeat with the remaining sheets to cover the entire surface of the pan. If excess phyllo is hanging from the edges of the pan, gently tuck the excess into the sides of the pan. Chill the pie for 30 minutes.

5. Preheat the oven to 350°F. With a sharp knife, score the top layers of phyllo into serving squares, about ¼-inch deep.

6. Bake the pie on the middle rack for 45 minutes or until the pie is golden. Let the pie cool for 15–20 minutes before serving.

Pastourma
Pastourma is air-cured beef that is rubbed in a paste made of garlic, fenugreek, and paprika. The best pastourma is offered at shops in Istanbul's spice market.

PRASSOPITA (LEEK PIE)

Serve this on the following day to allow the flavors time to meld. Refrigerate the pie once it has cooled to room temperature, and then cut and warm the slices as needed.

Serves 6

½ cup extra-virgin olive oil

3 or 4 large leeks, sliced thinly (upper dark-green stalks removed)

¼ cup green onion, finely chopped

3 large eggs

1½ cups milk

1 cup crumbled Greek feta cheese

¾ cup all-purpose flour

¼ cup fresh dill, finely chopped

1 teaspoon dried oregano

Fresh-ground pepper and pinch of salt

1. Preheat the oven to 350°F.

2. Heat olive oil in pan; sauté leeks about 5 minutes. Add onion; continue sautéing until both are soft and tender, another 3 minutes or so.

3. In a large bowl, beat eggs well; add milk, feta, flour, dill, oregano, pepper, salt, and sautéed leeks and onions; mix well.

4. Grease sides of a baking dish with olive oil; pour mixture into the dish. Bake about 1 hour.

5. Allow to cool before cutting. Can be served warm or at room temperature.

PATATOPITA (POTATO PIE)

This recipe incorporates halloumi cheese. Halloumi is a traditional Cypriot cheese made from sheep and goat's milk that has a texture similar to mozzarella, though saltier in flavor.

Serves 6

2½ pounds white potatoes

1 cup finely crumbled Greek feta cheese

1 cup finely shredded halloumi cheese

1 tablespoon finely chopped fresh mint leaves

Slight pinch nutmeg

Salt and pepper to taste

4 or 5 eggs, well beaten

2 tablespoons extra-virgin olive oil

1 cup dried bread crumbs

1. Preheat the oven to 350°F.

2. Wash and peel the potatoes; cut into small chunks. Boil in plenty of salted water until soft, about 30–40 minutes. Drain and place in a large mixing bowl; mash well and leave to cool slightly a few minutes.

3. Add cheeses, mint, nutmeg, salt, pepper, and eggs; incorporate well with potatoes, until entire mix is smooth and creamy.

4. Using 1 tablespoon oil, grease the pie baking pan well; spread a little less than half of the bread crumbs evenly across the bottom of the pan. Pour the potato pie mix into the greased pan; spread evenly.

5. Evenly distribute the rest of the bread crumbs across the top; spray remaining olive oil on top.

6. Bake for 40–45 minutes, or until the top is golden brown. Note: The pie will rise while in the oven and will settle when removed to cool, so don't be surprised by either state. Let stand 1 hour before slicing and serving.

Thank You, Columbus!

Potatoes, peppers, and tomatoes are all relatively recent imports to the Mediterranean region from the Americas.

SPANAKOTYROPITA (SPINACH AND CHEESE PIE)

Dandelion greens can be added to this recipe for a variation on the flavor.

Yields approximately 20 pieces

2 pounds fresh spinach

½ cup fresh dill, finely chopped

½ cup fennel leaves, finely chopped

2 large leeks, white part only, thinly sliced

2 green onions, diced

½ cup extra-virgin olive oil, divided

1 pound Greek feta cheese, crumbled

2 eggs, lightly beaten

Salt and fresh-ground pepper to taste

1 package commercial phyllo

1. Preheat the oven to 350°F.

2. Wash the spinach well; chop coarsely and set aside to drain well. Wash, drain, chop, and combine dill and fennel in a mixing bowl.

3. In a large frying pan, sauté the leeks and diced green onions in 2 tablespoons olive oil until soft; set aside in a mixing bowl 10 minutes to cool. Add dill and fennel, feta, eggs, salt, and pepper; mix thoroughly.

4. Spread out the phyllo sheet. Lightly brush the sheet entirely with olive oil; spread a line of cheese and vegetable mix along the length of one edge. Roll lengthwise into a long cigar shape with the filling inside. Curl each cigar-shaped package into a spiral; place on a lightly greased baking sheet.

5. Bake for 45 minutes, until golden brown. Serve hot or cold.

AEGEAN TYROPITA (NO-PASTRY CHEESE PIE)

Any fine or specialty cheese shop in most major cities will stock the requisite Greek cheeses for this recipe.

Serves 6

4 eggs

1½ cups grated kefalograviera (saganaki) cheese

1½ cups grated Graviera cheese

1 cup strained/pressed yogurt

1 cup all-purpose flour

⅓ cup extra-virgin olive oil, divided

1 teaspoon dried oregano

¼ teaspoon fresh-ground pepper

¼ cup dry bread crumbs

1. Preheat the oven to 350°F.

2. In a large mixing bowl, beat the eggs. Add the cheeses, yogurt, flour, all of the olive oil (except 1 tablespoonful), oregano, and pepper; mix thoroughly.

3. Grease a shallow baking pan with a 1 tablespoon olive oil. Evenly sprinkle bread crumbs to cover the bottom; pour in the mixture and spread evenly.

4. Bake for 50–60 minutes, until the top is slightly browned. Let cool slightly before cutting to serve.

FOCACCIA

Cooked vegetables or fresh herbs can be added to this recipe to make different flavored focaccias. Also, you can shape the dough into roll form for individual sandwiches.

Serves 6

1 teaspoon olive oil

½ cup rye flour

1½ cups all-purpose unbleached flour

½ teaspoon baking powder

½ teaspoon baking soda

¾ cup water

1. Preheat the oven to 375°F. Brush a small loaf or cake pan with some of the oil.

2. Mix together the remaining oil and all the other ingredients. Dust a work area with flour, and knead the dough. Place in a pan and let rise for at least 1 hour in a warm place.

3. Place the pan in the oven and bake for 45 minutes or until done.

Herb-Flavored Focaccia

Focaccia bread has become a popular favorite for use in pizzas and as a delicious accompaniment to Italian or any meals. To make the bread more crispy, drizzle a little olive oil on the crust before baking; to make it softer, brush the crust with oil immediately after it comes out of the oven. Focaccia, a wonderful sandwich bread alternative, can transform a simple entrée into a special treat.

FRY BREAD

Once you have become a pro at making traditional fry bread, stir things up a bit by substituting buttermilk for the water.

Serves 6

½ cup all-purpose unbleached flour

¼ cup wheat flour

¼ cup cornmeal

¼ teaspoon salt

⅓ cup water

½ cup olive oil, divided

1. Sift together the flours, cornmeal, and salt. Using a dough hook or your hands, combine the flour mixture with the water and 2 tablespoons of the oil.

2. On a lightly floured surface, roll out the dough ⅛-inch thick and cut into desired shapes.

3. Heat the remainder of the oil in a heavy-bottomed skillet (preferably cast iron) over medium-high heat. Fry the dough until light golden brown, then drain each on a rack covered with paper towels.

Fry Bread Anytime

You can serve fry bread with just about any meal. For instance, if you serve it with a little butter and honey, you can pass it off as a dessert. Or, try shaping the bread into doughnuts before frying. Dip into powdered sugar once they have cooled enough and you'll have homemade doughnuts for breakfast!

FLATBREAD

Flatbread is often served with cheese, soup, or salad. However, you could get a little more creative and use flatbread as pizza crust.

Serves 6

¼ cup spelt flour

¼ cup wheat flour

½ cup all-purpose unbleached flour

¼ teaspoon salt

¼ cup water

2 tablespoons olive oil, divided

1. Sift together the flours and salt. Using a dough hook or your hands, combine the flour mixture with the water and 1 tablespoon of the oil.

2. On a floured surface, roll out the dough ⅛-inch thick and cut into desired shapes.

3. Heat the remaining oil in a heavy-bottomed skillet (preferably cast iron) over medium-high heat and cook the flatbread on each side for 1–2 minutes.

CHAPTER 4

APPETIZERS AND SIDES

LAMB RIBS

Serve lamb ribs with a side of homemade Tzatziki (see recipe in Chapter 2).

Serves 4

1 tablespoon onion powder

1 tablespoon garlic powder

2 tablespoons lemon-pepper seasoning

1 teaspoon ground bay leaves

2 teaspoons ground allspice

2 teaspoons dry thyme

1 tablespoon salt

2 tablespoons sweet paprika

4 racks lamb ribs, excess fat trimmed and silver skin removed

2 teaspoons dried oregano

2 large lemons, cut into wedges

1. In a medium bowl, add onion powder, garlic powder, lemon pepper, bay, allspice, thyme, salt, and paprika. Thoroughly combine the spice mix. Rub the mix all over the ribs. Make sure the spices are distributed evenly over the meat. Allow the spices to penetrate the ribs in the refrigerator for 3 hours or for 1 hour at room temperature.

2. Preheat the oven to 425°F. If the ribs were in the refrigerator, allow them to return to room temperature before placing them on a parchment-lined baking sheet. Cover the ribs with aluminum foil and bake for 45 minutes; lower the heat to 375°F and cook for 15 minutes more. Remove the foil and bake for another 30 minutes.

3. Remove sheet from the oven and tent the ribs with foil for 5 minutes. Cut the ribs, sprinkle them with dried oregano, and serve them with lemon wedges.

How to Remove the Silver Skin

Silver skin is the membrane that covers the bones on a rack of ribs. Removing this skin allows the rub or marinade to penetrate the meat more easily. If your butcher hasn't already removed the silver skin, you can do it yourself. Run a small knife underneath the silver skin to loosen it from the ribs and then pull it off. It should peel away easily in one piece.

OCTOPUS MEATBALLS

Ouzo is the perfect drink for this appetizer! Octopus can be prepared in many different ways, but it must first be tenderized. Braising octopus is an easy method to accomplish this.

Serves 6

2 tablespoons extra-virgin olive oil, plus more for frying

1 medium onion, peeled and finely chopped

2 cloves garlic, peeled and minced

1 tablespoon red or white wine

1 pound braised octopus, liquid discarded (see Grilled Octopus recipe in Chapter 10)

1 teaspoon dried oregano

½ teaspoon finely chopped fresh mint

¼ cup finely chopped fresh parsley

2 tablespoons bread crumbs (optional)

1 medium starchy potato, peeled, cooked, and grated

1 teaspoon salt

½ teaspoon pepper

1 cup all-purpose flour

2 large lemons, cut into wedges

1. In a medium skillet over medium heat, add 2 tablespoons oil and heat for 30 seconds. Add onion and cook for 3–4 minutes until translucent. Add garlic and wine. Remove from heat and allow onion mixture to cool.

2. Place the cooled onion mixture in a food processor with octopus, oregano, mint, and parsley. Pulse ingredients into a mixture that is well blended. If the mixture is too wet, add bread crumbs to help bind the mixture.

3. In a large bowl, combine the octopus mixture with the grated potato. Season with salt and pepper. Using your hands, roll the octopus mixture into small meatballs (about 1 inch) and lightly dredge them in flour.

4. In a deep frying pan over medium-high heat, add 1 inch of oil. Bring the oil temperature up to 350°F. Adjust the heat to keep the temperature at 350°F while frying. Fry the octopus balls (in batches) until they are golden brown (about 1 minute per side). Place the balls on a tray lined with paper towels to soak up any excess oil.

5. Serve warm or at room temperature with lemon wedges.

GOAT CHEESE–STUFFED ONIONS

A crumbled goat cheese feta will also work well here.

Serves 4

4 medium onions, peeled

1 teaspoon salt

1 cup soft goat cheese

1 clove garlic, peeled and minced

2 teaspoons fresh thyme leaves

½ teaspoon pepper

¼ cup extra-virgin olive oil

¼ cup warm heavy cream

3 scallions or 12 chives, ends trimmed and chopped

1 teaspoon sweet paprika

1. Preheat the oven to 375°F. Place a large pot over high heat, fill two-thirds with water, and bring the water to a boil. Cut into each onion along the length and right through to the center. Do not cut past the center of the onion. When the water comes to a boil, add the salt and reduce the heat to medium. Carefully drop onions into the boiling water and simmer for 5–6 minutes or until they are soft to the touch and have opened up like a clam. Remove the onions with a slotted spoon and allow them to cool for about 10 minutes.

2. Carefully peel back each layer of each onion until you are left with the heart of the onion. Remove the hearts (you can use the hearts in another dish). Continue to peel the onions until you have a plate of onion shells.

3. In a bowl, combine the cheese, garlic, thyme, and pepper. To fill the onion shells, open a shell and place 1 tablespoon of the cheese mixture inside. Wrap the onion shell around the filling and place the onion upright in a shallow, medium baking dish. Fill the remaining onions and fit them snugly into the dish.

4. Drizzle the onions with the oil and bake for 25 minutes or until just browned. Spoon the heavy cream over the onions. Sprinkle with the scallions and paprika and serve immediately.

Cheeses of Greece

Most Greek cheeses are made of goat's milk, sheep's milk, or a combination of the two. Greeks have been making cheese for thousands of years, and today they eat the most cheese of all Europeans. There are almost fifty varieties of Greek cheese from the Aegean Islands alone!

POTATO CROQUETTES WITH SMOKED CHEESE

There are a variety of smoked cheeses available now. Look for smoked Gouda, Gruyère, Cheddar, mozzarella, and Greek Metsovone in your local cheese shop.

Serves 6

4 large potatoes, peeled and cut into chunks

1½ teaspoons salt, divided

4 cloves garlic, peeled

4 tablespoons unsalted butter, softened

1 cup plus 2 tablespoons whole milk, divided

½ cup chopped fresh chives or scallions

1 teaspoon dried oregano

¾ teaspoon pepper

1 cup grated smoked Metsovone cheese or smoked Gouda

1 large egg

½ cup fine cornmeal

Extra-virgin olive oil for frying

1. In a large pot over high heat, add potatoes, ½ teaspoon salt, garlic, and enough water to cover the potatoes by 1 inch. Cover pot and bring the water to a boil. Reduce heat to medium and cook potatoes for 15 minutes or until they are fork-tender. Drain the potatoes and garlic and return them to the empty pot.

2. In a small pot over medium heat, add the butter and 1 cup milk. Cook for 3 minutes until the butter has melted and the milk is warm. Reserve.

3. Mash the potatoes and garlic. Gradually add the warm butter-milk mixture and continue to mash until the potatoes are smooth. Stir in chives, oregano, the remaining salt, and pepper. Allow the mashed potatoes to cool completely. When the mashed potatoes have cooled, stir in the cheese.

4. Roll potato mixture into 1-inch balls. You should have about thirty balls. In a small bowl, add the egg and remaining milk and beat. Put the cornmeal into a medium bowl. Dip each ball into the egg mixture and then roll it in the cornmeal.

5. Add 1 inch of oil to a deep frying pan over medium-high heat. Bring the oil temperature to 350°F. Adjust the heat to keep the temperature at 350°F while frying. Fry the balls (in batches) until they are golden, about 1 minute per side. Transfer the balls to a tray lined with paper towels to soak up any excess oil. Serve warm.

BAKED OYSTERS WITH TOMATOES, CAPERS, AND FETA

A fresh raw oyster topped with a squeeze of lemon is a great treat. If you're trying oysters for the first time, baking them is a good introduction to this delicious shellfish.

Serves 4

¼ cup extra-virgin olive oil

½ cup thinly sliced scallions, ends trimmed

2 cloves garlic, peeled and sliced

3 medium plum tomatoes, chopped

½ teaspoon smoked paprika

¼ cup dry white wine

2 teaspoons capers

1 teaspoon fresh thyme leaves

¼ teaspoon red pepper flakes

½ cup bread crumbs

1 cup crumbled feta cheese

12 medium-size fresh oysters, shucked and bottom shells reserved

1 large lemon, cut into wedges

1. Preheat the oven to 450°F. In a large skillet over medium heat, add the oil and heat for 30 seconds. Add scallions, garlic, and tomatoes. Simmer for 5–6 minutes. Add paprika and wine, and simmer for another 2–3 minutes or until most of the liquid evaporates. Add the capers, thyme, and red pepper flakes. Take the skillet off the heat and allow the ingredients to cool for 15 minutes.

2. Add the bread crumbs and feta to the cooled topping mixture. Line a baking sheet with the oysters in their bottom shells. Divide the topping mixture evenly over the oysters.

3. Bake the oysters on the middle rack for 15–20 minutes or until the tops are golden brown. Serve the oysters hot or warm with lemon wedges.

Buying and Preparing Oysters

Buy oysters from a trusted fishmonger. Ask your fishmonger what type of oyster they are, where they are from, and any tips for shucking them. Fresh oysters can be refrigerated for up to 1 day before using. After shucking an oyster, always smell it to check for spoilage. The oyster should smell of the sea—if it has a fishy smell, throw it away.

DOLMADES GIALANTZI

Dolmades are a Greek and Turkish dish that consists of savory rice stuffed into grape leaves and baked in a sauce.

Serves 12

¼ cup plus 2 tablespoons extra-virgin olive oil, divided

1 medium onion, chopped

1 cup long-grain rice

1 teaspoon tomato paste, diluted in ½ cup warm water

½ cup chopped fresh parsley

½ cup chopped fresh dill

¼ cup chopped fresh mint

⅓ cup pine nuts

1 tablespoon fresh lemon juice

2½ teaspoons salt

¾ teaspoon pepper

40 medium jarred grape leaves, rinsed and stemmed

1½ cups hot Basic Vegetable Stock (see recipe in Chapter 2)

2 medium lemons, thinly sliced

1. In a large skillet over medium-low heat, add 2 tablespoons oil and heat for 30 seconds. Add onions and cook for 5–7 minutes or until translucent. Stir in rice and cook for 3 minutes. Stir in tomato paste. Cook for another 3–4 minutes or until most of the liquid has been absorbed by the rice. Take the skillet off the heat, stir in parsley, dill, mint, pine nuts, and lemon juice. Season with salt and pepper and allow the rice mixture to cool.

2. Preheat the oven to 325°F. Place a grape leaf on a work surface (seam-side up) and place 1 teaspoon of the rice mixture in the middle bottom part of the leaf. Fold the bottom of the leaf over the filling, and then tuck in the sides of the leaf. Roll the leaf into a cigar shape. Repeat with remaining leaves. Place the stuffed leaves snugly into a medium roasting pan (with a lid).

3. Pour the remaining oil and the stock over the stuffed leaves. Top with a layer of lemon slices. Cover the pan and bake for 30–35 minutes. Remove the lemon slices before serving. Serve at room temperature.

Grape Leaves

If you don't pick your own grape leaves, there are many jarred options available in Greek or Middle Eastern grocery stores. Try a few different brands to see which one you like best. Remember to rinse the jarred grape leaves before using them.

CHEESE SAGANAKI

Kefalotyri is a firm sheep's milk cheese from Greece. You can also substitute any firm aged sheep's milk cheese. Ask your grocer to suggest one for you.

Serves 2

1 (4" × 4" × ½") piece of kefalotyri cheese, rind removed

½ cup all-purpose flour

1½ tablespoons extra-virgin olive oil

1 ounce Metaxa brandy, brandy, or ouzo

1 large lemon wedge

1. Heat a medium cast-iron pan over medium-high heat for 5 minutes. Dip the cheese in a bowl of water and then dredge the cheese in the flour. Shake off any excess flour.

2. Add oil to the pan and heat for 30 seconds. Add the cheese and fry for 2 minutes. Carefully flip the cheese with a spatula and fry for another 2 minutes.

3. Turn off the heat, pour the brandy (from a glass, never the bottle) over the cheese, and carefully ignite the brandy with a lighter. Be careful here because the flame might reach high, so keep your head back. Squeeze the wedge of lemon over the cheese to douse the flame. Serve immediately.

Take Care When Lighting Cheese Saganaki

Never pour the brandy directly from the bottle into a pan that is near an open flame because the flame can follow the stream of alcohol back into the bottle and this can cause it to explode. Always pour the small amount of brandy you are using into a cup and use that instead of the bottle. Keep the bottle away from open flames.

KEFTEDES (GREEK MEAT PATTIES)

You can use a variety of ground meats to make these grilled Keftedes. These meat patties are also wonderful fried. Dredge them in a little flour and fry them in extra-virgin olive oil for a delicious treat.

Serves 6

2 pounds lean ground beef

2 medium onions, peeled and grated

2 slices bread, soaked in water, hand squeezed, and crumbled

1 tablespoon minced garlic

2 large eggs, beaten

2 teaspoons dried oregano

2 tablespoons chopped fresh parsley

1 teaspoon chopped fresh mint

⅛ teaspoon ground cumin

2½ teaspoons salt

¾ teaspoon pepper

1. In a large bowl, combine all the ingredients and mix well. Use your hands to form 2-inch patties with the meat mixture; place them on a tray. You'll get approximately sixteen patties. Wrap the tray with plastic wrap and refrigerate for at least 4 hours or overnight.

2. Preheat a gas or charcoal grill to medium-high heat. Bring the meat patties to room temperature before grilling. Place them on the hot grill and cook for 3–4 minutes per side. Serve immediately.

Greek Oregano

In Greek, *oregano* means "joy of the mountain." Greek oregano has wider and fuzzier leaves than the common variety. When dried, it has an unmistakable and distinct pungent aroma. Whenever possible, use Greek oregano in your dishes.

ROASTED RED PEPPERS

Roasted peppers can be stored in the freezer for up to 6 months. To protect the peppers from freezer burn, leave the charred skin on. Thaw the peppers overnight in the refrigerator and peel the charred skin off the peppers before using.

Serves 4

6 large red bell peppers

¼ cup extra-virgin olive oil

½ teaspoon salt

1. Preheat a gas or charcoal grill to medium-high. Place peppers on the grill and char them on all sides. Place the peppers in a bowl and cover tightly with plastic wrap. Cool for 20 minutes. Remove the charred skins and discard. Slit the peppers in half; remove and discard the seeds and stem.

2. Place peppers on a serving tray. Drizzle with oil and season with salt. Serve at room temperature.

ROASTED RED PEPPER DIP

If you don't have time to roast peppers, use drained, jarred roasted red peppers. You can find them in most grocery stores.

Serves 4

2 large red peppers

1 medium-hot banana pepper

1 scallion, ends trimmed

1 clove garlic, peeled

4 sun-dried tomatoes, packed in olive oil, rinsed

1 cup crumbled feta cheese

1 cup coarsely chopped fresh basil

⅓ cup extra-virgin olive oil

1. Preheat a gas or charcoal grill to medium-high heat. Place peppers on the hot grill and char them on all sides. Place peppers in a bowl and cover tightly with plastic wrap. Cool for 20 minutes. Remove the charred skins and discard. Slit peppers in half; remove and discard the seeds and stem.

2. Add peppers, scallion, garlic, sun-dried tomatoes, feta, and basil to a food processor and pulse until smooth. With the processor running, slowly add oil. Serve at room temperature.

BOUYIOURDI

Bouyiourdi is a hot, cheesy Greek fondue that's perfect with crusty bread.

Serves 4

1 large tomato, diced, divided

½ cup grated kasseri or Gouda cheese, divided

½ cup crumbled feta cheese

1 small banana pepper, sliced into ¼-inch slices

1 tablespoon extra-virgin olive oil

¼ teaspoon red pepper flakes

½ teaspoon oregano

1. Preheat the oven to 400°F. Place half of the diced tomato on the bottom of a medium ramekin. Top the tomatoes with ¼ cup kasseri and then the feta. Top the cheeses with the remaining diced tomatoes. Top the tomatoes with the remaining kasseri and peppers. Drizzle oil over the peppers and sprinkle with red pepper flakes and oregano.

2. Cover the ramekin tightly with foil and bake for 20 minutes or until the cheese is bubbling. Serve immediately.

MELITZANOSALATA (EGGPLANT DIP)

You will need either a charcoal or a gas grill, as well as a mortar and pestle, to prepare this dish with finesse.

Serves 4

1 large eggplant, skin pierced several times with a fork

1 clove garlic, peeled

1 teaspoon salt

1 tablespoon red wine vinegar

½ cup extra-virgin olive oil

2 tablespoons finely chopped fresh parsley

1. Preheat a gas or charcoal grill to medium-high heat. Place the eggplant on the grill and cook for 20–30 minutes or until the skin is completely charred and the inside is soft. Let the eggplant cool for 10 minutes. Cut the eggplant open (lengthwise) and scoop out the softened flesh, discarding the charred skin.

2. In a medium-size mortar, add garlic and salt and mash with a pestle into a fine paste. Add the eggplant and vinegar and mash until smooth.

3. Slowly add oil to the eggplant mixture and continue to mash until the oil is completely incorporated. Stir in parsley and adjust seasoning, if necessary. Serve at room temperature.

FRIED CALAMARI

Frozen, cleaned calamari (squid) is readily found in most major supermarkets and will work well for this dish. Thaw the frozen calamari in the refrigerator overnight.

Serves 4

1 pound calamari (squid), tubes and tentacles cleaned and quill removed

1 cup all-purpose flour

½ cup fine cornmeal

1½ teaspoons salt, divided

¾ teaspoon pepper

Extra-virgin olive oil for frying

1 large lemon, cut into wedges

1. Cut calamari tubes into ½-inch rings. Pat rings and tentacles dry with paper towels.

2. In a medium bowl, combine flour, cornmeal, 1 teaspoon salt, and pepper. Dredge calamari in the flour mixture. Shake off any excess flour.

3. Add 2 inches of oil to a deep frying pan over medium-high heat. Bring the oil temperature to 365°F. Adjust the heat to keep the temperature at 365°F while frying. Fry the calamari (in batches) for 3–4 minutes until they are lightly golden. Do not fry calamari for longer or they will become tough. Place the calamari on a tray lined with paper towels to soak up any excess oil. Sprinkle the remaining salt over the calamari immediately after frying.

4. Serve warm or at room temperature with lemon wedges.

How to Clean a Squid

To clean a squid, pull the head and tentacles away from the body. Remove the thin, clear quill and innards. Peel the skin from the body. Cut the tentacles away from the head just below the eyes and beak. Discard the quill, innards, skin, and head. Rinse the squid pieces well and pat dry with a paper towel.

OUZO-CURED SALMON

You don't want any bones in this dish, so inspect the salmon with your fingers to see if there are any hidden pin bones. Use a small, clean pair of needle-nose pliers to remove any bones that you find. Serve the cured salmon on its own or on toasted bread.

Serves 4

2 tablespoons coarse salt

1 tablespoon sugar

2 teaspoons pepper

1 teaspoon ground anise or ground fennel

1 teaspoon red pepper flakes

1 tablespoon grated orange or lemon zest

1 pound whole salmon, scaled, filleted, and pin bones removed

2 ounces ouzo

1 cup chopped fresh fennel fronds

1. In a small bowl, combine salt, sugar, pepper, anise, red pepper flakes, and zest. Reserve.

2. Place one salmon fillet on a large piece of plastic wrap (about three to four times the length of the fillet) with the skin-side down, pink flesh facing up. Pour ouzo over the fillet.

3. Rub the spice mixture over the salmon flesh. Make sure to cover as much of the exposed flesh as possible. Top the spice mixture with fennel. Carefully place the second fillet flesh-side down on top of the fennel (making a sandwich of the fillets).

4. Wrap the salmon tightly with the plastic wrap and place it on a large tray (deep enough to catch the juices that will seep out during the curing process).

5. Place a heavy weight (cans of tomatoes or apple juice will work fine) on top of the salmon and refrigerate it for at least 24 hours and up to 4 days (the longer you leave it, the better the flavor).

6. Unwrap the salmon, rinse it off, and pat it dry with paper towels. Using a sharp knife, thinly slice the fillets on the diagonal. Serve cool or at room temperature. Unused cured salmon can be kept wrapped in the refrigerator for up to 1 week.

Ouzo

Ouzo is the national drink of Greece. It's made by pressing grapes, blending the juice with herbs and spices, and boiling the mixture in copper stills. It is then cooled and stored for a few months before being diluted to contain about 40 percent alcohol.

FRIED PEPPERS

Using a variety of different colored peppers makes this simple dish spectacular.

Serves 4

1 pound long, slender red or green peppers (sweet or hot), rinsed and dried

¼ cup extra-virgin olive oil

1 teaspoon salt

1 tablespoon red or white wine vinegar

1. Poke the peppers with a fork a few times all over. Heat the oil in a large skillet over medium-high heat. Fry the peppers (in batches) for 3–4 minutes per side until the skins are lightly golden.

2. Transfer the peppers to a tray lined with paper towels and season them with salt. Serve on a plate with a drizzle of the remaining oil and the vinegar. Serve warm or at room temperature.

Eat More Peppers

Did you know peppers are fruits, not vegetables? Peppers originated in Mexico and South America and were introduced to Spain in the late 1400s. They were quickly adopted by and grown in other European countries. From there, peppers spread to Africa and Asia.

BAKED FETA

Choose plum or Roma tomatoes for cooking as they have less water and fewer seeds and are usually sweeter than the garden-variety tomato. Don't forget to serve lots of crusty bread with this dish to sop up all the tasty juices.

Serves 4

2 tablespoons extra-virgin olive oil, divided

1 (4" × 4" × 1") slab feta cheese

1 large tomato, thinly sliced

1 large banana or sweet pepper, stemmed, seeded, and thinly sliced

¼ teaspoon red pepper flakes

¼ teaspoon dried oregano

1. Preheat the oven to 400°F. In a small baking dish, put 1 tablespoon oil and the feta. Top the feta with alternating layers of tomato and pepper slices. Drizzle on the remaining oil and sprinkle red pepper flakes and oregano over the vegetables.

2. Cover the baking dish tightly with foil and bake for 20 minutes. Serve immediately.

SHRIMP SAGANAKI

Saganaki refers to the two-handled cooking vessel (baking dish or frying pan) used to serve this appetizer. You'll need lots of crusty bread for this dish.

Serves 4

¼ cup extra-virgin olive oil

½ cup sliced mushrooms

¼ finely chopped red onion, peeled

¼ cup diced green bell peppers, stemmed and seeded

¼ cup diced red bell peppers, stemmed and seeded

1 medium tomato, diced

½ cup crumbled feta cheese

1 teaspoon dried oregano

¼ teaspoon red pepper flakes

1 ounce ouzo

⅓ teaspoon salt

8–10 large head-on shrimp, deveined

¼ cup grated mozzarella

1. Set the oven to broil. Add the oil to a medium skillet over medium-high heat and heat for 30 seconds. Add the mushrooms and sauté for 2–3 minutes or until they have browned. Add the onions, peppers, and tomato. Reduce heat to medium and simmer for 5–7 minutes. Remove the skillet from the heat and stir the feta, oregano, red pepper flakes, ouzo, and salt into the sauce.

2. Put the sauce into a medium baking dish. Add the shrimp, nestling them slightly into the sauce. Top with the mozzarella. Bake under the broiler for about 5–6 minutes or until the shrimp have turned pink and the cheese becomes a golden brown.

Shrimp Shells

Don't throw out your shrimp shells! Store shells in the freezer and then use them to create the delicious Seafood Stock in Chapter 2.

TARAMOSALATA (CAVIAR DIP)

Tarama, sometimes called the poor man's caviar, is made from cod or carp roe. Resist the temptation to use extra-virgin olive oil in this dish because the strong flavor will interfere with the delicate flavor of the tarama.

Serves 12

9 slices white bread

5 ounces carp roe caviar

½ cup chopped onion, peeled

1½ cups light olive oil, divided

¼ cup fresh lemon juice

¼ cup cold water

1. Soak the bread in room-temperature water for 10 seconds and then squeeze the water out with your hands. Reserve the bread and discard the water.

2. In a food processor, put the caviar and onion. Process for 2 minutes to combine. Add the bread and process for 2–3 minutes or until the mixture is smooth.

3. With the processor running, slowly add ¾ cup oil (add it slowly so the mixture won't split). Add lemon juice and cold water and process to combine.

4. With the processor running, slowly add the remaining oil. Serve cold or at room temperature. Leftovers can be stored in a sealed container in the refrigerator for up to 4 weeks.

MUSSELS SAGANAKI

This mussel dish is a specialty of Thessaloniki, Greece, where much of the local cuisine is spicy. You may use sweet peppers if you wish to tone down the heat.

Serves 2

¼ cup extra-virgin olive oil

1 medium-size hot banana pepper, stemmed, seeded, and sliced thinly

2 medium tomatoes, chopped

½ teaspoon salt

1 pound fresh mussels, scrubbed and beards removed

⅓ cup crumbled feta cheese

2 teaspoons dried oregano

1. In a medium pot over medium heat, add oil and heat for 30 seconds. Add peppers, tomatoes, and salt, and cook 2–3 minutes.

2. Add mussels and cover. Increase the heat to medium-high and allow the mussels to steam 5–6 minutes. Discard any mussels that haven't opened.

3. Add feta and oregano and shake the pan to combine them into the sauce. Serve hot.

CRETAN DAKOS

Dakos, or rusks, are hard twice-baked bread. You can find rusks at Greek or Middle Eastern grocers.

Serves 4

4 medium rusks

1 clove garlic, peeled

¼ cup extra-virgin olive oil

1 large tomato, skinned and grated

¼ cup crumbled feta cheese

1 teaspoon dried oregano

1. Sprinkle some water over each rusk to soften it slightly. Then firmly rub the garlic clove over each rusk to infuse it with garlic flavor.

2. Drizzle oil evenly over the rusks and let them absorb the oil for 4–5 minutes.

3. Top rusks with tomato, feta, and a sprinkle of oregano. Serve at room temperature.

OLIVE AND RED-PEPPER DIP

Serve with flatbread or toasted pita.

Serves 4

½ cup pitted green olives

1 Roasted Red Pepper (see recipe in this chapter)

1 teaspoon balsamic vinegar

⅔ cup soft bread crumbs

2 cloves garlic, peeled and smashed

½ teaspoon red pepper flakes

⅓ cup extra-virgin olive oil

1. In a food processor, combine all the ingredients except for the oil. Pulse to combine, but leave the mixture chunky.

2. With the processor running, slowly add the oil until it is well combined. Serve the dip cool or at room temperature.

HUMMUS

Chickpeas are full of protein and zinc, and they are low in fat. They make this dish both tasty and healthy.

Serves 6

2 cups canned chickpeas, drained

4 cloves garlic, peeled and smashed

2 chopped scallions, ends trimmed

1 Roasted Red Pepper (see recipe in this chapter)

½ cup tahini (sesame-seed paste)

2 tablespoons lemon juice

¼ teaspoon red pepper flakes

½ cup extra-virgin olive oil

2 teaspoons salt

1. In a food processor, add chickpeas, garlic, scallions, roasted red pepper, tahini, lemon juice, and red pepper flakes. Process the chickpea mixture until smooth.

2. With the processor running, slowly add the oil until it's completely incorporated. Season with salt. Serve cool or at room temperature.

SANTORINI FAVA (SPLIT-PEA DIP)

Fava, in the Greek food sense, has nothing to do with fava beans. Rather, it's a dip made from split peas. Serve this dip with toasted pita bread.

Serves 4

3 cups water

1 cup dried yellow split peas, rinsed

½ cup chopped onions, peeled

2 cloves garlic, peeled and smashed

2 bay leaves

1 teaspoon red wine vinegar

½ cup plus 1 tablespoon extra-virgin olive oil, divided

2 teaspoons fresh thyme leaves

1 teaspoon salt

½ teaspoon pepper

2 tablespoons finely chopped red onions

½ teaspoon dried oregano

1. In a medium pot over medium-high heat, add water, peas, onions, garlic, and bay leaves. Cover the pot and bring the mixture to a boil. Reduce heat to medium-low and simmer for 15–20 minutes or until the peas are tender.

2. Strain the water and remove the bay leaves. Combine the pea mixture and the vinegar in a food processor. Process until the mixture is smooth. With the processor running, slowly add ½ cup oil.

3. Remove the dip from the processor and stir in the thyme. Season it with salt and pepper.

4. Sprinkle red onions and oregano on top and drizzle with the remaining oil. Serve warm or at room temperature.

Split Peas

Split peas are very high in dietary fiber and protein. They are an excellent and healthy alternative to meat proteins. Unlike other dried beans, you don't need to presoak them before cooking. Just give them a rinse and pick out any shriveled or broken beans, stones, or debris, and they are ready to cook.

DEEP-FRIED ZUCCHINI

These zucchini chips are perfect with Tzatziki (see recipe in Chapter 2).

Serves 6

Sunflower oil for frying

¾ cup all-purpose flour

¼ cup cornstarch

1 teaspoon salt, divided

¼ teaspoon pepper

4 medium zucchini, trimmed and thinly sliced (⅛ inch)

1. In a deep skillet over medium-high heat, bring 3 inches of oil to 370°F.

2. In a large bowl, combine the flour, cornstarch, ½ teaspoon salt, and pepper. Lightly dredge the zucchini in the flour and shake off any excess flour.

3. Fry the zucchini (in batches) for about 2 minutes or until golden. Place the fried zucchini on a tray lined with paper towels to soak up any excess oil. Season with the remaining salt and serve immediately.

HTIPITI (SPICY FETA DIP)

This spicy dip is pronounced "huh-tee-pee-tee" in Greek. It's fun to say and delicious to eat.

Serves 4

2 hot banana peppers

1 cup crumbled feta cheese

1 cup ricotta cheese

3 tablespoons strained Greek yogurt

¼ cup extra-virgin olive oil

1. Preheat a gas or charcoal grill to medium-high. Place the peppers on the grill and char them on all sides. Place the peppers in a large bowl and cover tightly with plastic wrap. Cool peppers for 20 minutes. Remove the charred skins and discard. Slit the peppers in half; remove and discard the seeds and stem. Finely mince the peppers.

2. In a medium bowl, thoroughly combine feta, ricotta, yogurt, and oil. Stir in the minced peppers. Serve cool or at room temperature.

GRILLED HALLOUMI WITH A ROASTED RED-PEPPER SAUCE

You can buy halloumi cheese in most cheese shops and Greek grocery stores. If you have any leftover sauce, serve it with pasta and shrimp.

Serves 6

¼ cup extra-virgin olive oil

⅓ cup chopped red onions

1 clove garlic, peeled and smashed

1 Roasted Red Pepper (see recipe in this chapter)

½ cup crushed canned tomatoes

½ teaspoon salt

⅛ teaspoon red pepper flakes

½ teaspoon dried oregano

12 (¼-inch) slices halloumi cheese

3 medium pitas, cut into four triangles big enough to hold a slice of cheese

1. Heat the oil in a small skillet over medium heat for 30 seconds. Add the onions and garlic and cook for 2–3 minutes or until onions are softened. Add the pepper and tomatoes, increase the heat to medium-high, and bring to a boil. Reduce the heat to medium, add salt, and simmer for 7–10 minutes or until sauce has thickened.

2. Cool the sauce for 10 minutes and then process it in a food processor until smooth. Stir in red pepper flakes and oregano. Adjust seasoning if necessary.

3. Preheat the gas or charcoal grill to medium-high. Place the cheese slices on the grill and cook for 1–1½ minutes per side. The cheese should be soft but still intact.

4. Place each piece of grilled cheese over a pita triangle and top with a dollop of the warm sauce. Serve immediately.

Halloumi Cheese

Halloumi cheese comes from Cyprus. It is made from sheep's milk and it is known as the "squeaky" cheese because of the sound it makes when you chew it.

BAKED KOLOKITHOKEFTEDES (ZUCCHINI PATTIES)

These baked zucchini fritters are great with a side of Feta-Yogurt Sauce (see recipe in Chapter 2).

Serves 6

3 medium zucchini, trimmed and grated

1 teaspoon salt

6 tablespoons extra-virgin olive oil, divided

6 scallions, ends trimmed and finely chopped

1 clove garlic, peeled and minced

1 large egg, beaten

2 tablespoons chopped fresh mint

1 tablespoon chopped fresh dill

1 tablespoon chopped fresh parsley

½ cup bread crumbs

¼ cup Graviera or Gruyère cheese

½ cup crumbled feta cheese

½ teaspoon pepper

1 tablespoon baking powder

1. Put the zucchini and salt into a colander. Cover the colander with plastic wrap and place it over a bowl to catch the drained water. Refrigerate the zucchini for at least 3 hours. Squeeze any remaining liquid from the zucchini with your hands or wring out in a clean tea towel. Try to get the zucchini as dry as possible.

2. Preheat the oven to 425°F. Heat 3 tablespoons oil in a medium skillet over medium heat for 30 seconds. Add the scallions and garlic and cook for 5–7 minutes. Take the skillet off the heat and allow the scallion mixture to cool.

3. In a large bowl, combine the cooled scallion mixture, egg, mint, dill, parsley, bread crumbs, Graviera, feta, pepper, and baking powder. If the mixture is too wet, add a few more bread crumbs. If the mixture is too dry, add a little more oil.

4. Using your hands, form the zucchini mixture into small patties, each about 3 inches wide. You should have enough for twelve to fourteen patties. Place the patties on a greased baking sheet and brush the tops with the remaining oil.

5. Bake for 8–10 minutes on the middle rack. Flip the patties over and bake for another 8–10 minutes or until they are golden. Serve them warm or at room temperature.

CRISPY FRIED ATHERINA (SMELTS)

Greeks love to eat smelts, but if you can't find them, use fresh anchovies.

Serves 4

2 pounds small whole smelts, heads and guts removed

2 teaspoons salt, divided

½ teaspoon pepper

1 teaspoon sweet paprika

½ cup rice flour

1 cup all-purpose flour

Sunflower oil for frying

1 tablespoon grated lemon zest

1 tablespoon grated lime zest

1 large lemon, cut into wedges

1 large lime, cut into wedges

1. Pat the smelts with paper towels to dry. In a large bowl, combine 1 teaspoon salt, pepper, and paprika, and then toss the smelts in the seasoning. Combine the flours in a medium bowl and then add them to the large bowl; toss again to coat the smelts in the flour. Shake off any excess flour from the smelts.

2. In a deep skillet over medium-high heat, bring 3 inches of oil to 360°F. Adjust the heat to keep the temperature at 360°F while frying.

3. Fry the smelts (in batches) for 3 minutes or until they are golden. Place them on a tray lined with paper towels to soak up excess oil. Season with the remaining salt.

4. Sprinkle the lemon and lime zests over the smelts. Serve immediately with lemon and lime wedges.

Smelts

Did you know smelts are found in both the ocean and in fresh water? Although the smelts of the Mediterranean are a slightly different species from the freshwater fish found in the Great Lakes, both work wonderfully in this dish. Choose smaller ones so you can eat the whole thing!

SPICY CHICKEN WINGS

Be sure to have a cool drink on hand when serving these wings. Try a Greek beer! Serve with some lemon wedges for a fresh hit of citrus.

Serves 4

4 cloves garlic, peeled and minced

1 small onion, grated

1 tablespoon grated lemon zest

1 tablespoon lemon juice

¼ teaspoon ground cinnamon

¼ teaspoon smoked paprika

½ teaspoon ground allspice

1 teaspoon pepper

2 teaspoons salt

2 tablespoons fresh thyme leaves

¼ cup extra-virgin olive oil

2 pounds chicken wings, patted dry

1. In a large bowl, combine all the ingredients except the chicken wings. Add the chicken wings and make sure they are completely coated in the marinade.

2. Marinate the wings for at least 4 hours or preferably overnight in the refrigerator. Take the wings out 20 minutes before grilling, so they come up to room temperature. Remove excess marinade from the wings.

3. Preheat a gas or charcoal grill to medium-high. Place the wings on the grill and cook for 4–5 minutes per side or until the chicken juices run clear. Serve immediately.

PHYLLO-WRAPPED SHRIMP

Serve these shrimp with a spicy cocktail sauce.

Serves 4

12 medium-size fresh shrimp, shelled (tails on) and deveined

2 tablespoons extra-virgin olive oil

½ teaspoon salt

½ teaspoon pepper

2 cloves garlic, peeled and minced

½ teaspoon sweet paprika

Sunflower oil for frying

4 sheets phyllo pastry

1 teaspoon cornstarch, dissolved in 1 teaspoon room-temperature water

1. Slit the inside curve of each shrimp three or four times to straighten it out. In a medium bowl, combine the oil, salt, pepper, garlic, and paprika. Toss the shrimp in the mixture. Reserve.

2. In a deep skillet over medium-high heat, bring 2 inches of oil to 360°F. Adjust the heat to keep the temperature at 360°F while frying.

3. Cut the phyllo sheets into 6" × 4" × 4" triangles and lay them out on a work surface. Work quickly because you don't want the phyllo to dry out. Place a shrimp near the left corner of the phyllo with the tail exposed and the body lying inside the phyllo. Fold the phyllo over the shrimp and tuck it tightly under the top of the shrimp. Fold the top part of the phyllo over to cover the shrimp. Finally, roll the phyllo up until the roll is complete. Dab your finger into the cornstarch paste and seal the end of the phyllo. Repeat with the remaining shrimp.

4. Fry shrimp rolls (in batches) for 3 minutes or until they are golden and the shrimp is cooked. Place them on a tray lined with paper towels to soak up excess oil. Serve immediately.

TALTSENES (ROASTED PEPPERS, EGGPLANT, AND TOMATO DIP)

The Greek word taltsenes *refers to pounding or mashing with a mortar and pestle. This richly flavorful dish should be served with crusty breads and salty cheeses.*

Serves 6

1 medium tomato

2 medium Italian eggplants or 4 long Japanese eggplants

2 medium-size red shepherd peppers

2 teaspoons salt, divided

2 or 3 cloves garlic, peeled and minced

1 teaspoon red wine vinegar

¾ cup extra-virgin olive oil

1. Preheat a gas or charcoal grill to medium-high. Wrap the tomato in foil. Pierce the skins of the eggplants a few times with a knife. Place the eggplants, peppers, and tomato on the grill. Cook the eggplants for 20–30 minutes or until the skin is completely charred and the inside is soft. Grill the peppers until they are charred on all sides. Grill the tomato in foil for 20 minutes.

2. Place the charred peppers in a medium bowl and cover it tightly with plastic wrap. Allow the peppers to cool for 15 minutes. Using your hands, remove the charred skins and discard them. Slit the peppers in half; remove and discard the seeds and stem. Chop the peppers.

3. Let the eggplants cool for 10 minutes. Cut open each eggplant lengthwise and scoop out the softened flesh, discarding the charred skin. Peel and discard the skin off the tomato and chop the flesh.

4. In a mortar, add ½ teaspoon salt and the garlic. Pound the garlic into a mash with the pestle. Using the pestle, blend in the eggplant flesh and vinegar. Blend in the peppers. Blend in the tomato. The mixture should not be completely smooth.

5. Stir the oil in slowly and continue to blend until it's well incorporated. Season the dip with the remaining salt and serve at room temperature.

Mortar and Pestle

A mortar and pestle is a worthwhile investment for your kitchen. It can be used to mix an array of dips and dressings and grind spices and nuts.

SCORTHALIA

This dip is a cousin to the famous garlic yogurt dip known as Tzatziki (see recipe in Chapter 2) and is an excellent accompaniment for vegetable and fish dishes.

Serves 4–6

3 large potatoes, peeled

6 or 7 cloves garlic, peeled and finely shredded

⅓ cup Greek extra-virgin olive oil

⅓ cup vinegar

1 tablespoon dried Greek oregano

Salt and pepper to taste

1. Fill a medium-size saucepan with water and dash of salt. Bring to boil.

2. Cut peeled potatoes into eighths and add to boiling water. Boil potatoes until soft; drain and put in a medium- to large-size mixing bowl.

3. Using a potato masher or large fork, thoroughly mash potatoes. Add garlic, olive oil, vinegar, oregano, salt, and pepper; resume mashing and stirring to incorporate all ingredients.

4. Ensure there are no lumps of potato remaining. When uniform and creamy, set aside to cool. Serve at room temperature.

FETA AND ROASTED RED PEPPER PIQUANTE

This dip should be refrigerated until needed, and is best served with some warm pita bread.

Serves 4–6

½ pound Greek feta cheese

1–1½ tablespoons dried chili pepper flakes

2 roasted red peppers

4 tablespoons extra-virgin olive oil

1 teaspoon fresh-ground black pepper

1. Crumble feta into a food processor or blender.

2. Add chili pepper flakes to processor. (This dip ought to be spicy but not red hot, so adjust the amount of chili pepper flakes accordingly.)

3. Remove seeds and skins from roasted red peppers; add to processor.

4. Add olive oil and 1 or 2 pinches of pepper to processor.

5. Purée until smooth throughout.

Love of Olive Oil

The most characteristic aspect of the Mediterranean diet is the ubiquitous presence of the olive and its juice in the foods that comprise the traditional cuisines that evolved under its influence.

FETA FRITTERS

Sprinkle these fritters with lemon juice and use some chopped fresh mint as a garnish when serving.

Serves 4–6

2 pounds white potatoes

3 tablespoons extra-virgin olive oil, divided

1 medium-sized onion, finely diced

¼ cup fresh dill, finely chopped

2 tablespoons fresh mint, finely chopped

1 tablespoon dried oregano

1 teaspoon fresh-ground black pepper

½ cup dried bread crumbs

1 cup crumbled Greek feta cheese

2 eggs, well beaten

Flour for dredging

Juice of 1 lemon

1. Peel potatoes and cut into quarters; boil in salted water until soft (approximately 20 minutes). In a large mixing bowl, mash potatoes thoroughly. Add 1 tablespoon olive oil, onions, dill, mint, oregano, fresh-ground pepper, and bread crumbs; mix well.

2. Let mixture stand 5 minutes to cool slightly. Add feta and eggs; mix until everything is well incorporated. Put bowl in freezer 20 minutes to chill mixture.

3. Remove from freezer; spoon out small portions and roll with fingers into balls (about the size of Ping-Pong balls). Place balls on a flat baking sheet covered with wax paper; slightly flatten each ball into a little cake with fingers.

4. Roll each fritter in flour to cover completely and arrange on pan; place pan in freezer for another 5 minutes to firm before frying.

5. Heat 2 tablespoons olive oil in a large frying pan; start frying fritters in batches over medium-high heat about 1 minute per side, until golden brown. Use a small spatula or fork to turn in pan. Sprinkle generously with lemon juice and serve immediately.

VILLAGE-STYLE ZUCCHINI FRITTERS

You do not need to peel the zucchini, but you must peel the potato for use in this recipe.

Yields 12–14 pieces

1 medium-size zucchini

1 medium-size potato

½ white onion

Olive oil for frying

2 eggs

2 tablespoons fresh mint leaves, finely chopped

1 tablespoon dried oregano

1 large fresh clove garlic, pressed or finely shredded

1 tablespoon Greek extra-virgin olive oil

½ cup dried bread crumbs

2 tablespoons all-purpose flour

Salt and pepper to taste

Pinch of baking soda or ½ teaspoon baking powder

1. Wash the zucchini and potato; shred entirely into a large mixing bowl using a grater or shredder. Finely chop the onion; add to bowl.

2. Heat the frying oil in a large pan—depth of oil should be no more than ½ inch—over medium heat. Allow 3–4 minutes for the oil to heat thoroughly.

3. Beat the eggs well; add to the mixing bowl along with the mint, oregano, garlic, 1 tablespoon extra-virgin olive oil, bread crumbs, flour, salt and pepper, and baking soda or powder. Mix well, until a thick batterlike consistency is achieved. Zucchini will begin to seep water immediately upon shredding—work quickly so mixture does not become watery. If it is thin, add more bread crumbs or flour to thicken slightly. Note: If using baking soda, make sure to only use a slight pinch so fritters won't be bitter.

4. Using a large spoon, add portions of the mixture to the hot oil in small clumps, making sure to form them as small pancakes. It is easier to make this dish with a large frying pan so you can control the shape of the clumps.

5. Cook for about 3–4 minutes on one side; carefully turn with a small spatula or large fork and cook on other side and cook for another 3–4 minutes.

6. Remove from the pan when golden brown; set aside on a plate/tray lined with paper towels or napkins to drain.

SFOUGATO (AEGEAN OMELET)

For Greeks, eggs are not limited to a breakfast food; they often make an appearance at the lunch or dinner table as an appetizer or main course.

Serves 4

1 cooking onion, finely diced

4 tablespoons all-purpose flour

¼ cup bread crumbs

2 tablespoons fresh mint, finely chopped

½ cup crumbled Greek feta cheese

Salt and pepper to taste

1 tablespoon dried thyme

6–8 eggs

2 tablespoons extra-virgin olive oil

1. Preheat the oven to 350°F. In a mixing bowl, add onion, flour, bread crumbs, mint, cheese, salt, pepper, and thyme; mix well.

2. In a separate bowl, add eggs; beat well.

3. Add olive oil to a large frying pan over medium-high heat. When the oil is hot, add eggs to the cheese and bread crumb mixture; combine well, then pour into the pan.

4. Using a wooden spoon, stir until thickened; cook one side for 4–5 minutes. Flip it, turn down heat to medium, and cook for another 4–5 minutes, until done.

5. When the omelet is cooked, turn off the heat and place the pan in the oven for 5 minutes. Serve immediately.

TOMATO FRITTERS

Peel tomatoes by dropping them in boiling water until their skins start to shrivel. Then remove from water and carefully peel away the skins, as tomatoes will be hot.

Yields 24 pieces

8 whole, cooked tomatoes, peeled and diced

½ pound Greek feta cheese, crumbled

1 egg, beaten

¾ cup all-purpose flour

2 onions, grated

¼ cup fresh mint, finely chopped

1 teaspoon dried oregano

¼ cup dry bread crumbs

Salt and pepper

Oil for frying

1. Remove as many seeds as possible from the diced tomatoes; place tomatoes in colander and set aside to drain 15 minutes.

2. In a large mixing bowl, combine tomatoes, feta, egg, flour, onions, mint, oregano, bread crumbs, salt, and pepper; mix together thoroughly until smooth and fluffy. Refrigerate and chill mixture 1 hour.

3. Heat the oil in a saucepan; take spoonfuls of chilled mixture and carefully drop into the oil. Turn using a spatula until both sides are nicely browned, approximately 5–6 minutes; remove with a slotted spoon and place on a platter lined with paper towels to drain. Serve immediately on their own or with Tzatziki (see recipe in Chapter 2).

FRESH MOZZARELLA

There is a world of difference between this fresh and moist cheese and what you buy in the stores wrapped in plastic.

Yields 1 pound

2 gallons water

¼ cup kosher salt

1 pound mozzarella cheese curd

1. Mix the water with the salt in a large saucepot and bring to a slow simmer. While the water comes to a simmer, thinly slice or grate the mozzarella curd.

2. Place the curd in the simmering water, stir with a wooden spoon, and remove from heat. Stir every few minutes until the curd begins to form a ball and stretches when stirred. Continue to stir for approximately 5–10 minutes, then let it sit for 15 minutes or until the curd and whey fully separate.

3. Using a slotted spoon, transfer the curd to a colander lined with cheesecloth, and let the whey drain from the curd mixture. Press the curd again to remove any remaining whey. Continue pressing until it is just cool enough (but still hot) to knead into a ball with your hands. While the cheese is still hot, stretch it and fold it back onto itself; repeat this until it will not stretch anymore. When it begins to stretch like taffy, it is almost done. Mold into a ball or string or desired shape. You can serve it immediately at room temperature or wrap it in plastic wrap, refrigerate, and serve later. It will keep for up to a month refrigerated.

Having Difficulty?

If you are having difficulty shredding the cheese, put it in the freezer for a few minutes. When you take it out it will be much more workable.

GARLIC FETA SPREAD

This dip is best refrigerated until needed, and is best accompanied by some fresh crusty bread.

Serves 6–8

½ pound Greek feta cheese, crumbled

3 cloves garlic, pressed

2 tablespoons extra-virgin olive oil

2 tablespoons fresh parsley, finely chopped

1 teaspoon dried oregano

Fresh-ground pepper

1. Combine all the ingredients; mash and mix well or put everything into a food processor and blend at low speed until smooth.

2. Refrigerate before/after serving. Serve with warm pita bread.

OVEN-DRIED TOMATOES

This homemade version of sun-dried tomatoes is a simple and healthy snack that can be eaten alone on crackers or used in many different recipes.

Serves 6

6 plum tomatoes

3 cloves garlic

¼ bunch fresh basil

Fresh-cracked black pepper

Kosher salt, to taste

1. Preheat the oven to 200°F.

2. Cut the tomatoes into ⅓-inch-wide slices. Lay out each slice in a single layer on a sheet pan. Mince the garlic, and finely chop the basil. Sprinkle the tomatoes with the garlic, basil, black pepper, and salt.

3. Cook in the oven for approximately 8 hours. Then remove and serve on top of Flatbread (see recipe in Chapter 3).

SMOKED TROUT HORS D'OEUVRES

Smoked trout lends itself well to this type of use. Not only does the appetizer taste good, it offers spectacular eye appeal as well.

Serves 6

¾ pound smoked trout

12 slices French bread

¼ bunch chives

1 fresh plum tomato

3 ounces provolone cheese

Fresh-cracked black pepper

1 teaspoon extra-virgin olive oil

1. Remove the skin and bone from the trout, then gently flake the trout with a fork. Lightly toast the bread. Chop the chives and finely chop the tomato. Grate the cheese.

2. Mound a small spoonful of trout on each piece of toast and place on a serving platter. Carefully top with provolone, then sprinkle with chopped tomatoes. Shake chives over the top of each. Sprinkle pepper over each and drizzle with oil before serving.

VEGETABLE KABOBS

Serving kabobs as an appetizer at parties is a good idea because guests can easily handle the food without using cutlery.

Serves 6

12 scallions

1 large red pepper

1 large yellow pepper

1 large green pepper

12 large button mushrooms

1 tablespoon olive oil

Fresh-cracked black pepper

Kosher salt, to taste

1. Cut standard wooden skewers in half for appetizer-size portions, then soak the skewers in water for a minimum of 1 hour.

2. Preheat grill or broiler.

3. Trim off the roots and dark green parts of the scallions. Dice the peppers into large pieces.

4. Thread the vegetables onto the skewers, and brush all sides of the vegetables with oil. Season with pepper and salt.

5. Place the skewers on the grill or under the broiler, paying close attention as they cook, as they can easily burn. Cook until the vegetables are fork-tender.

Soaking the Skewers

When using wooden skewers in cooking, always soak them in water for an hour before spearing the food items. Soaking the skewers allows you to place them on the grill for a time without them burning.

FRESH HERB DIP WITH EGGPLANT

The dip can be used as a sauce and is great over grilled meats or veggies.

Yields 2 cups

1 large eggplant

3 cloves garlic

1 tablespoon olive oil

½ cup Yogurt Cheese (see recipe in this chapter)

1 tablespoon each of fresh parsley, basil, and rosemary

Fresh-ground black pepper

Kosher salt, to taste

1. Slice the eggplant in half lengthwise and mince the garlic. Brush the cut side of the eggplant with the oil, sprinkle with garlic, and roast on foil in the oven at 375°F or place on the grill for 10 minutes. Place in a plastic bag for 5 minutes (the steam in the bag will help loosen the skin), then remove the skin if desired.

2. Spoon the eggplant pulp into a blender, and pulse. Add the yogurt cheese ¼ cup at a time, and blend until it reaches the consistency of a thick sauce. Add the herbs, pepper, and salt, and stir to combine.

3. Refrigerate for at least 2 hours before serving.

A Simple Appetizer

Instead of using a spread with the bread you serve, try serving a plate of extra-virgin olive oil to be used as a dipping sauce. This gives a wonderful flavor and is as simple as it gets.

MUSHROOMS STUFFED WITH CREAMY CRAB

If you choose the larger and more expensive portobello mushrooms for this dish, you can also use this as an entrée.

Yields about 45 mushroom caps

1 tablespoon olive oil

1 clove garlic, minced

2 tablespoons red pepper, diced

1 tablespoon yellow onion, diced

2½ pounds button mushrooms

10 ounces crabmeat

1 egg white

1 tablespoon nonfat plain yogurt

Fresh-cracked black pepper

Salt, to taste

1 large sprig fresh sage, chopped

1. Preheat the oven to 350°F. Spray a baking sheet with oil.

2. Heat the oil in a sauté pan over medium heat. Sauté the garlic, red peppers, and onions until tender.

3. Clean the mushrooms and remove the stems from the caps. Finely chop the stems; set the whole caps aside.

4. Combine the vegetable mixture, chopped stems, crabmeat, egg white, yogurt, pepper, salt, and sage.

5. Stuff the mushroom caps with the crab mixture and arrange on the prepared sheet pan; bake for about 15 minutes.

CHICKEN MEATBALLS WITH FRUIT SAUCE

This is a tasty change of pace. The fruit complements the chicken beautifully.

Serves 6

Olive oil

2 slices toasted Italian bread

1 pound ground chicken

¼ cup dried cranberries

¼ cup chopped pecans

1 egg

¼ teaspoon cinnamon

¼ teaspoon curry powder

Pinch of kosher salt

Fresh-cracked black pepper

½ cup Apple Chutney (see recipe in Chapter 2)

1. Preheat the oven to 350°F. Brush a baking dish with oil.

2. Soak the bread in water and then squeeze out the liquid. Mix together the soaked bread and all the remaining ingredients in a bowl. Shape the mixture into small balls. Place the balls in the prepared baking dish. Cover with foil and bake for about 20 minutes. Serve with Apple Chutney.

Artist at Work

Always keep a pastry brush or a small natural bristle paintbrush handy as one of your basic kitchen tools. They are great for getting just the right amount of oil in a pan or for brushing food with a light layer of oil before cooking.

HADDOCK FISH CAKES

This version of a familiar fish cake has the fresh flavor of haddock. Serve this with a spicy sauce or with just lemon.

Serves 6

1 pound haddock

2 leeks

1 red pepper

2 egg whites

Pinch of kosher salt

Fresh-cracked black pepper

1 tablespoon olive oil

1. Finely shred the raw fish with a fork. Dice the leeks and red pepper. Combine all the ingredients except the oil in a medium-size bowl; mix well. Form the mixture into small oval patties.

2. Heat the oil in a medium-size sauté pan. Place the cakes in the pan and loosely cover with the lid; sauté the cakes for 4–6 minutes on each side. Drain on a rack covered with paper towels; serve immediately.

LAMB PATTIES

The lamb can be served rare to medium-rare, but the egg must be thoroughly cooked.

Serves 6

1 shallot

2 cloves garlic

½ pound ground lamb

1 egg white

¼ cup dried currants

¼ cup pistachio nuts

½ teaspoon ground cinnamon

Fresh-cracked black pepper, to taste

Pinch of kosher salt

1. Preheat the oven to 350°F.

2. Peel and mince the shallot and garlic; mix with the lamb, egg, currants, nuts, and cinnamon. Season with pepper and salt.

3. Form the mixture into small ovals. Place them in a baking dish and bake for approximately 15 minutes.

MARINATED PORTOBELLO MUSHROOMS

Portobello mushrooms have such a meaty flavor, they can be used in place of meat in many recipes.

Serves 6

6 portobello mushrooms

1 teaspoon extra-virgin olive oil

2 teaspoons balsamic vinegar

Pinch of iodized salt

Fresh-cracked black pepper

¼ bunch marjoram

¼ bunch oregano

1. Remove the stems from the caps of the mushrooms and scrape out the black membrane. Slice the stems in half.

2. Mix together the remaining ingredients. Combine the caps and stems with the marinade in a container (plastic tub or sealable bag); marinate for at least 3 hours.

3. Preheat the oven to 400°F.

4. Roast the mushrooms for 15–20 minutes on an oven rack. Cut the caps into small wedges and serve.

SHREDDED VEGETABLE PATTIES

You can also make the patties extra thin and sauté them extra crispy so you can munch them like chips.

Serves 6

2 carrots

2 small zucchini

1 red onion

3 stalks celery

1 egg white

2 tablespoons all-purpose flour

2 ounces Romano cheese

1 tablespoon olive oil

Fresh-cracked black pepper, to taste

1. Finely shred all the vegetables and mix them with the egg white, flour, and cheese in a medium-size bowl. Form the mixture into small ovals.

2. Heat the oil over medium heat in a sauté pan. Place the patties in the oil and sauté until lightly golden brown. Turn the patties over and sauté the other sides until golden brown.

3. Drain on a rack covered with paper towels. Sprinkle with black pepper and serve with your favorite sauce as an accompaniment.

ROASTED GARLIC SERVED ON CROSTINI

There are countless variations of the classic roasted garlic served on crostini. Try adding herbs like thyme, sage, or rosemary.

Serves 6

1 bulb garlic

2 tablespoons virgin olive oil

½ bunch fresh parsley

½ loaf baguette

1. Preheat the oven to 375°F.

2. Cut off the top quarter of the garlic bulb. Rub both cut sides of garlic with olive oil, then place the top back on the bulb and wrap in foil. Place in the oven and bake until the cloves are fork tender (the same tenderness as a baked potato), about 5–10 minutes.

3. While the garlic cooks, chop the parsley. Slice the baguette thinly on the bias. Brush with the oil and place on a baking sheet. Toast until light brown.

4. Serve the bulb intact on a platter surrounded by crostini and sprinkled with parsley.

YOGURT CHEESE

This requires overnight refrigeration, and the fresh flavor of the yogurt produces an equally light cheese, which has many uses.

Serves 6

32 ounces nonfat plain yogurt

½ bulb garlic, minced

Fresh-cracked black pepper

½ bunch parsley, chopped

Mix together all the ingredients. Place the mixture in a colander lined with cheesecloth, then place the colander in a large bowl to catch the whey. Refrigerate overnight. When you are ready to serve, remove the colander from the refrigerator and dispose of the whey and cheesecloth. Slice and serve.

OLIVE CHEESE BREAD

Your guests will love the strong and unique flavor of these appetizers.

Serves 6

¼ pound pitted cured olives

1 clove garlic

2 tablespoons pine nuts

1½ tablespoons olive oil

1 long loaf crusty bread

¼ pound Gorgonzola cheese

Process the olives, garlic, pine nuts, and olive oil as finely as possible. Slice the bread into ¼-inch-thick slices. Spread the olive mixture on the bread and top with Gorgonzola. Serve as is or flash under broiler until the cheese begins to bubble.

FLATBREAD WITH OLIVE TAPENADE

Try using different types of olives for another flavor, or mix together black and green olives for a colorful version.

Serves 6

Flatbread

½ cup all-purpose flour

¼ cup whole-wheat flour

¼ cup spelt flour

¼ teaspoon iodized salt

½ cup water

Tapenade

¼ cup roasted garlic (see Roasted Garlic Served on Crostini recipe in this chapter)

½ cup kalamata olives (pitted)

Fresh-cracked black pepper, to taste

1. Sift together the flours and salt. Add water and mix on medium-low speed with dough hook or by hand until completely incorporated; let the dough rest in refrigerator for at least 1 hour.

2. Roll out the dough to ¼-inch thickness and cut into a 3-inch circle.

3. Heat a medium-size sauté pan over medium-high heat. Place the bread in the sauté pan and cook for 3 minutes on each side, until cooked through.

4. Using a food processor or blender, purée the garlic, olives, and black pepper. To serve, spread the tapenade onto the flatbread.

BRUSCHETTA WITH MARINATED RED PEPPER

Try using any of your summer veggies to create this delicious dish.

Serves 6

3 red peppers

1 teaspoon extra-virgin olive oil

1 teaspoon balsamic vinegar

¼ bunch fresh oregano, chopped

12 (1½-inch-thick) slices baguette

1½ ounces manchego cheese (Romano or Parmesan can be substituted)

Fresh-cracked black pepper, to taste

1. Preheat the oven to 400°F.

2. Coat the whole peppers with a bit of the oil and place on a baking sheet; roast until the skin blisters, approximately 10 minutes. Remove the peppers from the oven and immediately place in a plastic bag; let sit for a minimum of 5 minutes. Remove the peppers from the bag and peel off and discard the skin. Purée the peppers in a blender, then add the vinegar and continue to process into a smooth paste. Mix in the chopped oregano. Let stand for at least 1 hour (can be prepared a day in advance and refrigerated).

3. Use a pastry brush to coat the bread slices lightly with the remaining oil. Toast until lightly golden brown.

4. Spread the puréed pepper on the toasted bread and sprinkle with cheese and black pepper.

EGGPLANT ROULADES

These can be fastened with toothpicks or small skewers to hold the roulades together. Remember to soak your skewers in water first.

Serves 6

2 small, thin Italian eggplants

1 teaspoon olive oil

¼ cup all-purpose flour

2 egg whites

¼ cup bread crumbs

¼ cup nonfat yogurt

½ cup low-fat ricotta

4 ounces part-skim mozzarella cheese, shredded

1½ tablespoons grated Romano cheese

¼ bunch fresh oregano, chopped

Fresh-cracked black pepper, to taste

1 cup tomato sauce

1. Preheat the oven to 375°F.

2. Slice the eggplants into thin slices lengthwise. Pour the oil in the bottom of a baking dish. Dip the eggplant slices in the flour, then in the egg whites, then in the bread crumbs; place in oiled baking dish. Bake for approximately 3 minutes on each side until golden brown.

3. While the eggplant cooks, mix together the yogurt, cheeses, oregano, and black pepper. When the eggplants are cooked, remove from oven and drain on rack. Then spread the cheese mixture on 1 side of the eggplant slices and roll up.

4. Coat the bottom of the baking dish with tomato sauce and place the rolled eggplants inside the dish, letting some of the sauce come up the sides of the eggplant rolls. Lightly spoon some more sauce over the top. Bake for approximately 10 minutes.

SESAME CHEESE PUFFS

Try either a sweet or savory sauce for dipping.

Serves 6

4 tablespoons sesame seeds, plus extra for coating

½ cup flour

½ teaspoon baking powder

Fresh-cracked black pepper, to taste

2 egg whites

2 egg yolks

3 ounces Parmesan cheese, grated

¼ cup fontina cheese, grated

Olive oil for frying

1. Preheat the oven to 350°F.

2. Spread the 4 tablespoons of sesame seeds on a baking pan and toast lightly, about 5 minutes.

3. Combine the flour, baking powder, and pepper. Beat the egg whites until stiff. In a separate bowl, beat the egg yolks and mix in the grated cheeses and toasted seeds. Combine the yolk and flour mixture, then fold it into the whites.

4. Line a sheet pan with parchment paper or foil. Form the cheese mixture into balls by rounded spoonfuls, or pipe with a pastry bag; coat the balls with sesame seeds. Chill until firm, about 30 minutes.

5. Fry in 1 inch of olive oil until golden; drain on a rack covered with paper towels. Serve with a sauce of your choice.

AMARANTH GREENS

These beautiful red, purple, and green leaves will brighten any dinner table. If you can't find amaranth greens, use dandelion greens.

Serves 4

3 teaspoons salt, divided

3 cups amaranth greens, thoroughly washed and roughly chopped

½ cup extra-virgin olive oil

1 tablespoon lemon juice

1. Fill a large pot two-thirds with water and set it over medium-high heat. Bring the water to a boil, and add 2 teaspoons of salt and the amaranth. Lower the heat to medium and cook for 10–12 minutes or until the amaranth stems are fork-tender. Drain the amaranth and discard the cooking water.

2. In a medium bowl, combine the amaranth, oil, and lemon juice. Season the greens with the remaining salt, and serve warm.

Amaranth Greens

Amaranth greens, which grow wild in the Mediterranean region, are loaded with iron and are good for your blood. Look for amaranth at Asian markets. Young amaranth greens can be eaten raw, but mature greens need to be cooked because they are bitter.

ARAKAS LATHEROS (GREEN PEAS WITH TOMATOES AND MINT)

This vegetarian dish and many others in Greek cuisine are called ladera, *which means "in oil."*

Serves 4

3 tablespoons extra-virgin olive oil, divided

1 tablespoon unsalted butter

4 scallions, ends trimmed and thinly sliced

18 ounces fresh peas

2 medium tomatoes, grated into a purée

3 tablespoons chopped fresh dill

1 teaspoon salt

½ teaspoon pepper

1 cup hot water

1 tablespoon chopped fresh mint

1. Heat 2 tablespoons of oil in a medium skillet over medium heat for 30 seconds. Add the butter and scallions. Cook for 2 minutes until the scallions are softened. Add the peas and cook for another 2 minutes. Add the tomatoes, dill, salt, pepper, and hot water. Cover and cook for 30 minutes or until all the water is absorbed and only the oil remains.

2. Serve this dish warm topped with the mint and the remaining oil.

FETA FRIES

Making the perfect fries involves great ingredients and proper techniques. Potatoes fried in olive oil are an amazing treat. You won't want fries any other way.

Serves 6

3 cups olive oil

4 large Yukon gold potatoes, peeled and cut into strips

2 teaspoons salt

½ cup Feta-Yogurt Sauce (see recipe in Chapter 2)

1. Heat the oil in a medium deep pot over medium-high heat until its temperature reaches 275°F. Adjust the heat to keep the temperature at 275°F while frying. Add the potatoes and fry for 8 minutes or until they are fork-tender. Remove the potatoes with a slotted spoon and allow them to cool for at least 10 minutes. The fries won't be crispy at this point; just cooked.

2. Reheat the oil to 375°F. Adjust the heat to keep the temperature at 375°F while frying the potatoes for a second time. Add the cooked potatoes and fry them until they are golden and crispy.

3. Place the fries on a tray lined with paper towels to soak up excess oil, and season them with the salt.

4. Serve the fries hot with the Feta-Yogurt Sauce either spooned over them or on the side for dipping.

Frying with Olive Oil

Olive oil has a smoke point of 410°F, well above the 365°F–375°F range that is ideal for frying. So don't shy away from frying with delicious olive oil.

SAUERKRAUT RICE

This side dish is savory and a little tangy, with just a hint of smoky flavor from the paprika. It's perfect when paired with roast pork.

Serves 6

3 cups water

2½ teaspoons salt, divided

1½ cups long-grain rice, rinsed

1 (32-ounce) jar sauerkraut or choucroute, drained

¼ cup unsalted butter

1 small onion, peeled and chopped

1½ teaspoons sweet paprika

½ teaspoon smoked paprika

¾ teaspoon pepper

1. Bring water to a boil in a medium pot over medium-high heat. Add 2 teaspoons salt and the rice to the boiling water, reduce the heat to medium, and cook for 20–25 minutes.

2. Taste the sauerkraut. If it is too tart, rinse it under cold water and drain it again.

3. Melt the butter in a medium skillet over medium heat, and add the onions. Cook the onions for 4–5 minutes until they soften. Add the sauerkraut, sweet paprika, and smoked paprika, and cook for another 2 minutes. Stir in the rice and cook for another 2 minutes.

4. Season the rice with the remaining salt and pepper. Serve warm.

RICE WITH GRAPE LEAVES, RAISINS, AND PINE NUTS

This is a deconstructed version of rice-stuffed grape leaves. Serve the rice as a side with a fish or chicken main course. The grape leaves used here are jarred and can be found in Greek or Middle Eastern grocery stores.

Serves 4

¼ cup extra-virgin olive oil

1 small onion, peeled and chopped

1 clove garlic, peeled and minced

1 cup long-grain and wild rice mix

¼ cup chopped fresh parsley

2 teaspoons finely chopped fresh lemon verbena or mint

4 tablespoons fresh lemon juice, divided

2 tablespoons sultana raisins

2 tablespoons pine nuts

6 grape leaves, stemmed, rinsed, and sliced into thin ribbons

3 cups hot Chicken or Turkey Stock or Basic Vegetable Stock (see recipes in Chapter 2)

¼ cup chopped fresh dill

1 teaspoon salt

½ teaspoon pepper

1. Preheat the oven to 400°F. Heat the oil in a medium skillet over medium heat for 30 seconds. Add the onions and garlic, and cook for 5 minutes or until the onions soften. Stir in the rice and coat every grain with the oil. Remove from heat and set aside.

2. In a medium baking dish, combine the rice mixture, parsley, lemon verbena, 2 tablespoons lemon juice, raisins, pine nuts, and grape leaves. Stir in the stock. Bake the dish for 35–40 minutes uncovered or until all the liquid is absorbed by the rice.

3. Add the dill and remaining lemon juice. Fluff the rice with a fork, and season it with the salt and pepper.

Wild Rice

Wild rice is not actually rice; it is a grass. Wild rice is usually black and has a nutty taste and chewy texture. It is a high-protein grain rich in B vitamins and potassium.

GRATIN OF ZUCCHINI AND SQUASH

This is a delicious, comforting dish from Istanbul. It goes well with roast chicken or pork.

Serves 6

¼ cup plus 1 tablespoon unsalted butter, divided

1 large onion, peeled and chopped

½ large carrot, peeled and grated

1 medium-size sweet banana pepper, stemmed, seeded, and chopped

2 large zucchini, trimmed and cut into ¼-inch slices

1½ cups summer squash, peeled, seeded, and diced

2 teaspoons salt, divided

¾ teaspoon pepper, divided

2 teaspoons fresh thyme leaves

2 scallions, ends trimmed and chopped

½ cup chopped fresh dill

2 tablespoons chopped fresh parsley

½ cup all-purpose flour

1½ cups warm whole milk

1¼ cups grated aged white Cheddar, divided

⅛ teaspoon ground nutmeg

1. Preheat the oven to 375°F. In a large skillet over medium heat, add ¼ cup butter, onions, carrots, and peppers. Cook the vegetables for 10 minutes or until they soften.

2. Add the zucchini, squash, 1 teaspoon salt, ½ teaspoon pepper, and thyme. Cover the skillet and cook for 10–15 minutes or until the zucchini and squash are tender.

3. Add the scallions, dill, and parsley, and cook uncovered for 2 minutes.

4. Stir in the flour and cook for 2 minutes. Stir the milk slowly into the vegetables and cook until the sauce becomes creamy. Stir in 1 cup of cheese. Add the nutmeg and season the vegetables with the remaining salt and pepper. Keep warm.

5. Grease a medium baking dish with the remaining butter. Pour the vegetable mixture into the baking dish and top with the remaining cheese. Bake the dish on the middle rack of the oven for 30–40 minutes or until the top is golden brown. Allow the gratin to cool for 10 minutes and serve warm.

ASPARAGUS GRATIN

Asparagus tastes best when it's consumed in season. Remember to trim or peel the woody ends; they are fibrous and unpleasant to eat.

Serves 6

1 teaspoon salt, plus most to taste

2 pounds asparagus, woody ends trimmed

2 tablespoons unsalted butter, divided

2 tablespoons all-purpose flour

1½ cups warm whole milk

½ cup grated Metsovone or Gouda cheese

¼ cup grated Romano cheese

½ teaspoon pepper

½ cup bread crumbs

1. Preheat the oven to 375°F. Fill a large pot two-thirds with water and set it over medium-high heat. Bring the water to a boil, and add the 1 teaspoon salt and asparagus. Return the water to a boil and cook the asparagus for 2 minutes. Remove the asparagus from the water and place it in an ice bath to stop it from cooking further. When the asparagus has cooled, remove it from the ice bath and set it aside.

2. Melt 1 tablespoon butter in a medium skillet over medium heat. Then stir in the flour and cook for 2 minutes. Add the milk and keep stirring until the sauce thickens to a creamy texture. Take the sauce off the heat and stir in the cheeses. Season the sauce with salt to taste, and pepper, and keep it warm.

3. Grease a large baking dish with the remaining butter and lay asparagus lengthwise in the dish with half of the tips pointing in one direction and the other half pointing in the opposite direction. Pour the sauce over the asparagus, leaving the tips of the spears exposed. Sprinkle the bread crumbs over the sauce. Bake the asparagus for 30 minutes or until the top is golden brown. Serve it hot.

Asparagus in Ancient Times

Asparagus is derived from the Greek word meaning "sprout" and this plant has grown in the Mediterranean region since antiquity. It was used for medicinal purposes and as an aphrodisiac. Today, it's a delicious part of the Mediterranean diet.

POTATOES AU GRATIN WITH ONIONS

This is an easy dish to make ahead of time that will taste great even after you reheat it. To shake things up, try using different cheeses and herbs.

Serves 6

4 medium Yukon gold potatoes, skin on, scrubbed, and thinly sliced

1 medium red onion, thinly sliced

3 tablespoons fresh thyme leaves

2 tablespoons chopped fresh parsley

5 tablespoons unsalted butter, divided

⅓ cup all-purpose flour

1½ cups whole milk

2 cloves garlic, peeled and minced

1 bay leaf

½ cup grated aged Cheddar

½ cup grated Graviera or Gruyère cheese

⅛ teaspoon ground nutmeg

1½ teaspoons salt

¾ teaspoon black pepper

½ cup bread crumbs

1. Preheat the oven to 375°F. Into a large bowl, combine the potatoes, onions, thyme, and parsley. Reserve.

2. Melt 4 tablespoons of butter in a medium skillet over medium heat. Then stir in the flour and cook for 2 minutes. Add the milk, garlic, and bay leaf, and keep stirring until the sauce thickens to a creamy texture. Remove the skillet from the heat and stir in the cheeses. Add the nutmeg and season with the salt and pepper. Keep the sauce warm.

3. Grease a large baking dish with the remaining butter. Spoon a ladle of sauce on the bottom of the dish; remove the bay leaf. Add an overlapping layer of potatoes. Sprinkle some of the sliced onions over the potatoes. Spoon a couple of ladles of sauce over the onions. Repeat this pattern with the remaining sauce, potatoes, and onions. Finish with a final layer of sauce. Sprinkle the top with the bread crumbs.

4. Bake the casserole for 30–40 minutes or until the top is golden brown. Let it rest for 5 minutes before serving.

SAFFRON COUSCOUS

This bright yellow dish is a delicious side for fish or seafood. Add some chopped grilled vegetables to the couscous and you have a fantastic vegetarian main dish.

Serves 6

2¼ cups water

½ teaspoon salt

⅛ teaspoon saffron threads

2 tablespoons unsalted butter, divided

1½ cups couscous, uncooked

1. In a medium pot over medium-high heat, combine the water, salt, saffron, and 1 tablespoon of butter. Bring the mixture to a boil, and then remove it from the heat. Stir in the couscous and cover the pot. Let the couscous stand for 5 minutes or until all the liquid has been absorbed.

2. Fluff the couscous with a fork, and stir in the remaining butter. Adjust the seasoning with salt, if necessary. Serve this dish warm or at room temperature.

Saffron

Saffron is a spice derived from the dried stigmas of crocus plants. The crocus must be picked by hand so that the delicate stigmas are kept intact. Because of this, saffron is the most expensive spice in the world. Thankfully, a little goes a long way to add rich flavor and bright color to a dish.

ROASTED CARROTS WITH HONEY AND THYME

The honey brings out the sweetness of the carrots.

Serves 4

8 medium carrots, peeled, halved lengthwise

⅓ cup extra-virgin olive oil

1 teaspoon grated orange zest

1 tablespoon honey

2 tablespoons dry white wine

1 teaspoon salt

½ teaspoon pepper

2 teaspoons fresh thyme leaves

1. Preheat the oven to 400°F. In a large bowl, combine the carrots, oil, zest, honey, wine, salt, pepper, and thyme. Make sure the carrots are well coated. Empty the contents of the bowl evenly onto a baking tray.

2. Bake the carrots on the middle rack of the oven for 25–30 minutes or until they are tender. Serve immediately or warm.

GREEK ROASTED POTATOES

Lemony roast potatoes are a must for any Greek feast and are often paired with roast lamb, beef, or chicken.

Serves 6

8 large Yukon gold or russet potatoes, peeled and sliced lengthwise into wedges

½ cup extra-virgin olive oil

2–3 tablespoons fresh lemon juice

½ teaspoon pepper

1½ teaspoons salt

1 teaspoon dried oregano

½ cup hot water

1. Preheat the oven to 425°F. In a large bowl, combine the potatoes, oil, lemon juice, pepper, salt, oregano, and water. Make sure the potatoes are well coated.

2. Empty the bowl into a deep roasting pan. Bake on the middle rack for 20 minutes. Stir the potatoes and bake for another 20–25 minutes or until the potatoes are fork-tender.

HERB AND LEMON COUSCOUS

Change up the herbs and use whatever you have on hand. Serve this side with fish or chicken.

Serves 6

2¼ cups water

½ teaspoon salt

2 teaspoons grated lemon zest

1 tablespoon fresh lemon juice

2 tablespoons extra-virgin olive oil, divided

1½ cups couscous, uncooked

1 tablespoon finely chopped fresh parsley

1 tablespoon finely chopped fresh chives

1 tablespoon finely chopped fresh mint

1. In a medium pot over medium-high heat, combine the water, salt, lemon zest, lemon juice, and 1 tablespoon oil. Bring the mixture to a boil, and then remove from heat. Stir in the couscous. Cover and let it stand for 5 minutes or until the couscous has absorbed the liquid.

2. Fluff the couscous with a fork. Stir in the parsley, chives, mint, and remaining oil. Serve the couscous warm or at room temperature.

CRISPY ROASTED POTATOES

These potatoes are crispy outside and fluffy inside. Serve them with a Sunday roast of lamb or pork.

Serves 6

12 medium Yukon gold potatoes, peeled

3½ teaspoons salt, divided

½ cup extra-virgin olive oil

4 cloves garlic, peeled and minced

1. In a large pot over medium-high heat, put the potatoes, 1 teaspoon of salt, and just enough water to cover the potatoes by 1 inch. Bring the water to a boil, and then reduce the heat to medium. Cook for 10 minutes (the potatoes will finish cooking in the oven).

2. Preheat the oven to 425°F. In a medium roasting pan, combine the oil and garlic.

3. Drain the potatoes and add them to the pan. Sprinkle the potatoes with the remaining salt and toss them gently to coat them in the oil and garlic.

4. Roast the potatoes on the middle rack for 20 minutes. Remove the pan from the oven; using a masher, gently flatten the potatoes until they are about 1-inch thick. Spoon some oil from the pan over the potatoes and roast them for another 10 minutes or until golden.

5. Serve the potatoes immediately so they stay crispy.

GRILLED ASPARAGUS WITH ROASTED PEPPERS AND FETA

Keep an eye on the asparagus while grilling because they burn easily.

Serves 4

½ pound asparagus, woody ends trimmed

4 tablespoons extra-virgin olive oil, divided

½ teaspoon salt

¼ teaspoon pepper

3 tablespoons vegetable oil

1 Roasted Red Pepper (see recipe in this chapter)

½ cup crumbled feta cheese

1. In a large bowl, combine the asparagus, 2 tablespoons olive oil, salt, and pepper. Toss to coat the asparagus.

2. Preheat a gas or charcoal grill to medium-high. When the grill is ready, dip a clean tea towel in the vegetable oil and wipe the grill's surface with the oil.

3. Grill asparagus 2 minutes per side. Arrange on a platter and top with the Roasted Red Pepper. Sprinkle the cheese on top and drizzle with the remaining oil.

STEAMED CAULIFLOWER

You can use broccoli instead of the cauliflower, or try both for a colorful side dish.

Serves 6

1 head cauliflower, leaves removed, trimmed, and cut into florets

⅓ cup extra-virgin olive oil

1 tablespoon fresh lemon juice

1 teaspoon salt

¼ cup chopped fresh chives

1. Pour water into a large pot with a steaming basket until the water barely touches the basket. Bring the water to a boil over medium-high heat, add the cauliflower, and cover the pot. Steam the cauliflower for 15 minutes until it is cooked but not mushy.

2. In a large bowl, whisk the oil, lemon juice, salt, and chives. Toss the cauliflower in the dressing, and adjust the seasoning with salt, if necessary

Preparing a Cauliflower

To prepare a cauliflower, first remove the leaves and trim away any brown spots. Turn the cauliflower over and cut off the florets by turning a small knife downward and around the stalk to release the florets.

BEANS WITH ROASTED GARLIC, CAPERS, AND PARSLEY

Yellow beans or a combination of green and yellow beans would also work in this recipe.

Serves 6

1 pound green wax beans, trimmed

2½ teaspoons salt, divided

1 cup fresh parsley leaves

3 tablespoons capers, rinsed

1½ teaspoons grated lemon zest

1 teaspoon Dijon mustard

⅓ cup extra-virgin olive oil

1 whole head garlic, roasted and cloves extracted (see Roasting Garlic sidebar)

1 teaspoon dried oregano

1–2 teaspoons red wine vinegar

½ teaspoon pepper

1. Fill a large pot two-thirds with water and bring the water to boil over medium-high heat. Add the beans and 1½ teaspoons of salt. Bring the water back to a boil, and then reduce the heat to medium. Cook the beans for 6–7 minutes or until the beans are cooked, but not soft. Remove the beans from the water and place them in an ice bath to stop further cooking. When the beans are cool, remove them from the ice bath and set them aside.

2. In a food processor, combine the parsley, capers, lemon zest, mustard, and oil. Process the ingredients to make the dressing.

3. In a large bowl, combine the beans, garlic, oregano, vinegar, and dressing. Toss the beans to coat them, and then season them with the remaining salt and pepper.

Roasting Garlic

Roasting garlic is easy. Preheat the oven to 350°F. Cut the top off a whole head of garlic; remove just enough to expose the cloves inside. Place the garlic in a sheet of aluminum foil and lightly drizzle it with olive oil and then add a sprinkle of salt. Wrap the garlic in the foil and roast it for 35–50 minutes. Allow the garlic to cool. Remove each clove with a knife, or squeeze the whole head until the cloves pop out.

SAUTÉED MUSHROOMS WITH BRANDY AND CREAM

Evaporated milk can be used as a lighter alternative to heavy cream in this dish. Try Metaxa brandy from Greece . . . it has a touch of honey!

Serves 4

1 tablespoon unsalted butter

1 tablespoon extra-virgin olive oil

1 pound cremini mushrooms, cleaned and halved

1 medium shallot, finely chopped

1 clove garlic, peeled and minced

1 teaspoon fresh thyme leaves

2 tablespoons chopped fresh parsley, divided

½ teaspoon salt

¼ teaspoon pepper

1 ounce brandy

2 tablespoons heavy cream

1. Heat the butter and oil in a large skillet over medium-high heat for 30 seconds. Add the mushrooms, shallots, and garlic. Stirring frequently, sauté the mushrooms for 5–6 minutes.

2. Reduce the heat to medium, and add the thyme, 1 tablespoon parsley, salt, and pepper. Cover the skillet and cook for 3 minutes. Remove the lid and continue cooking until most of the liquid has evaporated.

3. Add the brandy and cook for 2 minutes. Stir in the cream and let the sauce thicken for 1 minute.

4. Serve the mushrooms with a sprinkle of the remaining parsley.

Spend a Little More

Cremini mushrooms are a little more expensive than regular button mushrooms, but they are worth the price. Cremini mushrooms are darker and have a firmer texture than button mushrooms. Cremini mushrooms taste richer and nuttier as well.

KATSAMAKI

Most people are familiar with Italian polenta; this is the Greek version.

Serves 6

2½ cups Chicken or Turkey Stock or Basic Vegetable Stock (see recipes in Chapter 2)

1 cup cornmeal

¼ cup grated kefalotyri or other sharp goat's milk cheese

½ teaspoon pepper

1. Heat the stock in a medium pot over medium-high heat until almost boiling.

2. Slowly whisk in a steady stream of cornmeal. Continue to whisk to remove any lumps until you get a smooth porridge-like consistency. Remove the pot from the heat.

3. Stir in the cheese and season the dish with pepper. Serve it immediately.

BRAISED LENTILS

Always wait to salt lentils until the end of cooking because the salt can make them tough.

Serves 6

¼ cup extra-virgin olive oil

¼ cup finely chopped red onions

½ cup finely chopped celery

½ cup finely chopped peeled carrots

1½ cups dried green or brown lentils, rinsed

1 bay leaf

2 sprigs fresh oregano

2 sprigs fresh parsley

4 cups Chicken or Turkey Stock or Basic Vegetable Stock (see recipes in Chapter 2)

1½ teaspoons salt

½ teaspoon pepper

1. Heat the oil in a medium pot over medium-high heat for 30 seconds. Add the onions, celery, and carrots. Cook for 2–3 minutes until the vegetables soften. Add the lentils, bay leaf, oregano, parsley, and stock. Cover the pot, and reduce the heat to medium-low. Cook for 30–40 minutes or until almost all the liquid is absorbed.

2. Discard the bay leaf, oregano, and parsley, and season the lentils with salt and pepper.

BAKED POTATO À LA GREQUE

Serve these baked potatoes with grilled meat.

Serves 4

4 large baking potatoes, skins on and scrubbed

½ cup plus 2 tablespoons extra-virgin olive oil, divided

1 cup crumbled feta cheese

2 tablespoons whole milk

1½ teaspoons grated lemon zest

2 tablespoons cream cheese

2 teaspoons dried oregano

½ tablespoon salt

¼ teaspoon pepper

¼ cup chopped scallions, ends trimmed

1. Preheat the oven to 350°F. Pierce each potato with a fork several times on each side to allow the steam to escape. Place the potatoes on a baking sheet and rub the skins with 2 tablespoons of oil. Bake the potatoes on the middle rack of the oven for 90 minutes.

2. In a medium bowl, combine the feta and milk. With a fork, mash the feta into the milk. Stir in the lemon zest, cream cheese, and oregano.

3. Cut a slit halfway down and lengthwise into the top of each potato. Squeeze the ends of the potatoes to open them up. Drizzle the remaining oil over the potatoes and season them with salt and pepper. Top each potato with the feta sauce and the scallions.

SAVORY ISRAELI COUSCOUS CARROT CAKE

The flavors of the nutty couscous and the sweet carrots make a wonderful combination.

Serves 6

1½ teaspoons olive oil, divided

6 carrots

1 shallot

2 sprigs rosemary, leaves only

1 whole egg

1 egg white

1 cup cooked couscous

¼ cup skimmed milk

1½ cups whole-wheat flour

½ teaspoon baking powder

¼ teaspoon iodized salt

1. Preheat the oven to 375°F. Brush a layer-cake pan with a quarter of the oil.

2. Peel and grate the carrots. Mince the shallot.

3. Combine the carrots and shallots with the rosemary, eggs, couscous, the remaining oil, and the milk. In a separate bowl, sift together the flour, baking powder, and salt and, in batches, slowly stir into wet mixture.

4. Place in the prepared cake pan and bake for 45 minutes.

Baking Tip
To prevent overbrowning the top of the cake while baking, cover it with foil halfway through the cooking time.

BROWNED MIXED POTATO PANCAKES

This is an alternate version of the classic potato pancake. For even more variety, try other types of potatoes when available.

Serves 6

1 large sweet potato

1 large baking potato

1 tablespoon olive oil

Peel and shred the potatoes. Form into small patties. Heat a small sauté pan to medium-high heat and brush with oil. Place the potato patties in the sauté pan. Let brown on each side; serve immediately.

CHAPTER 5

SOUPS, SALADS, AND SANDWICHES

SOUPS

COLD CUCUMBER SOUP

Make this soup when you have an abundance of cucumbers from your garden. This soup comes together quickly using a food processor.

Serves 4

2 cloves garlic, peeled and minced

1 tablespoon red wine vinegar

2 slices white bread, crusts removed

1 large English cucumber, ends trimmed and grated

1½ cups plain yogurt

1½ cups cold water

4 tablespoons extra-virgin olive oil, divided

¼ cup plus 2 tablespoons chopped fresh dill, divided

¾ teaspoon salt

1 cup ½-inch-cubed English cucumber

1. In a food processor, add the garlic, vinegar, and bread. Process until the mixture becomes a paste. Add the grated cucumber and yogurt and process again.

2. With the processor running, slowly add the water in a steady stream. Add more water if you want the soup to be thinner. Add 2 tablespoons oil, ¼ cup dill, and the salt. Pulse a few times to blend into the soup.

3. Transfer the soup into a container with lid. Cover it and refrigerate until chilled.

4. Before serving, stir the soup. Ladle it into bowls and top with the cubed cucumber, remaining dill, and remaining oil. Serve cold.

Food Processors

With the limited amount of time people have to spend in the kitchen, a food processor is a wise investment. It chops, slices, grates, and even kneads. Save yourself some time and energy. There are many affordable models out there, so find one that's right for you.

LENTIL SOUP

Lentils have been consumed in the Mediterranean region for centuries, and lentil soup is a regular meal in many Mediterranean homes. Serve with crusty bread, olives, and pickled vegetables.

Serves 8

2 cups brown lentils, rinsed

½ cup extra-virgin olive oil

2 medium onions, peeled and chopped

1 large carrot, peeled, halved, and cut into ½-inch slices

1 large red pepper, stemmed, seeded, and chopped

3 bay leaves

¾ cup tomato sauce

1 tablespoon sweet paprika

8 cloves garlic, peeled (3 smashed and 5 minced)

8 cups water

2 tablespoons dried oregano

2½ teaspoons salt

¼ cup red wine vinegar

1. In a large pot over medium-high heat, add the lentils and enough water to cover them by 1 inch. Bring the water to a boil and cook for 1 minute. Drain the lentils.

2. Return the lentils to the empty pot, and add oil, onions, carrots, peppers, bay leaves, tomato sauce, paprika, and smashed garlic. Add 8 cups water and bring the soup to a boil.

3. Cover and reduce the heat to medium-low. Cook for 50–60 minutes or until the lentils are tender. Remove the bay leaves and the smashed garlic. Add the minced garlic, oregano, salt, and vinegar. Cook for another 2 minutes. Serve hot.

CHICKPEA SOUP

Try puréeing this soup for more formal dinners and serve with sautéed shrimp as a garnish. Keep in mind, you'll have to start this soup the night before to rehydrate the chickpeas.

Serves 8

2 cups dried chickpeas

½ cup extra-virgin olive oil

2 large onions, peeled and chopped

3 or 4 cloves garlic, peeled and minced

1 medium carrot, peeled and finely chopped

1 stalk celery, ends trimmed and finely chopped

3 bay leaves

1 teaspoon sweet paprika

1 tablespoon fresh thyme leaves

¼ cup chopped fresh parsley

½ large lemon, sliced

8 cups Chicken or Turkey Stock or Basic Vegetable Stock (see recipes in Chapter 2)

2⅓ teaspoons salt

½ teaspoon pepper

1 teaspoon dried oregano

1. To rehydrate chickpeas, put them in a bowl and cover them with at least 2 inches of water. Leave them to rehydrate overnight, and then strain and rinse the chickpeas before using.

2. In a large pot over medium heat, add the oil and heat for 30 seconds. Add onions, garlic, carrot, celery, bay leaves, paprika, and thyme. Reduce heat to medium-low and cook for 15 minutes or until the vegetables are softened.

3. Add the chickpeas, parsley, lemon, and stock. Increase heat to medium-high and bring to a boil. Reduce heat to medium-low and partially cover (leave the lid slightly ajar). Cook for 2–3 hours or until the chickpeas are tender and the soup is thickened. Season with salt and pepper.

4. Remove bay leaves and serve hot with a sprinkle of oregano on top.

Sunday Chickpea Soup

Each Saturday night on the Greek island of Sifnos, ladies would carry a large earthenware vessel full of rehydrated chickpeas with olive oil and aromatics to the local bakery to slow-cook in the oven overnight. The soup would be ready Sunday just after church service.

ARTICHOKE SOUP

Artichokes are part of the thistle family. They grow wild in the Mediterranean.

Serves 8

18 large fresh artichokes, outer layers peeled, trimmed, halved, and chokes removed

6 tablespoons fresh lemon juice, divided

¼ cup extra-virgin olive oil

6 leeks, ends trimmed, thoroughly cleaned, cut lengthwise, and sliced

1½ teaspoons salt, divided

½ teaspoon pepper, divided

3 large potatoes, peeled and quartered

10 cups Basic Vegetable Stock (see recipe in Chapter 2)

½ cup strained Greek yogurt

½ cup chopped fresh chives

1. In a large bowl, combine artichokes, enough water to cover them, and 3 tablespoons of lemon juice. Reserve.

2. Heat the oil in a large pot over medium heat for 30 seconds. Add the leeks, ½ teaspoon salt, and ¼ teaspoon pepper. Cook for 10 minutes or until the leeks are softened.

3. Drain the artichokes and add them to the leeks along with the potatoes and stock. Increase the heat to medium-high and bring the soup to a boil. Add the remaining salt and pepper and reduce heat to medium-low. Cook for 40–45 minutes. Take the pot off the heat.

4. Using an immersion blender or a regular blender, carefully purée the soup until smooth. Add the remaining lemon juice and adjust seasoning with more salt and pepper, if necessary.

5. Serve soup with a dollop of yogurt and a sprinkle of chives.

GIOUVARLAKIA SOUP

This hearty soup is a one-pot meal.

Serves 4

1 pound lean ground beef

1 medium onion, peeled and grated

3 large eggs, divided

⅓ cup plus ½ cup Arborio rice, divided

1 teaspoon ground allspice

⅛ teaspoon grated nutmeg

1½ teaspoons salt, divided

1½ teaspoons pepper, divided

8 cups Chicken or Turkey Stock (see recipe in Chapter 2)

1 tablespoon flour

2 tablespoons water

3 tablespoons fresh lemon juice

1. In a large bowl, combine beef, onion, 1 egg, ⅓ cup rice, allspice, nutmeg, ½ teaspoon salt, and ½ teaspoon pepper. Roll the mixture into 1-inch balls. Reserve.

2. Add the stock to a large pot over medium-high heat and bring to a boil. Reduce the heat to medium. Add the meatballs (carefully), the remaining rice, the remaining salt, and the remaining pepper. Cover and cook for 20 minutes. Take the pot off the heat.

3. In a large bowl, whisk together flour and water until you get a slurry. Whisk in the remaining eggs and lemon juice. Continuing to whisk vigorously, slowly add a ladle of soup liquid into the egg-lemon mixture. Continue whisking and slowly add another 3 or 4 ladles of soup (one at a time) into the egg-lemon mixture.

4. Slowly stir the egg-lemon mixture back into the soup.

5. Allow the soup to cool for 5 minutes and then serve it immediately.

GREEK GAZPACHO

Roasted peppers add a sweetness and smokiness to a typical gazpacho recipe. Olive-oil ice cubes provide a unique garnish.

Serves 4

2 slices day-old white bread

1 tablespoon dried oregano

3 or 4 cloves garlic, peeled and smashed

2 tablespoons chopped fresh parsley

¼ cup red wine vinegar

¼ cup extra-virgin olive oil

1 large Roasted Red Pepper (see recipe in Chapter 4)

1 large roasted green bell pepper (see Roasted Red Peppers recipe in Chapter 4)

2 medium-size red onions, peeled and roughly chopped

1 large English cucumber, seeded and chopped

4 large ripe tomatoes, roughly chopped

¾ cup sun-dried black olives, pitted

6 cups vegetable cocktail beverage

1 teaspoon pepper

1 cup cubed feta cheese

4–6 olive-oil ice cubes (see Olive-Oil Ice Cubes sidebar)

1. Place bread, oregano, garlic, and parsley into a food processor. Process the ingredients until they form a wet paste. Add vinegar and oil and pulse until incorporated. Empty the contents of the processor into a large bowl. Reserve.

2. Add peppers, onions, cucumber, tomatoes, and olives to the food processor. Pulse until the ingredients are coarsely chopped. Add this mixture to the reserved bread-garlic mixture.

3. Stir in the vegetable cocktail beverage and the pepper. Cover with plastic wrap and chill for at least 3 hours.

4. Serve cold, topped with feta and olive-oil ice cubes.

Olive-Oil Ice Cubes

Fill the ice-cube tray's compartments halfway with extra-virgin olive oil. Place the tray in the freezer to harden. Use them as a garnish for any cold savory soups.

FASSOULADA (GREEK NAVY BEAN SOUP)

This is a hearty vegetarian soup. Try using a pressure cooker for this recipe. Pressure cookers are safe and they cut the cooking time in half! You'll have to start this soup the night before to rehydrate the beans.

Serves 6

1 cup small dry (white) navy beans

1 large stalk celery, ends trimmed, halved lengthwise, and sliced into ½-inch pieces

1 large carrot, peeled, halved, and sliced into ½-inch pieces

2 medium onions, peeled and chopped

½ cup tomato purée

½ cup extra-virgin olive oil

2 bay leaves

1 medium chili pepper, stemmed and finely chopped

2 teaspoons smoked paprika

8 cups water

2½ teaspoons salt

1. To rehydrate the beans, add them to a bowl large enough to hold them and cover them with at least 2 inches of water. Let them rehydrate overnight, and then strain and rinse the beans before using them.

2. In a large pot over medium-high heat, add the rehydrated beans, celery, carrot, onions, tomato purée, oil, bay leaves, chili pepper, paprika, and water. Cover and bring to a boil.

3. Lower heat to medium and cook the soup for 2 hours or until the beans are soft. Take the pot off the heat and season the soup with salt.

4. Remove the bay leaves before serving. Serve hot.

Bay Leaves

Bay leaves are a favorite Mediterranean aromatic for cooking. The leaves come from a tree that grows throughout the Mediterranean, and they add a savory note in soups, roasts, and sauces. Fresh bay leaves are more aromatic, but dried bay leaves are just as good.

HEARTY WINTER VEGETABLE SOUP

Serve this soup with crusty bread and a glass of red wine. It's wonderful when eaten by a warm fire.

Serves 8

¼ cup extra-virgin olive oil

1 large leek, ends trimmed, thoroughly cleaned, cut lengthwise, and sliced

5 or 6 cloves garlic, peeled and minced

2 large carrots, peeled and diced

3 stalks celery, ends trimmed and diced

1 large red bell pepper, stemmed, seeded, and diced

3 bay leaves

3 sprigs thyme

2 teaspoons salt, divided

1 teaspoon pepper, divided

1 sweet potato, peeled and grated

1 cup shredded white cabbage

1 cup halved broccoli florets

1 cup halved cauliflower florets

9–10 cups Basic Vegetable Stock (see recipe in Chapter 2)

2 cups chopped romaine lettuce

1 cup pasta of your choice

1. Add the oil to a large pot over medium heat and heat for 30 seconds. Add the leeks, garlic, carrots, celery, bell pepper, bay leaves, and thyme. Season with ½ teaspoon salt and ¼ teaspoon pepper. Cover and cook for 10 minutes or until the vegetables are softened.

2. Add the sweet potato and cook for 2 minutes. Add the cabbage, broccoli, and cauliflower. Cook for another minute.

3. Add the stock, increase the heat to medium-high, and bring the soup to a boil. Reduce the heat to medium-low and cook for 15 minutes. Add the lettuce and pasta and cook for another 20–25 minutes.

4. Season with remaining salt and pepper. Remove thyme stems and bay leaves. Serve hot.

Leeks

Leeks are part of the onion family and are wonderful for making soups. They do need thorough cleaning, as dirt often gets in between the layers. To clean them properly, cut the ends off the leeks, and cut them in half lengthwise. Run them under cold water while running your fingers back and forth between the layers to remove grit.

VRASTO

This soup is made of simmered vegetables and veal. It's finished with an egg-lemon mixture Greeks call avgolemono.

Serves 6

2 pounds veal shoulder, cut into chunks

1½ teaspoons salt, divided

1 teaspoon pepper, divided

8 cups plus 2 tablespoons water

¼ cup extra-virgin olive oil

6 small onions, peeled and halved

3 large carrots, peeled and roughly chopped

4 stalks celery, ends trimmed and roughly chopped

5 large potatoes, peeled (1 grated and 4 roughly chopped)

1 tablespoon all-purpose flour

2 large eggs

3 tablespoons fresh lemon juice

1. Season the veal with ½ teaspoon salt and ½ teaspoon pepper. Add the veal and 8 cups water to a pressure cooker. Secure the lid and crank the heat to high. When the seal forms, you will hear the cooker whistle. Turn the heat to medium and cook for 20–30 minutes. Take the pressure cooker off the heat and release the pressure according to the manufacturer's instructions. If you don't have a pressure cooker, place the veal and water in a large pot over medium heat. Cover and cook for 90 minutes. Reserve the veal and the liquid.

2. Add the oil to a large pot over medium heat and heat for 30 seconds. Add the onions, carrots, and celery. Cook for 15 minutes or until the vegetables have softened. Add potatoes and the veal cooking liquid (you should have 8 cups or more). Increase the heat to medium-high and bring the soup to a boil. Reduce the heat to medium-low and cook for 30 minutes.

3. Add the cooked veal and season it with the remaining salt and pepper. Cook for 5 minutes to warm the veal through. Take the pot off the heat.

4. In a large bowl, whisk the flour with 2 tablespoons water. Whisk in the eggs and lemon juice. Continuing to whisk vigorously, slowly add a ladle of soup liquid into the egg-lemon mixture. Continue whisking and slowly add another 3 or 4 ladles of soup one at a time.

5. Slowly stir the egg-lemon mixture back into the soup. Let the soup cool for 5 minutes before serving. Serve hot.

Beef Instead of Veal

If you don't like veal, you can always use beef instead. Beef won't be as tender as veal, so you'll need to cook it a bit longer. It will be just as tasty.

GREEK FISHERMAN'S SOUP

You will need cheesecloth for this soup to wrap up the fish, spices, and shrimp shells. Cheesecloth is found in most supermarkets. Serve this soup with toasted garlic bread.

Serves 6

3 bay leaves

4 or 5 allspice berries

6 or 7 peppercorns

4 sprigs fresh thyme

1 pound medium shrimp, peeled, deveined, and shells reserved

2 medium-size red mullets or 1 whole red snapper or scorpion fish, cleaned and gutted

½ cup extra-virgin olive oil

2 large leeks, ends trimmed, thoroughly cleaned, cut lengthwise, and sliced

4 cloves garlic, peeled and smashed

3 medium carrots, peeled and chopped

2 stalks celery, ends trimmed and chopped

3 large potatoes, peeled and diced

⅛ teaspoon saffron threads

2 teaspoons tomato paste

½ cup tomato purée

1 cup dry white wine

8–9 cups water

1 teaspoon salt

½ teaspoon pepper

1 pound fresh clams, scrubbed and rinsed

1 pound mussels, scrubbed and beards removed

1 pound whitefish fillets (bass, haddock, halibut, whiting), cut into bite-size pieces

½ cup chopped fresh parsley

1 large lemon cut into wedges

1. Wrap bay leaves, allspice, peppercorns, and thyme in cheesecloth and tie it tightly into a bundle. Wrap the reserved shrimp shells in cheesecloth and tie it tightly into another bundle. Wrap the mullet in cheesecloth and tie it tightly into another bundle.

2. Heat oil in a large pot over medium-high heat for 30 seconds. Reduce heat to medium and add leeks, garlic, carrots, and celery. Cook for 5 minutes. Add the spice bundle and the shrimp-shell bundle and lower the heat to medium. Cook for 10 minutes.

3. Stir in the potatoes, saffron, tomato paste, and tomato purée, and cook for 2 minutes. Add the wine and water, and increase the heat to medium-high. Bring the mixture to a boil, and then reduce the heat to medium-low. Season with the salt and pepper, cover, and cook for 30 minutes.

4. Add the mullet bundle and cook for 15 minutes. Carefully remove the mullet, unwrap it, and remove its flesh (discard the bones and skin). Reserve. Add the clams to the pot, return the heat to medium-high, and bring the soup to a boil. Turn the heat off, and add the mussels, shrimp, whitefish, and reserved mullet flesh. Cover the pot and allow the fish to cook in the residual heat for 10 minutes.

5. Remove the spice and shrimp-shell bundles. Discard any clams and mussels that have not opened. Add the parsley and serve the soup hot with lemon.

LEEK AND POTATO SOUP

This soup never goes out of style. It satisfies every time the cold weather returns.

Serves 8

¼ cup extra-virgin olive oil

3 leeks, ends trimmed, thoroughly cleaned, cut lengthwise, and sliced

2 bay leaves

1 teaspoon dried thyme

3 russet potatoes, peeled and grated

8 cups Chicken or Turkey Stock or Basic Vegetable Stock (see recipes in Chapter 2)

½ cup heavy cream or evaporated milk

2½ teaspoons salt

1 teaspoon pepper

½ cup chopped fresh chives

1. Add the oil to a large pot over medium heat and heat for 30 seconds. Add the leeks, bay leaves, and thyme. Cook for 10–15 minutes or until the leeks soften.

2. Add the potatoes and cook for another 5 minutes. If the mixture gets dry or gluey, add some water or stock.

3. Add the stock and the increase heat to medium-high. Bring the soup to a boil, reduce the heat to medium-low, and cook for 30–40 minutes. Remove the bay leaves.

4. Using an immersion blender or a regular blender, carefully purée the soup until it is smooth. Add the cream, and season with salt and pepper.

5. Serve hot and topped with chives.

ROASTED YELLOW BELL PEPPER SOUP

Try using orange or red bell peppers to make a brilliant colored soup. Garnish with strained Greek yogurt and cubed roasted beets.

Serves 6

¼ cup extra-virgin olive oil

1 leek (white part only), ends trimmed, thoroughly cleaned, cut lengthwise, and sliced

1 medium carrot, peeled and diced

½ stalk celery, ends trimmed and diced

4 cloves garlic, peeled and smashed

1½ teaspoons salt, divided

½ teaspoon pepper, divided

2 medium Yukon gold potatoes, peeled and diced

1 teaspoon sweet paprika

1 teaspoon fresh thyme leaves

4 large roasted yellow bell peppers (see Roasted Red Peppers recipe in Chapter 4)

1 small hot banana pepper, stemmed, seeded, and chopped

4 cups Basic Vegetable Stock or Chicken or Turkey Stock (see recipes in Chapter 2)

½ cup sliced fresh basil leaves

½ cup heavy cream

½ cup grated Graviera (or Gruyère) cheese

1. Add the oil to a large pot over medium heat and heat for 30 seconds. Add the leeks, carrot, celery, and garlic. Season with ½ teaspoon salt and ¼ teaspoon pepper. Reduce the heat to medium-low and cook for 10 minutes or until the leeks soften.

2. Add the potatoes, paprika, and thyme. Cook for 2 minutes. Add the roasted peppers, banana pepper, and stock. Increase the heat to medium-high and bring the soup to a boil. Reduce the heat to medium-low, cover, and cook for another 20 minutes.

3. Add the basil. Using an immersion blender or a regular blender, carefully purée the soup until it is smooth. Add cream, cheese, and remaining salt and pepper. Stir until the cheese is melted and the soup smooth.

4. Serve hot.

ZESTY CABBAGE SOUP

Eliminate the chili pepper in this recipe if you don't like spicy food.

Serves 4

¼ cup extra-virgin olive oil

3 medium onions, peeled and chopped

1 large carrot, peeled, quartered, and sliced

1 stalk celery, ends trimmed and chopped

3 bay leaves

1 teaspoon smoked paprika

3 cups sliced white cabbage

1 teaspoon fresh thyme

3 cloves garlic, peeled and minced

1 large Roasted Red Pepper (see recipe in Chapter 4), chopped

1 small can white navy beans, rinsed

1½ cups vegetable cocktail beverage

7 cups Basic Vegetable Stock (see recipe in Chapter 2)

1 dried chili pepper

2 medium zucchini, ends trimmed, halved lengthwise, and sliced thin

1 teaspoon salt

½ teaspoon pepper

1. Heat the oil in a large pot over medium heat for 30 seconds. Add the onions, carrots, celery, and bay leaves. Cook for 7–10 minutes or until the vegetables are soft.

2. Add the paprika, cabbage, thyme, garlic, Roasted Red Pepper, and beans. Stir to combine all the ingredients and cook for 2 minutes.

3. Add the vegetable cocktail beverage, stock, and chili pepper. Increase the heat to medium-high and bring the soup to a boil. Reduce the heat to medium-low, cover, and cook for 40–45 minutes.

4. Add the zucchini and cook another 5 minutes. Season with salt and pepper; remove the bay leaves.

5. Serve hot.

Cabbage

Cabbage is an underrated vegetable that should be used more. It's a good source of fiber and vitamin C. It's a great colon cleanser and a detoxifier for the entire body.

CALDO VERDE

This comforting soup is Portugal's national dish. It literally means "Green Soup." Try to find Portuguese chouriço, which is a cured pork sausage. If you can't find it, you can substitute Spanish chorizo. Serve this soup with crusty bread and some white wine.

Serves 8

8 cups Chicken or Turkey Stock (see recipe in Chapter 2)

1 teaspoon salt

2 cloves garlic, peeled and smashed

2 large onions, peeled and quartered

1½ pounds potatoes, peeled and halved

4 tablespoons extra-virgin olive oil, divided

8 ounces chouriço (whole)

2 cups water

2 cups finely shredded kale

1. In a large pot over medium-high heat, combine the stock, salt, garlic, onions, potatoes, 2 tablespoons oil, chouriço, and water. Bring the mixture to a boil, reduce the heat to medium, and cook for 45–50 minutes or until the potatoes are tender when pierced with a fork.

2. Remove the chouriço; slice thinly and reserve.

3. Using an immersion blender or a regular blender, carefully purée the soup until it is smooth. If using a regular blender, transfer the soup back to the pot and add the kale. Cook over medium heat for 5 minutes or until the kale is wilted. Adjust the seasoning with salt, if necessary.

4. To serve, ladle the soup into bowls and garnish each bowl with a few slices of chouriço and a drop of the remaining oil.

Portuguese Chouriço Versus Spanish Chorizo
These cured sausages are similar in many ways; they are usually made with pork shoulder, paprika, black pepper, garlic, and salt. The proportions of the ingredients differ. The chorizo has more paprika while the chouriço has more garlic and black pepper. Also the type of paprika used is different. The chorizo uses a smoked paprika and the chouriço uses a sweet paprika.

GREEK EASTER SOUP

This soup is traditionally served on the Greek Easter, the most significant religious feast for Greeks. This soup is usually made with the viscera of lamb or goat, but this recipe uses lamb meat instead.

Serves 10

2 pounds lamb shoulder

1 tablespoon plus 1½ teaspoons salt, divided

10 cups water

¼ cup extra-virgin olive oil

12 scallions, ends trimmed and sliced

½ head romaine lettuce, finely chopped

½ cup Arborio rice

½ cup finely chopped parsley

1 cup finely chopped dill, divided

1 teaspoon pepper

2 large eggs

6 tablespoons fresh lemon juice

1 large lemon cut into wedges

1. Season lamb with 1 tablespoon salt. Put lamb and 10 cups of water into a pressure cooker. Secure the lid and crank the heat to high. When the seal forms, the cooker will whistle. Reduce heat to medium and cook for 1 hour. Take the cooker off the heat and release the pressure. If you don't have a pressure cooker, place the lamb and water in a large pot over medium heat. Cover and cook for 2½ hours (add more water if necessary).

2. Remove the meat from the lamb and discard any bones. Discard any fat and cartilage, and chop the lamb into bite-size pieces. Reserve the lamb and liquid.

3. Add the oil to a large pot over medium heat and heat for 30 seconds. Add the scallions and lettuce. Cook for 5 minutes or until the scallions are softened. Add the lamb and liquid, rice, parsley, and ½ cup dill. Increase heat to medium-high. Bring the soup to a boil, and then reduce the heat to medium-low. Cook for 25–30 minutes or until the rice is cooked. Season with remaining pepper and remaining salt. Take the pot off the heat.

4. In a large bowl, whisk together the eggs and lemon juice. Continuing to whisk vigorously, slowly add a ladle of soup liquid into the egg-lemon mixture. Continue whisking and slowly add another 3 or 4 ladles of soup (one at a time) into the egg-lemon mixture. Slowly stir the egg-lemon mixture back into the soup.

5. Adjust the seasoning if necessary. Stir in the remaining dill; serve the soup hot with lemon wedges on the side.

WEDDING SOUP

This Italian classic is served at weddings or on other special occasions.

Serves 6

3 slices Italian bread, toasted

¾ pound lean ground beef

1 large egg, beaten

1 medium onion, peeled and chopped

3 cloves garlic, peeled and minced

¼ cup chopped fresh parsley

1 tablespoon finely chopped fresh oregano

1 tablespoon finely chopped fresh basil

1 teaspoon salt

½ teaspoon pepper

½ cup grated Parmesan cheese, divided

8 cups Chicken or Turkey Stock (see recipe in Chapter 2)

1 cup roughly chopped fresh spinach, stems removed, and steamed until wilted

1. Preheat the oven to 375°F. Wet the toasted bread with water and then squeeze out all the liquid.

2. In a large bowl, combine beef, bread, egg, onion, garlic, parsley, oregano, basil, salt, pepper, and ¼ cup Parmesan. Mix well. Form the mixture into 1-inch balls. Place the balls on a parchment-lined baking sheet and bake for 20–30 minutes. Place the meatballs on a tray lined with paper towels to absorb excess oil.

3. In a large pot over medium-high heat, bring the stock to a boil, and then reduce heat to medium-low. Add the spinach and meatballs and cook for 30 minutes.

4. Ladle the soup into serving bowls and sprinkle with remaining cheese.

CARROT-THYME SOUP

If your carrots are not sweet enough for your liking, try adding a sweet potato to this soup. You can also top the soup with grated cheese.

Serves 6

1 tablespoon extra-virgin olive oil

2 pounds carrots, peeled and chopped

1 large onion, peeled and chopped

4 large potatoes, peeled and chopped

3 cloves garlic, peeled and minced

6 cups Basic Vegetable Stock (see recipe in Chapter 2)

1 teaspoon fresh thyme leaves

1 teaspoon salt

½ teaspoon pepper

1. Add oil to a large pot over medium-high heat, and heat for 30 seconds. Add the carrots, onions, potatoes, and garlic. Reduce heat to medium and cook for 10 minutes or until the vegetables are softened.

2. Add the stock and increase the heat to medium-high. Bring the soup to a boil, and then reduce the heat to medium and cook for 50–60 minutes.

3. Using an immersion blender or a regular blender, purée the soup until smooth. Be careful because the soup is very hot, so purée it with care. If you used a blender, return the soup to the pot.

4. Add the thyme, salt, and pepper. Cook over medium heat for another 15 minutes. Serve hot.

DANDELION AND WHITE BEAN SOUP

If you like the taste of dandelion greens, try them in a salad!

Serves 6

1 teaspoon extra-virgin olive oil

2 onions, peeled and chopped

3 medium carrots, peeled and chopped

3 stalks celery, ends trimmed and chopped

4 cloves garlic, peeled and minced

8 cups Basic Vegetable Stock (see recipe in Chapter 2)

1 bay leaf

¼ cup chopped fresh parsley

2 teaspoons fresh thyme leaves

1 teaspoon salt

½ teaspoon pepper

2 cups fresh dandelion greens, steamed until wilted

1 cup cooked cannellini beans

¼ cup grated Romano or Parmesan cheese

1. Add the oil to a large pot over medium heat and heat for 30 seconds. Add the onions, carrots, celery, and garlic. Cook for 5 minutes or until vegetables soften.

2. Add the stock, increase the heat to medium-high, and bring the soup to a boil. Reduce the heat to medium and cook for 1½ hours.

3. Add the bay leaf, parsley, thyme, salt, and pepper. Cook for 30 minutes. Add the dandelion greens and beans. Cook for another 15 minutes. Remove the bay leaf.

4. Serve the soup with a sprinkle of cheese on top.

Dandelion Greens

Dandelions grow in the Mediterranean countryside. Many people forage for the young, tender plants in the spring when they are not too bitter. Try dandelions in your salads or boil them and toss them in a little olive oil and lemon juice.

STRACCIATELLA (ITALIAN EGG-DROP SOUP)

This soup is hearty enough to stand on its own as a main dish.

Serves 6

1 tablespoon extra-virgin olive oil

1 large onion, peeled and chopped

1 medium shallot, peeled and finely chopped

6 cloves garlic, peeled and minced

8 cups Chicken or Turkey Stock (see recipe in Chapter 2)

1 bay leaf

½ cup chopped fresh parsley

2 teaspoons fresh thyme leaves

1 pound fresh spinach, finely sliced

2 large eggs

4 large egg whites

1 teaspoon salt

½ teaspoon pepper

¼ cup grated Parmesan cheese

1. Put the oil into a large pot over medium heat, and heat for 30 seconds. Add the onion, shallot, and garlic. Cook for 3 minutes or until the onion is softened.

2. Add the stock, bay leaf, parsley, and thyme; simmer for 30–45 minutes. Remove the bay leaf. Add the spinach and cook for 5 minutes or until the spinach is wilted.

3. In a small bowl, whisk the eggs and egg whites. Stir the eggs into the soup and cook 5 minutes. Season with salt and pepper. Serve topped with a sprinkle of grated Parmesan.

BEET SOUP

To add some creaminess to this flavorful soup, add a dollop of strained Greek yogurt in each bowl.

Serves 6

2 large beets

1 tablespoon plus ¼ cup extra-virgin olive oil, divided

3 medium onions, peeled and sliced

3 cloves garlic, peeled and smashed

2 medium carrots, peeled and sliced

2 stalks celery, sliced

2 cups finely sliced white cabbage

1 cup tomato purée

½ cup chopped fresh parsley

6–8 cups Beef Stock or Veal Stock (see recipe in Chapter 2)

2 large potatoes, peeled and cut into cubes

2 teaspoons salt

½ teaspoon pepper

¼ cup red wine vinegar

½ cup chopped fresh dill

1. Preheat the oven to 450°F. Rub the beets with 1 tablespoon oil. Wrap them in aluminum foil and place them on a baking sheet. Bake for 45 minutes or until fork-tender. Peel the skins off the beets with the back of a knife and discard. Chop the beets into ½-inch chunks.

2. Add the remaining oil to a large pot over medium heat, and heat for 30 seconds. Add the onions, garlic, carrots, and celery, and cook for 15 minutes. Add the cabbage, tomato purée, parsley, and beets. Cook for another 5 minutes.

3. Add the stock and potatoes, increase the heat to medium-high, and bring the soup to a boil. Reduce the heat to medium-low and cook for 45–60 minutes or until the potatoes are cooked. Season with salt and pepper.

4. Stir in the vinegar and dill and serve.

PUMPKIN SOUP

In the summer, Mediterranean residents are all about zucchini, but in the winter months, pumpkin gets the spotlight. This comforting soup is perfect for those cold winter nights. Serve with a dollop of Feta-Yogurt Sauce (see recipe in Chapter 2).

Serves 6

¼ cup unsalted butter

1 large onion, peeled and chopped

2 tablespoons grated ginger

2 cloves garlic, peeled and minced

8 cups Basic Vegetable Stock (see recipe in Chapter 2)

3 cups skinned, seeded, and chopped pumpkin

3 tablespoons chopped parsley

2 teaspoons salt

½ teaspoon pepper

⅛ teaspoon ground nutmeg

¼ cup chopped fresh chives

1. Add the butter to a large pot over medium heat, and let it melt. Add the onions, ginger, and garlic. Reduce the heat to medium, and cook for 5 minutes or until onions soften.

2. Add the stock, pumpkin, and parsley. Increase the heat to medium-high and bring the soup to a boil. Reduce the heat to medium-low, cover the pot, and cook for 40–45 minutes. Season with the salt, pepper, and nutmeg.

3. Using an immersion blender or a regular blender, carefully purée the soup until it is smooth.

4. Stir in the chives and serve.

AVGOLEMONO SOUP WITH CHICKEN AND RICE

Try substituting rice with orzo or hand-crushed nests of vermicelli pasta. You can also use leftover roast chicken in this recipe.

Serves 8

10 cups Chicken or Turkey Stock (see recipe in Chapter 2)

⅓ cup finely diced carrot

⅓ cup finely diced celery

⅓ cup Arborio or Carolina rice

2½ teaspoons salt

2 large eggs

3 tablespoons fresh lemon juice

2 cups cooked and shredded skinless chicken, at room temperature

1. Add the stock to a large pot over medium-high heat and bring it to a boil. Add the carrots, celery, and rice, and return the mixture to a boil. Boil for 10–15 minutes, and take the pot off the heat. Season with salt.

2. In a large bowl, whisk together eggs and lemon juice. Continuing to whisk vigorously, slowly add a ladle of soup liquid into the egg-lemon mixture. Continue whisking and slowly add another 3 or 4 ladles of soup (one at a time) into the egg-lemon mixture.

3. Slowly stir the egg-lemon mixture back into the soup. Stir in the chicken so the meat heats through.

4. Let the soup cool for 5 minutes before serving. Serve hot.

FASOLADA (WHITE BEAN SOUP)

This thick soup is considered one of the national dishes of Greece and has been a staple food in that country for centuries.

Serves 4

1 pound dried haricot (white kidney) beans

2 medium-size carrots, sliced into discs

2 medium-size cooking onions, diced

2 stalks celery, thinly sliced

1 cup tomato sauce or 3 finely diced tomatoes

1 medium-size parsnip, thinly sliced

1 tablespoon dried rosemary

1 tablespoon dried thyme

3 bay leaves

¼ cup olive oil

4 tablespoons finely chopped fresh parsley

4–6 cloves garlic, whole or halved

Salt and pepper to taste

1. Soak beans overnight in roughly three times their volume of water. Dump beans into colander; rinse well before use.

2. Put 3 quarts of water in pot; add beans and bring to boil over high heat. Skim away surface foam as it develops. Boil beans 15 minutes, continuing to skim away surface foam using a wooden spoon. At the 15-minute mark, skim off the last bit of foam; dump into colander to strain and rinse the beans. Rinse pot well.

3. Put another 3 quarts of fresh water in pot; bring to a boil and add beans. After 5 minutes, skim any remaining surface foam that may develop; add all remaining ingredients. Stir well.

4. When it has resumed boiling, cover pot with lid slightly ajar; let simmer over low heat 2 hours, or until beans are soft. Stir occasionally and check to ensure there is ample liquid in the pot to keep the beans from sticking to the bottom. Note: Though it is technically a soup, you do not want a very runny soup, nor do you want one that is thick and gooey, so monitor the water content of the pot and add a cup or so if necessary. Remove bay leaves before serving.

KAKAVIA (FISH SOUP)

Feel free to add some shrimp, scallops, or any other favorite seafood to this recipe for variation.

Serves 6

2 medium-size onions, diced

2 medium-size potatoes, cubed

2 stalks celery, finely chopped

2 medium-size carrots

1 tablespoon dried marjoram

Salt and pepper

2 pounds fresh cod, cut into pieces

2 pounds fresh grey mullet, deboned and cut into pieces

1 pound mussels, cleaned and bearded

¼ cup fresh parsley, roughly chopped

½ cup extra-virgin olive oil

Juice of 1 lemon

1. Put 6 pints water in large pot; bring to a boil. Add chopped vegetables, marjoram, salt, and pepper; cover and boil for 30 minutes.

2. Wash and thoroughly clean fish and mussels. When pot has boiled 30 minutes, add fish and mussels and parsley; boil for another 20 minutes.

3. Using a slotted spoon, remove fish and mussels from pot; set aside on plate.

4. Strain the stock through a sieve; push softened vegetables through a sieve using a wooden spoon. Return the strained stock to the pot; add olive oil and lemon juice and bring to a boil. Add the fish and mussels; simmer for 3–5 minutes. Serve hot.

TAHINI SOUP

Tahini is a ground sesame paste that has been used in cooking throughout the eastern Mediterranean for many centuries. Most well-stocked supermarkets should carry a brand of tahini, or visit a Middle Eastern grocery where they are sure to have it in stock.

Serves 4–6

4–5 pints water

2 cups orzo pasta

Salt and pepper

½ cup tahini

Juice of 2 lemons

1. Bring water to a boil in large pot. Add pasta, salt, and pepper; stir well. Cover and simmer until cooked, about 10 minutes. Remove pot from heat.

2. Add tahini to a mixing bowl; slowly add lemon juice while whisking constantly. Once lemon juice has been incorporated, take about ½ cup hot broth from the pot and slowly add to the tahini-lemon mixture while whisking, until creamy smooth.

3. Pour the mixture into the pot with the pasta; mix well. Serve immediately.

BAKALIAROS AVGOLEMONO (COD EGG–LEMON SOUP)

If you're using salted cod, make sure to soak the cod in water for at least 24 hours, making sure to change the water several times, to remove the salt.

Serves 4

⅓ cup olive oil

2 or 3 celery stalks, sliced

1 medium-size onion, diced

3 medium-size potatoes, peeled and cubed

Salt and fresh-ground pepper to taste

½ tablespoon corn flour

1½ pounds fresh, frozen, or salted cod (thick-cut pieces)

2 eggs

2 lemons

1. In a large pot, bring 4 cups of water to boil; add olive oil, celery, onion, potatoes, salt, and fresh-ground pepper. Cover and simmer 15 minutes.

2. Dilute corn flour in ½ cup of warm water. Add to pot; stir well. Immediately add cod to pot; cover and boil a further 5–6 minutes.

3. Separate egg whites from yolks; put whites in a large mixing bowl. Whisk whites stiff; add yolks while continuing to whisk. Slowly add lemon juice while stirring mixture constantly with a whisk.

4. Slowly add 2 ladlefuls of hot broth from the pot into the egg-lemon froth in the mixing bowl while continually whisking, to achieve a uniform creamy consistency.

5. Remove the pot from heat and add contents of the mixing bowl to the pot; cover and let stand a few minutes before serving.

SALADS

TUNA SALAD WITH TOASTED PINE NUTS

Tarragon is an herb from southern France that has a delicate anise flavor. Use it in fish and chicken dishes.

Serves 4

1 (5-ounce) can tuna, packed in olive oil, drained and flaked

1 medium shallot, diced

3 tablespoons chopped fresh chives

1 tablespoon chopped fresh tarragon

1 stalk celery, trimmed and finely diced

2–3 tablespoons mayonnaise

1 teaspoon Dijon mustard

¼ teaspoon salt

⅛ teaspoon pepper

¼ cup toasted pine nuts

1. In a medium bowl, toss the tuna, shallot, chives, tarragon, and celery.

2. In a small bowl, combine the mayonnaise, mustard, salt, and pepper. Stir the mayonnaise mixture into the tuna mixture. Stir in the pine nuts. Serve cool or at room temperature.

WATERMELON AND FETA SALAD

Purslane is a green, crisp, and slightly tangy herb eaten in Greece. If you can't find purslane, substitute pea shoots or watercress.

Serves 4

4¼ cups cubed (¾-inch) watermelon, divided

⅓ cup sliced red onions

⅓ cup purslane leaves

1½ cups cubed (¾-inch) feta

¼ cup fresh mint leaves

1 teaspoon honey

1 tablespoon fresh lemon juice

¼ cup extra-virgin olive oil

1. In a large bowl, combine 4 cups of the watermelon, onions, purslane, and feta.

2. Place the remaining watermelon, mint, honey, lemon juice, and oil in a food processor. Process until the dressing is well incorporated.

3. Pour the dressing over the salad and toss gently with your fingers to combine. Serve cool or at room temperature.

BULGUR SALAD WITH NUTS, HONEY, CHEESE, AND POMEGRANATE

Bulgur is a whole-wheat grain that has been cracked and parboiled. Try it in place of rice. You can find pomegranate molasses in Greek or Middle Eastern grocery stores.

Serves 4

1 cup coarse (#3) bulgur wheat

1 teaspoon salt

½ cup extra-virgin olive oil

¼ cup chopped toasted almonds (see Toasting Nuts sidebar)

¼ cup chopped toasted walnuts

¼ teaspoon ground allspice

¼ cup pomegranate molasses

2 teaspoons red wine vinegar

2 teaspoons honey

2 scallions, ends trimmed, thinly sliced

1½ cups baby arugula, washed and dried

¼ cup chopped fresh mint

1 cup crumbled goat cheese

¼ teaspoon pepper

1. Fill a medium pot two-thirds with water and set it over medium-high heat. Bring the water to a boil. Add bulgur and salt. Boil for 6 minutes. Strain the bulgur.

2. While the bulgur is still warm, add oil, nuts, allspice, molasses, vinegar, and honey. Mix well.

3. Add the scallions, arugula, mint, cheese, and pepper. Toss to combine. Adjust seasoning with more salt and pepper, if necessary.

4. Serve at room temperature.

Toasting Nuts

To toast nuts, add them to a dry frying pan over medium-high heat. Stir them with a wooden spoon constantly for 5–6 minutes or until just golden. Keep stirring; never walk away from the pan until the nuts are toasted to your liking. Nuts go from toasted to burned in the blink of an eye. Always cool the toasted nuts before using them.

CREAMY COLESLAW

This version of coleslaw uses a little mayonnaise, but is big on healthful, protein-rich Greek yogurt. Leftover coleslaw can be covered and stored for up to five days in a refrigerator.

Serves 6

1½ teaspoons salt

1 tablespoon sugar

¼ cup red wine vinegar

½ large head cabbage, stalk removed and thinly sliced

1 large peeled carrot, grated

2 scallions, ends trimmed and thinly sliced

2 cloves garlic, peeled and minced

½ cup extra-virgin olive oil

¼ cup mayonnaise

½ cup strained Greek yogurt

Salt and pepper to season (optional)

1. In a large bowl, whisk together sugar, salt, and vinegar. Add the cabbage, carrot, scallions, and garlic. Toss to combine. Let the vegetables sit for 5 minutes.

2. To the vegetables, add the oil, mayonnaise, and yogurt. Stir to combine and coat the vegetables in the creamy dressing.

3. Adjust the seasoning with more salt and pepper, if necessary. Serve the coleslaw cool or at room temperature.

ARUGULA, PEAR, AND GOAT CHEESE SALAD

Arugula is a peppery salad green that is sometimes called "rocket" in grocery stores.

Serves 4

2 medium pears, cored and cut into wedges

2 tablespoons fresh lemon juice, divided

1 tablespoon balsamic vinegar

⅓ cup extra-virgin olive oil

¼ cup chopped fresh chives

½ teaspoon salt

⅛ teaspoon pepper

3 cups arugula, rinsed and dried

½ cup chopped unsalted pistachios

½ cup crumbled goat cheese

1. In a small bowl, toss the pears with 1 tablespoon of the lemon juice. In a large bowl, whisk remaining lemon juice, vinegar, oil, chives, salt, and pepper.

2. Toss the arugula in the dressing and plate it on a serving platter. Arrange the pears over the arugula and sprinkle the top with pistachios and cheese. Drizzle any remaining dressing over the salad and serve.

GREEK VILLAGE SALAD

An authentic Greek salad contains no lettuce of any kind. Use the best extra-virgin olive oil in your pantry for this dish. Resist using any kind of vinegar; the acidity from the tomatoes is enough.

Serves 4

4 medium-size ripe tomatoes, cut into wedges

½ English cucumber, halved and sliced into ½-inch slices

1 medium cubanelle (green) pepper, stemmed, seeded, halved, and cut into slices

1 small red onion, peeled, halved, and thinly sliced

⅛ teaspoon salt

⅓ cup extra-virgin olive oil

1½ cups cubed feta cheese

1 teaspoon dried oregano

8 kalamata olives

1. On a serving plate, arrange tomatoes and cucumbers. Next add peppers and onions. Season vegetables with salt.

2. Drizzle oil over the vegetables. Top with feta and sprinkle with oregano.

3. Finally, top the salad with the olives and serve at room temperature.

STRAWBERRY AND FETA SALAD WITH BALSAMIC DRESSING

The sweet strawberries complement the tart and briny feta very well.

Serves 4

1 teaspoon Dijon mustard

3 tablespoons balsamic vinegar

1 clove garlic, peeled and minced

¾ cup extra-virgin olive oil

½ teaspoon salt

⅛ teaspoon pepper

4 cups salad greens, rinsed and dried

1 pint ripe strawberries, hulled and halved

1½ cups crumbled feta cheese

1. In a small bowl, whisk the mustard, vinegar, garlic, oil, salt, and pepper to make the dressing.

2. In a large bowl, combine the salad greens and the dressing. Plate the salad on a serving platter and top with the strawberries and feta.

3. Drizzle any remaining dressing over the salad and serve.

CREAMY CAESAR SALAD

This recipe makes more dressing than you'll need for this salad. Add as much or as little dressing as you prefer. Leftover dressing can be stored in the refrigerator for up to one week.

Serves 6

2 cloves garlic, peeled and chopped

3 egg yolks

1 tablespoon Dijon mustard

3 tablespoons Worcestershire sauce

1 tablespoon anchovy paste or 2 anchovy fillets

½ cup grated Parmesan cheese, divided

2 tablespoons fresh lemon juice, divided

½ teaspoon salt

1 teaspoon pepper

1 tablespoon water

1 cup light olive oil

1 head romaine lettuce, washed, dried, and chopped

½ cup chopped cooked bacon

1 cup croutons

1. Place the garlic, egg yolks, mustard, Worcestershire sauce, anchovy paste, ¼ cup Parmesan cheese, 1 tablespoon lemon juice, salt, pepper, and water into the food processor. Process until the dressing is combined and thick. With the processor running, slowly add the oil until it is well incorporated. Taste the dressing and adjust the seasoning with more salt and pepper, if necessary.

2. In a large bowl, combine the lettuce and the remaining lemon juice. Add just enough dressing to coat the lettuce (add more if you want to make it creamier). Toss in the bacon and croutons. Top the salad with the remaining Parmesan. Serve with extra dressing.

Make Your Own Croutons

Croutons are easy to make and add a delicious crunch to any salad. All you need is leftover bread, some olive oil, and an oven. Cut up leftover bread into cubes or chunks. Toss them with just enough olive oil to lightly coat the bread but not soak it. Lay the bread on a baking sheet and bake it in a preheated 350°F oven for 30 minutes or until the croutons are crunchy.

POLITIKI CABBAGE SALAD

This dish comes from the Byzantine city of Constantinople, or modern-day Istanbul. Because cabbage is so plentiful, cabbage salads are made often in the Mediterranean.

Serves 4

1 teaspoon sugar

1 teaspoon salt

¼ cup red wine vinegar

4 cups shredded white cabbage

½ cup grated peeled carrot

½ cup thinly sliced red pepper

¼ cup celery, diced

¼ cup extra-virgin olive oil

⅛ teaspoon red pepper flakes

Salt and pepper to season (optional)

1. In a large bowl, whisk sugar, salt, and vinegar. Add the cabbage, carrot, pepper, and celery. Toss to combine. Let the vegetables sit for 15–20 minutes. The vegetables will begin to release liquid.

2. Using your hands, squeeze out any excess liquid from the vegetables and place them in a separate large bowl.

3. To the vegetables, add the oil and red pepper flakes. Toss to coat the vegetables in the oil. Adjust the seasoning with more salt and pepper, if necessary. Serve the salad cool or at room temperature.

ARUGULA SALAD WITH FIGS AND SHAVED CHEESE

Don't get too hung up on finding fresh figs—dried ones will also work well, or you can use any seasonal fruit.

Serves 6

1 tablespoon honey

1 teaspoon Dijon mustard

3 tablespoons balsamic vinegar

1 small clove garlic, peeled and minced

1 teaspoon salt

½ teaspoon pepper

⅔ cup extra-virgin olive oil

5 cups arugula leaves, rinsed and dried

12 fresh (ripe) figs, stemmed and quartered

1 cup walnuts, roughly chopped

¼ cup shaved Graviera or Gruyère cheese

1. In a large bowl, whisk honey, mustard, vinegar, garlic, salt, and pepper. Slowly whisk in the oil until well incorporated.

2. Add the arugula and figs. Toss the salad to combine the ingredients and to coat them in the dressing.

3. Sprinkle the salad with walnuts and cheese, and serve.

ASPARAGUS SALAD

Top this salad with your favorite cheese.

Serves 4

1 pound asparagus, rinsed and woody ends trimmed

1 teaspoon salt

1 tablespoon fresh lemon juice

1 clove garlic, peeled and minced

1 tablespoon grated lemon zest

1 teaspoon fresh thyme leaves

2 tablespoons chopped fresh parsley

½ teaspoon pepper

¼ cup extra-virgin olive oil

Salt and pepper to season (optional)

1. Using a vegetable peeler, shave the asparagus into long, thin strips. In a medium bowl, combine the shaved asparagus, salt, and lemon juice. Set aside for 15 minutes.

2. In a small bowl, whisk garlic, zest, thyme, parsley, pepper, and oil. Season with salt and pepper, if desired.

3. Add the dressing to the asparagus and toss to coat. Serve the salad cool or at room temperature.

SPINACH SALAD WITH APPLES AND MINT

Use any variety of apples you like for this salad. Always include at least one tart apple.

Serves 4

⅓ cup extra-virgin olive oil

10 fresh mint leaves, chopped

1 large orange, peeled and segmented, juice reserved

1 large grapefruit, peeled and segmented, juice reserved

1 tablespoon fresh lime juice

¾ teaspoon salt

¼ teaspoon pepper

1 large red apple, cored and cut into thin slices

1 large green apple, cored and cut into thin slices

⅓ cup finely chopped red onion

1 stalk celery, trimmed and chopped

4 cups baby spinach, washed and dried

1. Put the oil and mint into a food processor. Process until well incorporated. Set aside and let the mint infuse the oil.

2. In a large bowl, whisk together reserved orange juice, grapefruit juice, lime juice, salt, pepper, and olive oil–mint infusion. Add the apple slices, onion, and celery. Toss the salad to coat in the dressing.

3. Add the spinach and toss again to combine with the salad and dressing. Top the salad with orange and grapefruit segments, and serve.

TOMATO SALAD WITH FRIED FETA

Keep your fried cheese warm in a preheated 280°F oven until you are ready to serve.

Serves 4

1 large egg

1 teaspoon whole milk

¼ cup all-purpose flour

1½ cups feta cheese, cut into ½-inch cubes

1 tablespoon fresh lemon juice

1⅔ cups extra-virgin olive oil, divided

1 teaspoon Dijon mustard

1 tablespoon balsamic vinegar

1 teaspoon honey

2 teaspoons dried oregano

1 teaspoon salt

¼ teaspoon pepper

2 medium-size ripe tomatoes, sliced into ½-inch slices

4 cups salad greens, rinsed and dried

1 small red onion, thinly sliced

½ cup kalamata olives

1. In a small bowl, beat the egg and milk. Put the flour into another small bowl. Dip the feta cubes in the egg mixture and then dredge them in the flour. Shake off any excess flour. Refrigerate the dredged feta for at least 30 minutes.

2. Into a small jar with a lid, put the lemon juice, ⅔ cup oil, mustard, vinegar, honey, oregano, salt, and pepper. Close the jar and shake vigorously until the dressing is well incorporated.

3. Add the remaining oil to a medium nonstick frying pan and heat on medium for 1 minute. Add the feta (in batches) and fry until the cubes are lightly golden on all sides (20–30 seconds per side). Place the feta on a tray lined with paper towels to absorb any excess oil.

4. In a large bowl, place the tomatoes, greens, onions, and olives. Shake the dressing and then add it to the salad. Toss to combine the ingredients.

5. Top the salad with the fried feta. Serve immediately.

TOMATO SALAD WITH ROASTED GARLIC, BASIL, AND PINE NUT DRESSING

This recipe makes a nice addition to any summer meal.

Serves 4

½ medium red onion, peeled and thinly sliced

4 large ripe tomatoes, cut into wedges

1 teaspoon salt

½ teaspoon pepper

6 cloves roasted garlic (see Roasted Garlic Served on Crostini recipe in Chapter 4)

⅓ cup pine nuts, toasted

½ cup sliced fresh basil

¼ cup extra-virgin olive oil

¼ cup kalamata olives, pitted and sliced

1. In a large bowl, gently toss the onion and tomatoes. Season them with salt and pepper.

2. Place the garlic, pine nuts, and basil into a mortar. Using the pestle, grind the ingredients to make a paste. Add the oil and mix to combine the dressing.

3. Add the dressing to onions and tomatoes. Gently toss to coat. Top the salad with olives and serve.

POTATO SALAD

This salad is ideal for serving in the summer. It comes together easily and can be made ahead of time. It's delicious served with grilled fish.

Serves 6

6 large Yukon gold potatoes, skins on

1½ teaspoons salt

½ teaspoon pepper

½ cup extra-virgin olive oil

¼ cup Dijon mustard

2 tablespoons capers, drained and chopped

¼ cup red wine vinegar

2 tablespoons chopped fresh parsley

3 scallions, ends trimmed and finely chopped

½ cup chopped fresh dill

1 tablespoon fresh lemon juice

1. Place a large pot of water over medium-high heat. Add the potatoes and bring the water to a boil. Cook for 30 minutes. Let potatoes cool for 10 minutes, and then peel them. Cut the potatoes into chunks.

2. In a large bowl, whisk the remaining ingredients until they are well incorporated.

3. Add the potatoes to the dressing and toss to coat. Serve the salad warm or at room temperature.

ARTICHOKE SALAD

Try topping this salad with fried calamari or grilled shrimp.

Serves 4

2 medium onions, peeled and chopped, divided

1 medium carrot, peeled and diced, divided

1 tablespoon finely chopped celery

2 tablespoons fresh lemon juice

1 teaspoon salt

8 canned or jarred artichokes, rinsed and halved

½ cup extra-virgin olive oil, divided

1 red bell pepper, stemmed, seeded, and chopped

2 medium zucchini, ends trimmed and diced

½ cup fresh peas or thawed frozen peas

1 teaspoon salt

½ teaspoon pepper

10 pitted kalamata olives, sliced

¼ cup finely chopped capers

½ cup chopped fresh mint

1. Add 3 inches of water to a large deep skillet and bring it to a boil over medium-high heat. Add 2 tablespoons onions, 1 tablespoon carrots, celery, lemon juice, and salt. Return to a boil. Add the artichokes and reduce the heat to medium-low. Cook the artichokes for 3 minutes or until tender. Remove the artichokes with a slotted spoon, discard the cooking liquid, and place the artichokes in an ice bath to stop the cooking process. When the artichokes have cooled, remove them from the ice bath and reserve.

2. In a large skillet over medium-high heat, add ¼ cup of the oil and heat for 30 seconds. Add the remaining onions, remaining carrots, and peppers. Reduce heat to medium and cook for 5–6 minutes. Add the zucchini and cook for 2 minutes. Add the peas and cook for another 2 minutes. Season with salt and pepper. Remove from heat and allow the vegetables to cool.

3. In a bowl, combine the cooled vegetables, remaining oil, olives, capers, and mint. Adjust the seasoning with more salt and pepper, if necessary.

4. To serve, place 3 or 4 artichokes on each plate and top with the vegetables. Serve the salad at room temperature.

CHICKPEA SALAD WITH ROASTED RED PEPPERS AND GREEN BEANS

Try using a combination of red, green, yellow, or orange peppers for a change of color!

Serves 6

3 cloves garlic, peeled and minced

1 teaspoon Dijon mustard

2 tablespoons red wine vinegar

1 teaspoon salt, divided

½ teaspoon pepper, divided

½ cup extra-virgin olive oil

1 cup canned chickpeas, drained and rinsed

1 pound green beans, trimmed and blanched for 5–6 minutes

2 Roasted Red Peppers (see recipe in Chapter 4), stemmed, peeled, seeded, and cut into ribbons

1 cup pickled cauliflower florets, halved

2 cups salad greens, washed and dried

¼ cup chopped fresh parsley

2 teaspoons dried oregano

12 kalamata olives, pitted

1. In a large bowl, whisk garlic, mustard, vinegar, ½ teaspoon salt, and ¼ teaspoon pepper. Slowly whisk in oil until it is well incorporated.

2. Add the chickpeas, beans, Roasted Red Peppers, and cauliflower. Toss to coat them in the dressing.

3. Add the greens, parsley, oregano, and olives, and season them with the remaining salt and pepper. Toss the salad to combine the ingredients and serve.

Kalamata Olives

Kalamata is a region in Greece that is famous for its olives and its olive oil. Kalamata olives have a distinct brown-green color and are briny and meaty.

WARM MUSHROOM SALAD

This is a wonderful, hearty winter salad.

Serves 4

⅔ cup extra-virgin olive oil, divided

2 cups sliced cremini mushrooms

2 cups sliced king mushrooms

6 cloves garlic, peeled and smashed

2 bay leaves

1 teaspoon chopped fresh rosemary

1 teaspoon fresh thyme leaves

1 teaspoon salt, divided

½ teaspoon pepper, divided

1 teaspoon Dijon mustard

2 tablespoons balsamic vinegar

1 tablespoon fresh lemon juice

4 cups salad greens, washed and dried

¼ cup pumpkin seeds

½ cup crumbled goat cheese

¼ cup crispy fried onions (see Crispy Fried Onions sidebar)

1. Heat ⅓ cup oil in a large cast-iron pan over medium-low heat for 30 seconds. Add the mushrooms, garlic, bay leaves, rosemary, thyme, ½ teaspoon salt, and ¼ teaspoon pepper. Stirring occasionally, cook the mushrooms for 20 minutes, then remove bay leaves.

2. In a small jar with a lid, place the remaining oil, mustard, vinegar, lemon juice, and remaining salt and pepper. Close the jar and shake it vigorously until the dressing is well incorporated.

3. In a large bowl, add the greens and dressing and toss them to combine. Divide and plate the greens, and then top them with the warm mushrooms. Sprinkle the salad with the pumpkin seeds, cheese, and crispy fried onions. Drizzle the remaining dressing over the salads. Serve them warm or at room temperature.

Crispy Fried Onions

Crispy fried onions are tasty and easy to make. Use them as a topping for salads, potatoes, and meats. Slice a medium onion as thinly as possible. Toss the onion slices in a little cornstarch; shake off any excess. Heat some olive oil in a pan, place the onions in the hot oil, and fry until they are golden and crispy. Sprinkle the onions with salt and allow them to cool.

SUN-DRIED TOMATO VINAIGRETTE

Use this dressing with spinach or peppery salad greens.

Serves 4

⅓ cup sun-dried tomatoes, packed in olive oil, rinsed and finely chopped

2 tablespoons balsamic vinegar

1 teaspoon garlic powder

1 teaspoon dried oregano

¼ teaspoon pepper

½ teaspoon salt

⅓ cup extra-virgin olive oil

1. In a small bowl, whisk all the ingredients until they are well incorporated.

2. Keep the dressing refrigerated until it is needed.

CREAMY FETA DRESSING

Spoon this dressing over olive oil fries, a baked potato, or a vegetable tray.

Serves 4

⅓ cup crumbled feta cheese

2 teaspoons water

¾ cup plain yogurt

2 tablespoons mayonnaise

2 tablespoons evaporated milk

1 teaspoon dried oregano

1 clove garlic, peeled and minced

2 tablespoons chopped fresh chives

⅛ teaspoon pepper

1. Place the feta and water in a medium bowl. Using a fork, mash the feta into a paste.

2. Add the remaining ingredients and mix them until they are well incorporated. Keep the dressing refrigerated until it is needed.

KALAMATA OLIVE DRESSING

This dressing is wonderful with romaine lettuce, cherry tomatoes, and grilled halloumi cheese.

Serves 4

¼ cup chopped red onions

1 clove garlic, peeled and smashed

½ cup pitted kalamata olives

2 sun-dried tomatoes, packed in olive oil, rinsed and chopped

½ teaspoon dried oregano

2 tablespoons red wine vinegar

1 tablespoon balsamic vinegar

1 teaspoon Dijon mustard

½ teaspoon pepper

⅔ cup extra-virgin olive oil

1. Add all the ingredients to a food processor, and process until they are well incorporated.

2. Refrigerate the dressing until it is needed.

CUCUMBER AND DILL DRESSING

This dressing pairs wonderfully with salad greens, ripe tomatoes, and some peppery radish slices.

Serves 4

½ medium English cucumber, grated

¾ teaspoon salt, divided

½ cup strained Greek yogurt

¼ cup whole milk

2 tablespoons mayonnaise

2 teaspoons fresh lemon juice

1 scallion (white part only), ends trimmed and thinly sliced

1 clove garlic, peeled and minced

2 tablespoons chopped fresh dill

¼ teaspoon pepper

1. Place cucumber and ¼ teaspoon salt in a fine-mesh strainer over a medium bowl. Strain for 30 minutes. Squeeze any remaining water from the cucumber.

2. Combine the cucumber and remaining ingredients in a medium bowl. Stir well to incorporate the ingredients.

3. Adjust the seasoning if necessary. Refrigerate the dressing in a tight jar for up to 1 week.

POMEGRANATE DRESSING

Toss this dressing with baby dandelion greens and top with crumbled feta or goat cheese. Pomegranate molasses can be found in Greek and Middle Eastern grocers.

Serves 8

½ cup unsweetened pomegranate juice

1 clove garlic, peeled and minced

1 cup extra-virgin olive oil

¾ teaspoon salt

⅓ teaspoon pepper

1 teaspoon Dijon mustard

2 tablespoons pomegranate molasses

1. Combine all the ingredients in a jar with a lid. Close the jar and shake it vigorously until the ingredients are well incorporated.

2. Adjust the seasoning with more salt and pepper, if necessary. Serve the dressing at room temperature.

GRILLED EGGPLANT SALAD

This salad is best served cold and is even tastier the next day after the flavors of the eggplant and tomato mixture have a chance to coalesce. Do not add salt to the tomato mix until you are ready to serve.

Serves 4

1 large eggplant

2 tablespoons salt, plus more to taste

2 or 3 tomatoes

Small bunch of parsley, finely chopped

2 cloves garlic, pressed or very finely diced

Pepper to taste

1 tablespoon dried oregano

¼ cup extra-virgin olive oil

1. Slice eggplant into discs along length—not too thin and not too thick, about ¼ inch thickness is ideal. Fill a large mixing bowl or pot with water, add 2 tablespoons of salt, and mix well; place eggplant discs in salt bath and set a plate over the top to weigh them down. Soak for 20–30 minutes. Mix periodically to ensure salty water soaks them completely.

2. Dice tomatoes; place in bowl. Add parsley, garlic, salt, pepper, oregano, and 2–3 tablespoons olive oil; mix well and set aside.

3. Light a grill and set on high temperature. When grilling surface is ready, spray or wipe with vegetable oil.

4. Using your hands and working quickly over the grill, brush (or spray) downward-facing side of each slice of eggplant with a little olive oil; place across grill, starting from the top left rear section and filling the entire surface in rows. Once all the eggplant discs are on the grill, give the upward-facing sides a brush (or spray) of olive oil. Grill until visibly softened around the edges and centers, approximately 6–8 minutes. Allow each side a few minutes to cook through and absorb oil, but watch them carefully.

5. Brush with olive oil again; turn over. Grill another few minutes; give final brushing of oil. Leave on grill another minute or so; remove onto platter or dish.

6. Arrange several eggplant discs on a serving plate, top with chopped tomato mixture, sprinkle with oregano, and serve with crusty bread.

LAHANOSALATA (CABBAGE SALAD)

If you do not have any yogurt on hand, you can use a couple of tablespoons of mayonnaise as a substitute for the dressing in this recipe.

Serves 4

⅓ of a white cabbage

2 large carrots

½ cup Greek-style strained yogurt

¼ cup extra-virgin olive oil

2 tablespoons fresh lemon juice (or vinegar)

½ teaspoon dried oregano

1 tablespoon chopped fresh dill

Salt and pepper to taste

1. Wash cabbage well; peel carrots. Shred cabbage finely with a sharp knife. Shred carrots into ribbons using a mandoline or the large holes on a grater; add to shredded cabbage.

2. Toss shredded cabbage and carrots well.

3. In a food processor/blender, add yogurt, olive oil, lemon juice, oregano, dill, salt, and pepper; blend together until smooth and creamy.

4. Pour the dressing over the top of individual servings or mix well into the entire salad before serving. Garnish with chopped dill and a kalamata olive or two.

Long Before Caffeine . . .
Dill seeds were chewed by the ancient Greeks as a form of stimulant to cause wakefulness, as well as to freshen breath.

TARAMOSALATA/TARAMA (FISH ROE SALAD)

The pink coloring of the carp roe in this recipe is a food dye. In Greece, taramosalata can often be beige in color, as undyed roe is often used.

Serves 6–8

½ loaf two-day-old white bread

½ cup carp roe

1 large onion, grated

Juice of 2 lemons

2 cups extra-virgin olive oil

Cucumber slices, for garnish

Tomato slices, for garnish

Olives, for garnish

1. Remove the outside crust and soak the inner bread in water; squeeze well to drain and set aside.

2. Place fish roe in a food processor/blender; mix a minute or so to break down eggs.

3. Add grated onion to the processor; continue mixing.

4. Add moistened bread in stages to the processor/blender; mix well.

5. Slowly add lemon juice and olive oil while constantly mixing. Note: When adding olive oil and lemon juice, add in a slow and alternate fashion by first adding some lemon juice then some olive oil and so on, until both are incorporated into the tarama.

6. Refrigerate before serving to firm up the tarama. Garnish with cucumber, tomato slices, and/or olive(s); serve with warm pita bread.

GRILLED HALLOUMI SALAD

Halloumi cheese is a specialty from the island of Cyprus. It is a firm cheese that holds its shape well when heated. It is usually served grilled or fried and adds a wonderful chewy texture to any salad.

Serves 4

10–12 kalamata olives, pitted and finely chopped or ground to a pulp

¼ cup extra-virgin olive oil

2 tablespoons balsamic vinegar

1 tablespoon dried oregano

1 medium carrot, shredded

¼ of a small green cabbage, shredded

1 large tomato

1 bunch fresh rocket greens (arugula), finely cut

1 head romaine lettuce, finely cut

2 stalks fresh green onion, finely sliced (green stalk included)

½ pound halloumi cheese, thick sliced

1. Prepare the dressing by pitting and grinding or finely chopping olives; combine pulp with olive oil, vinegar, and oregano. Mix well; set aside.

2. Wash all the vegetables well. Peel carrot; use a mandoline to finely shred cabbage and carrot into a large salad bowl. Chop tomato into sections; add to the bowl. Finely cut rocket and lettuce; add to the bowl. Finely slice green onions; add to salad.

3. Fire up a grill; grill the halloumi until it noticeably starts to soften and grill marks appear. Make sure to flip the cheese so both sides are scored with grill marks. When the cheese is done, remove from heat and immediately cut into cubes; add to salad. Pour dressing over the salad; mix well. Serve immediately.

Changing Diets

A growing number of people who inhabit the Mediterranean basin are eschewing their traditional eating patterns for a less healthy but more convenient "Western" diet. As a result, health issues have risen exponentially.

GRILLED BANANA PEPPER SALAD

If you don't like hot peppers, make sure to choose sweet banana peppers for this recipe.

Serves 6

6 hot banana peppers (AKA Hungarian or wax peppers)

½ cup Greek feta cheese, crumbled

2 tablespoons extra-virgin olive oil

2 tablespoons wine vinegar

1 teaspoon dried oregano

1. Grill peppers until they are soft and their skins are charred, approximately 8–10 minutes; peel.

2. Spread peppers flat on a serving dish; add feta over top of peppers.

3. Drizzle a little olive oil and some wine vinegar over everything.

4. Finish with a sprinkle of oregano, and serve.

DANDELION GREENS

Be sure to wash these greens well and cut away all of the root stalk when cleaning, as it is tough and does not become tender when cooked.

Serves 6

4 pounds dandelion greens

½ cup extra-virgin olive oil

½ cup fresh lemon juice

Salt and pepper to taste

1. Cut away and discard stalks of dandelion greens; wash thoroughly.

2. Bring a large pot of water to a rolling boil; add greens and stir. Cook over high heat until the greens are tender, about 8–10 minutes; remove and drain well.

3. Combine olive oil, lemon juice, salt, and pepper; use as a dressing for the greens. Can be served warm or cold, as a side for grilled fish, or on their own with some crusty bread, kalamata olives, and feta. Garnish with fresh minced garlic.

SLICED TOMATO SALAD WITH FETA AND BALSAMIC VINAIGRETTE

This dish is all about presentation, so take your time with it and your guests will be pleased with the way it looks as well as how it tastes!

Serves 4–6

4 large tomatoes, washed and sliced into round slices

¼ pound Greek feta cheese, crumbled

1 teaspoon dried oregano

¼ cup extra-virgin olive oil

2 tablespoons balsamic vinegar

Fresh-ground black pepper

1. Wash and slice tomatoes into rounds approximately ¼-inch thick. Arrange slices in a slightly overlapping circle pattern on a large presentation platter.

2. Cover tomatoes with a layer of feta cheese, making sure to spread the cheese over all the tomato slices; then sprinkle oregano over top of the cheese.

3. Combine olive oil and balsamic vinegar; pour over cheese and tomatoes. Sprinkle with fresh-ground pepper and serve.

Everything Has Its Time

Traditional eating patterns are based on seasonal availability of fresh ingredients and do not rely on canning, preservatives, and refrigeration.

SANDWICHES

ROASTED RED PEPPER AND FETA SANDWICHES

This is a lovely vegetarian sandwich.

Serves 4

4 Roasted Red Peppers (see recipe in Chapter 4)

1 teaspoon extra-virgin olive oil

¼ teaspoon salt

4 sandwich buns, lightly toasted

¾ cup crumbled feta cheese

1. Combine the peppers, oil, and salt in a medium bowl. Divide the peppers over each bottom of the sandwich bun.

2. Top with the feta and cap with top sandwich bun. Serve.

GRILLED HALLOUMI SANDWICHES

Place pita bread in a microwave for 30 seconds to puff it up and help make a pocket.

Serves 4

¼ cup extra-virgin olive oil

½ teaspoon Dijon mustard

1 tablespoon fresh lemon juice

½ teaspoon honey

1 tablespoon chopped fresh mint

⅛ teaspoon dried oregano

½ teaspoon pepper

8 slices (about ¼-inch thick) halloumi cheese

4 medium Middle Eastern–style pita breads (pocket), warmed with the pocket open

½ cup baby spinach, washed and dried

¼ cup sliced red or green peppers, stemmed and seeded

¼ cup chopped pitted kalamata olives

½ cup sliced pickled red onions (see Quick Pickled Red Onions sidebar)

1. Put the oil, mustard, lemon juice, honey, mint, oregano, and pepper into a jar with a lid. Close the jar and shake it vigorously until the ingredients are well incorporated. Adjust the seasoning with more salt and pepper, if necessary. Reserve.

2. Preheat a gas or charcoal grill to medium-high. Place the cheese slices on the grill and cook for 1–1½ minutes per side. The cheese should be soft, but still intact.

3. For each sandwich, insert two slices of halloumi into each pita. Stuff the pocket with the baby spinach, peppers, and chopped olives. Top the sandwiches with the pickled red onions and a spoonful of the dressing.

Quick Pickled Red Onions

Quick pickled red onions make a great garnish for sandwiches and salads. Combine a thinly sliced medium-size red onion, 1 teaspoon sugar, ½ teaspoon salt, and 1 tablespoon red wine vinegar. Allow the onions to "pickle" for about 15 minutes and then strain them. Pickled red onions can be refrigerated for 1 week.

STEAK SANDWICHES WITH MUSHROOMS AND CHEESE

Make this sandwich when you have leftover grilled beef.

Serves 4

2 tablespoons extra-virgin olive oil

1 clove garlic, peeled and minced

1 cup sliced cremini mushrooms

½ teaspoon salt

⅛ teaspoon pepper

½ teaspoon fresh thyme leaves

½ teaspoon chopped fresh rosemary

½ cup Taltsenes (see recipe in Chapter 4)

4 sandwich buns

1 pound grilled flank steak, thinly sliced

½ cup grated Provolone cheese

1. Preheat the oven to 450°F. Heat the oil in a medium skillet over medium heat for 30 seconds. Add the garlic, mushrooms, salt, and pepper. Cook the mushrooms for 8–10 minutes until they soften. Add the thyme and rosemary, and take the skillet off the heat. Reserve.

2. For each sandwich (divide evenly for four sandwiches), smear the Taltsenes dip on the bottom bun and then top it with the steak. Top the steak with the mushrooms and cheese.

3. Place the sandwiches (without the top bun) on a baking sheet and bake them for 5 minutes or until the cheese is melted.

4. Place the top bun on each sandwich and serve warm.

CALAMARI SANDWICHES WITH SMOKY YOGURT SAUCE

Instead of sandwich buns, try toasted Italian ciabatta bread for this sandwich.

Serves 4

½ cup Homemade Greek Yogurt (see recipe in Chapter 1)

1 clove garlic, peeled and minced

2 tablespoons mayonnaise

¼ teaspoon smoked paprika

1½ teaspoons grated lemon zest

1 small pickle, finely chopped

1 tablespoon finely chopped capers

1 tablespoon chopped fresh parsley

1 tablespoon finely chopped chives

1 tablespoon chopped fresh dill

⅛ teaspoon cayenne pepper

1 teaspoon fresh lemon juice

4 sandwich buns, toasted

4 leaves romaine lettuce, shredded

1 pound Fried Calamari (see recipe in Chapter 4)

1 large tomato, sliced

1. In a small bowl, combine the yogurt, garlic, mayonnaise, paprika, zest, pickle, capers, parsley, chives, dill, cayenne pepper, and lemon juice. Mix the sauce and reserve it.

2. Evenly spread the sauce on both the bottom and top buns. Add lettuce to the bottom bun and top it with the Fried Calamari. Top the calamari with the tomato slices.

3. Add the top bun and serve.

Smoked Paprika

Smoked paprika is made by air-drying red peppers and then wood-smoking them. The smoked peppers are ground into a powder. A little goes a long way with smoked paprika. Don't add too much or it will overpower any dish.

TUNA PANINI

This is like making a marinated sandwich!

Serves 6

1 hard-boiled egg

1 red onion

1 medium apple

¼ teaspoon lemon juice

1 cup water

1 pound cooked or canned tuna

¼ cup chopped walnuts

2 tablespoons extra-virgin olive oil

1 tablespoon balsamic vinegar, or to taste

Kosher salt, to taste

Fresh-cracked black pepper, to taste

1 small loaf Italian bread

1 head green or red leaf lettuce

1. Medium-dice the egg and onion. Dice the apple and toss it in the lemon juice and water; drain.

2. Mix together the tuna, egg, onion, apple, nuts, oil, and vinegar; season with salt and pepper. Cut the bread in half lengthwise, then layer the lettuce and mound the tuna mixture on top.

3. Wrap the loaf tightly with plastic wrap and refrigerate for 1 hour. Slice into 6 equal portions and serve.

OPEN-FACED GRILLED CHEESE

This recipe makes for a delightful lunch when served with a fresh salad.

Serves 6

1 pear

1 teaspoon lemon juice

1 cup water

6 large slices raisin-pumpernickel bread

1 tablespoon extra-virgin olive oil

6 thick slices Swiss cheese (1 ounce each)

Kosher salt, to taste

Fresh-cracked black pepper, to taste

1. Preheat broiler.

2. Dice the pear and toss it in the lemon juice and water; drain thoroughly.

3. Brush the bread with the oil and toast lightly. Place the cheese on the bread, sprinkle with diced pears, and season with salt and pepper.

4. Place under broiler until the cheese melts and the pears brown slightly, approximately 2 minutes.

CAESAR SANDWICH

You must purchase pasteurized egg yolks to prevent salmonella.

Serves 6

3 cloves roasted garlic (see Roasted Garlic Served on Crostini recipe in Chapter 4)

1 anchovy fillet (optional)

1 ounce pasteurized egg yolks

½ teaspoon dry mustard

Fresh-cracked black pepper

½ cup extra-virgin olive oil

1 large head romaine lettuce

6 slices crusty Italian bread

2 ounces Parmesan cheese, grated

1. Prepare the dressing by mashing together the garlic and anchovy. Add the yolks and seasonings. Whisk in the olive oil.

2. Clean and dry the lettuce, then toss the lettuce with the dressing.

3. Place on bread and sprinkle with Parmesan.

WATERCRESS SANDWICHES

This recipe is a slight twist on the classic watercress tea sandwiches.

Serves 6

6 slices marble (rye-pumpernickel mix) bread

3 ounces Brie cheese

3 bunches watercress leaves

1. Lightly toast the bread; let cool. Spread each slice with the Brie.

2. Clean and lay out the watercress leaves on three slices, then top each with the remaining three slices. Cut each sandwich into six small pieces. Serve three each with Pumpkin Soup (see recipe in this chapter).

Diet Breads

For those of you watching your weight or counting calories, you may want to try out some of the fat-free or low-calorie breads available in the market. Most are just as tasty, and you probably won't be able to tell the difference.

WARM OPEN-FACED TURKEY SANDWICH

Now you don't have to wait for Thanksgiving to have delicious turkey sandwiches!

Serves 6

½ baguette

1 yellow onion

2 stalks celery

½ cup mushrooms

1 tablespoon olive oil

6 ounces turkey Demi-Glace Reduction Sauce (see recipe in Chapter 2)

2 ounces warm turkey

Fresh-cracked black pepper, to taste

Kosher salt, to taste

1. Slice the baguette in half lengthwise. Slice the onion and finely slice the celery and mushrooms.

2. Heat the oil to medium temperature in a small saucepan, then add the onions, celery, and mushrooms. Cover and simmer at medium-low heat until the vegetables are wilted.

3. Heat the demi-glace. Place the cooked vegetables on the baguette and layer with warm turkey. Season with pepper and salt, to taste.

4. To serve, cut into 6 portions and ladle with demi-glace.

WILTED ARUGULA ON FLATBREAD

You can use slices of extra-crispy bacon in place of the pancetta.

Serves 6

1 teaspoon olive oil

2 ounces pancetta

3 cups fresh arugula

12 slices Flatbread (see recipe in Chapter 3)

Fresh-cracked black pepper

Heat the oil to medium temperature in a medium-size saucepan. Add the pancetta, and brown. Add the arugula, wilt, and immediately mound on the flatbread; add pepper to taste. Serve with Gorgonzola or your favorite cheese.

GREEK PITA

You must use feta with care; while it adds wonderful flavors, remember that it is salty.

Serves 6

2 European cucumbers

1 large red onion

¼ bunch oregano

2 anchovy fillets (optional)

6 pita bread

3 ounces feta cheese

1 tablespoon olive oil

Fresh-cracked black pepper

1. Peel and dice the cucumbers and thinly slice the onion. Chop the oregano. Mash the anchovy fillets.

2. Cut a slit into each pita and stuff with cucumber, onion, oregano, and feta.

3. Drizzle with oil and sprinkle with mashed anchovy and black pepper.

SESAME-GINGER-ENCRUSTED TUNA CARPACCIO

Rice cakes make a nice alternative to bread.

Serves 6

1 tablespoon fresh-minced ginger

3 cloves garlic

½ teaspoon soy sauce

1 tablespoon sesame oil, divided

¼ cup sesame seeds

1 pound fresh tuna steak

1 apple, any type

1 bunch scallions

6 rice cakes

1. Mix together the ginger, garlic, soy, ½ tablespoon sesame oil, and the sesame seeds. Encrust the tuna with the seed mixture.

2. Heat a sauté pan on highest heat; sear the outside of the tuna very quickly. Wrap the tuna in plastic wrap and freeze solid.

3. Remove from plastic wrap and, using a very sharp knife, slice the tuna as thinly as possible. Thinly slice the apple and slice the scallions on an extreme bias.

4. Brush the rice cakes with the rest of the sesame oil, and layer with tuna, apple, and scallions.

CURRIED CHICKEN ON LAVASH

Lavash is another type of flatbread that originally comes from Armenia.

Serves 6

Lavash

1 cup whole-wheat flour

¼ cup water

Pinch of iodized salt

1 tablespoon olive oil

Chicken

1 medium-size yellow onion

3 cloves garlic

1 carrot

1 tablespoon olive oil

¾ pound chicken

2 tablespoons curry powder

¼ teaspoon red pepper flakes

Fresh-cracked black pepper

½ cup Chicken or Turkey Stock (see recipe in Chapter 2)

1. Mix together all the lavash ingredients, except the oil, with a dough hook or by hand. Heat the oil to medium temperature in a sauté pan. Roll the lavash into eight 1-inch-thin discs and cook each in the pan for approximately 5 minutes on each side, lightly browning each side.

2. To prepare the chicken, peel and chop the onion, garlic, and carrot. Heat the oil to medium temperature in a saucepan. Sauté the vegetables, then add the chicken, seasoning, and stock. Simmer for 1 hour.

3. Serve the chicken on top of the lavash.

Pita, Please

Pita is a great bread to use for sandwiches. The bread opens up into a pocket, which you can stuff with your favorite goodies. For on-the-go convenience, pita is a pleaser. Try it with the sandwich recipes in this chapter.

ALMOND-ENCRUSTED SALMON ON TOAST POINTS

Serrano peppers have such a thin skin that you don't need to bother removing it.

Serves 6

6 flour or corn tortillas

1 serrano pepper

¼ cup almonds

1 teaspoon chili powder

1 pound salmon fillet

¼ cup milk

1 tablespoon extra-virgin olive oil, plus extra for drizzling

Honey, for drizzling

1. Toast the tortillas under the broiler.

2. Mince the serrano and finely chop the almonds; mix together the serrano, almonds, and chili powder.

3. Clean the salmon in ice water, cut it into 6 portions, then dip it into the milk. Dredge in the almond mix.

4. Heat the 1 tablespoon olive oil to medium temperature and cook the salmon on each side for approximately 5 minutes, until thoroughly cooked.

5. Serve on tortillas, drizzled with extra-virgin olive oil and honey.

Herb Gardens

If you enjoy Mediterranean cooking, you may want to consider planting an herb garden. This will allow you to have fresh herbs at your fingertips to use in all your Mediterranean recipes.

CALZONE

You can also use chicken or turkey sausage for a different flavor. Serve with Tomato Salad with Roasted Garlic, Basil, and Pine Nut Dressing (see recipe in this chapter).

Serves 6

3 ounces dried sausage (soppressata)

3 ounces pepperoni

¼ bunch oregano, chopped

6 large basil leaves

1 tablespoon olive oil

1 recipe Flatbread dough (see recipe in Chapter 3)

½ cup part-skim ricotta

3 ounces part-skim mozzarella

Kosher salt, to taste

Fresh-cracked black pepper

1. Preheat the oven to 375°F.

2. Finely dice the sausage, pepperoni, oregano, and basil. Brush a baking sheet with oil.

3. Roll the dough out to ½-inch thickness and spread with ricotta, mozzarella, sausage, and pepperoni. Sprinkle with the spices.

4. Fold the dough in half and place on the prepared baking sheet; bake for approximately 30 minutes. Slice into 6 equal portions.

SOUVLAKI WITH TZATZIKI

You can serve the lamb rare or medium-rare to suit your preference.

Serves 6

1 teaspoon olive oil

1 pound diced boneless lamb (fat removed)

Fresh-cracked black pepper, to taste

¼ cup dry red wine

¼ bunch fresh oregano

6 pitas

1 cup Tzatziki (see recipe in Chapter 2)

1. Heat the oil in a sauté pan on high heat. Season the lamb with pepper. Sear the lamb quickly, then add the wine. Allow the wine to reduce by half.

2. Remove the pan from the heat and toss in the chopped oregano.

3. Place on pitas and serve with Tzatziki.

SLICED OPEN-FACED LONDON BROIL

Horseradish is a nice accompaniment for beef. Try it in other recipes as well.

Serves 6

1 pound London broil

¼ cup mustard

Fresh-cracked black pepper, to taste

6 slices hearty grain bread

1 tablespoon extra-virgin olive oil

½ cup brown Demi-Glacé Reduction Sauce (see recipe in Chapter 2)

¼ cup horseradish

1. Preheat grill or broiler.

2. Rub the steak with mustard and season with pepper. Grill to desired doneness. Let rest for 1–2 minutes, then slice thinly on bias.

3. While the steak cooks, toast the bread and brush with oil. Heat the demi-glacé.

4. To serve, layer the meat on the bread with horseradish and drizzle with demi-glacé.

FISH CLUB SANDWICH

This Fish Club Sandwich is a refreshing variation on the common club sandwich.

Serves 6

6 slices pancetta or bacon

12 very thin slices whole-grain bread

1 tablespoon extra-virgin olive oil

12 lettuce leaves

2 tomatoes

1 red onion

¾ pound grilled fish

1. Cook the pancetta until it's crisp. Toast the bread lightly and brush with oil. Shred the lettuce, slice the tomatoes, and thinly slice the onion.

2. Layer the fish, veggies, and pancetta on the bread. Cut each sandwich into 4 sections

GRILLED VEGETABLE HERO

This sandwich is sure to please your vegetarian friends.

Serves 6

6 club rolls

1 eggplant

1 red pepper

1 Vidalia onion

1 tablespoon extra-virgin olive oil

3 ounces goat cheese (optional)

Fresh-cracked black pepper

1. Preheat a grill pan on the stovetop over medium-high heat. Slice the eggplant, pepper, and onion approximately 1-inch thick; toss in olive oil. Place on the grill pan and cook until al dente.

2. Brush the rolls with oil. Layer the veggies on the rolls.

3. Sprinkle with cheese and pepper, and serve.

FRESH MOZZARELLA AND TOMATO SALAD ON BAGUETTE

You can put the salad and cheese on the bread and bake it to make pizza.

Serves 6

1 baguette

6 ounces Fresh Mozzarella (see recipe in Chapter 4)

1½ cups Tomato Salad with Roasted Garlic, Basil, and Pine Nut Dressing (see recipe in this chapter)

Slice the bread in half lengthwise. Shred the mozzarella on top of the bread slices. Spoon the salad on top.

Cheese Choices

If you are a cheese lover, you know that most sandwiches are just not complete without cheese. Feel free to experiment with different cheeses on the sandwiches listed in this chapter. But don't just stick with your favorites. Try cheese you've never used before; you may just find a new favorite.

ROASTED GARLIC POTATO SALAD LETTUCE ROLLS

It's perfectly fine to cook red potatoes with the skin on—there's no need to peel them.

Serves 6

6 cooked Idaho potatoes or 12 small red-skinned potatoes

½ bulb roasted garlic (see Roasted Garlic Served on Crostini recipe in Chapter 4)

1 yellow onion

¼ cup extra-virgin olive oil

2 tablespoons balsamic vinegar

¼ bunch parsley, chopped

Fresh-cracked black pepper, to taste

Kosher salt, to taste

1 head large-leaf lettuce

Chop the potatoes and mash them with the garlic; mix together with the onion, olive oil, vinegar, and parsley. Adjust seasoning to taste. Place the potato salad on lettuce leaves, then roll up.

NUT BUTTER AND HONEY ON WHOLE GRAIN

Walnuts and almonds work great in this recipe, although any of your favorite nuts are fine to use.

Serves 6

2 cups nuts (shelled)

12 slices whole-grain bread (toast if desired)

6 tablespoons honey

Purée the nuts until a smooth paste forms; spread onto bread and drizzle with honey.

Allergies Alert

Many people have allergies to nuts or garlic, which are common ingredients in Mediterranean cooking. If you will be serving guests, be sure to find out ahead of time whether any allergies exist.

VEGETABLE PITA

Use fresh seasonal vegetables and either roast or grill them for this recipe.

Serves 6

1 large red onion

1 large head lettuce (any type)

6 ounces Hummus (see recipe in Chapter 4)

6 large pitas

4½ cups vegetables of your choice

2 tablespoons extra-virgin olive oil

Thinly slice the onion and shred the lettuce. Spread hummus on each pita. Layer with onion, lettuce, and roasted vegetables. Drizzle with olive oil, and serve.

PEANUT-COCONUT-GRILLED CHICKEN SANDWICH

This fresh sandwich is perfect for a light lunch on a busy day.

Serves 6

¼ cup peanut butter

½ cup coconut milk

¼ cup Chicken or Turkey Stock (see recipe in Chapter 2)

1 pound boneless, skinless chicken breasts

6 slices whole-grain bread

½ fresh pineapple

1. Mix together the peanut butter, coconut milk, and stock. Marinate the chicken in this mixture for 4 hours, then remove the chicken and reserve the marinade.

2. Preheat grill.

3. Grill the chicken on each side for approximately 10 minutes.

4. While the chicken is grilling, thoroughly cook the marinade over medium heat in a small saucepan until it is reduced by half.

5. Toast the bread. Slice the chicken on the bias and fan it over the toast. Slice the pineapple and place the slices on top of the chicken.

CHAPTER 6

PASTA AND RICE ENTRÉES

PASTA DOUGH

Cooking time varies according to thickness of dough; thicker dough needs to cook longer.

Serves 6

¾ cup semolina

1 cup unbleached all-purpose flour

Pinch of iodized salt

1 whole egg

1 egg white

1 tablespoon extra-virgin olive oil

½ tablespoon cold water

1. Sift together semolina, flour, and salt. Scramble eggs and mix together with oil and water.

2. Mix with a dough hook at medium speed for 2 minutes until a ball forms. Let the dough rest for 1 hour in the refrigerator.

3. Roll out and form as desired.

4. Bring 1 gallon of water to boil and cook dough approximately 4–8 minutes until al dente.

SPAGHETTI WITH TOMATO AND BASIL

This pasta dish tastes like summer in a bowl. Use ripe summer tomatoes and fresh basil from the garden for best results.

Serves 4

1 tablespoon plus 1½ teaspoons salt, divided

1 pound spaghetti

¼ cup plus 2 tablespoons extra-virgin olive oil, divided

8 cloves garlic, peeled and minced

1 (28-ounce) can whole tomatoes, hand crushed

½ teaspoon pepper

1 cup sliced fresh basil leaves

1 cup grated Romano cheese, divided

1. Fill a large pot two-thirds with water and place over medium-high heat. Add 1 tablespoon salt and bring the water to a boil. Add the pasta and cook for about 6–7 minutes or until al dente (follow the package's cooking times).

2. In a large skillet over medium heat, heat ¼ cup oil for 30 seconds. Add garlic and cook for 2 minutes, or until you begin to smell the garlic. Add tomatoes (include the liquid) and increase the heat to medium-high. Bring it to a boil, and then reduce the heat to medium-low. Season the tomato sauce with the remaining salt and pepper and cook for 10–12 minutes or until sauce has thickened.

3. Reserve ¼ cup of the pasta cooking water and drain the pasta. Add the pasta to the sauce and stir it to combine. If the sauce is a little thin or dry, stir in the reserved pasta water. Add the basil and stir to combine.

4. Add ¾ cup cheese and toss to combine.

5. Serve the pasta topped with remaining cheese and a drizzle of the remaining oil.

Al Dente

Al dente means "to the tooth" in Italian. It refers to pasta that is cooked but not soft. The cooked pasta should be slightly firm and still hold its shape. Perfectly cooked pasta is the best vehicle for a delicious sauce.

LINGUINE CARBONARA

Try a new type of pasta today. The Italians have hundreds of different pasta shapes. The possibilities are endless!

Serves 4

1 tablespoon salt

1 pound linguine pasta

4 large egg yolks

2 teaspoons pepper

1 cup grated Romano cheese, divided

¾ cup diced bacon or pancetta

3 tablespoons water

¼ cup extra-virgin olive oil

¼ cup diced red onion

2 cloves garlic, peeled and smashed

¼ cup dry white wine

1. Fill a large pot two-thirds with water and place it over medium-high heat. Add salt and bring the water to a boil. Add the pasta and cook for 6–7 minutes or until al dente (follow the package's cooking times).

2. In a small bowl, whisk the egg yolks, pepper, and ¾ cup of the Romano. Set aside.

3. Add the bacon and 3 tablespoons of water to a large skillet over medium-high heat. The water will evaporate and the bacon will crisp up. Cook the bacon until it is crispy but not hard. Remove the bacon with a slotted spoon and reserve it. Discard all but 1 tablespoon of bacon fat from the skillet.

4. Add the oil to the skillet and heat for 30 seconds on medium. Add the onions and garlic, and cook for 1–2 minutes. Add the wine and deglaze the pan for 2 minutes. Take the skillet off the heat and stir in the reserved bacon.

5. Reserve ¼ cup of the pasta cooking water and drain the pasta. In the skillet, add the pasta, pasta water, and egg mixture. The residual heat of the hot pasta and pasta water should cook and bind the egg mixture into a thick and creamy sauce. Serve topped with the remaining cheese.

Pasta Water

Adding a little of the pasta cooking water to the sauce helps the sauce thicken (because of the starches in the water) and helps the sauce stick to the pasta better.

PENNE ALL'ARRABBIATA

This dish is zesty from the red pepper flakes and gooey from melted mozzarella. It is a quick and easy dinner to pull together.

Serves 6

1 tablespoon plus 1 teaspoon salt, divided

1 pound penne rigate

¼ cup extra-virgin olive oil

1 medium onion, peeled and diced

6 cloves garlic, peeled and minced

2 cups canned whole tomatoes, hand crushed

½ teaspoon pepper

1 cup grated mozzarella cheese

1 teaspoon red pepper flakes

1 cup fresh basil, hand torn

½ cup grated Romano or Parmesan cheese

1. Fill a large pot two-thirds with water and place it over medium-high heat. Add 1 tablespoon salt and bring the water to a boil. Add the pasta and cook it for 8–9 minutes or until al dente (follow the package's cooking times).

2. Heat the oil in a large skillet over medium heat for 30 seconds. Add the onions and garlic. Reduce the heat to medium-low and cook for 5 minutes or until onions soften. Add the tomatoes (including the liquid) and the remaining salt and pepper. Cook for 20 minutes or until the sauce has thickened.

3. Reserve ¼ cup of the pasta cooking water and drain the pasta. Add the pasta to the sauce and stir to combine. If the sauce is a little thin or dry, stir in the reserved pasta water. Add the mozzarella, red pepper flakes, and basil. Stir until the mozzarella has melted.

4. Serve the penne topped with Romano cheese.

Penne Rigate

Penne rigate is a short, thick, ridged, hollow pasta. It is perfect for a thick tomato sauce because it allows the sauce to stick to the outside ridges and fills the inside. Every bite is a burst of flavor!

PASTA SALAD WITH FETA, SUN-DRIED TOMATOES, AND SPINACH

Pasta salads are great for backyard entertaining, picnics, or potluck dinners. Use bow-tie pasta because it makes it easy to grab a forkful of all the ingredients with one stab! Bow-tie pasta is also known as farfalle, *the Italian word for "butterflies," because of its shape.*

Serves 4

1 tablespoon plus 1 teaspoon salt, divided

1½ cups farfalle (bow-tie pasta)

1 cup chopped baby spinach, rinsed and dried

8 sun-dried tomatoes, sliced

1 cup grated and peeled carrot

2 scallions, ends trimmed and thinly sliced

1 clove garlic, peeled and minced

1 medium dill pickle, diced

⅓ cup extra-virgin olive oil

2 tablespoons red wine vinegar

½ cup strained Greek yogurt

½ teaspoon pepper

1 teaspoon chopped fresh oregano

¼ cup chopped fresh basil

1 cup diced feta cheese

¼ cup chopped fresh chives

1. Fill a large pot two-thirds with water and place it over medium-high heat. Add 1 tablespoon salt and bring the water to a boil. Add the pasta and cook for 6–7 minutes or until al dente (follow the package's cooking times). Drain the pasta in a colander and cool it under cold running water.

2. In a large bowl, combine the spinach, tomatoes, carrot, scallions, garlic, and pickle. Add the pasta and toss the ingredients to combine them.

3. In a medium bowl, whisk the oil, vinegar, yogurt, remaining salt, and pepper. Add the dressing to the pasta and toss it to combine and coat evenly. Toss in the oregano, basil, and feta.

4. Sprinkle the salad with chives. Serve it cool or at room temperature.

PASTA WITH CHERRY TOMATOES, FETA, HALLOUMI, AND BASIL

Use any ripe chopped tomato if you can't find cherry tomatoes.

Serves 4

1 tablespoon plus ½ teaspoon salt, divided

1 pound broad egg noodles

¼ cup extra-virgin olive oil

1 pint ripe cherry tomatoes, halved

¼ teaspoon pepper

6 or 7 cloves garlic, peeled and minced

1 cup diced halloumi cheese

1 cup sliced fresh basil leaves

1½ cups crumbled feta cheese, divided

½ cup strained Greek yogurt

½ teaspoon red pepper flakes

1. Fill a large pot two-thirds with water and place it over medium-high heat. Add 1 tablespoon salt and bring the water to a boil. Add the noodles and cook them for 6–7 minutes or until al dente (follow the package's cooking times).

2. In a large skillet over medium heat, add the oil and heat for 30 seconds. Add tomatoes, remaining salt, and pepper. Cover the skillet and cook for 5 minutes. Uncover and mash the tomatoes slightly to release their juices. Add the garlic and cook for 10 minutes or until the sauce thickens.

3. Reserve ¼ cup of the pasta cooking water and then drain the pasta. Add the pasta to the sauce and stir to combine. If the sauce is a little thin or dry, stir in the reserved pasta water. Stir in the halloumi and basil.

4. In a medium bowl, combine 1 cup of feta, yogurt, and red pepper flakes. Mash everything together with a fork. Add the feta mixture to the pasta and stir until the sauce is creamy.

5. Top with the remaining feta and serve immediately.

Basil

Basil in Greek is *basilikos*, which means "king." In the Mediterranean, there's no doubt that basil is the king of herbs. There are many varieties to be found, so try as many as you can to find your favorite.

LOBSTER PASTA

Lobster pasta is a delicious indulgence. It's the perfect dish for a romantic dinner for two.

Serves 2

1½-pound live lobster, refrigerated until needed

2 tablespoons plus ½ teaspoon salt, divided

½ pound long pasta (spaghetti, linguine, fettuccine, or bucatini)

1 tablespoon unsalted butter

2 tablespoons extra-virgin olive oil, divided

⅓ cup diced red onions

1 clove garlic, peeled and minced

2 tablespoons finely diced celery

2 tablespoons finely diced, peeled carrots

1 bay leaf

½ cup puréed plum tomatoes

1 teaspoon tomato paste

2 tablespoons dry white wine

1 tablespoon brandy

¼ teaspoon pepper

2 tablespoons chopped fresh dill

⅛ teaspoon cinnamon

1. Place a large pot (big enough to hold the lobster) of water over medium-high heat, and bring the water to a boil. Add 1 tablespoon salt and the lobster. Cover, return to a boil, and cook for 5–7 minutes. To stop the cooking process, place the lobster in an ice bath.

2. When the lobster is cool enough to handle, place it on a cutting board inside a baking tray. Tear the claws, knuckles, and tail off the body. Cut the tail lengthwise in half and remove the meat. Crack open the claws and knuckles to remove the meat. Cut the meat into chunks and reserve along with the juices.

3. Heat another large pot of water over high heat. Add 1 tablespoon salt and bring the water to a boil. Add the pasta and cook for about 6–7 minutes or until al dente.

4. Heat the butter and 1 tablespoon of oil in a large skillet over medium heat. Add the onions, garlic, celery, carrots, and bay leaf. Cook for 5 minutes or until the onions are softened. Add the tomato purée, tomato paste, wine, and reserved lobster juices. Increase heat to medium-high and bring to a boil; decrease the heat to medium-low and simmer for 5–10 minutes or until sauce has thickened. Add the brandy and lobster pieces, and stir to combine. Season with the remaining salt and pepper and remove the bay leaf.

5. Drain the pasta. Add the pasta to the sauce and stir to combine. Stir in the dill and cinnamon. Drizzle with the remaining oil and serve immediately.

Storing Lobsters

Lobsters don't live for more than a day out of salt water, so you should cook them the day you buy them. Cooked lobster will keep in the refrigerator for up to 3 days. The best way to keep lobsters alive at home is to refrigerate them until you are ready to cook.

SPAGHETTI WITH BROWN BUTTER AND FETA

Brown butter has a lovely nutty taste. This recipe can be easily doubled or tripled.

Serves 2

1¼ teaspoons salt, divided

½ pound spaghetti

¼ cup unsalted butter

3 teaspoons extra-virgin olive oil, divided

2 cloves garlic, peeled and smashed

2 tablespoons grated kefalotyri or Romano cheese

2 tablespoons crumbled feta cheese

¼ teaspoon pepper

1. Fill a large pot two-thirds with water, and place it over medium-high heat. Add 1 teaspoon of the salt and bring the water to a boil. Add the pasta and cook for 6–7 minutes or until al dente (follow the package's cooking times).

2. Add the butter, oil, and garlic to a small skillet over medium heat. Whisk as you brown the butter. A little past the melting point, the butter's milk solids will begin to foam. The butter will turn from a golden yellow to a chestnut brown very quickly. When the butter is chestnut brown, take the pan off the heat. This should take 1–2 minutes. Remove the garlic and discard it.

3. Drain the pasta. Add the pasta to the brown butter and stir to combine the ingredients. If the spaghetti appears a bit dry, add a little more oil. Add the kefalotyri and 1 tablespoon of the feta and continue to toss until the cheeses have blended in with the butter. Season with the remaining salt and pepper.

4. Serve the pasta topped with the remaining feta and drizzled with the remaining oil.

PASTITSIO

This is one of Greece's most comforting dishes. Penne pasta will work in a pinch, but try to find Misko #2 pasta for an authentic dish.

Serves 6

1 tablespoon salt

1 pound Misko #2 or bucatini pasta

8 cups Béchamel Sauce (see recipe in Chapter 2)

6 cups Greek Meat Sauce (see recipe in Chapter 2)

½ cup grated kefalotyri or Romano cheese

1. Fill a large pot two-thirds with water, and place it over medium-high heat. Add 1 tablespoon salt and bring the water to a boil. Add the pasta and cook for 6–7 minutes or until al dente (follow the package's cooking times). Drain the pasta. Reserve.

2. Preheat the oven to 350°F. Mix 1 ladle of Béchamel Sauce into the Greek Meat Sauce. Mix 3 ladles of the Béchamel Sauce into the reserved pasta. This will ensure the Pastitsio stays moist.

3. In a large baking dish, add enough Béchamel Sauce to cover the bottom of the dish. Spread half of the pasta evenly over the Béchamel Sauce. Pour all of the Greek Meat Sauce evenly over the pasta. Top evenly with the remaining pasta. Pour the remaining Béchamel Sauce evenly over the second layer of pasta.

4. Sprinkle with the grated cheese and bake in the middle rack for 45–60 minutes or until the top is golden brown.

5. Allow the dish to rest for 30–45 minutes before serving.

MAKARONIA WITH TARAMA

Tarama is fish roe and can be found at Greek or Middle Eastern grocery stores.

Serves 4

1 tablespoon salt

1 pound spaghetti

⅓ cup extra-virgin olive oil

1 cup coarse bread crumbs

¼ cup finely chopped blanched almonds

1 ounce ouzo

4 tablespoons tarama (fish roe)

2 cloves garlic, peeled and minced

¼ cup chopped fresh parsley

½ cup chopped fresh scallions, ends trimmed

2 tablespoons grated lemon zest

1 teaspoon dried oregano

1 tablespoon fresh lemon juice

¼–½ teaspoon red pepper flakes

1. Fill a large pot two-thirds with water and place it over medium-high heat. Add the salt and bring the water to a boil. Add the pasta and cook for 6–7 minutes or until al dente (follow the package's cooking times).

2. Heat the oil in a small skillet over medium heat for 30 seconds. Add the bread crumbs and almonds, and stir for 2 minutes to brown. Add the ouzo, tarama, and garlic, and cook for another 2 minutes or until the ouzo is absorbed.

3. Take the skillet off the heat, and add the parsley, scallions, zest, and oregano. Drain the pasta and add it to the skillet. Toss to combine all the ingredients and to coat the pasta.

4. Add the lemon juice and red pepper flakes, and toss to combine. Serve immediately.

SHRIMP, MACARONI, AND FETA

This dish combines elements of Shrimp Saganaki (see recipe in Chapter 4) with macaroni and cheese. It will be an instant classic in your home.

Serves 8

1 tablespoon plus ½ teaspoon salt, divided

2½ cups elbow macaroni

1 or 2 red chilies, stemmed, seeded, and chopped

3 cloves garlic, peeled (2 whole, 1 minced), divided

¼ cup chopped fresh parsley

1¼ cups sliced fresh basil, divided

½ cup extra-virgin olive oil, divided

½ teaspoon honey

2 tablespoons fresh lemon juice

¼ cup unsalted butter

1 small red onion, finely chopped

1 cup sliced button mushrooms

1 teaspoon sweet paprika

6 medium-size ripe plum tomatoes, peeled and puréed

¼ teaspoon pepper

¼ cup dry white wine

1 ounce ouzo

1 cup heavy cream or evaporated milk

1 cup crumbled plus 1 cup cubed feta cheese, divided

24 medium shrimp, peeled and deveined

1 teaspoon dried oregano

1. Fill a large pot two-thirds with water, and place it over medium-high heat. Add 1 tablespoon salt and bring the water to a boil. Add the pasta and cook for 6–7 minutes or until al dente (follow the package's cooking times).

2. Preheat the broiler. Put the chilies, whole garlic, parsley, ¼ cup of basil, ¼ cup of oil, honey, lemon juice, and ¼ teaspoon of the salt in a food processor, and pulse until all the ingredients are well incorporated. Reserve.

3. In a large skillet over medium heat, heat the remaining oil for 30 seconds. Add butter, onions, minced garlic, mushrooms, and paprika. Cook for 5 minutes or until the onions are soft. Add the tomatoes, and season with the remaining salt and pepper. Simmer for 5–7 minutes. Add the wine and ouzo, and cook until most of the liquid has evaporated.

4. Add the cream and crumbled feta, and cook for 3 minutes or until the sauce has thickened. Drain the pasta and stir the pasta into the cream-tomato sauce. Add the remaining basil and toss to combine.

5. Add the pasta to a medium baking dish and top it with the shrimp and cubed feta. Broil for 5 minutes or until the shrimp turn pink and the cheese is melted. Drizzle with the reserved parsley-basil sauce and sprinkle with oregano. Let cool for 5 minutes before serving.

Tomatoes

It's hard to imagine Mediterranean cuisine without tomatoes. Their bright flavor and rich color make them a staple ingredient in most dishes. Tomatoes came to Europe via the explorer Hernando Cortés, in the 1500s, after he discovered the Aztecs eating them.

SHRIMP AND PASTA OF ST. NICHOLAS

This recipe can easily be doubled to serve twelve or increased even more for larger numbers of hungry guests.

Serves 6

1 tablespoon plus ¾ teaspoon salt, divided

1 pound linguine

24 medium shrimp, shelled, deveined, and shells reserved

¼ teaspoon pepper

⅓ cup extra-virgin olive oil

1 medium onion, peeled and finely chopped

6 cloves garlic, peeled and minced

¼ cup dry white wine

2 cups canned plum tomatoes, puréed

¼ teaspoon red pepper flakes

½ cup chopped fresh parsley

¼ cup chopped fresh basil

1. Fill a large pot two-thirds with water, and place it over medium-high heat. Add 1 tablespoon of the salt and bring the water to a boil. Add pasta and cook for 6–7 minutes or until al dente (follow the package's cooking times).

2. Wrap the reserved shrimp shells in cheesecloth and tie it up tightly. Season the shrimp with ¼ teaspoon of the salt and the pepper. Heat the oil in a large skillet over medium-high heat for 30 seconds. Add the shrimp and cook for 1 minute on each side or until they are pink. Remove them from the skillet, leaving the oil in the skillet, and reserve.

3. Reduce the heat to medium and add the onion, garlic, and shrimp shells. Cook for 5–7 minutes or until onions are softened. Add the wine and cook for 5 minutes.

4. Add the tomatoes, increase the heat to medium-high, and bring the sauce to a boil. Decrease the heat to medium and cook for 20 minutes or until the sauce thickens. Remove the shrimp shells and discard them. Adjust the seasoning with more salt and pepper, if necessary.

5. Drain the pasta and add it to the sauce. Toss to combine the ingredients and to coat the pasta with the sauce. Take the skillet off the heat and add the cooked shrimp, red pepper flakes, parsley, and basil. Toss them to combine the ingredients and serve immediately.

LINGUINE WITH TAPENADE

Serve this delicious tapenade on its own as a topping for toast.

Serves 6

1 cup oil-cured pitted olives

2 tablespoons capers, rinsed and drained

1½ tablespoons fresh rosemary leaves

1 clove garlic, peeled and smashed

2 anchovy fillets, packed in oil

½ teaspoon sugar

⅔ cup plus 2 tablespoons extra-virgin olive oil, divided

1 pound linguine, cooked

½ cup grated kasseri or sheep's milk cheese

1 tablespoon chopped fresh chives

1. Place the olives, capers, rosemary, garlic, anchovy, sugar, and ⅔ cup of oil into a food processor. Process the ingredients until they are well incorporated but not smooth. The tapenade should still have texture.

2. Toss pasta with the remaining oil and cheese. Arrange the pasta on a serving platter, and top it with the tapenade and chives. Serve.

PASTA AND CANNELLINI BEANS

Any type of pasta or bean works for this recipe, also known as pasta fagiole.

Serves 6

1 cup dried cannellini beans

1 quart water

6 cloves garlic

1 shallot

2 fresh plum tomatoes

2 sprigs thyme, leaves only

2 sprigs oregano

8 large basil leaves

1 teaspoon olive oil

1 quart Red Wine Vegetable Stock (see recipe in Chapter 2)

1 dried bay leaf

Fresh-cracked black pepper, to taste

1 pound cooked pasta

¼ cup grated Romano cheese

1. Soak the beans overnight in the water; rinse and drain.

2. Mince the garlic and shallot. Chop the tomatoes, thyme, and oregano. Slice the basil.

3. Heat the oil over medium heat in a large stockpot; quick sauté the garlic and shallots, then add the beans and stock. Simmer on low heat for approximately 3 hours with lid ajar.

4. Add the bay leaf, thyme, and oregano; simmer for 30 minutes more.

5. Add the tomatoes and black pepper; cook for another 30 minutes.

6. Remove from heat, remove the bay leaf, and add the basil. Serve over warm pasta and sprinkle with grated cheese.

SEAFOOD RAVIOLI

Stuffed dough can be found in all cultures. The most famous of the Mediterranean types is ravioli. It can be stuffed with just about anything.

Serves 6

Ravioli Stuffing

½ pound shrimp

½ pound scallops

¼ bunch fresh cilantro

3 cloves garlic

Fresh-cracked black pepper, to taste

Kosher salt, to taste

Vinaigrette Sauce

1½ tablespoons extra-virgin olive oil

Juice of 1 lime

1 cup Seafood Stock (see recipe in Chapter 2)

¼ bunch fresh cilantro leaves

Fresh-cracked black pepper, to taste

Kosher salt, to taste

2 cups Pasta Dough (see recipe in this chapter)

1. Peel the shrimp. Roughly chop the shrimp and scallops. Chop the cilantro and mince the garlic.

2. Mix together all the stuffing ingredients.

3. Whisk together all the vinaigrette ingredients.

4. Roll the dough to ⅛- to ¼-inch thickness. Cut into 2-inch squares and place ½–1 teaspoon of seafood mixture into center of squares. Moisten edges of dough with water, then fold the dough from corner to corner, forming a triangle shape; seal tightly.

5. Cook the ravioli in 1–2 gallons of salted, boiling water to desired doneness. Strain and serve with vinaigrette ladled over the top.

COCKLES AND PASTA

You can substitute small clams for cockles if you like.

Serves 6

16 cockles

½ cup white wine (Pinot Grigio or Sauvignon Blanc)

Juice of 1 lemon

1 cup Seafood Stock (see recipe in Chapter 2)

1½ pounds cooked pasta

Fresh-cracked black pepper, to taste

1½ tablespoons extra-virgin olive oil

1. Clean the cockles (or small clams) thoroughly.

2. In a medium-size saucepot, bring the wine, lemon juice, and stock to a simmer and let reduce by half the amount.

3. Add the cockles (or clams), and cook for 2–3 minutes. (Discard any cockles/clams that do not open.) Add the cooked pasta. Sprinkle with pepper and drizzle with oil before serving.

What Are Cockles?

Cockles are like small clams, with heart-shaped shells. The meat has a tendency to be gritty and hold sand, so be sure you wash them thoroughly.

PASTA WITH ARUGULA AND BRIE

Removing the rind from Brie is an optional step, depending on personal preference.

Serves 6

6 cloves roasted garlic (see Roasted Garlic Served on Crostini recipe in Chapter 4)

4 heads arugula

6 ounces Brie cheese

1¼ pounds pasta

1 teaspoon extra-virgin olive oil

Fresh-cracked black pepper

1. Remove the roasted garlic from peels. Rip the arugula into bite-size pieces. Cut the Brie into small pieces (since Brie is very soft, shape does not matter).

2. Cook the pasta until al dente; drain. Just as the pasta is done, toss all the ingredients together in a bowl. Serve as is (the heat from the cooked pasta will wilt the arugula and melt the Brie adequately).

SPINACH BARLEY GNOCCHI

For an easy way to create the traditional gnocchi shape, gently press the gnocchi against floured fork tines and roll the gnocchi down the fork.

Serves 6

¼ cup cooked spinach

¼ cup cooked barley

1 whole egg

1 egg white

½ teaspoon extra-virgin olive oil

1 teaspoon dry white wine

½ cup semolina

½ cup unbleached all-purpose flour

Pinch of iodized salt

1. In a blender or food processor, purée the spinach and barley, then add the eggs, oil, and wine; continue to blend until thoroughly smooth.

2. Sift together the semolina, flour, and salt. Incorporate the spinach mixture with the flour mixture.

3. Bring 1 gallon of water to a boil. While the water comes to a boil, form gnocchi mix into ½-teaspoon oval-shaped dumplings. (You can make grooved imprints on them with a fork if you like.) Drop the gnocchi into the boiling water and cook for approximately 8 minutes, until al dente.

Preparing Dough

Whenever preparing any type of dough, use flour to prevent sticking. However, you don't want a lot of excess flour on the final product, so be certain to brush all the flour off before cooking.

PASTA AND SPINACH CASSEROLE

If you enjoy macaroni and cheese, you'll likely love this fancier version. The good ol' mac and cheese just won't ever be the same.

Serves 6

3 heads fresh spinach

1 shallot

3 cloves garlic

3 ounces goat cheese

3 ounces firm tofu

2 tablespoons olive oil, plus extra for greasing

2½ tablespoons all-purpose unbleached flour

2 cups skim milk

3 cups cooked pasta

¼ cup chopped Spanish olives

Fresh-cracked black pepper, to taste

1. Preheat the oven to 350°F.

2. Steam the spinach. Mince the shallot and garlic. Crumble the goat cheese and cut the tofu into small cubes.

3. Heat the 2 tablespoons oil over medium heat in a medium-size saucepan, then add the flour to form a roux. Whisk in the milk, and cook until thickened to make white sauce.

4. Grease a casserole pan and ladle in the white sauce. Layer the pasta, spinach, cheese, tofu, olives, shallots, garlic, pepper, and more white sauce (in that order). Continue to layer until all ingredients are used.

5. Bake, covered, for approximately 15–20 minutes until heated through. Uncover and brown for 5–10 minutes longer.

SPAGHETTI WITH FRESH MUSSELS, PARSLEY, AND LEMON

Try using fresh clams or shrimp in place of mussels in this dish.

Serves 6

½ cup extra-virgin olive oil

8 cloves garlic, thinly sliced

3 pounds fresh mussels, cleaned and beards removed

¼ cup plus 2 tablespoons chopped fresh parsley, divided

½ cup dry white wine

¼ cup fresh lemon juice

1 pound spaghetti, cooked

1½ teaspoons grated lemon zest

½–1 teaspoon red pepper flakes

¼ teaspoon pepper

½ teaspoon salt

1. Heat oil in a large skillet over medium-high heat. Add garlic and cook for 1 minute or until light brown. Add mussels and ¼ cup parsley. Cook for 2 minutes while stirring. Add wine and cook for another 2 minutes. Add lemon juice and cover the skillet. Cook for 4–5 minutes. Uncover and discard any unopened mussels.

2. Add pasta, zest, red pepper flakes, pepper, and salt to the mussels. Toss to combine the ingredients and to coat the pasta. Sprinkle with the remaining parsley and serve immediately.

GARIDOMAKARONADA WITH OUZO AND FRESH TOMATO

Garidomakaronada *is a compound word in Greek meaning "pasta and shrimp." The long, thick, hollow bucatini allows this aromatic seafood sauce to get right into the pasta.*

Serves 4

1 tablespoon plus ½ teaspoon salt, divided

1 pound bucatini

16 medium-size shrimp, heads on, body shelled and deveined

½ teaspoon pepper, divided

¼ cup extra-virgin olive oil

1 large onion, peeled and finely chopped

3 cloves garlic, peeled and smashed

4 large, very ripe tomatoes, skinned and puréed

1½ tablespoons tomato paste

1 ounce ouzo

½ teaspoon red pepper flakes

2 tablespoons chopped fresh parsley

1. Fill a large pot two-thirds with water, and place it over medium-high heat. Add 1 tablespoon of the salt and bring the water to a boil. Add the pasta and cook for 6–7 minutes or until al dente (follow the package's cooking times).

2. Season the shrimp with ¼ teaspoon salt and ¼ teaspoon pepper. Heat the oil in a large skillet over medium-high heat for 30 seconds. Add the shrimp and cook for 1 minute on each side or until they are pink. Remove the shrimp from the skillet, leaving the oil in the skillet, and reserve.

3. Reduce the heat to medium and add the onions and garlic. Cook for 5 minutes or until the onions soften. Add the tomatoes and tomato paste. Increase the heat and bring the sauce to a boil. Reduce the heat to medium-low and cook for 15–20 minutes or until the sauce has thickened. Stir in the ouzo and season with the remaining salt and pepper. Take the skillet off the heat.

4. Drain the pasta and add it to the sauce along with the red pepper flakes and cooked shrimp. Toss to combine the ingredients and to coat the pasta.

5. Sprinkle with the parsley and serve immediately.

Red Pepper Flakes

Red pepper flakes are made from hot peppers that are dried and crushed. Most red pepper flakes include the seeds, which are the hottest part of the pepper. Depending on the peppers used, some brands are hotter than others. Be careful when you first use them. Only add a little at a time to make sure the dish is not too hot for your taste. You can always add more heat, but you can't take it away.

PASTA WITH MUSHROOM BOLOGNESE

If you love mushrooms and want to serve them as a main dish for a weekday meal or a dinner party, this pasta dish is for you.

Serves 4

1 tablespoon plus 1 teaspoon salt, divided

1 pound rigatoni or ziti

¼ cup extra-virgin olive oil

1 cup finely chopped onion

4 or 5 cloves garlic, peeled and minced

1 medium carrot, peeled and grated

1 stalk celery, trimmed and finely chopped

3 cups chopped assorted mushrooms

2 or 3 bay leaves

½ teaspoon pepper

¼ cup dried porcini mushrooms, rehydrated in 2 cups of hot water for 10 minutes, then drained

½ cup dry white wine

¼ teaspoon fresh grated nutmeg

2 cups canned plum tomatoes, puréed

1 teaspoon fresh thyme leaves

1 teaspoon dried oregano

2 tablespoons chopped fresh parsley

⅓ cup grated Parmesan cheese

1. Fill a large pot two-thirds with water, and place it over medium-high heat. Add 1 tablespoon of the salt and bring the water to a boil. Add the pasta and cook for 6–7 minutes or until al dente (follow the package's cooking times).

2. Heat the oil in a large skillet over medium-high heat for 30 seconds. Add the onions, garlic, carrot, celery, assorted mushrooms (not the porcini), and bay leaves. Cook for 8–10 minutes while stirring. Season with the remaining salt and pepper, and reduce the heat to medium. Cook for another 5 minutes or until most of the liquid evaporates.

3. Chop the rehydrated porcini mushrooms and add them to the sauce. Add the wine and nutmeg, and cook until most of the liquid evaporates.

4. Add the tomatoes and thyme. Increase the heat to medium-high and bring to a boil. Reduce the heat to medium-low and cook for 20–30 minutes or until the sauce thickens. Adjust the seasoning with more salt and pepper, if necessary. Remove the bay leaves and stir in the oregano.

5. Drain the pasta and add it to the sauce. Toss to combine the ingredients and coat the pasta. Sprinkle the top with parsley and cheese. Serve immediately.

OCTOPUS AND PASTA BAKE

For this dish, the octopus is braised in its own liquid. This concentrated juice becomes an intense stock, which is the undertone for this complex, flavorful sauce.

Serves 4

2-pound octopus, cleaned and beak removed

⅓ cup plus 2 tablespoons extra-virgin olive oil, divided

1 large onion, peeled and grated

2 cloves garlic, peeled and minced

1 medium carrot, peeled and finely chopped

1 stalk celery, trimmed and finely chopped

2 bay leaves

1 cinnamon stick

1½ tablespoons tomato paste, diluted in ½ cup hot water

½ cup dry white wine

½ cup tomato purée

1 pound elbow macaroni, cooked according to package directions

1 cup chopped fresh dill

¼ teaspoon salt

¼ teaspoon pepper

1. Place the octopus in a large pot over medium-high heat. Cover the pot and cook for 5 minutes or until the liquid from the octopus is released. Lower the heat to medium and cook for 45 minutes or until the octopus is fork-tender. Remove the pot from the heat. Reserve the octopus and 1 cup of the braising liquid.

2. Preheat the oven to 400°F. Heat ⅓ cup of the oil in a large skillet over medium-high heat for 30 seconds. Add the onions, garlic, carrot, celery, bay leaves, and cinnamon. Cook for 5 minutes or until the vegetables soften.

3. Add the tomato paste and cook for 2 minutes. Add the wine, the reserved braising liquid, and the tomato purée. Bring the sauce to a boil, reduce the heat to medium, and cook for 10 minutes.

4. Pour the sauce into a large deep casserole dish. Add the pasta and dill, and stir to combine. Season the pasta with salt and pepper. Place the octopus on top of the pasta. Bake for 20–30 minutes or until most of the liquid has been absorbed by the pasta.

5. Discard the bay leaves and the cinnamon stick. Serve the dish drizzled with the remaining oil.

GIOUVETSI WITH VEAL

You can change the meat in this orzo dish to suit your taste. Use either lamb or chicken.

Serves 6

1½-pound veal shoulder, cut into 1½-inch pieces

¾ teaspoon salt, divided

½ teaspoon pepper, divided

2 cups water

½ cup extra-virgin olive oil

1 medium onion, peeled and finely chopped

2 cloves garlic, peeled and smashed

1 medium-size red pepper, stemmed, seeded, and finely chopped

2 cups orzo

1 teaspoon smoked paprika

½ cup tomato purée

6 cups Veal Stock, Chicken or Turkey Stock, or Basic Vegetable Stock (see recipes in Chapter 2)

½ cup grated kefalotyri or Romano cheese

1. Season the veal with ¼ teaspoon of salt and ¼ teaspoon of pepper. Put the veal and 2 cups of water into a pressure cooker. Secure the lid and crank the heat to high. As soon as the seal forms, the cooker will whistle. Turn the heat to medium, and cook the meat for 30 minutes. Take the pressure cooker off the heat, and release the pressure according to the manufacturer's instructions. If you don't have a pressure cooker, place the water and the veal in a large pot over medium heat, cover it, and cook for 90 minutes.

2. Preheat the oven to 375°F. Heat the oil in a large skillet over medium-high heat for 30 seconds. Add the onions, garlic, and red pepper. Cook for 5 minutes or until the onions soften.

3. Add the uncooked orzo and the paprika. Stir to combine the ingredients and coat the orzo for 5 minutes. Add the tomato purée and the stock, and bring the mixture to a boil; then take it off the heat. Season with the remaining salt and pepper.

4. Put the orzo mixture and the veal into a large, deep casserole dish. Stir to combine the ingredients. Bake for 45 minutes or until the orzo has absorbed most of the liquid and the top is golden brown.

5. Allow to cool for 10 minutes. Top the dish with cheese and serve.

Orzo

Orzo is a type of pasta that has a distinct rice shape. Although invented by the Italians, this pasta is very popular in Greece and in other Mediterranean countries.

MUSHROOM RISOTTO

Add some healthy greens to this risotto, such as asparagus, peas, green beans, or baby spinach. Pick whatever is in season!

Serves 4

¼ cup extra-virgin olive oil

1 small red onion, peeled and finely diced

2 cloves garlic, peeled and minced

⅓ cup bacon, finely chopped

1½ cups sliced cremini mushrooms

1 teaspoon fresh thyme leaves

2 bay leaves

½ teaspoon salt

½ teaspoon pepper

1 cup Arborio rice

½ cup dry white wine

3½–4 cups hot Chicken or Turkey Stock (see recipe in Chapter 2)

4 tablespoons unsalted butter

½ cup grated Parmesan cheese

1. Heat the oil in a medium-heavy skillet over medium heat for 30 seconds. Add the onions, garlic, bacon, mushrooms, thyme, bay leaves, salt, and pepper. Cook for 5–6 minutes or until mushrooms brown and the bacon is crisp.

2. Add the rice and stir to coat each grain in the oil. Add the wine and stir until the rice has absorbed the wine.

3. Add 1 ladle of stock and stir until it is absorbed by the rice. Keep adding 1 ladle of stock at a time, stirring until the stock is absorbed by the rice. After 3½ cups of stock, check the rice for doneness. It should be cooked but still al dente (it should have some firmness). If needed, add the remaining stock, 1 ladle at a time, until the rice is al dente.

4. Stir in the butter, 1 tablespoon at a time. Stir in the cheese. Remove the bay leaves and discard them.

5. Adjust the seasoning with more salt and pepper, if necessary. Serve immediately.

Risotto

The classic Italian risotto is rice that is cooked slowly in broth until it reaches a creamy consistency. It is a comfort food that is worth the time and effort needed to prepare it. Cooking risotto is not hard. It simply requires time, patience, and the proper technique.

BAKED RICE WITH RED PEPPERS

You can also switch out the peppers for another vegetable such as mushrooms.

Serves 4

1 cup long-grain rice, rinsed

½ cup diced red bell pepper

¼ cup extra-virgin olive oil

2½ cups hot Basic Vegetable Stock (see recipe in Chapter 2)

1 teaspoon salt

¼ teaspoon pepper

1. Preheat the oven to 400°F. In a medium casserole dish, combine the rice, peppers, and oil. Toss to make sure the rice and peppers are coated in the oil.

2. Stir in the stock, and season with salt and pepper.

3. Bake, uncovered, for 40–45 minutes or until all the liquid is absorbed by the rice. Serve warm.

SPANAKORIZO WITH GREEN OLIVES AND FETA

Spanakorizo *means "spinach with rice." This makes a great vegetarian meal.*

Serves 4

½ cup extra-virgin olive oil

1 medium onion, peeled and diced

2 cloves garlic, peeled and minced

1 cup long-grain rice, rinsed

2 pounds fresh spinach, chopped

1½ cups Basic Vegetable Stock (see recipe in Chapter 2)

½ cup plus 1 tablespoon chopped fresh dill, divided

2 tablespoons fresh lemon juice

1½ teaspoons salt

½ teaspoon pepper

¼ cup crumbled feta cheese

¼ cup chopped pitted green olives

1. Heat the oil in a medium-size heavy-bottomed pot over medium heat for 30 seconds. Add the onions and garlic, and cook for 5 minutes or until the onions are softened.

2. Add the rice and stir to coat each grain in the oil. Add the spinach (in batches) and stir until it is wilted. Add the stock and ¼ cup of the dill. Cover and cook for 20 minutes or until most of the liquid is absorbed.

3. Add the lemon juice, ¼ cup dill, salt, and pepper. Fluff the rice and transfer it to a serving platter. Top with the feta, olives, and remaining dill. Serve immediately.

RISOTTO WITH SMOKED EGGPLANT

Roasting an eggplant over the grill gives it a distinct smoky flavor.

Serves 4

⅓ cup extra-virgin olive oil

1 small onion, peeled and finely chopped

1 clove garlic, peeled and minced

1 bay leaf

1 cup Arborio rice

⅓ cup dry white wine

1 large eggplant, roasted and flesh reserved

2–2½ cups hot chicken or vegetable stock

1 cup finely chopped zucchini

¼ cup grated Romano or Parmesan cheese

1 teaspoon salt

½ teaspoon pepper

2 tablespoons chopped fresh chives

1. Heat the oil in a large skillet over medium heat for 30 seconds. Add the onions, garlic, and bay leaf, and cook for 5 minutes or until the onions are soft. Add the rice and stir to coat each grain in oil.

2. Add the wine and stir until the rice has absorbed the wine. Add the eggplant and stir it into the rice.

3. Add a ladle of stock and stir until it is absorbed by the rice. Keep adding 1 ladle of stock at a time and stir until it is absorbed by the rice. After 2 cups of stock, check the rice for doneness. It should be cooked, but it should still be al dente (it should have some firmness). If needed, add the remaining stock, 1 ladle at a time, until the rice is al dente.

4. Stir in the zucchini, and cook for 1 minute. Stir in the cheese, and season with the salt and pepper. Remove the bay leaf and discard it.

5. Stir in the chives and serve the risotto immediately.

Roasting an Eggplant

Pierce the outside of the eggplant a few times with a knife. Place the eggplant on a hot gas or charcoal grill. Grill the eggplant for 20–30 minutes or until the skin is completely charred and the inside is soft. Let it cool for 10 minutes. Cut the eggplant open lengthwise and scoop out the softened flesh, discarding the charred skin.

DOMATORIZO (TOMATO RICE)

Add a few golden raisins and pine nuts to this recipe for some extra texture and varied flavor.

Serves 4

1 large onion, finely chopped

½ cup extra-virgin olive oil

1 cup Arborio rice

1 cup fresh tomato juice (or strained tomato pulp)

3 tablespoons dry white wine

2 cups water

1 tablespoon tomato paste

Salt and pepper to taste

¼ cup pine nuts and/or golden sultana raisins (optional)

½ cup crumbled or cubed Greek feta cheese

1 pinch dried Greek oregano

1 green onion

1. In a medium-size saucepan, sauté onion in olive oil until soft; add rice and continue to stir into onion at high heat for 2 minutes.

2. Add tomato juice and wine to the rice; let simmer for a few minutes, stirring often to keep it from sticking to the pan's bottom.

3. In a separate, smaller saucepan, mix 2 cups water with tomato paste and bring to boil. Add to the simmering rice along with salt and pepper to taste (and the optional pine nuts and raisins); stir well. Cover; simmer over medium-low heat for 15 minutes. Make sure to occasionally stir the rice (about every 2–3 minutes or so) to ensure it does not stick to the bottom of the pan.

4. When the rice is cooked, remove the saucepan from the heat; cover with a cotton cloth before covering with a lid. Let stand 10–15 minutes.

5. Spoon the rice into serving bowls and add some feta on top. Sprinkle feta with a pinch of dried Greek oregano and garnish with finely slivered or chopped green onion.

GRANDMA'S PLIGOURI (BULGUR MEDLEY)

Blanched almonds and raw walnuts can also be added as a garnish when serving this dish.

Serves 4

1 medium-size onion, diced

1 tablespoon butter

1 tablespoon extra-virgin olive oil

½ cup chopped button mushrooms

1 small handful golden raisins (sultanas)

¼ cup pine nuts

2 cups Basic Vegetable Stock or Chicken or Turkey Stock (see recipes in Chapter 2) (or water with a bouillon cube)

1 teaspoon ground cumin

Salt and pepper to taste

1 cup medium bulgur

1 tablespoon petimezi (concentrated Greek grape must syrup, called Sapa by Italians) or honey

½ cup roasted chestnuts, peeled and cut in half (approximately 12 chestnuts)

1 teaspoon sesame seeds (raw and/or black)

1. In a medium-size saucepan, sauté onion in butter and olive oil over medium heat until soft, 3 minutes or so.

2. Add mushrooms, raisins, and pine nuts to the pan; continue to sauté for another 2 minutes, stirring regularly.

3. Add stock, cumin, salt, and pepper. Turn heat to medium-high and bring to a boil; add bulgur and petimezi and cook while stirring well for about 3 minutes. (Note: If you cannot find any petimezi, some Greek thyme honey makes a good substitute.)

4. Add chestnuts; stir well. Cover and lower the heat to medium-low; allow to simmer for 20 minutes or so, until all the liquid is absorbed.

5. Uncover and stir thoroughly from the bottom and sides; cover with a tea or paper towel before replacing the lid (to eliminate any steam-water built up in the lid from running back into the pan when uncovered for serving). Remove from heat and set aside for 10 minutes. Garnish with sesame seeds, both black and raw, then serve.

PRASSORIZO (LEEKS AND RICE)

Try adding some crumbled feta cheese with a sprinkling of lemon over the top of this dish when serving.

Serves 4–6

6 large leeks

5 cups water

4 green onions, chopped

⅓ cup fresh dill, finely chopped

¼ cup fresh mint, finely chopped

½ tablespoon dried thyme

Salt and fresh-ground pepper to taste

1 cup white/Italian-style/Arborio rice

⅓ cup extra-virgin olive oil

1 lemon

1. Wash leeks well and cut white ends into thick slices; do not use the green part of the leeks.

2. Add 5 cups water to a large saucepan and bring to a boil. Add leeks, green onions, dill, mint, thyme, salt, and pepper; cook uncovered over medium heat for about 20 minutes.

3. Once leeks are noticeably soft, add rice and stir well. Cover and simmer over medium-low heat for about 20 minutes, stirring occasionally.

4. Add olive oil; cook 3–4 more minutes. Serve warm with lemon juice sprinkled over top.

Eat Your Veggies

In Mediterranean countries, vegetables are not only used as garnishes or sides to mains, they also comprise entire meals in themselves.

MAKARONADA (SPAGHETTI WITH MEAT SAUCE)

Well-stocked cheese shops should carry Greek myzithra cheese. Use it if you can find it, for an authentic flavor.

Serves 4

⅓ cup extra-virgin olive oil

1 white onion, diced

1 pound lean ground veal

Salt and pepper to taste

¼ cup white wine

1½ cups strained tomato sauce or ¼ cup tomato paste diluted in 1½ cups water

1 medium-sized cinnamon stick

2 bay leaves

1 clove garlic, whole

1 pound spaghetti-style pasta

Grated myzithra cheese (or Parmesan)

1. Heat olive oil in a large pan; sauté onion until soft. Add ground veal; stir well to break up thoroughly. Keep stirring over medium-high heat for 5 minutes, or until meat is browned.

2. Once the meat is browned, add salt and pepper, wine, and tomato sauce; mix well. Bring to a boil.

3. Add cinnamon stick, bay leaves, and garlic clove, and cover with sauce; reduce heat to medium-low. Cover the pot, leaving it slightly uncovered to allow water to evaporate as steam; simmer for 30 minutes. The sauce should reduce so that the water is steamed away and the tomato- and cinnamon-hinted olive oil is left behind with the meat. When ready, the meat will have absorbed all of the liquid. Remove bay leaves and cinamon stick.

4. Boil and strain pasta. Sprinkle generously with grated myzithra cheese; spoon meat sauce over top. Make sure to stir sauce first to get some orange-tinted olive oil in each helping.

PILAFI (RICE PILAF)

For presentation purposes, a bundt cake–style mold can be used for this recipe, and the cavity in its center may be filled with sautéed mushrooms and onions, or even cubed and lightly sautéed vegetables of your choice.

Serves 4–6

5 cups Basic Vegetable Stock (see recipe in Chapter 2) (or equivalent water and stock cubes)

2 tablespoons butter

2 tablespoons extra-virgin olive oil

1 bay leaf

Salt and fresh-ground pepper to taste

2 cups of white/Italian style/Arborio rice

1. In a large saucepan, add stock, butter, olive oil, bay leaf, salt, and pepper; bring to a boil. Add rice and stir well; once it has resumed boiling, cover and reduce heat to medium-low. Simmer for 20 minutes, stirring occasionally with a wooden spoon so the rice does not stick to the bottom of the pan.

2. Once the water has been fully absorbed, uncover and fluff rice with a fork. Cover and remove from heat; let stand for 5 minutes.

3. Uncover the pan and remove the bay leaf. Spoon rice into a mold; let stand a couple of minutes before turning pilaf out onto presentation plate.

SAM'S GREEK RIGATONI

Capers also make a good addition to this dish.

Serves up to 4

½ pound rigatoni shape pasta

¾ cup kalamata black olives

10 sun-dried tomatoes

½ pound Greek feta cheese

⅓ cup extra-virgin olive oil

1 tablespoon dried oregano

Fresh-ground black pepper

1. Bring salted water to boil; cook pasta according to directions on package.

2. Pit and chop olives into pieces (not too small). Chop sun-dried tomatoes into ribbons. Cut feta into small cubes.

3. Heat olive oil in a large sauté pan.

4. Drain pasta well; add to the heated olive oil in the sauté pan. Add feta and sun-dried tomatoes; heat through by tossing repeatedly for a couple of minutes until cheese just starts to melt.

5. Season with oregano and pepper; give a couple more tosses to the pan and serve hot.

Serious Cheese Eaters!

Feta cheese accounts for well over half of the roughly 60 pounds of cheese the average Greek consumes in a year. No other nation eats as much cheese, not even the French.

CHAPTER 7

VEGETABLE AND LEGUME ENTRÉES

TOMATO-AND-FETA STUFFED PEPPERS

If you're brave, try this dish with hot banana peppers. Serve these peppers with crusty bread and ouzo.

Serves 4

1½ teaspoons salt, divided

8 (5-inch) sweet peppers or banana peppers

2 cups crumbled feta cheese

3 large ripe tomatoes, seeded and cut into ¼-inch strips

½ cup extra-virgin olive oil, divided

1 teaspoon dried oregano

1. Preheat the oven to 400°F. Fill a medium-size pot with water and bring it to a boil. Add 1 teaspoon of salt to the water and allow it to return to a boil. Add the peppers and simmer over medium-low heat for 5–6 minutes, and then remove them from the water with a slotted spoon. Run the peppers under cold water until just cool. Pat the peppers dry.

2. Place a pepper on your work surface. Leaving the top intact, slice the pepper open (lengthwise) and carefully remove seeds (optional). Insert enough feta cheese into the opening of the pepper to line the entire length. Insert strips of tomato along the feta. Try and enclose the filling as much as possible. Repeat with the remaining peppers.

3. Place the peppers in a small baking dish that will tightly hold them. Drizzle tops of the peppers with ¼ cup oil and then sprinkle with the oregano and remaining salt. Cover with foil and bake for 20 minutes. Remove the foil and bake uncovered for another 5 minutes or until most of the liquid has evaporated.

4. Drizzle remaining oil over peppers and serve hot.

ARTICHOKES À LA POLITA

Recipes with the term polita *refer to dishes from Constantinople/Istanbul.*

Serves 4

¼ cup extra-virgin olive oil

2 medium onions, peeled and sliced

4 medium potatoes, peeled and cut into thirds

3 carrots, peeled and cut into 2-inch pieces

1 tablespoon tomato paste

12 medium artichokes, outer layers peeled, trimmed, halved, and chokes removed

2½ teaspoons salt

¾ teaspoon pepper

1 cup peas, frozen (thawed) or fresh

½ cup chopped fresh dill

1 large lemon, cut into wedges (optional)

1. Heat the oil in a large pot over medium-high heat. Stir in onions, potatoes, and carrots. Reduce the heat to medium and cover. Simmer for 15–20 minutes.

2. Add the tomato paste, artichokes, salt, pepper, and enough water to cover the vegetables. Bring to a boil, cover the pot, and reduce the temperature to medium. Cook for 10 minutes or until the artichokes are tender.

3. Gently stir in the peas and dill. Take the pot off the heat, and allow the peas to cook for 5 minutes. Serve hot with lemon wedges.

OKRA STEW

To prevent okra from becoming slimy, trim blemishes from the stems and keep the okra intact during cooking.

Serves 4

¼ cup extra-virgin olive oil

2 medium onions, peeled and sliced

1½ pounds okra (fresh or frozen), stems trimmed

½ cup canned plum tomatoes, hand-crushed

½ cup chopped fresh parsley

3 or 4 cloves garlic, peeled and sliced

5 or 6 allspice berries

2 cups Basic Vegetable Stock (see recipe in Chapter 2)

2½ teaspoons salt

¾ teaspoon pepper

4 large potatoes, peeled and cut in half

1. Heat oil in a large pot over medium-high heat. Add the onions and sauté for 2 minutes. Cover the pan, reduce the heat to medium-low, and simmer for 10 minutes.

2. Add the okra, tomatoes, parsley, garlic, allspice, and stock. Increase the heat to medium-high and bring the mixture to a boil. Season with salt and pepper.

3. Cover, reduce heat to medium-low, and simmer for 20 minutes. Add the potatoes and cook for another 25 minutes or until fork-tender. Serve warm.

CAULIFLOWER STIFADO WITH KALE AND KALAMATA OLIVES

This is a vegetarian version of stifado, a Greek dish usually made with beef. Kale is high in beta carotene, vitamin C, and calcium.

Serves 4

1 head cauliflower, leaves removed and trimmed

½ cup extra-virgin olive oil

1 medium onion, peeled and sliced

3 or 4 cloves garlic, peeled and minced

2 or 3 bay leaves

1 large red bell pepper, stemmed, seeded, and chopped

1½ tablespoons tomato paste

3 tablespoons chopped fresh rosemary

1 cup pearl onions, blanched and skins removed

6 or 7 small potatoes, skin on, washed and cut in half

3–4 cups hot Basic Vegetable Stock (see recipe in Chapter 2) or water

2½ teaspoons salt

¾ teaspoon pepper

3–4 cups kale, stemmed and washed

1 cup kalamata olives

1 teaspoon dried oregano

1 tablespoon red wine vinegar

1. Turn the cauliflower over and cut off the florets (run a small knife down and around the stalk).

2. Heat the oil in a large pot over medium-high heat for 30 seconds. Add cauliflower and cook for 5 minutes or until the cauliflower is browned. Remove the cauliflower with a slotted spoon and set aside.

3. Reduce the heat to medium, and add the onions, garlic, bay leaves, and peppers to the pot. Cook for 5–6 minutes. Add tomato paste, rosemary, pearl onions, and potatoes. Stir and cook for 1 minute.

4. Add enough stock or hot water to cover the potatoes. Add salt and pepper. Cover the pot and simmer for 20 minutes.

5. Uncover the pot, and add the cauliflower (stem-side down) and kale. Cover the pot, and simmer for another 10 minutes or until the kale wilts. Add the olives. Simmer uncovered for 5 minutes or until the sauce thickens to your liking.

6. Add the oregano and red wine vinegar. Do not stir the pot or the cauliflower might break up. Shake the pot back and forth to mix. Remove bay leaves. Serve hot.

POTATOES PLAKI

Plaki *is a Greek term referring to a dish of tomatoes and vegetables baked in extra-virgin olive oil. Potatoes are not just a side dish; they can be the star attraction! Serve with crusty bread to dip into the sauce.*

Serves 6

6 large Yukon gold or other yellow potatoes, peeled and quartered

2 or 3 cloves garlic, peeled and smashed

1 medium onion, peeled and chopped

½ large red bell pepper, stemmed, seeded, and sliced into ¼-inch slices

½ large green bell pepper, stemmed, seeded, and sliced into ¼-inch slices

½ medium carrot, peeled, halved lengthwise, and sliced

1 large ripe tomato, passed through a box grater (or ¾ cup vegetable cocktail)

1 teaspoon sweet paprika

2 bay leaves

1 teaspoon crushed red pepper flakes

1 teaspoon dried oregano

1 cup hot Basic Vegetable Stock (see recipe in Chapter 2)

2 teaspoons salt

1 teaspoon pepper

⅓ cup extra-virgin olive oil

1. Preheat the oven to 425°F. In a deep, medium-size baking dish, add the potatoes, garlic, onions, red pepper, green pepper, carrot, tomato, paprika, bay leaves, red pepper flakes, and oregano. Stir to combine the ingredients. Stir in the hot Basic Vegetable Stock. Season with salt and pepper.

2. Drizzle the oil over the vegetables. Place the baking dish on middle rack of the oven and bake for 45–50 minutes, or until the tops of the potatoes are crisp but there is still some sauce in the dish.

3. Allow the dish to cool for 5 minutes; remove the bay leaves, then serve hot.

BAKED GIGANTES BEANS

Gigantes beans are also known as elephant or butter beans. Turn leftovers into an appetizer by warming up the beans and serving them on toasted bread.

Serves 8

16 ounces dried gigantes beans

1 large carrot, peeled, halved lengthwise, and cut into ½-inch pieces

1 large stalk celery, trimmed and diced

3 bay leaves

4 cloves garlic, peeled and smashed

½ cup extra-virgin olive oil

2 large onions, peeled and chopped

½ cup tomato sauce

1½ tablespoons tomato paste

1 teaspoon smoked paprika

1 teaspoon salt

½ teaspoon pepper

1 cup finely chopped fresh parsley

¼ cup finely chopped fresh dill

1. Preheat the oven to 375°F. Place the beans in a large pot. Fill the pot with enough water to cover the beans. Bring the water to a boil, and then reduce heat to medium and cook for 2 minutes. Drain the beans and place them back in the empty pot. Add the carrot, celery, bay leaves, and garlic. Fill the pot with enough water to cover the ingredients by 1 inch. Bring to a boil, and then the reduce heat to medium and cook for 45 minutes or until the beans are soft. Take the pot off the heat and set it aside.

2. Heat the oil in a large skillet over medium heat for 30 seconds. Add the onions and cook them for about 5 minutes or until they soften but are not brown. Stir in the tomato sauce, tomato paste, paprika, salt, pepper, and parsley. Set the skillet aside.

3. Using a slotted spoon, transfer the bean and vegetable mixture into a large casserole dish. Reserve the liquid from the beans. Carefully stir the onion mixture into the beans.

4. Pour in enough of the reserved liquid to cover everything in the casserole dish. Adjust the seasoning with salt and pepper, if necessary. Bake for 30–35 minutes.

5. Remove the dish from the oven, and stir in the dill. Place the dish back into the oven, and bake for another 10–15 minutes or until most of the liquid is gone and the top is just golden.

ROASTED BEETS WITH ALMOND-POTATO SKORDALIA

This dish is a perfect entrée, but can also be served as a side!

Serves 4

2 or 3 medium beets, trimmed but unpeeled

3 tablespoons extra-virgin olive oil, divided

½ teaspoons salt

2 tablespoons red wine vinegar

1 tablespoon fresh thyme leaves

2 cups Almond-Potato Skordalia (see recipe in Chapter 2)

3 scallions, ends trimmed and thinly sliced

¼ cup sliced almonds

1. Preheat the oven to 400°F. Place beets in the center of a large sheet of aluminum foil; drizzle them with 1 tablespoon of the oil. Tightly wrap the beets in the foil and place them on a baking sheet.

2. Bake beets for 30 minutes. Allow them to cool for 10 minutes. Unwrap the foil and discard it. Using the back of a knife, peel off the beet skins and slice the beets into wedges. In a large bowl, toss the beets, salt, remaining oil, vinegar, and the thyme. Reserve.

3. To plate, mound the skordalia on a platter and top it with the beets. Spoon some of the beet dressing over the top and garnish the dish with the scallions and the almonds.

ITALIAN GREEN BEANS WITH POTATOES

Switch up the nuts in this dish with either almonds or hazelnuts. This is a great recipe to use up leftover baked or boiled potatoes.

Serves 6

1 tablespoon extra-virgin olive oil

1¼ pounds Italian green beans, trimmed

2 cloves garlic, peeled and minced

2 large potatoes, peeled, cooked, and diced

½ cup Basic Vegetable Stock (see recipe in Chapter 2)

½ teaspoon dried oregano

¼ cup chopped fresh parsley

1 teaspoon salt

½ teaspoon pepper

¼ cup chopped walnuts, toasted

1. Heat the oil in a large skillet over medium heat for 30 seconds.

2. Add the beans, garlic, potatoes, stock, oregano, parsley, salt, and pepper. Cook for 8–10 minutes or until the beans are tender.

3. Adjust the seasoning with more salt and pepper, if necessary. Sprinkle the walnuts over the beans and serve.

ZUCCHINI PIE WITH HERBS AND CHEESE

This is a fantastic savory pie. Serve it with a simple green salad for a perfect brunch or lunch dish.

Serves 12

½ cup extra-virgin olive oil

12 scallions, ends trimmed and finely chopped

4 medium zucchini, 3 diced and 1 thinly sliced into rounds

½ teaspoon salt

5 large eggs

1 cup self-rising flour

1 teaspoon baking powder

1 cup strained Greek yogurt

1 cup crumbled feta cheese

1 cup grated kasseri (or Gouda) cheese

1 teaspoon pepper

2 teaspoons sweet paprika, divided

1 cup chopped fresh dill

1. Preheat the oven to 350°F. Heat the oil in a large skillet over medium heat for 30 seconds. Add the scallions, diced zucchini, and salt. Cook for about 20 minutes to soften the vegetables and evaporate half of their released liquids. Take the skillet off the heat and reserve.

2. Crack the eggs into a large bowl and whisk for 2 minutes. Stir in the flour and baking powder. Stir in the Greek yogurt. Stir in the cheeses and softened vegetables. Stir in the pepper, 1½ teaspoons of paprika, and the dill.

3. Pour the mixture into a large, deep, greased baking dish. Top the vegetables with zucchini slices and sprinkle with the remaining paprika.

4. Place the dish on the middle rack and bake for 1 hour. Allow the pie to cool for about 15 minutes before cutting it into slices and serving.

Cheese Substitutions

Kasseri cheese is a Greek sheep's milk cheese that is often served on its own. If you can't find kasseri, Gruyère or Gouda works just as well.

POTATO AND FENNEL GRATIN

Use evaporated milk instead of heavy cream to reduce the fat content without sacrificing flavor or richness.

Serves 10

1 tablespoon unsalted butter, softened

¼ cup extra-virgin olive oil

4 cups sliced fennel, trimmed and outer layer removed

1 large onion, peeled and sliced

4 or 5 large Yukon gold potatoes, peeled and thinly sliced

1 cup heavy cream

1 cup whole milk

1 tablespoon fresh thyme leaves

1 teaspoon salt, divided

½ teaspoon pepper, divided

2½ cups grated Gouda cheese, divided

½ cup bread crumbs

1. Preheat the oven to 375°F. Grease a large, deep baking dish with the butter.

2. Heat the oil in a large skillet over medium heat for 30 seconds. Add the fennel and onions. Cook the vegetables for 15 minutes or until they are soft and translucent. Set aside.

3. In a large bowl, combine the potatoes, cream, milk, and thyme. Layer the bottom of the baking dish with one-third of the potato slices (leave cream/milk in bowl for later). Spread half of the fennel mixture evenly over the potatoes. Sprinkle ½ teaspoon of the salt and ¼ teaspoon of the pepper over the fennel mixture and top with 1 cup of the cheese. Repeat another potato layer, another fennel and cheese layer, and finish with a final layer of potatoes.

4. Pour enough of the cream/milk over the baking dish to just cover the gratin. Using your fingers, press down gently to even out and compact the potatoes. Sprinkle the remaining cheese evenly over the top. Sprinkle the bread crumbs over the top.

5. Bake the gratin for 90 minutes or until the potatoes are very tender and the top is brown and bubbling. Allow the gratin to cool for 20 minutes before slicing and serving.

Fabulous Fennel

Fennel is a versatile and healthful vegetable. It is rich in potassium, iron, vitamin C, and dietary fiber! Fennel's sweet anise, or licorice, flavor mellows as it cooks so it pairs deliciously with potatoes.

EGGPLANT ROLL-UPS

This is the same concept as lasagna roll-ups. Instead of rolling up lasagna sheets, use eggplant slices. Serve this dish with a simple green salad and red wine.

Serves 6

5 ounces ricotta cheese

5 ounces feta cheese, crumbled

1 large egg

½ cup pine nuts, toasted

3 tablespoons bread crumbs

1 tablespoon chopped fresh mint

1 tablespoon chopped fresh dill

1 teaspoon salt, divided

1 teaspoon pepper, divided

¼ cup plus 2 tablespoons extra-virgin olive oil, divided

1 medium onion, peeled and chopped

3 cloves garlic, peeled and minced

1 (28-ounce) can whole plum tomatoes, hand crushed

1 tablespoon chopped fresh parsley

1 teaspoon dried oregano

4 long, slender Japanese eggplants

16 medium slices mozzarella cheese

1. In a large bowl combine ricotta, feta, egg, pine nuts, bread crumbs, mint, dill, ¼ teaspoon salt, and ¼ teaspoon pepper. Set aside.

2. Heat ¼ cup oil in a large skillet over medium heat. Add the onions and garlic, and cook for 5–7 minutes or until softened. Stir in tomatoes and bring to a boil. Reduce the heat to medium and simmer for 10 minutes until the sauce thickens. Stir in the parsley, oregano, ¼ teaspoon salt, and ¼ teaspoon pepper. Remove the sauce from the heat and set it aside.

3. Set the oven to broil. Cut the eggplants lengthwise into 16 (¼-inch) slices. Brush both sides of the slices with the remaining oil and season them with the remaining salt and pepper. Place the slices on a baking sheet, and broil them on one side for 3 minutes. Allow the eggplant to cool slightly. Preheat the oven to 350°F.

4. Spread half of the tomato sauce on the bottom of a large casserole dish. Spread 2 tablespoons of the cheese filling on the surface of each eggplant slice, and roll it up to form a bundle. Place the eggplant roll-up in the dish (seam-side down) on top of the tomato sauce. Repeat with the remaining eggplant slices. Pour the remaining tomato sauce over the roll-ups.

5. Top each roll-up with a slice of mozzarella cheese. Bake for 30–45 minutes or until the mozzarella is brown and bubbling. Serve immediately.

Bitter Eggplants

Eggplants are at their best when consumed in season and may become bitter when out of season. To remove the bitterness, slice the eggplant in half and sprinkle the white flesh with coarse salt. Set the eggplant on a plate, flesh-side down, for 15 minutes. The salt will draw out some of the bitter liquid.

VEGETABLE TOURLOU WITH BEANS

Tourlou *means "mixed-up vegetables" in Greek. Make your own version of tourlou by choosing your favorite vegetables for the dish. Tourlou is even tastier when it is made the day before serving. Some crusty bread and a slab of feta cheese would pair nicely with this dish.*

Serves 6

¾ cup extra-virgin olive oil, divided

2 large onions, peeled and sliced

5 or 6 cloves garlic, peeled and minced

2 teaspoons salt, divided

1 teaspoon pepper, divided

2 large zucchini, sliced

2 long, slender Japanese eggplants, sliced

6 medium plum or Roma tomatoes, chopped

1 cup chopped fresh parsley

1 tablespoon fresh thyme leaves

1 cup chopped fresh basil

1 pound green beans, trimmed, blanched, at room temperature (see Blanching Vegetables sidebar)

1. Preheat the oven to 375°F. Heat ½ cup of the oil in a large skillet over medium heat for 30 seconds. Add the onions, garlic, ¼ teaspoon of the salt, and ¼ teaspoon of the pepper. Cook the mixture for 6–7 minutes or until the onions are translucent. Spread the onion mixture evenly over the bottom of a medium casserole dish.

2. In a medium bowl, combine the zucchini, eggplant, tomatoes, parsley, thyme, and the remaining oil. Season with the remaining salt and the pepper. Top the onion mixture with the vegetables, and stir to combine the ingredients.

3. Cover the dish with aluminum foil and bake for 1 hour. Remove the foil and sprinkle the top with basil. Allow the tourlou to cool for 10 minutes before serving it. Vegetables can be cooled completely, stored in the refrigerator, and reheated the next day.

4. To serve the tourlou, place the beans on the bottom of a plate or platter, and then top them with the warm vegetable mixture (including juices).

Blanching Vegetables

Blanching refers to a cooking technique in which vegetables are first boiled briefly in salted water; then, the cooking process is stopped quickly by plunging or "shocking" the vegetables in ice water. This technique keeps vegetables tender and preserves their bright natural colors.

CATALAN POTATOES

This dish comes from Barcelona, the capital of Catalonia, a province of Spain

Serves 6

½ cup extra-virgin olive oil

6 cloves garlic, peeled, 3 whole and 3 minced

1 large red onion, peeled and chopped

2 large Idaho or russet potatoes, peeled and sliced into ¼-inch slices

1 teaspoon salt, divided

½ teaspoon pepper, divided

4 medium plum tomatoes, peeled, seeded, and diced

1. Heat the oil in an 8-inch or 9-inch cast-iron pan over medium heat for 30 seconds. Add the 3 whole garlic cloves. Cook the garlic for 8 minutes or until brown. Discard the garlic.

2. Add the onions to the pan; cook them for 10–12 minutes or until lightly browned. Remove the onions from the pan with a slotted spoon and reserve.

3. In the pan, layer half of the potato slices on top of the oil. Season the potatoes with ½ teaspoon of the salt and ¼ teaspoon of the pepper. Top the potatoes with an even layer of the reserved onions, tomatoes, and remaining garlic. Top with the remaining potato slices and season with the remaining salt and pepper.

4. Cook for 15 minutes or until the bottom potato layer is browned. Flip the potatoes over from the pan onto a wide plate. Using the plate, slide the potatoes back into the pan (bottom-side up). Press down on the potatoes with a spatula.

5. Cook the potatoes for another 15 minutes or until the bottom layer is brown and the potatoes are tender throughout. Slide the potatoes from the pan onto a serving platter and serve immediately.

Cleaning a Cast-Iron Pan

Cleaning is an important step to keep your cast-iron pan in tiptop shape for a lifetime. Never use soap or steel wool, and never put your pan in the dishwasher! Wash your pan while it is still hot or warm with hot water and a sponge or brush. Dry the pan completely. Using a paper towel, lightly coat the inside of the pan with a little vegetable oil before storing it in a dry place.

SPINACH AND FETA GRATIN

If you can't find Graviera cheese, then Gruyère is a great substitution in this dish.

Serves 6

2 teaspoons salt, divided

2 pounds fresh spinach, thoroughly washed

¼ cup extra-virgin olive oil

2 medium onions, peeled and sliced

¼ cup all-purpose flour

2 cups whole milk

4 large eggs, beaten

½ cup chopped fresh dill

½ cup grated Graviera or Gruyère cheese

⅛ teaspoon grated nutmeg

1 teaspoon pepper

½ cup crumbled feta cheese

1. Preheat the oven to 375°F. Fill a large pot halfway with water. Bring the water to a boil over high heat. Add 1 teaspoon of the salt and the spinach (in batches). Boil the spinach for 6–7 minutes and then drain it. Reserve.

2. Heat the oil in a large skillet over medium for 30 seconds. Add the onions and the remaining salt. Cover and cook the onions for about 5 minutes, and then remove them from the heat. Allow the onions to cool.

3. In a large bowl, combine the cooled onions, spinach, flour, and milk. Stir in the eggs, dill, Graviera cheese, nutmeg, and pepper. Put the spinach mixture in a deep, medium-size baking dish. Top the spinach mixture evenly with the feta.

4. Bake on the middle rack of the oven for 35–40 minutes.

EGGPLANT PARMESAN

You can make this dish lighter by not frying the eggplant, but you won't get the same delicious result. Frying the eggplant coated in the egg and bread crumbs will make this a favorite dish.

Serves 10

½ cup extra-virgin olive oil plus more for frying, divided

2 medium onions, peeled and finely chopped

6–8 cloves garlic, peeled and minced

2 teaspoons salt, divided

1 teaspoon pepper, divided

2 (28-ounce) cans puréed tomatoes

1 cup all-purpose flour

4 large eggs

½ cup whole milk

3 cups bread crumbs

2 large eggplants, peeled and sliced lengthwise into ¼-inch slices

1¼ cups torn fresh basil, divided

½ cup grated Parmesan or Romano cheese, divided

1 cup grated mozzarella cheese, divided

16 medium slices mozzarella cheese

1. Heat ½ cup oil in a large skillet over medium heat for 30 seconds. Add the onions, garlic, 1 teaspoon salt, and ½ teaspoon pepper. Cook for 5–7 minutes or until softened. Add the tomatoes, increase the heat, and bring to a boil. Lower to medium-low and simmer for 10 minutes or until the sauce thickens. Set aside.

2. In a medium bowl, combine flour with remaining salt and pepper. In a second medium bowl, beat the eggs with milk. Put the bread crumbs in a third medium bowl. Dredge each eggplant slice in the flour mixture, then the eggs, and finally the bread crumbs. Set aside.

3. Heat ½ inch of the oil in a large skillet over medium-high heat for 1 minute. Fry eggplant slices in batches on both sides for 1–2 minutes or until just golden. Set slices on a baking sheet lined with paper towels.

4. Preheat the oven to 350°F. Set aside 1 cup of tomato sauce. To a large, deep baking dish add a couple of ladles of tomato sauce. Top with a layer of eggplant slices. Top the slices with one-quarter of the remaining tomato sauce. Sprinkle ¼ cup basil, 2 tablespoons Parmesan, and ¼ cup grated mozzarella over the tomato sauce. Continue repeating the layers three more times. Top the last layer with sliced mozzarella.

5. Place the dish on the middle rack of the oven and bake it for 25–30 minutes or until the cheese is brown and bubbling. Allow the dish to cool for 15–20 minutes. Serve it with the reserved warm tomato sauce and garnish with the remaining fresh basil.

IMAM BAILDI

This wonderful stuffed-eggplant dish can be served on its own or as a side dish. Be sure to have your very best extra-virgin olive oil on hand so your guests can drizzle some over their eggplant.

Serves 6

6 medium eggplants, stems removed

3 teaspoons salt, divided

½ cup extra-virgin olive oil, divided

4 medium onions, peeled and sliced thinly, divided

1 green bell pepper, seeded and sliced

5 or 6 whole allspice berries, wrapped tightly in thin cheesecloth

1 (14-ounce) can whole tomatoes, hand crushed

1 teaspoon pepper

10 cloves garlic, peeled and thinly sliced

2 teaspoons dried oregano

1 teaspoon fresh thyme leaves

½ cup chopped fresh parsley

2 medium tomatoes, sliced thinly

1. Preheat the oven to 375°F. Cut the eggplants in half lengthwise. Using a spoon, hollow out the eggplants leaving a ¼-inch-thick shell. Reserve the flesh. Evenly sprinkle 1½ teaspoons salt over the hollowed-out shells. Place the eggplants flesh-side down on a plate. Coarsely chop the scooped-out flesh, place it in a strainer, and sprinkle with ½ teaspoon salt. Set aside.

2. Heat ¼ cup oil in a large skillet over medium-high heat for 30 seconds. Add two-thirds of the onions, peppers, and allspice. Cook for 1 minute. Reduce the heat to medium and cover. Cook for 10–15 minutes or until the vegetables are softened.

3. Stir in the chopped eggplant, crushed tomatoes, and remaining salt and pepper. Cook 20–30 minutes or until reduced to a thick, chunky sauce. Remove the allspice. Adjust the seasoning with more salt and pepper, if necessary. Stir in the garlic, oregano, thyme, and parsley.

4. Place the inverted eggplant shells upright in a large, shallow baking dish. Pat the insides dry with a paper towel. Spoon the vegetable sauce evenly into each eggplant shell. Pour enough hot water around the eggplants to come halfway up the sides.

5. Cover each eggplant with tomato slices and the reserved sliced onions. Drizzle the remaining oil evenly over the eggplants. Bake for 45–60 minutes or until most of the water has evaporated and the tops are golden brown. Serve warm.

The Fainting Priest

Imam Baildi, which means "Fainting Priest," is originally a Turkish dish, but it is also very popular in Greece. The story behind Imam Baildi is that when a Muslim priest (or imam) tasted this dish of olive oil, sweet eggplant, and vegetables for the first time, he fainted because it was so delicious.

ZUCCHINI BLOSSOMS WITH RICE

Serve these delightful zucchini blossoms with Feta-Yogurt Sauce (see recipe in Chapter 2).

Serves 6

30–35 zucchini blossoms, washed, stemmed, and small outer leaves removed

½ cup extra-virgin olive oil, divided

1 large onion, peeled and chopped

2 cloves garlic, peeled and minced

2 medium tomatoes, peeled and grated

1 cup Arborio rice, rinsed

¼ cup dry white wine

2 medium zucchini (1 trimmed and grated, and 1 trimmed and thinly sliced)

½ cup chopped fresh parsley

2 tablespoons chopped fresh mint

2 tablespoons chopped fresh dill

2 teaspoons salt

1 teaspoon pepper

2 cups hot Basic Vegetable Stock (see recipe in Chapter 2)

1. Place the blossoms in a large bowl with warm water for 10 minutes. Rinse the blossoms under cool tap water and set them upside-down to dry.

2. Heat ¼ cup of the oil in a large skillet over medium heat for 30 seconds. Add the onions, garlic, and tomatoes. Simmer for 5–7 minutes or until the onions are translucent. Stir in the rice, wine, and grated zucchini. Simmer for another 15 minutes. If most of the cooking liquid has dried up, add 2 tablespoons of hot water. Stir in the parsley, mint, and dill, and then take the skillet off the heat. Season with salt and pepper. Preheat the oven to 350°F.

3. Line the bottom of a large baking dish (with lid) with sliced zucchini. Gently open a zucchini blossom and insert 1 teaspoon of the rice mixture. Fold the petals inward to seal the filling and place the blossom in the dish. Repeat this process for the remaining blossoms. Arrange the blossoms in a taut, circular pattern in the dish.

4. Add the stock and drizzle the blossoms with the remaining oil. Place an inverted (ovenproof) plate over the blossoms, and cover the baking dish. Bake 30–40 minutes or until the rice has cooked. Serve warm or at room temperature.

PATATES LEMONATES (LEMON POTATOES)

Yukon gold potatoes are preferable when preparing this recipe.

Serves 4–6

2½ pounds potatoes, washed and peeled

½ cup Greek extra-virgin olive oil

Salt and pepper to taste

Juice of 2 lemons

1 tablespoon finely shredded lemon rind

1 heaping tablespoon dried oregano

1. Preheat the oven to 375°F.

2. Cut potatoes into thin wedges slightly bigger than fries but not too big, as you want them to cook through and crisp slightly on outside.

3. Spray or sprinkle olive oil to coat the bottom and sides of a deep-walled, medium-size baking pan (stone bakeware works best).

4. Spread potato slices evenly across the bottom of the pan; liberally sprinkle salt and fresh-ground pepper on top.

5. Add enough water to almost but not quite cover the bottom layer of potatoes. Add lemon juice and lemon rind; using your hands, mix potatoes well in the pan to ensure an even soaking and help spread salt, pepper, and lemon zest.

6. Pour remaining olive oil over top of potatoes, making sure to cover all of them; sprinkle oregano over everything. Bake for approximately 50 minutes; mix potatoes well at the halfway mark, to guarantee a thorough and even baking. When potatoes are visibly crisping at edges it is time to remove the pan or turn the oven off.

MEATLESS MOUSSAKA

For best results and perfect slices, bake the moussaka early and allow it to cool completely. Reheat the moussaka at 300°F for 15 minutes, then slice it and serve.

Serves 8

2 large eggplants, stemmed and cut into ½-inch slices

3 large zucchini, stemmed and cut into ½-inch slices

½ cup extra-virgin olive oil, divided

4 teaspoons salt, divided

1½ teaspoons pepper, divided

4 medium potatoes, peeled and quartered

¼ cup unsalted butter, softened

1 cup whole milk, hot

2 large eggs, beaten

½ cup Greek yogurt

¾ cup grated kefalotyri cheese or Pecorino Romano cheese, divided

⅛ teaspoon grated nutmeg

1 medium onion, peeled and finely chopped

2 cups tomato sauce

2 bay leaves

3 or 4 allspice berries

½ teaspoon dried oregano

1 cup bread crumbs, divided

1. Preheat the oven to 375°F. Brush both sides of the eggplant and zucchini slices with ¼ cup of the oil and season them with 1½ teaspoons of salt and ½ teaspoon of pepper. Place the slices on a baking sheet. Bake them for 15 minutes, flip the slices over, and bake them for another 10 minutes. Place the baked slices on a tray lined with paper towels to absorb excess oil. Reserve.

2. In a medium pot over high heat, put the potatoes, 1 teaspoon of the salt, and enough water to cover the potatoes by 1 inch. Cover the pot and bring the water to a boil. Reduce the heat to medium and cook the potatoes for 15 minutes or until they are fork-tender. Drain the potatoes and return them to the empty pot. Add the butter and milk and mash the potatoes. Season them with ½ teaspoon salt and ½ teaspoon pepper. Remove the pot from the heat and allow the potatoes to cool. Once the potatoes are cooled, add the eggs and yogurt, and whip the potatoes using a hand mixer. Stir in ½ cup of the cheese and the nutmeg.

3. Heat the remaining oil in a large skillet over medium heat for 30 seconds. Add the onions and cook them for 5 minutes. Add the tomato sauce, bay leaves, and allspice. Increase the heat to medium-high and bring the sauce to a boil. Reduce the heat to medium-low and season the sauce with the remaining salt and pepper. Cook for 15–20 minutes or until the sauce thickens. Remove the bay leaves and allspice from the sauce. Add the oregano. Remove the skillet from the heat.

4. To assemble the moussaka, line the bottom of a greased large, deep baking dish with ⅓ cup of the bread crumbs. Layer the eggplant slices over the bread crumbs so they completely cover the bottom of the dish. Spread half of the tomato sauce evenly over the eggplant slices. Sprinkle another ⅓ cup of the bread crumbs over the sauce. Layer the zucchini slices over the bread crumbs to completely cover the surface. Top the zucchini slices with the remaining sauce and bread crumbs.

5. Evenly spread the cooled mashed potatoes over the entire surface of the dish. Sprinkle the remaining cheese over the mashed potatoes. Bake on the middle rack of the oven for 30–40 minutes or until the top is golden. Allow the moussaka to cool for at least 30 minutes before slicing it and serving.

ARTICHOKE MOUSSAKA

Béchamel is an easy sauce to make and can be used to top all sorts of casseroles. This dish uses kefalotyri cheese, a sharp Greek sheep's milk cheese.

Serves 6–8

8–10 medium artichokes, outer layers peeled, trimmed, and choke removed

3 tablespoons fresh lemon juice

½ cup extra-virgin olive oil

2 large potatoes, peeled and cut into ⅛-inch thick slices

2 teaspoons salt, divided

1 teaspoon pepper, divided

2 large onions, peeled and thinly sliced

2 cups fresh peas or thawed frozen peas, divided

1 cup bread crumbs, divided

1 recipe Béchamel Sauce, divided (see recipe in Chapter 2)

2 tablespoons chopped fresh oregano or 1 teaspoon dried oregano, divided

¼ cup chopped fresh dill, divided

1 cup crumbled feta cheese, divided

¼ cup grated kefalotyri cheese or Pecorino Romano cheese

1. In a medium bowl, put the artichokes, lemon juice, and enough water to cover the artichokes. Set it aside. Heat the oil in a large skillet over medium-high heat for 30 seconds. When the oil is hot, fry the potato slices (in batches) for 5–7 minutes or until they are golden and cooked through. Transfer the fried potatoes to a tray lined with paper towels, and season with 1 teaspoon of the salt and ¼ teaspoon of the pepper. Reserve.

2. Discard all but ¼ cup of the oil from the skillet and heat it to medium. Add half of the onions and 1 cup of the peas. Season them with ½ teaspoon salt and ¼ teaspoon pepper. Place the artichokes on top of the onions and peas. Top the artichokes with the remaining layer of onions and peas. Season with the remaining salt and pepper, and cover the skillet. Simmer the ingredients for about 15 minutes or until the artichokes are fork-tender. Uncover the skillet, and cook off the excess liquid for 5 minutes. Then set it aside. Preheat the oven to 350°F.

3. To assemble the moussaka, line the bottom of a greased large, deep baking dish with ¼ cup of the bread crumbs. Layer the bottom of the dish with the potatoes, slightly overlapping each other. Spread half of the Béchamel Sauce over the potatoes.

4. Transfer the top layer of onions and peas from the skillet to the dish and spread them evenly over the Béchamel Sauce. Sprinkle 1 tablespoon oregano, 2 tablespoons dill, ¼ cup bread crumbs, and ½ cup feta over the onions and peas. Transfer the artichokes from the skillet to the dish and spread them evenly over the top. Sprinkle ¼ cup of the bread crumbs evenly over the artichokes. Spread the final layer of onions and peas over the artichokes. Top with the remaining oregano, dill, bread crumbs, and feta.

5. Pour the remaining Béchamel Sauce over the layers and sprinkle the top with the kefalotyri cheese. Bake on the middle rack of the oven for 35–40 minutes or until the top is golden. Allow the moussaka to cool for at least 30 minutes before slicing and serving.

REVITHIA STO FOURNO (BAKED CHICKPEAS)

Canned or dried chickpeas can be used for this recipe. Dried chickpeas must be soaked overnight and boiled for 30 minutes before use.

Serves 2–4

1 (16.9-ounce) can chickpeas

¼ cup extra-virgin olive oil

4–6 whole cloves garlic

1 large bay leaf

1 cup water

1 tablespoon dried savory (or dried marjoram)

1 teaspoon dried thyme leaves

Salt and pepper to taste

1 large onion, quartered and thinly sliced

Juice of 1 lemon

1. Preheat the oven to 325°F.

2. Add chickpeas, olive oil, garlic cloves, bay leaf, and water to a small, high-walled, earthenware/Pyrex baking vessel. Sprinkle half of the dried savory, all of the thyme leaves, salt, and pepper over chickpeas; mix slightly to disperse herbs and seasonings.

3. Arrange sliced onion on top of chickpeas; sprinkle remaining dried savory on top.

4. Cover with a lid or aluminum foil; bake for 1½–2 hours.

5. Remove from the oven and let cool for 5–10 minutes while still covered. Remove the lid; add lemon juice, mix well, and serve.

Cooks and Poets

The ancient food writer Athenaeus claimed there was no difference between a poet and a cook as both were artists who enchanted the senses with their imagination and creativity.

MELITZANES YIAHNI (BRAISED EGGPLANT)

This eggplant dish is best served over a bed of rice.

Serves 4

2 large eggplants

¼ cup extra-virgin olive oil

1 medium-sized yellow onion, diced

3 cloves garlic, minced or pressed

2 cups pulped fresh tomatoes

1 cup water

1 tablespoon dried oregano

Salt and pepper to taste

2 tablespoons finely chopped fresh basil

2 tablespoons sesame seeds

1. Wash eggplant and cut into small cubes; place in a colander and sprinkle with salt. Place the colander over a plate; let stand for 30 minutes to drain the bitter juices.

2. Add 2 tablespoons of olive oil to a pan; add onion and sauté over medium heat until soft, about 5 minutes. Add garlic; mix 30 seconds. Add tomatoes and water; bring to a boil.

3. Rinse eggplant well and drain. Add to the pan with boiling sauce. Partially cover; simmer over medium-low heat for 30 minutes, until the eggplant is soft and the sauce has reduced. Stir occasionally; add oregano, salt, and pepper.

4. Add remaining olive oil to pan; stir well. Let simmer for another 15 minutes over medium-low heat. Just before removing from the stove, add basil and give a few quick stirs.

5. Serve hot over a bed of rice and garnish with sesame seeds.

BRIAMI (BAKED VEGETABLE MEDLEY)

Feel free to add radishes, peppers, sweet potatoes, or any other vegetable that takes your fancy to add more variety to this dish.

Serves 4

2 large eggplants, cubed

2 zucchini, cubed

2 large potatoes, cubed

2 large parsnips, peeled and thickly sliced

2 large carrots, peeled and thickly sliced

1 pound white button mushrooms, thickly sliced

1 large yellow onion, sliced

1 large red pepper, cut into strips

6 cloves garlic, cut in half

½ cup extra-virgin olive oil

1 tablespoon fresh rosemary, finely chopped

½ tablespoon dried oregano

Salt and pepper to taste

1. Preheat the oven to 400°F.

2. Wash eggplant and cut into small cubes; place in a colander and sprinkle with salt. Place the colander over a plate and let stand for 30 minutes to drain the bitter juices.

3. Wash and cut remaining vegetables; set aside until eggplant has drained.

4. Rinse eggplant and combine all the vegetables and garlic in a large baking dish; add olive oil and mix well. Sprinkle with rosemary, oregano, salt, and pepper; add enough water to cover the bottom half of the baking dish and contents.

5. Bake uncovered for 50–60 minutes, or until the water has been absorbed. Make sure to stir the vegetables at least once halfway through the cooking time, or as needed.

6. Serve warm.

CHICKPEA RISSOLES

These rissoles can be served warm or at room temperature with a tomato sauce or dip of your choosing.

Serves 4

1 pound chickpeas (soaked overnight if dry)

1 egg

1 tablespoon dried oregano or finely chopped fresh

3 tablespoons finely chopped fresh mint

3 tablespoons flour

1 teaspoon pepper

½ teaspoon salt

3 tablespoons bread crumbs

Vegetable oil for deep-frying

1. Boil chickpeas for 30 minutes, or until soft; drain and purée with egg, oregano, mint, flour, pepper, and salt.

2. Scrape chickpea purée into a mixing bowl. Add bread crumbs; mix well.

3. Spread a sheet of wax paper on the counter/cutting board. Spoon about ⅓ of the chickpea mixture in an even line along the horizontal center of the wax paper. Fold over the bottom half of wax paper and, using the flat of your hand, roll mixture into a long cylindrical shape (similar to using a sushi roller). Cut resulting cylindrical shape into 3 equal pieces or "sausages." Repeat to use up the rest of the chickpea mixture.

4. Place rissoles into sizzling oil; fry for 5–6 minutes, making sure to turn often if the oil does not completely cover the rissoles. Remove with a slotted spoon; set on paper towels a few minutes to drain.

BEETS WITH YOGURT

This recipe does not require the yogurt, as the beets can be eaten on their own.

Serves 2–4

2 pounds fresh red beets

3 cloves garlic, finely minced

¼ cup extra-virgin olive oil

¼ cup red wine vinegar

Salt and fresh-ground pepper

1 cup strained yogurt

1. Remove leaves from beets, leaving approximately 1 inch of stem along with the lower root, if still attached. Wash beets gently in cold water, making sure not to break the skin.

2. Place beets in a pot of cold water; cover and bring to a boil. Cook on medium heat until beets are cooked yet still firm, usually about 45–50 minutes.

3. Drain beets and run under cold water to cool for handling. Peel the skin away and slice into discs.

4. Combine beets, garlic, oil, and vinegar in a mixing bowl; toss thoroughly. Add salt and pepper. Cover and refrigerate for 2 hours. Serve with a good dollop of yogurt on the side.

Open-Air Markets

From Madrid to Athens, open-air markets bursting with seasonal produce are the preferred shopping sources for fresh vegetables, fruits, and herbs.

BLACK-EYED PEAS AND SWISS CHARD

Though Swiss chard is usually used in this dish, it is possible to substitute beet leaves when beets are in season.

Serves 4

1 cup dry black-eyed peas

¼ cup extra-virgin olive oil

1 teaspoon dried oregano

Salt and pepper

2 pounds Swiss chard

Juice of 1 lemon

1. Soak peas overnight. Drain and rinse before using.

2. Bring a pot of water to boil; simmer peas for 15 minutes.

3. Drain water from the pot. Add fresh water, olive oil, oregano, and salt and pepper; bring to a boil again. Simmer on medium-low heat for 30 minutes.

4. Chop Swiss chard leaves into ribbons; add to the pot after 30 minutes. Simmer for another 5 minutes.

5. Sprinkle with lemon juice. Serve warm or cold.

LENTIL-STUFFED PEPPERS

Use both red and yellow bell peppers for variety in color and flavor.

Serves 6

2 medium yellow onions

2 stalks celery

2 carrots

6 sprigs oregano

1 tablespoon olive oil

1 cup Basic Vegetable Stock (see recipe in Chapter 2) plus 3 cups, divided

3 cups red lentils

6 bell peppers

3 ounces feta cheese

Fresh-cracked black pepper, to taste

1. Finely dice the onions and celery. Peel and finely dice the carrots. Reserve the top parts of the oregano sprigs and chop the remaining leaves.

2. Heat the oil over medium heat in a large saucepot. Add the onions, carrots, and celery; sauté for 5 minutes, then add 1 cup Basic Vegetable Stock and the lentils. Simmer for 15–20 minutes, until the lentils are fully cooked.

3. Cut off the tops of the peppers, leaving the stems attached, and remove the seeds. Place the peppers in a shallow pot with the 3 cups Basic Vegetable Stock. Cover and simmer for 10 minutes, then remove from heat.

4. In a bowl, mix together the lentil mixture, the chopped oregano, feta, and black pepper; spoon the mixture into the peppers. Serve the peppers with the stem tops ajar. Garnish with reserved oregano tops.

KIDNEY BEAN CASSEROLE

Feel free to substitute any type of bean and vegetable purée to better suit your taste.

Serves 6

1 teaspoon olive oil

¼ bunch celery

1 yellow onion

½ head romaine lettuce

1 cup puréed carrots

1 cup Basic Vegetable Stock (see recipe in Chapter 2)

1 cup cooked kidney beans

½ cup cooked barley

3 sprigs thyme, leaves only

½ teaspoon dried oregano leaves

½ teaspoon chili powder

Fresh-cracked black pepper, to taste

1. Preheat the oven to 325°F. Grease a casserole or loaf pan with the oil.

2. Slice the celery and onion. Shred the romaine lettuce.

3. Blend together the carrot purée and stock.

4. In the prepared dish, layer the beans, celery, onions, barley, herbs, spices, and the carrot-stock mixture; cover and bake for 30–45 minutes. Serve topped with shredded romaine.

Using Thyme

When using thyme for flavoring, remove the whole cleaned sprigs after cooking. If you wish to leave the thyme in, strip the stem of its leaves and add only the leaves to your dish. Or, you could even use thyme as a garnish.

LENTIL AND WALNUT CHILI

If you purchase already-shelled walnuts, be sure to spread them out on a flat surface and search for leftover shell fragments before using them.

Serves 6

2 cups red lentils

½ cup walnuts

2 shallots

4 cloves garlic

2 poblano peppers

1 tablespoon olive oil

1½ cups Basic Vegetable Stock (see recipe in Chapter 2)

2½ cups Fresh Tomato Sauce (see recipe in Chapter 2)

1 teaspoon cumin

1½ tablespoons chili powder

1 tablespoon honey

½ cup plain nonfat yogurt (optional)

1. Lay out the lentils on a baking sheet and pick out any stones. Chop the walnuts and slice the shallots. Mince the garlic and dice the peppers.

2. Heat the oil over medium heat in a saucepot. Add the shallots, garlic, and peppers; sauté for 1–2 minutes. Add all the remaining ingredients except the lentils and yogurt. Simmer for 1 hour, then add the lentils and cook for 30 minutes longer.

3. Ladle into bowls. Serve with a dollop of yogurt.

It's Not Hot, It's Chili

Fruity, smoky, citrusy, woodsy . . . these are just a few words to describe the flavors of various chilies. Make dried chilies ready for use by toasting them in a 350°F oven for 5 minutes, until they soften, become fragrant, and smoke lightly. Then, soak them in enough water to cover for 1 hour, and purée in a blender with just enough soaking liquid to make a thick purée circulate in the blender vase. For less "heat," remove the seeds before soaking.

RED LENTIL LASAGNA

This recipe puts a distinctive twist on the traditional veggie lasagna. But if you crave cheese, any kind can be added to this recipe.

Serves 6

1 tablespoon olive oil

2 cups Béchamel Sauce (see recipe in Chapter 2)

1 pound cooked lasagna noodles

½ cup crumbled firm tofu

½ cup cooked red lentils

¼ cup peeled and shredded carrots

1 yellow onion, chopped

4 cloves garlic, minced

½ cup cooked chopped spinach

1 sprig fresh oregano, chopped

1 sprig fresh marjoram, chopped

Fresh-cracked black pepper, to taste

1. Preheat the oven to 325°F.

2. Brush a casserole dish with the olive oil. Alternate all the ingredients in the dish in layers, starting with a thin layer of sauce to moisten the bottom before the first layer of noodles, and ending with the Béchamel Sauce on top. Cover tightly and bake for 30–45 minutes. Cool slightly, cut, and serve.

All about Lentils

Unlike beans, lentils do not need to be presoaked, but they do need to be washed several times in warm water. Lentils are often used as a meat substitute and are a good source of iron. Lentils can be used in salads and soups, and can be combined with other vegetables and dishes.

GRILLED PORTOBELLO MUSHROOMS

These Grilled Portobello Mushrooms are guaranteed to fill you up!

Serves 6

6 portobello mushrooms

3 cloves garlic

1 tablespoon olive oil

Kosher or coarse sea salt, to taste

Fresh-cracked black pepper, to taste

1. Preheat the grill to medium temperature. Clean off the mushrooms with damp paper towels or a mushroom brush, and scrape out the black membrane on the underside of the cap. Mince the garlic.

2. Mix together the oil and garlic; dip each mushroom in the oil and place on a rack to drain. Season with salt and pepper, and grill on each side until fork-tender.

3. To serve, slice on the bias and fan out on serving plates.

RATATOUILLE

There are no limits to the types of vegetables that can be added to ratatouille. Get creative and experiment!

Serves 6

1 small eggplant

1 small zucchini squash

1 small yellow squash

½ leek

1 plum tomato

1 shallot

2 cloves garlic

2 sprigs marjoram

¼ cup kalamata olives

½ teaspoon olive oil

1 cup Basic Vegetable Stock (see recipe in Chapter 2)

Fresh-cracked black pepper, to taste

1. Large-dice the eggplant, zucchini, yellow squash, leek, and tomato. Finely dice the shallot and garlic. Mince the marjoram and chop the olives.

2. Place all the ingredients in a saucepot and cook over low heat for 1½ hours.

Summer and Winter Squash

You will often hear yellow squash referred to as "summer squash." Squash is normally divided into two groups: summer squash and winter squash. Summer squashes have thin skins and soft seeds. Winter squashes have tough skins and hard seeds.

VEGETABLE TERRINE

To spice up this dish, add a poblano chili pepper in place of the red bell peppers.

Serves 6

1 medium-size baked sweet potato

1 large par-baked baking potato

1 medium-size yellow onion

3 red bell peppers

1 large eggplant

4 cloves garlic

1 head escarole

2 tablespoons olive oil

1 tablespoon curry powder

Fresh-cracked black pepper, to taste

¼ cup chopped unsalted cashew nuts

1. Preheat the oven to 375°F.

2. Peel and mash the sweet potato. Peel and slice the baking potato into 1-inch-thick slices. Thickly slice the onion. Cut the peppers in half and remove the seeds. Slice the eggplant lengthwise into 1-inch slices. Mince the garlic. Steam the escarole.

3. Brush the onion, peppers, and eggplant with the oil, then sprinkle with curry and black pepper; roast in the oven until al dente, approximately 10–20 minutes.

4. Grease a loaf pan with the remaining oil. Line the pan with the eggplant, allowing the slices to drape up and over the sides of the pan. Then layer the remainder of the ingredients and sprinkle with remaining curry and drizzle with oil. Fold over the eggplant slices to seal the terrine.

5. Seal tightly with plastic wrap and place something heavy on top to press the ingredients firmly together. Refrigerate for at least 4 hours.

6. Cut into 2-inch slices to serve.

ZUCCHINI PARMESAN

You may use plain or preseasoned bread crumbs for this recipe. Also, try adding thin-sliced fresh basil or chopped oregano for flair and extra flavor.

Serves 6

3 medium zucchini

2 egg whites

1 cup skim milk

½ cup bread crumbs

1 teaspoon olive oil

2 cups Long-Cooking Traditional Tomato Sauce (see recipe in Chapter 2)

6 ounces part-skim mozzarella cheese, shredded

Fresh-cracked black pepper, to taste

1. Preheat the oven to 375°F.

2. Slice the zucchini into ½-inch-thick coins. Beat the egg whites and mix with the milk. Brush a baking sheet with the oil. Dip the zucchini into the egg mixture, then into the bread crumbs, and shake off excess; place on baking sheet and bake for 10–15 minutes, until the zucchini are just fork-tender.

3. Ladle the sauce into a large casserole or baking dish. Cover the bottom of the dish with a single layer of zucchini, then top with the cheese, then sauce. Repeat the process until you have used all the ingredients; bake for 5–10 minutes, until the cheese has melted and begins to brown on top. Top with black pepper, to taste, and serve.

Parmesan

Parmesan is best known as a type of cheese, but the term "Parmesan" also loosely refers to a type of cooking—for example, Chicken Parmesan. Any type of Parmesan dish indicates the presence of some type of cheese, but not necessarily Parmesan cheese.

SQUASH AND GOAT CHEESE NAPOLEON

For a bit of excitement, consider using kalamata olives in place of the commonplace pitted, black olives.

Serves 6

1 medium-size yellow squash

1 medium zucchini squash

1 tablespoon olive oil

1 leek

1 cup fresh spinach

3 cloves garlic

¼ cup pitted, black olives, chopped

2 plum tomatoes

¼ cup dry red wine

½ cup Red Wine Vegetable Stock (see recipe in Chapter 2)

Fresh-cracked black pepper, to taste

6 ounces goat cheese, crumbled

1. Heat grill to medium-high temperature.

2. Slice the squashes lengthwise. Coat a pan with some of the olive oil and grill the squashes for approximately 1–2 minutes on each side until al dente.

3. Thinly slice the leek and spinach. Mince the garlic and olives. Dice the tomatoes.

4. Heat the remaining oil over medium heat in a large saucepan. Add the leek and garlic; sauté for 2 minutes. Add the spinach; sauté 1 more minute. Add the tomatoes, and sauté for 1 minute. Add the wine and stock, and reduce by half.

5. To serve, layer the ingredients, starting with squashes, then leek mixture, then pepper, olives, and goat cheese—repeating until you've used all the ingredients.

BRAISED OKRA WITH TOMATO

Keep in mind that feta cheese tends to impart a salty taste, so you probably won't need to add any salt to this recipe.

Serves 6

1½ pounds okra

8 plum tomatoes

2 shallots

4 cloves garlic

1 tablespoon olive oil

¼ cup dry red wine

½ cup Basic Vegetable Stock (see recipe in Chapter 2)

4 sprigs oregano, leaves only

4 ounces feta cheese, crumbled

Fresh-cracked black pepper, to taste

1. Preheat the oven to 375°F.

2. Remove the tops of the okra. Cut the tomatoes into wedges. Fine-dice the shallots and mince the garlic.

3. Heat the oil in a Dutch oven (or other heavy-bottomed pan with a lid) over medium-high heat. Add the okra, shallots, and garlic; sauté for 2 minutes. Add the wine, and reduce by half. Add the stock and oregano; bring to simmer, cover, and place in the oven for 15–20 minutes.

4. Remove from oven and add the feta and pepper. Adjust seasoning to taste, then serve.

Storing Olive Oil

Olive oil should be kept away from sunlight and heat. It does not need to be refrigerated. If the oil gets too cold, it will become cloudy but will return to its normal color when it returns to room temperature.

CHAPTER 8

LAMB, BEEF, AND PORK ENTRÉES

LAMB EXOHIKO

These are phyllo bundles of tender lamb, spinach, red peppers, and sharp sheep's milk cheese. This is a great dish for leftover lamb.

Serves 4

2 tablespoons extra-virgin olive oil

4 cups fresh spinach, blanched, drained, and chopped

4 or 5 scallions, ends trimmed and chopped

1 clove garlic, peeled and minced

¼ cup dry white wine

¾ teaspoon salt

½ teaspoon pepper

2 tablespoons chopped fresh dill

1 teaspoon dried oregano

8 sheets phyllo pastry, thawed, at room temperature

½ cup melted butter

2 cups diced cooked lamb meat

4 (¼-inch) slices ripe medium-size tomato

4 (¼-inch) slices kefalotyri or Romano cheese

4 (¼-inch) slices red bell pepper, stemmed and seeded

1. Heat the oil in a large skillet over medium heat for 30 seconds. Add the spinach, scallions, and garlic, and cook for 5–6 minutes. Add the wine, and cook for 2–3 minutes to reduce the wine. Season with salt and pepper. Add the dill and oregano, take the skillet off the heat, and reserve.

2. Preheat the oven to 350°F. Place the phyllo on a clean work surface, and cover sheets with a lightly damp tea towel to keep them from drying. Brush a sheet of phyllo with butter. Take a second sheet, place it on top of the first sheet, and brush it with butter.

3. Place one-fourth of the lamb on the phyllo about 5 inches from the bottom and leave 2 inches from the left and the right sides. Top the lamb with one-fourth of the spinach filling, a slice of tomato, a slice of cheese, and a slice of red pepper. Fold the bottom 5 inches of phyllo over the filling, and then fold in the left and right sides. Next, roll the phyllo to make a bundle. Place the bundle, seam-side down, on a baking sheet lined with parchment paper. Repeat this process three more times.

4. Brush the tops of the bundles with butter, and bake them on the middle rack for 25–30 minutes or until they are golden.

5. Serve immediately or warm.

LEMON VERBENA RACK OF LAMB

Lamb works wonderfully with lemon verbena, but you can always use lemon thyme in a pinch. Greek roast potatoes are a wonderful side for this easy rack of lamb dish.

Serves 4

2 (2-pound) racks lamb, silver skin removed and tied

¼ cup extra-virgin olive oil

2 cloves garlic, peeled and crushed

1 tablespoon Dijon mustard

1 teaspoon sweet paprika

1 tablespoon honey

2 teaspoons grated lemon zest

2 tablespoons chopped fresh parsley

2 tablespoons lemon verbena leaves

2 teaspoons fresh thyme leaves

3 teaspoons salt

1 teaspoon pepper

1. Place the lamb in a medium baking dish. In a food processor, put the oil, garlic, mustard, paprika, honey, zest, parsley, lemon verbena, and thyme. Process until the ingredients are well incorporated. Pour the marinade over the lamb and rub it all over to coat. Cover and marinate the lamb for 1 hour at room temperature. Season the lamb with salt and pepper.

2. Preheat the broiler. Place the lamb on a baking tray lined with parchment paper and roast it under the broiler for 5 minutes. Set the oven temperature to 450°F and roast for 25 minutes. Check the internal temperature of the lamb; it should read a minimum of 135°F. If you prefer the meat well done, roast the lamb for a few more minutes.

3. Tent the lamb with foil and let it rest for 5 minutes before serving.

Ask the Butcher

Ask the butcher to trim the rack of lamb and remove its silver skin. He or she will then tie the lamb into a crown rack, which will save some preparation time.

TANGY MAPLE-MUSTARD LAMB

Serve this lamb with a side of grilled vegetables and roasted potatoes or rice pilaf.

Serves 6

3 pounds lamb chops

¼ cup extra-virgin olive oil

2 tablespoons chopped fresh rosemary

2 cloves garlic, peeled and minced

1 teaspoon pepper

1 tablespoon Dijon mustard

¼ cup maple syrup

1 teaspoon orange zest

2 teaspoons salt

3 tablespoons vegetable oil

1 large lemon, cut into wedges

1. Put the lamb in a medium baking dish. In a medium bowl, whisk the oil, rosemary, garlic, pepper, mustard, maple syrup, and orange zest. Reserve ⅓ cup of the marinade to brush on the lamb after grilling. Pour the remaining marinade over the lamb and rub it all over to coat. Cover and marinate for 1 hour at room temperature or refrigerate overnight. Bring the lamb to room temperature, if it was refrigerated. Season the lamb with salt.

2. Preheat the gas or charcoal grill to medium-high. Brush the grill surface to make sure it is thoroughly clean. When the grill is ready, dip a clean tea towel in the vegetable oil and wipe the grill's surface with the oil. Place the lamb on the grill, and grill it 3–4 minutes a side for medium-rare or 4 minutes a side for medium. Brush the reserved marinade on the lamb chops and let them rest for 5 minutes.

3. Serve the lamb with the lemon wedges.

OSSO BUCO

To make it easy, ask the butcher to slice the veal shanks.

Serves 10

5 pounds veal shanks

2 teaspoons salt, divided

1 teaspoon pepper, divided

1 tablespoon extra-virgin olive oil

1 leek, ends trimmed, thoroughly cleaned, cut lengthwise, and sliced

3 large tomatoes, cut into wedges

4 medium onions, peeled and cut into large wedges

4 cloves garlic, peeled and smashed

2 stalks celery, ends trimmed and cut into chunks

2 medium carrots, peeled and cut into chunks

1 cup dry red wine

3 cups veal or beef stock

2 bay leaves

3 tablespoons chopped fresh parsley

1 tablespoon fresh thyme leaves

1 tablespoon chopped fresh rosemary

1. Preheat the oven to 325°F. Season the shanks with 1 teaspoon of salt and ½ teaspoon of pepper.

2. Heat the oil in a Dutch oven (with a lid) over medium-high heat for 30 seconds. Add the shanks and brown them for 3–4 minutes on both sides.

3. Add the leeks, tomatoes, onions, garlic, celery, and carrots. Brown the vegetables lightly. Add the wine and cook it for 2–3 minutes to let it reduce by half.

4. Add the stock, bay leaves, parsley, thyme, and rosemary. Bring the veal to a boil, cover it immediately, and place it in the oven. Braise the dish for 2–3 hours, until the meat is fork-tender and starts to separate from the bone. Remove the bay leaves.

5. Serve it hot or let it come to room temperature, refrigerate it, and reheat it the next day.

HÜNKAR BEGENDI WITH LAMB

This dish from Istanbul features tender pieces of lamb simmered in a tomato sauce and served on a bed of smoked eggplant purée.

Serves 6

2 pounds cubed lamb meat, rinsed and dried

2½ teaspoons salt, divided

1 teaspoon pepper, divided

2 tablespoons olive oil

1 large onion, peeled and thinly sliced

½ cup diced green pepper, stemmed and seeded

3 or 4 cloves garlic, peeled and minced

2 or 3 bay leaves

6 or 7 whole allspice berries

2 tablespoons puréed roasted red peppers

2 teaspoons fresh thyme leaves

2 tablespoons chopped fresh parsley

2 cups puréed tomatoes

2 cups hot water or lamb stock

2 large eggplants, charred and flesh reserved

2 tablespoons unsalted butter

2 tablespoons all-purpose flour

2 cups whole milk

½ cup grated kefalotyri or Romano cheese

3 tablespoons cream cheese

½ cup chopped fresh chives

1. Season the lamb with 1 teaspoon of salt and ½ teaspoon pepper. Heat the oil in a large skillet over medium-high heat for 30 seconds. Add the lamb cubes and brown them for 2–3 minutes on all sides. Add the onions, green peppers, garlic, bay leaves, and allspice, and reduce the heat to medium. Cook for 6–7 minutes.

2. Add the red peppers, thyme, parsley, tomatoes, and hot water or stock. Increase the heat to medium-high, and bring the mixture to a boil. Reduce the heat to medium, partially cover the skillet, and cook for 30–40 minutes. Uncover, season with 1 teaspoon of salt and ¼ teaspoon of pepper, and continue to cook until the sauce thickens. Take the skillet off the heat and keep warm.

3. Put the eggplant flesh in a mortar, and pound it with the pestle until it becomes creamy but still chunky. Reserve.

4. Melt the butter in a medium saucepan over medium heat. Add the flour and stir the mixture until it turns light brown. Continue to stir and slowly add the milk. Keep stirring until the milk thickens. Stir in the reserved eggplant and cheeses. Season with the remaining salt and pepper.

5. Serve a generous ladle of eggplant sauce on each plate and top with the lamb. Sprinkle the chives on top and serve warm.

MOUSSAKA

Moussaka is a classic and comforting Greek dish.

Serves 10

2 tablespoons salt

3 large eggplants, ends trimmed and cut into ½-inch slices

½ cup extra-virgin olive oil

1 cup bread crumbs, divided

6 cups Greek Meat Sauce (see recipe in Chapter 2)

1½ cups grated kefalotyri or Romano cheese, divided

4 cups Béchamel Sauce (see recipe in Chapter 2)

1. Sprinkle the salt over the eggplant slices, and leave them for 30 minutes to release their bitter liquid. Wipe the eggplants dry with a paper towel. Preheat the oven to 400°F.

2. Brush the eggplants with oil and place them on a baking sheet. Bake the eggplants for 6 minutes until softened. (The eggplant can also be grilled.) Transfer the eggplant to a tray lined with paper towels to soak up excess oil, and let them cool. Reduce the oven temperature to 375°F.

3. In a large casserole dish, place a layer of the eggplant on the bottom. Sprinkle ½ cup of bread crumbs over the eggplant. Spread half of the Greek Meat Sauce over the bread crumbs. Next sprinkle ½ cup cheese over the top. Add another layer of eggplant, the remaining bread crumbs, Greek Meat Sauce, and ½ cup of cheese.

4. Top the moussaka with the Béchamel Sauce. Sprinkle the remaining cheese on top, and bake for 30–40 minutes or until the top is golden.

5. Allow the moussaka to rest for 45 minutes before cutting and serving.

SLOW-COOKED PORK CHOPS IN WINE

Garlic mashed potatoes and some sautéed mushrooms are a great way to round out this dish.

Serves 4

¼ cup all-purpose flour

1½ teaspoons salt

½ teaspoon pepper

2 teaspoons sweet paprika

4 bone-in pork chops, rinsed and dried

¼ cup extra-virgin olive oil

½ cup dry white wine

1 cup Chicken or Turkey Stock or Basic Vegetable Stock (see recipes in Chapter 2)

2 bay leaves

6–8 large green olives, pitted and chopped

1 tablespoon fresh lemon juice

1 tablespoon fresh thyme leaves

1. Combine the flour, salt, pepper, and paprika in a medium bowl. Stir to combine the ingredients. Dredge the pork chops in the flour. Reserve the pork chops and discard the flour.

2. Heat the oil in a large skillet over medium-high heat for 30 seconds. Add the pork chops and brown them for 2–3 minutes per side. Remove the pork chops and reserve.

3. Add the wine, stock, and bay leaves. Stir and cook the sauce for 2–3 minutes, scraping up brown bits from the bottom of the pan. Put the pork chops back in the skillet. Cover it, and reduce the heat to medium-low. Cook for 30 minutes or until the pork is tender and the sauce has reduced by half.

4. Add the olives, lemon juice, and thyme. Season with more salt and pepper, if necessary.

5. Remove the bay leaves and serve.

PORK CHOPS IN WINE

Though boneless center-cut pork chops can be used in this recipe, it is recommended that you use chops with the bone in for optimum flavor and tenderness.

Serves 4

4 thick-cut pork chops

½ cup extra-virgin olive oil

1 cup white wine

½ cup hot water

1 tablespoon dried oregano

Salt and pepper to taste

1. Rinse pork chops well and pat dry with a paper towel.

2. Place 2 tablespoons olive oil in a frying pan; lightly brown pork chops.

3. Put remaining olive oil in a fresh pan and turn heat to medium-high. Cook pork chops 3–4 minutes per side, making sure to turn them over at least once.

4. Add wine; bring to a boil. Turn to medium and simmer for 10 minutes, turning the meat once.

5. Add ½ cup hot water to pan; bring to a boil and let simmer until the sauce has reduced. Sprinkle with oregano, salt, and pepper, and serve immediately.

BREADED PORK CHOPS

Raisins and apples are sure to complement pork in any form of preparation.

Serves 6

Cooking spray

3 slices raisin-pumpernickel bread

6 cloves garlic

½ cup applesauce

1 teaspoon olive oil

6 pork chops

Fresh-cracked black pepper, to taste

Kosher salt, to taste

1. Preheat oven to 375°F. Spray a baking sheet with cooking spray.

2. Toast the bread and grate into crumbs. Mince the garlic in a blender, then add the applesauce and oil, and blend until smooth.

3. Rub the chops with the garlic-applesauce mixture. Bread with pumpernickel crumbs and place on prepared baking sheet. Spray the chops with cooking spray and season with pepper and salt.

4. Bake for 20 minutes, then turn and bake for 20–40 minutes longer, depending on the thickness of the pork. Serve hot.

SMYRNA SOUTZOUKAKIA

Soutzoukakia are short, seasoned sausages without a casing. These sausages are served with a wonderful tomato sauce.

Serves 4

2 slices white bread

½ cup white wine, divided

1 pound lean ground beef

2 medium onions, peeled (1 grated, 1 diced), divided

4 cloves garlic, minced, divided

3 tablespoons finely chopped fresh parsley

½ teaspoon plus ⅛ teaspoon ground cumin, divided

1 teaspoon dried oregano

2½ teaspoons salt, divided

¾ teaspoon pepper, divided

1 large egg, beaten

½ cup extra-virgin olive oil, divided

1 bay leaf

1 (28-ounce) can plum tomatoes, puréed

⅛ teaspoon cinnamon

1. Soak the bread in ¼ cup of the wine, squeeze out the liquid, and crumble the bread. In a large bowl, mix the beef, bread, grated onion, 1 teaspoon of the garlic, parsley, ½ teaspoon of the cumin, oregano, 2 teaspoons of the salt, ½ teaspoon of the pepper, and the egg. Mix well and refrigerate for 1 hour.

2. Heat ¼ cup of the oil in a medium skillet over medium-high heat for 30 seconds. Add the diced onions, bay leaf, tomatoes, remaining garlic, remaining cumin, cinnamon, and remaining wine. Season with the remaining salt and pepper. Reduce the heat to medium-low and cook for 30 minutes.

3. Form the meat mixture into 3-inch, quenelle-shaped sausages. Preheat a gas or charcoal grill to medium-high. Place the sausages on the grill and grill them 3–4 minutes a side (if you prefer to fry them instead, lightly dredge them in flour before frying them in olive oil).

4. Place the sausages in the tomato sauce and cook for 10–15 minutes.

5. Remove the bay leaf and serve hot.

STUFFED PEPPERS WITH MEAT

Sweet red peppers, ground beef, herbs, and rice; a self-contained meal!

Serves 6

⅓ cup extra-virgin olive oil

2 medium onions, peeled and diced

3 cloves garlic, peeled and minced

1 cup finely chopped fresh parsley

1 cup finely chopped fresh dill

2 tablespoons finely chopped fresh mint

1 cup tomato sauce

1 cup long-grain rice

2 pounds lean ground beef

2½ teaspoons salt

¾ teaspoon pepper

2–3 cups hot water

1. Preheat the oven to 375°F. Heat the oil in a large skillet over medium-high heat for 30 seconds. Reduce the heat to medium, and add the onions and garlic. Cook for 10 minutes or until the onions soften. Add the parsley, dill, mint, and tomato sauce. Cook for 10 minutes or until the sauce thickens. Take the skillet off the heat and cool it for 5 minutes.

2. Add the rice and ground beef to the skillet. Season with the salt and pepper and cook until rice is soft and beef is browned.

3. Spoon the beef-rice mixture into the peppers and place them in a roasting pan that will hold all the peppers snugly. Add 2–3 cups of hot water, enough to fill the pan up to 1 inch on the sides of the peppers.

4. Bake on the middle rack of the oven for 70–80 minutes or until the pepper tops are golden and the rice is cooked.

5. Serve hot or at room temperature.

Red Shepherd's Peppers

Red shepherd's peppers are ideal for this dish, but you can also use green cubanelle peppers. Use bell peppers only as a last resort; they are thicker and take longer to cook.

ROAST PORK BELLY AND POTATOES

Pork belly is a wonderful cut that requires very little fuss.

Serves 12

10–12 medium Yukon gold potatoes, peeled and quartered

½ cup extra-virgin olive oil

½ cup hot Chicken or Turkey Stock or Basic Vegetable Stock (see recipes in Chapter 2)

2 tablespoons Dijon mustard

1 tablespoon lemon juice

10 sprigs fresh thyme plus 2 teaspoons fresh thyme leaves, divided

2 or 3 sprigs fresh rosemary

3 teaspoons salt, divided

1½ teaspoons pepper, divided

1 (3½-pound) pork belly, cut into ½-inch slices

2 teaspoons sweet paprika

1 teaspoon dried oregano

¼ cup diced smoked pork or bacon

1 head garlic, top third cut off

1. Preheat the oven to 400°F. In a roasting pan, put the potatoes, olive oil, stock, mustard, lemon juice, thyme sprigs, and rosemary. Toss to combine the ingredients and coat the potatoes. Season with 1 teaspoon of salt and ½ teaspoon of pepper and toss again. Reserve.

2. In a large bowl, combine the pork belly, remaining salt, remaining pepper, paprika, oregano, and thyme leaves. Toss to combine the ingredients and coat the pork.

3. Place the pork belly on the potatoes. Sprinkle the smoked pork over the potatoes and the pork belly. Nestle the garlic in the middle of the pan.

4. Bake on the middle rack for 30 minutes or until the tops of the pork are nicely browned. Turn the pork belly over and bake for another 20 minutes or until the pork is browned and the potatoes are cooked.

5. Serve immediately.

GREEK-STYLE RIBS

Take the classic Greek flavors of lemon and garlic, throw in some spices, and you have a tasty twist on pork ribs. Serve with some Tzatziki (see recipe in Chapter 2).

Serves 4

1 tablespoon onion powder

1 tablespoon garlic powder

2 tablespoons lemon pepper

1 teaspoon ground bay

1 teaspoon dry oregano

1 teaspoon dry thyme

1 tablespoon seasoning salt

2 tablespoons sweet paprika

2 racks pork baby-back ribs, silver skin removed

1. In a medium bowl, combine all the ingredients except the ribs. Rub the mix evenly over the ribs. Refrigerate for 3 hours or let sit for 1 hour at room temperature. Preheat the oven to 425°F.

2. Bring ribs to room temperature. Place them on a baking sheet lined with parchment paper. Cover with foil and bake for 45 minutes; lower the heat to 375°F and bake for 15 minutes. Remove foil and bake for another 30 minutes. Tent the ribs with foil for 5 minutes. Cut ribs and serve.

GRILLED LAMB CHOPS

Serve these chops with Politiki Cabbage Salad (see recipe in Chapter 5).

Serves 4

½ cup extra-virgin olive oil

3 cloves garlic, peeled and minced

1 teaspoon Dijon mustard

2 tablespoons chopped fresh parsley

1 tablespoon fresh thyme leaves

1 tablespoon fresh lemon juice

2 teaspoons pepper

2½ teaspoons salt

2 teaspoons dried oregano, divided

2½ pounds lamb chops

3 tablespoons vegetable oil

1 large lemon, cut into wedges

1. In a small bowl, thoroughly whisk the olive oil, garlic, mustard, parsley, thyme, lemon juice, pepper, salt, and 1 teaspoon of oregano. Reserve one-third of the marinade to brush on the lamb after grilling.

2. Place the lamb in a medium baking dish and top with two-thirds of the marinade. Rub the lamb to coat it in the marinade. Cover and refrigerate for 2 hours. Return the lamb to room temperature before grilling.

3. Preheat a gas or charcoal grill to medium-high heat. Brush the grill surface to make sure it is clean. When the grill is ready, dip a clean tea towel in the vegetable oil and wipe the grill surface with the oil. Place the lamb on the grill and cook for 3–4 minutes a side for medium-rare and 4 minutes a side for medium. Brush the reserved marinade on the lamb and let the chops rest for 5 minutes.

4. Sprinkle the chops with the remaining oregano and serve with the lemon wedges.

KONTOSOUVLI

This is slow rotisserie pork that is traditionally served at Greek Easter, but it is delicious anytime during grilling season. The meat is sliced off as the pork rotates on the grill.

Serves 10

1 medium onion, peeled and grated

2 or 3 cloves garlic, peeled and minced

1 tablespoon sweet paprika

2 teaspoons fresh thyme leaves

3 tablespoons dried oregano

½ cup dry red wine

1½ teaspoons pepper

3 teaspoons salt, divided

6 pound pork butt, cut into 4-inch chunks

2 large lemons, cut into wedges

1. In a large bowl, whisk the onions, garlic, paprika, thyme, oregano, red wine, pepper, and 2 teaspoons of salt. Add the pork; toss to combine the ingredients and coat the pork. Cover and refrigerate overnight. Bring the pork to room temperature before grilling.

2. Prepare the rotisserie. If using a charcoal pit, bring it to a medium heat. If using a gas grill, remove the grates and place a drip pan with water beneath the rotisserie. The drip pan will keep the grill clean and prevent flare-ups as the fat renders.

3. Skewer the meat (close to each other) on the rotisserie spit and secure at each end. Season the meat with the remaining salt. Put the spit over the heat and grill. Lower the lid on a gas grill. Check and replenish the drip pan with water every ½ hour (the charcoal grill doesn't need a drip pan).

4. After 1 hour, begin slicing off some of the outer layers of meat. Continue slicing off meat as the Kontosouvli cooks. Serve it with the lemon wedges.

PORK SOUVLAKI

This marinade can be used with other meats to make different kinds of souvlaki. It works great with beef shoulder or even lamb shoulder. If you are using wooden skewers, soak them for at least 2 hours or overnight.

Serves 8

1 large onion, peeled and grated

3 cloves garlic, peeled and minced

2 teaspoons salt

¾ teaspoon pepper

¼ cup plus 3 tablespoons vegetable oil, divided

4 teaspoons dried oregano, divided

2 pound boneless pork butt, fat trimmed and cut into 1-inch cubes

2 large lemons, cut into wedges

1. In a large bowl, whisk the onion, garlic, salt, pepper, ¼ cup oil, and oregano. Whisk to thoroughly combine the marinade. Add the pork and toss to coat the meat. Refrigerate the pork for at least 5 hours or overnight. Bring the pork to room temperature before grilling it.

2. Put the meat onto wooden or metal skewers. Add 4 pieces of pork per skewer.

3. Preheat the gas or charcoal grill to medium-high. Brush the grill surface to make sure it is thoroughly clean. When the grill is ready, dip a clean tea towel in the remaining oil and wipe the grill surface with the oil. Put the pork on the grill and cook it for 3–4 minutes a side or until the pork is cooked through.

4. Sprinkle the pork with the remaining oregano and serve it with the lemon wedges.

SPETSOFAI

This is a one-pan dish of spicy sausages, onions, peppers, and tomatoes. Pick your favorite sausage and enjoy Spetsofai with crusty bread and a dry red wine.

Serves 4

¼ cup extra-virgin olive oil, divided

4 (5-inch) fresh sausages

4 hot banana peppers, stemmed, seeded, and skins pierced

2 large red or yellow bell peppers, stemmed, seeded, and sliced

2 medium onions, peeled and sliced

3 or 4 cloves garlic, peeled and minced

2 large ripe tomatoes, skinned and grated

½ teaspoon salt

½ teaspoon pepper

2 teaspoons dry oregano

1. Heat 2 tablespoons of oil in a large skillet over medium-high heat for 30 seconds. Add the sausages and brown them for 2–3 minutes on all sides. Remove the sausages from the skillet and reserve.

2. Add the banana peppers and fry them on all sides until they are just brown, about 60–90 seconds per side. Remove the banana peppers and reserve.

3. Add the bell peppers, onions, garlic, and tomatoes. Bring the mixture to a boil and then reduce the heat to medium-low. Season it with salt and pepper. Return the sausages and banana peppers to the skillet. Cover and cook for 15–20 minutes or until the sauce thickens.

4. Remove the cover and add the oregano. Adjust the seasoning with salt and pepper, if necessary. Drizzle the remaining oil over the dish. Serve hot.

FASOLAKIA WITH VEAL

This all-in-one meal is great for the summer months when beans, tomatoes, and herbs are in season.

Serves 4

⅓ cup extra-virgin olive oil

3 medium onions, peeled and sliced

5 cloves garlic, peeled and sliced

½ cup chopped fresh parsley

¼ cup finely chopped fresh mint

½ cup chopped fresh dill

2 pounds fasolakia (runner beans), trimmed

3 large ripe tomatoes, skinned and grated

1 teaspoon salt

½ teaspoon pepper

2 pounds cooked veal or beef, cut into bite-size pieces

2 large potatoes, peeled and quartered

2–3 cups hot veal broth

1. Heat the oil in a large skillet over medium-high heat for 30 seconds. Add the onions and cook for 5 minutes or until they soften. Add the garlic, parsley, mint, dill, beans, and tomatoes. Bring the mixture to a boil and then reduce the heat to medium-low and cook for 30 minutes. Season with salt and pepper.

2. Add the veal, potatoes, and enough broth just to cover the ingredients. Cook for another 30 minutes or until the potatoes are cooked and the sauce thickens a little.

3. Adjust the seasoning with more salt and pepper, if necessary. Serve hot.

Fasolakia

Fasolakia are also known as runner beans. Runner beans are flat beans and can be found at farmers' markets and Asian grocers. If you can't find them, use regular green beans.

SLOW-ROASTED LEG OF LAMB

Choose bone-in lamb, use lots of garlic and herbs, and serve roast potatoes to accompany this succulent dish.

Serves 10

1 (6–8 pound) leg of lamb, bone in

1 head garlic, cloves peeled and sliced thinly

3 tablespoons extra-virgin olive oil

5 teaspoons salt

2 teaspoons pepper

2 teaspoons garlic powder

2 teaspoons sweet paprika

2 medium onions, peeled and quartered

2 or 3 sprigs fresh rosemary

10 sprigs fresh thyme

2–3 teaspoons dried oregano

2 or 3 bay leaves

⅓ cup fresh lemon juice

1 cup dry white wine

Hot water

1. Stick a paring knife into the lamb and make a hole; then slip a sliver of garlic into the hole. Repeat this process and insert as many slivers of garlic as you can into the leg.

2. Preheat the oven to 550°F or its highest temperature. Put the lamb in a roasting pan (that just fits the lamb) and rub 3 tablespoons of oil all over it. Season all sides with the salt, pepper, garlic powder, and paprika. Roast the lamb uncovered for 10–15 minutes or until browned. Flip the lamb over and roast it on the other side for 10–15 minutes or until browned. Remove the pan from the oven. Reduce the oven temperature to 350°F.

3. To the roasting pan, add the onions, any remaining slivers of garlic, rosemary, thyme, oregano, and bay leaves. Add the lemon juice, wine, and just enough hot water to rise one-third of the way up the lamb. Cover and roast the lamb for 2 hours. Baste the lamb after the first hour.

4. Turn the lamb over and roast for another hour. Add more hot water if necessary. The lamb should be deep brown, the bone will be exposed, and the meat should be separating from the bone.

5. Remove the bay leaves. Baste the lamb, and let it rest for 15–20 minutes before serving.

BRAISED SHORT RIBS KOKKINISTO

Kokkinisto *in Greek means "reddened," so always use tomato paste for consistent results.*

Serves 4

4 (8-ounce) thick beef short ribs

1½ teaspoons salt

½ teaspoon pepper

¼ cup all-purpose flour

½ cup extra-virgin olive oil, divided

½ stalk celery, ends trimmed and diced

½ medium carrot, peeled and diced

3 medium onions, peeled (1 whole, 1 diced), divided

5 or 6 cloves garlic, peeled

6 whole allspice berries

2 bay leaves

1 teaspoon smoked paprika

½ cup dry white wine

2 tablespoons tomato paste

1 teaspoon fresh thyme leaves

1 teaspoon fresh rosemary leaves

2 cups hot water

1. Season beef with salt and pepper and dredge in flour. In an ovenproof pot, just big enough to hold the ribs, heat 2 tablespoons of oil over medium-high heat for 30 seconds. Add the beef (in batches) and brown for 3 minutes on each side. Remove the beef and reserve.

2. Add the remaining oil to the pan and reduce heat to medium. Add celery, carrots, onions, garlic, allspice, bay leaves, and paprika. Stir and cook for 5–6 minutes to soften the vegetables. Preheat the oven to 350°F.

3. Add the wine and allow it to reduce for 3 minutes. Add the tomato paste, thyme, and rosemary. Return the beef to the pan and add the hot water. Cover and bake for 70–90 minutes.

4. Check the seasoning and adjust with salt and pepper, if necessary. Return the pot to the oven and bake for 30 minutes. Remove from the oven and uncover; remove the bay leaves. Serve hot.

LAMB ON THE SPIT

Spit-roasting an entire lamb is a Greek Easter tradition. For the best results, you will need a charcoal spit, and you should cook on a day that is warm, dry, and has little wind. You will also need butcher's twine and a long upholstery needle.

Serves 30

1 (15–20 pound) whole lamb

½ cup vegetable oil

1½ cups salt, divided

6 tablespoons pepper, divided

½ cup garlic powder

¼ cup lemon juice

¾ cup extra-virgin olive oil

½ cup dried oregano

½ cup Ladolemono (see recipe in Chapter 2)

1. Place the spit rod through the lamb (rear to head). If the head is still on the lamb, pierce the skull to help secure the spit. Break the hind legs, bending them backward, and tie them securely to the spit with butcher's twine. Repeat this step with the front legs and also securely bind the neck to the spit. Using butcher's twine and an upholstery needle, make a stitch across the length of the lamb's spine, looping around the spit. It's important that the stitch enters the meat near the spine, loops around the spit, and then the needle comes back out of the body near the spine again. Loop the twine through your stitch and continue securing the spine to the spit until you've reached the shoulder.

2. Rub the inside of the lamb with vegetable oil and sprinkle with ½ cup salt, 3 tablespoons pepper, and garlic powder. Using the butcher's twine and needle, stitch and close the opening to the cavity. Rub the exterior of the lamb with oil and season it well with ¾ cup salt and remaining pepper. Get a fire pit started with some kindling wood and newspaper. When some burning embers are present, add two bags of charcoal into the pit and allow 30 minutes for the charcoal to get white-hot.

3. Separate the hot coals into two piles: one underneath the shoulder end, and the other pile under the hind leg side. The midsection of the lamb cooks the fastest and there is enough residual heat from both piles to cook the midsection evenly. Every hour, replenish the pit with another bag of charcoal, with two piles at each end of the pit. When the older charcoals start losing heat, just push the newer charcoals over to the two main charcoal areas. The lamb should take 5–6 hours to cook through.

4. In a medium bowl, combine the lemon juice, olive oil, remaining salt, and oregano to make a basting marinade. Baste frequently for the last hour. The lamb will show signs of being done when the carcass starts to crack.

5. Transfer the lamb to a large baking tray, allow it to rest 15–20 minutes, and then cut away all butcher's twine and carve it into pieces. Drizzle the Ladolemono on the meat before serving.

CABBAGE ROLLS

Avgolemono is an egg and lemon sauce and a unique way to finish traditional cabbage rolls.

Serves 10

¼ cup extra-virgin olive oil

3 medium onions, finely diced

3 cloves garlic, minced

¼ cup tomato purée

1 pound lean ground beef

1 pound ground pork

1½ cups Arborio rice

1 cup chopped fresh parsley

1 cup chopped fresh dill

3 teaspoons salt

1 teaspoon black pepper

1 large cabbage, blanched, leaves separated and trimmed

3 cups Chicken or Turkey Stock or Basic Vegetable Stock (see recipes in Chapter 2)

4 tablespoons all-purpose flour

2 tablespoons water

3 large eggs

6 tablespoons fresh lemon juice

1. Heat the oil in a large skillet over medium-high heat. Reduce the heat to medium and add the onions and garlic. Cook for 10 minutes or until the onions soften. Take the skillet off the heat and stir in the tomato purée, beef, pork, rice, parsley, dill, salt, and pepper.

2. Place a cabbage leaf on a work surface. Add a generous tablespoon of filling near the bottom of the leaf. Fold the two ends of the leaf inward and roll it into a long, narrow bundle. Do not roll the leaf too tightly or the rice will break the cabbage as it expands. Repeat the process until all the filling is used.

3. Preheat the oven to 350°F. Place some leftover leaves on the bottom of a roasting pan. Place the cabbage rolls in concentric circles in the pan. Top with more loose cabbage leaves. Add the stock, cover, and bake on the lower rack for 90 minutes. Carefully pour any remaining liquid from the pan into a bowl. Reserve.

4. In a large bowl, whisk the flour and water to form a slurry. Whisk in the eggs and lemon juice. Continuing to whisk vigorously, slowly add a ladle of cabbage-roll liquid into the egg-lemon mixture. Continue whisking and slowly add another two ladles (one at a time) into the egg-lemon mixture.

5. Pour the avgolemono over the rolls and shake the pan to allow the sauce to blend in. Let the dish cool for 15 minutes before serving.

How to Blanch and Separate a Head of Cabbage

Bring a large pot of water to a boil with a little salt. Meanwhile, remove the outer leaves and the hard stalk (root) of the cabbage. Wash the cabbage and put it into the boiling water for 10 minutes. Carefully remove the cabbage from the water. Using tongs, peel away each leaf and unwrap the head of boiled cabbage. Remove the bottom part of the main rib from each leaf. Repeat this process with all the leaves. Cut the leaves in half if they are too big.

ZUCCHINI STUFFED WITH MEAT AND RICE

This is a great make-ahead dish that tastes even better the next day.

Serves 6

¼ cup extra-virgin olive oil

2 medium onions, peeled and finely diced

3 cloves garlic, peeled and minced

1½ cups chopped fresh parsley

¾ cup chopped fresh dill

½ cup chopped fresh mint

⅔ cup tomato sauce

¼ cup plus 2 tablespoons water plus 3 cups hot water, divided

1½ cups Arborio rice

2 pounds extra-lean ground beef

1 tablespoon salt

¾ teaspoon black pepper

10 medium zucchini, peeled, cut in half, and cored

4 tablespoons all-purpose flour

3 large eggs

6 tablespoons fresh lemon juice

1. Preheat the oven to 375°F. Heat the oil in a large skillet over medium-high heat for 30 seconds. Reduce the heat to medium and add the onions and garlic. Cook for 5–6 minutes or until the onions soften. Stir in the parsley, dill, and mint. Add the tomato sauce, ¼ cup of water, and the rice. Cook for 10 minutes while stirring. Stir in the beef, salt, and pepper. Take the skillet off the heat.

2. Stuff the zucchini with the filling. Place them in a roasting pan big enough to hold them in a single layer. Pour 3 cups of hot water into the roasting pan, cover it with a lid, and bake for 60 minutes. Carefully tilt the roasting pan and pour any remaining liquid from the pan into a bowl. Reserve the liquid and the zucchini.

3. In a large bowl, whisk the flour and 2 tablespoons of water to form a slurry. Whisk in the eggs and lemon juice. Continuing to whisk vigorously, slowly add a ladle of the reserved liquid into the egg-lemon mixture. Continue whisking and slowly add another 2 ladles (one at a time) into the egg-lemon mixture. Adjust the seasoning with salt, if necessary.

4. Pour the avgolemono over the zucchini and shake the pan to allow the sauce to blend in. Let it cool for 15 minutes before serving warm.

GREEK-STYLE FLANK STEAK

Serve some Greek-Style Chimichurri (see recipe in Chapter 2) sauce over this delicious steak.

Serves 4

¼ cup extra-virgin olive oil

7 or 8 cloves garlic, peeled and smashed

4 or 5 chopped scallions, ends trimmed

1 tablespoon Dijon mustard

⅓ cup balsamic vinegar

2 bay leaves

2 tablespoons fresh thyme leaves

2 tablespoons fresh rosemary leaves

1 teaspoon dried oregano

1½ teaspoons salt, divided

¾ teaspoon pepper, divided

1 (2-pound) large flank steak

3 tablespoons vegetable oil

1. In a food processor, process the olive oil, garlic, scallions, mustard, vinegar, bay leaves, thyme, rosemary, oregano, 1 teaspoon salt, and ½ teaspoon pepper. Thoroughly incorporate the ingredients in the marinade.

2. Rub the steak with the marinade and place in a medium baking dish. Cover and refrigerate for 3 hours. Return the steak to room temperature before grilling. Wipe most of the marinade off the steak and season with remaining salt and pepper.

3. Preheat a gas or charcoal grill to medium-high. Brush the grill surface to make sure it is thoroughly clean. When the grill is ready, dip a clean tea towel in the vegetable oil and wipe the grill surface with the oil. Place the meat on the grill and grill for 4 minutes a side.

4. Let the steak rest for 5 minutes before serving.

CHEESE-STUFFED BIFTEKI

If you can't find Greek Graviera cheese, use any other firm sheep's milk cheese.

Serves 6

2 pounds medium ground beef

2 medium onions, peeled and grated

3 slices of bread, soaked in water, hand squeezed, and crumbled

1 tablespoon minced garlic

1 teaspoon dried oregano

1 teaspoon chopped fresh parsley

¼ teaspoon ground allspice

2 tablespoons salt

1 teaspoon pepper

6 (1-inch) cubes Graviera cheese

3 tablespoons vegetable oil

1. In a large bowl, combine all the ingredients (except the cheese and vegetable oil) and mix thoroughly.

2. Using your hands, form twelve (4" × ½") patties with the meat. Place the patties on a tray, cover them with plastic wrap, and refrigerate for 4 hours or overnight. Allow the patties to come to room temperature before grilling.

3. Take a piece of cheese and place it on the middle of a patty. Place another patty on top and press them together to form one burger. Using your fingers, pinch the entire perimeter of the burger so that when you grill, the burger will hold together and the cheese will not leak out.

4. Preheat a gas or charcoal grill to medium-high. Brush the grill surface to make sure it is thoroughly clean. When the grill is ready, dip a clean tea towel in the vegetable oil and wipe the grill surface with the oil. Place the burgers on the grill and grill for 5 minutes a side.

5. Allow the burgers to rest for 5 minutes before serving.

MEATBALLS IN EGG-LEMON SAUCE

Ground beef, pork, or lamb can easily be used as a substitute for the veal in this recipe.

Serves 6

2 pounds lean ground veal

2 medium onions, finely diced

½ cup dry bread crumbs

1 egg, beaten, plus 2 eggs

¼ cup extra-virgin olive oil, divided

¼ cup fresh mint, finely chopped

¼ cup fresh parsley, finely chopped

1 teaspoon dried oregano

Salt and pepper to taste

4 cups Beef Stock or Veal Stock (see recipe in Chapter 2)

Juice of 1 lemon

1. Preheat the oven to 400°F.

2. In a large mixing bowl, combine meat, onions, bread crumbs, 1 beaten egg, 2 tablespoons olive oil, mint, parsley, oregano, salt, and pepper; mix together well with your hands.

3. Using your fingers, take up small pieces of meat mix and fashion into meatballs about the size of a golf ball. Place in rows in a baking dish greased with the remaining olive oil. Bake for 30–40 minutes, until cooked.

4. In a stockpot, bring stock to a boil. Add the meatballs; cover and simmer for 10 minutes.

5. Beat the 2 remaining eggs in a mixing bowl; slowly add lemon juice and some of the hot stock in slow streams as you beat them to achieve a frothy mix.

6. Pour egg-lemon mix into the pot with the meatballs. Cover and simmer for another 2–3 minutes and serve immediately.

The Good Old Days

At the start of the twentieth century, Greeks consumed less meat than any other European nation. By the start of the twenty-first century, they were vying with the French for top meat consumers per capita in Europe. A parallel rise in degenerative illnesses has prompted many Greeks to return to traditional eating habits.

AUBERGINE MEAT ROLLS

Ground beef, pork, or lamb can be substituted for the veal in this dish.

Serves 4–6

1 large, round eggplant

1 large white onion, finely diced

½ cup Greek extra-virgin olive oil, divided

2 cloves garlic, minced or pressed

1 pound lean ground veal

½ cup white wine (or Retsina)

2 cups strained tomato pulp/juice

1 teaspoon ground cumin

Salt and pepper to taste

Flour for dredging

1 cup shredded or grated Greek Graviera cheese (or mild Gruyère)

⅓ cup dried bread crumbs

2 tablespoons finely chopped fresh mint

⅓ cup pine nuts

1 egg

1. Preheat the oven to 350°F.

2. Wash eggplant thoroughly and remove stalk. Slice thinly along its length; aim for 12 slices. Salt both sides and spread in a flower pattern in a colander. Set aside to drain for 30 minutes. Remember to flip the slices at least once for better drainage.

3. In a large frying pan over medium-high heat, sauté onions in ¼ cup olive oil until soft; stir garlic in for 1 minute. Add meat and mix well; sauté for 8–10 minutes to brown it thoroughly. Set aside while you prepare tomato sauce.

4. Add wine, 2 cups tomato juice, cumin, salt, and pepper to a small pot; stir well to mix completely. Bring to a boil and simmer over medium-low heat for 30 minutes, stirring occasionally. Once sauce has completely reduced, remove frying pan from heat and set aside to cool.

5. Heat 3 tablespoons olive oil in a large fry pan. Lightly flour both sides of the eggplant slices; fry in batches until softened. Add olive oil to pan as needed, but do it in a thin stream around the entire circumference of the pan so it seeps toward the center. Shake the frying pan back and forth with each batch to keep eggplant slices from sticking to the bottom. Once the eggplant slices have been lightly fried, spread on paper towels in a pan.

6. Retrieve the cooled meat mixture. In a large mixing bowl, add cheese (leave aside a few tablespoonfuls of shredded cheese for use as a garnish later), bread crumbs, mint, pine nuts, and egg; mix well to combine with meat. Pick up an eggplant slice; place a heaping spoonful of meat mixture in the middle of one end. Roll up that end to complete a full end-to-end overlapping roll; use a toothpick to pin in place. Be sure not to press the center of the roll too hard, as you do not want the meat to protrude from the open sides.

7. Place rolls side by side in close rows in a deep-walled pan greased with olive oil. Spoon tomato sauce on top of rolls in single stripe right along the middle of the rolled slices; sprinkle cheese on top of the tomato sauce stripe.

8. Bake for 30 minutes. Let stand to cool for at least 10 minutes before serving. Garnish with a little more shredded cheese while still warm.

PORK WITH LEEKS AND CELERY

Only use the white ends of the leeks and not the green stalks for this dish.

Serves 4

2 pounds pork shoulder, chopped into cubes

1 onion, finely chopped

½ cup extra-virgin olive oil

½ cup white wine

2 cups water

2 pounds leeks

1 cup finely chopped celery

1 cup tomatoes, diced and sieved (fresh or canned)

1 teaspoon dried oregano

Salt and fresh-ground pepper

1. Wash pork well; chop into cubes and set aside to drain.

2. In a deep-walled pot, sauté onion in olive oil until slightly soft; add pork and brown thoroughly.

3. Add wine to the pot; bring to a boil, then cover and simmer for 15 minutes, stirring regularly. Remove pork; cover to keep warm and set aside.

4. Add water to the pan along with the leeks and celery; bring to a boil and simmer for 30 minutes over medium heat.

5. Return pork to the pot along with tomatoes, oregano, salt, and pepper; stir well. Bring to a boil and continue to simmer until the sauce is reduced and thickened, approximately 8–10 minutes. Serve immediately.

Longevity

The oldest olive tree in the world is situated in Vouves, Crete, and is thought to be approximately 3,500 years old.

STIFADO (BRAISED BEEF WITH ONIONS)

If you cannot find pearl onions, then use the smallest onions you can find to prepare this dish.

Serves 4

½ cup extra-virgin olive oil

2 pounds stewing beef, cubed

2 tablespoons tomato paste, diluted in 2 cups of water

2 tablespoons wine vinegar (or a sweet dessert wine like Madeira or Mavrodaphne)

14–16 pearl onions, peeled

6 cloves garlic, peeled

4 spice cloves

1 small cinnamon stick

1 tablespoon dried oregano

Salt and fresh-ground pepper

1. Add olive oil to a large pot over medium-high heat; add meat and brown well on all sides by stirring continuously so meat does not stick to the bottom of the pot.

2. Add tomato paste, wine vinegar, onions, garlic, cloves, cinnamon, oregano, salt, and pepper; mix well and turn heat to high. Bring to a boil.

3. Cover and turn heat down to medium-low; simmer for approximately 1 hour.

4. Serve immediately, accompanied by fresh bread for sauce.

BRAISED LAMB SHOULDER

Serve this dish with rice, plain spaghetti, or fried potatoes.

Serves 4

1½–2 pounds lamb shoulder

½ cup extra-virgin olive oil

½ cup hot water

2 cups tomatoes, diced and sieved (fresh or canned)

2 bay leaves

4 cloves garlic, peeled and minced

1 cinnamon stick

1 tablespoon dried thyme

Salt and pepper to taste

1. Wash meat well and cut into small pieces; include bones.

2. Heat olive oil in a pot; brown meat on all sides.

3. Add water, tomatoes, bay leaves, garlic, cinnamon, thyme, salt, and pepper; cover and bring to a boil, then turn heat down to medium-low.

4. Simmer for 1½ hours, stirring occasionally.

APRICOT-STUFFED PORK TENDERLOIN

You can use dried apricots instead of fresh. However, you'll probably want to rehydrate them slightly in red wine.

Serves 6

1½-pound pork tenderloin

1 shallot

3 cloves garlic

6 apricots

½ cup pecans

3 fresh sage leaves

Fresh-cracked black pepper, to taste

Kosher salt, to taste

Cooking spray

1. Preheat the oven to 375°F.

2. Butterfly the tenderloin by making a lengthwise slice down the middle, making certain not to cut completely through.

3. Mince the shallot and garlic. Remove pits and slice apricots. Chop the pecans and sage.

4. Lay out the tenderloin. Layer all ingredients over the tenderloin and season with pepper and salt. Carefully roll up the loin and tie securely.

5. Spray a rack with cooking spray, then place the tenderloin on the rack and roast for 1–1½ hours. Let cool slightly, then slice.

STEWED SHORT RIBS OF BEEF

While you can certainly use any red wine that appeals to you, a Cabernet or Merlot wine is recommended.

Serves 6

12 plum tomatoes

2 large yellow onions

1½ pounds short ribs of beef

1 tablespoon ground cumin

Fresh-cracked black pepper, to taste

1 tablespoon olive oil

1 cup dry red wine

1 quart Hearty Red Wine Brown Stock (see recipe in Chapter 2)

1. Preheat the oven to 325°F.

2. Chop the tomatoes. Roughly chop the onions. Season the ribs with cumin and pepper.

3. Heat the oil over medium-high heat in a Dutch oven, and sear the ribs on all sides. Add the onions and sauté for 2 minutes, then add the tomatoes and sauté 1 minute more. Add the wine and let reduce by half.

4. Add the stock. When stock begins to boil, cover and place in oven for 1–1½ hours.

5. Drain the ribs and vegetables, reserving the stock. Keep the ribs and vegetables warm. Place the stock on the stove over high heat and let the sauce thicken to a gravy-type consistency.

SICILIAN STUFFED STEAK

For a spicier flavor, try using arugula instead of spinach leaves.

Serves 6

1 pound fresh baby spinach

5 eggs, divided

1 small yellow onion

4 cloves garlic

½ bunch Italian parsley

½ cup olive oil, divided

½ cup grated pecorino Romano cheese

¼ pound ground veal

Kosher salt, to taste

Fresh-cracked black pepper

2-pound round steak

½ pound prosciutto, diced

½ pound provolone or Asiago cheese, diced

1 cup dry red wine

1 cup veal stock

2 teaspoons tomato paste

1. Place the spinach in a saucepan and gently steam over medium heat until tender, about 8–10 minutes. Remove from heat and let cool. Drain and squeeze out as much water as possible.

2. Hard-boil 3 of the eggs, peel, and set aside. Finely dice the onion and mince the garlic. Chop the parsley.

3. Heat ¼ cup of the oil over medium heat in a sauté pan; sauté the onion and garlic until golden. Set aside.

4. Preheat the oven to 350°F.

5. Mix together the Romano cheese, ground veal, parsley, onion, and garlic. Season with salt and pepper. Add the 2 raw eggs and mix again. Spread the mixture evenly over the round steak. Place the slices of hard-boiled eggs in a row on top of the meat and the cheese mixture. Top with diced prosciutto, provolone, and spinach. Roll the meat tightly over stuffing and tie with string to secure it during cooking.

6. Brown the meat in the remaining oil until browned all over. Place in an ovenproof pan. In a saucepan, bring the wine, stock, and tomato paste to a boil. Pour this mixture over the meat and roast in the oven for 1½–2 hours, until the internal temperature reaches 165°F. Turn the meat often to baste.

7. Remove the meat from the pan and let stand for about 10 minutes before removing the string. Cut into slices and serve with the remaining juices.

SAUSAGE PATTIES

You can substitute some olive oil for pork fat, but keep in mind that the flavor will be compromised.

Serves 6

2 ounces pork fat

2 ounces pancetta

½ pound ground pork

½ pound ground veal

1 egg

1 tablespoon fresh-cracked black pepper, to taste

1 tablespoon dried sage

¼ teaspoon dried red pepper flakes

1 teaspoon ground cumin

Kosher salt, to taste

1 tablespoon olive oil

1. Finely dice the pork fat and pancetta. Mix together all the ingredients except the oil until thoroughly blended; form into patties.

2. Heat the oil over medium heat in a skillet. Brown the patties on each side, covered with a lid to ensure thorough cooking. Drain on a rack lined with paper towels, then serve.

CYPRIOT ORZO YIOUVETSI

This dish tastes best when cooked in a stoneware casserole, so if you have one available you will want to use it.

Serves 4

3 tablespoons Greek extra-virgin olive oil

1 pound lean ground veal

1 onion, grated or finely chopped

2 cloves garlic, finely chopped or pressed

1 cup fresh strained tomato sauce or
  2 tablespoons tomato paste diluted
  in 1 cup water

1 cinnamon stick

4 spice cloves

Salt and pepper to taste

4 cups Beef Stock (see recipe in Chapter 2)

1½ cups orzo pasta

1 teaspoon butter

1. Preheat oven to 350°F.

2. Heat olive oil in large saucepan over medium heat; add veal and break up with wooden spoon. Sauté 5–8 minutes, stirring constantly, until thoroughly browned.

3. Add onion, garlic, tomato sauce, cinnamon stick, cloves, salt, and pepper to saucepan with meat. Bring to a boil, stirring well; cover and simmer 15 minutes over medium-low heat.

4. In separate pan, bring stock to boil; cover and reduce heat to low.

5. When meat has cooked, remove cinnamon stick from pan. Add uncooked orzo pasta to hot stock for a couple of stirs; add stock to pan with meat sauce. Stir to mix thoroughly.

6. Butter sides and bottom of casserole; add yiouvetsi mixture. Bake uncovered 50–60 minutes, until liquid has been absorbed by pasta.

7. Stir well with wooden spoon only once, at about 25-minute mark (making sure to get into corners of dish); let it cook undisturbed for remainder of time. Look for surface of yiouvetsi to form a crust-like top layer, especially near edges.

8. Remove from oven and let sit for 15 minutes before serving.

CHAPTER 9

POULTRY ENTRÉES

ROOSTER BRAISED IN WINE (KOKKOROS KRASSATO)

Serve this savory dish with hollow pasta to catch all the sauce.

Serves 4

1 (3–4 pound) whole rooster or capon or whole chicken, cut into pieces and skinned (skin reserved)

2 teaspoons salt, divided

¾ teaspoon pepper, divided

½ cup plus 2 tablespoons extra-virgin olive oil, divided

1 cup canned puréed tomatoes

2½ teaspoons tomato paste

1 cup dry red wine

4 or 5 whole allspice berries

1 stick cinnamon

4 medium onions, peeled and halved

3 or 4 cloves garlic, peeled and smashed

1 cup hot Chicken or Turkey Stock (see recipe in Chapter 2) or hot water

1. Season the reserved skin and rooster pieces with 1 teaspoon of salt and ½ teaspoon of pepper. Brown the skin in a large pot over medium heat for 2 minutes. Cover the pot, and allow the skin to render its fat for 2–3 minutes. Uncover the pot, and continue to brown and crisp the skin. Flip the skin over and brown and crisp the other side. Transfer the skin to a tray lined with paper towels and reserve. Leave the fat in the pan.

2. To the pot, add 2 tablespoons of oil and heat for 30 seconds. Add the rooster and brown both sides for 4–5 minutes a side. Transfer the rooster from the pot to a plate and reserve.

3. To the pot, add the tomatoes, tomato paste, wine, and remaining ½ cup of oil. Increase the heat to medium-high and bring the sauce to a boil. Add the rooster, allspice, cinnamon, onions, garlic, and stock. Season with the remaining salt and pepper. Bring everything back to a boil, and then reduce the heat to medium-low. Cover and cook for 90 minutes.

4. Uncover the pot and cook for another 10–15 minutes to thicken the sauce. Adjust the seasoning with more salt and pepper, if necessary. Remove the cinnamon stick and serve hot. Garnish with a crumble of reserved chicken skins.

Roosters

The French have Coq au Vin, the Greeks have Kokkoros Krassato. Roosters are more active than hens and have more muscle, which can make their meat tough. Braising this bird with lots of wine, herbs, and spices will make it tender.

CHICKEN SOUVLAKI

These chicken skewers are traditionally served with lightly grilled pita bread and Tzatziki (see recipe in Chapter 2).

Serves 6

2 pounds boneless, skinless chicken thighs, cut into 1-inch cubes

⅓ cup extra-virgin olive oil

2 medium onions, peeled and grated

4 cloves garlic, peeled and minced

2 tablespoons grated lemon zest

1 teaspoon dried oregano

1 teaspoon chopped fresh rosemary leaves

2 teaspoons salt

1 teaspoon pepper

2 tablespoons fresh lemon juice

1. In a large bowl, combine the chicken, oil, onions, garlic, lemon zest, oregano, rosemary, salt, and pepper. Toss to make sure the chicken is well coated. Cover the bowl with plastic wrap and refrigerate for 8 hours or overnight. Take the chicken out of the refrigerator for 30 minutes before skewering.

2. Preheat the gas or charcoal grill to medium-high. Put the chicken onto wooden or metal skewers; each skewer should hold 4 pieces.

3. Place the skewers on the grill and grill for 3–4 minutes per side or until chicken is no longer pink inside.

4. Drizzle lemon juice over the skewers and serve.

GREEK-STYLE ROASTED CHICKEN WITH POTATOES

Roast chicken is a universal comfort food. This is a lemony Greek version with roasted potatoes.

Serves 4

4–6 Yukon gold potatoes, peeled and cut into wedges

½ cup plus 2 tablespoons extra-virgin olive oil, divided

2 tablespoons Dijon mustard

2½ teaspoons salt, divided

1 teaspoon pepper, divided

1 teaspoon dried oregano

3 tablespoons fresh lemon juice, divided

½ cup hot water

1 (3-pound) whole chicken, rinsed and dried

3 cloves garlic, peeled and smashed

3 sprigs fresh thyme plus ½ teaspoon dried thyme

3 sprigs fresh parsley

½ large lemon, quartered

½ teaspoon dried oregano

1. Preheat the oven to 375°F. Put the potatoes, ½ cup of oil, mustard, 1 teaspoon of salt, ½ teaspoon of pepper, oregano, 2 tablespoons of lemon juice, and hot water in a roasting pan. Toss the ingredients together to coat the potatoes. Reserve.

2. Into the chicken cavity, put the garlic, thyme sprigs, parsley, and lemon. Combine the remaining oil and lemon juice, and rub the mixture all over the surface of the chicken. Season the chicken with the remaining salt and pepper and then sprinkle with the dried thyme and oregano.

3. Place the chicken on the potatoes in the roasting pan. Roast on the middle rack for 90 minutes or until the internal temperature of the chicken reaches 180°F. Let the chicken rest for 15 minutes before serving.

4. Serve warm with the roasted potatoes.

ROAST CHICKEN WITH OKRA

The combination of chicken and okra is a classic Greek choice. This dish is ideal in the summer months when okra and tomatoes are in season.

Serves 4

1 (3-pound) whole chicken, cut into pieces, rinsed and dried

2 teaspoons salt, divided

¾ teaspoon pepper, divided

½ cup extra-virgin olive oil

2 large onions, peeled and sliced

1 pound fresh okra, rinsed and stems trimmed

4 large ripe tomatoes, skinned and grated

5 or 6 cloves garlic, peeled and sliced

4 or 5 whole allspice berries

½ cup chopped fresh parsley

1. Season chicken with 1 teaspoon of salt and ½ teaspoon of pepper.

2. Put the chicken in a large pot over medium-high heat with enough water to just cover it. Bring the water to a boil, reduce the heat to medium-low, and cook for 30 minutes. Skim the fat off the surface of the water and discard the fat. Remove the chicken from the pot and reserve the liquid. Preheat the oven to 375°F.

3. Heat the oil in a large skillet over medium heat for 30 seconds. Add the onions and cook for 7–10 minutes or until they are translucent. Add the okra and cook for 5 minutes. Add the tomatoes, garlic, allspice, and parsley, and cook for 5 minutes. Add just enough of the reserved liquid to cover the okra.

4. Transfer the contents of the skillet to a large baking dish. Place the chicken pieces on top and season with the remaining salt and pepper. Cover the baking dish.

5. Bake for 30 minutes. Uncover and bake for another 15 minutes. Allow the chicken to rest for 5–10 minutes before serving.

CHICKEN CACCIATORE

The name of this classic Italian dish means "Hunter's Chicken." It can also be made with rabbit. Serve with roast potatoes and some bread for soaking up the delicious sauce.

Serves 4

1 (3-pound) whole chicken, cut into 8 pieces, rinsed and dried

2 teaspoons salt, divided

1 teaspoon pepper, divided

¼ cup all-purpose flour

¼ cup extra-virgin olive oil

1 (6-inch) Italian sausage, casing removed and crumbled

2 medium onions, chopped

1 large carrot, peeled and chopped

1 stalk celery, trimmed and chopped

⅓ cup diced green pepper, stemmed and seeded

1 cup sliced cremini mushrooms

3 bay leaves

2 teaspoons chopped fresh rosemary

¼ cup chopped fresh parsley

1 tablespoon tomato paste

4 cloves garlic, peeled and smashed

1 cup dry white wine

1 (28-ounce) can whole tomatoes, hand crushed

½ cup hot Chicken or Turkey Stock (see recipe in Chapter 2)

1. Season the chicken with 1 teaspoon of salt and ½ teaspoon of pepper. Dredge the chicken in the flour. Set aside.

2. Heat the oil in a Dutch oven (or heavy-bottomed pot) over medium-high heat for 30 seconds. Add the chicken and brown for 3–4 minutes on each side. Remove the chicken and reserve.

3. Add the sausage to the pot and brown for 2 minutes. Lower the heat to medium and add the onions, carrots, celery, peppers, mushrooms, bay leaves, and rosemary. Cook the ingredients for 5–7 minutes or until the onions are translucent. Add the parsley, tomato paste, and garlic, and cook for 2 minutes. Add the wine and cook for 5–7 minutes. Add the tomatoes and stock, and cook for 2 minutes.

4. Put the chicken back in the pot and lower the heat to medium-low. Partially cover the pot and cook for 60–80 minutes or until the sauce is thick and chunky. Remove the bay leaves.

5. Allow the chicken to rest for 5–10 minutes before serving with the sauce.

CHICKEN GIOULBASI

This foolproof roast chicken is wrapped in parchment paper and stuffed with kefalotyri cheese. Serve with mashed potatoes or rice and a dollop of Homemade Greek Yogurt (see recipe in Chapter 1).

Serves 4

1 (3-pound) whole chicken, rinsed and dried

¼ cup extra-virgin olive oil

1 tablespoon grated lemon zest

3 tablespoons fresh lemon juice

1½ teaspoons salt

½ teaspoon pepper

½ teaspoon sweet paprika

2 teaspoons dried oregano

6 or 7 cloves garlic, peeled and smashed

¾ cup cubed kefalotyri or Romano cheese

½ large lemon, cut into wedges

1. Preheat the oven to 400°F. Take two pieces of parchment paper (each 2 feet long) and lay them on a work surface in a cross pattern. Place the chicken in the middle of the parchment paper.

2. In a small bowl, combine the oil, lemon zest, and lemon juice. Rub the oil-lemon mixture all over the chicken. Season the chicken with salt and pepper, and sprinkle with paprika and oregano. Place the garlic, cheese, and lemon wedges in the cavity of the chicken.

3. Wrap the parchment around the chicken, so it is completely enclosed. Use butcher's twine and tie the chicken into a bundle.

4. Place the chicken in a roasting pan and roast for 90–110 minutes or until the internal temperature of the chicken is 180°F.

5. Let the chicken rest for 15 minutes before unwrapping it; then serve.

GRAPE-LEAF CHICKEN STUFFED WITH FETA

These moist chicken breasts can be served with a side of couscous.

Serves 4

½ cup crumbled feta cheese

2 scallions, ends trimmed and finely chopped

4 sun-dried tomatoes, finely chopped

1 tablespoon chopped fresh lemon verbena or lemon thyme

¾ teaspoon pepper

4 boneless, skinless chicken breasts

1½ teaspoons salt

8 large jarred grape leaves, rinsed and stems removed

¼ cup extra-virgin olive oil

1. Preheat the oven to 375°F. In a medium bowl, combine the feta, scallions, tomatoes, lemon verbena, and pepper. Mash the ingredients with a fork and set them aside.

2. Using a sharp knife, cut a slit 3 inches wide in the middle of the thickest part of the chicken breast. The slit should penetrate two-thirds of the way into the chicken breast to create a pocket. Stuff one-quarter of the filling into the pocket. Repeat with the remaining chicken breasts. Season the chicken with salt.

3. Place 2 or 3 grape leaves on a work surface and place the chicken breast on top. Wrap the leaves around the chicken. Set the chicken, seam-side down, on a baking sheet lined with parchment paper. Brush the wrapped chicken on both sides with the oil. Repeat with the remaining chicken.

4. Bake on the middle rack for 20–25 minutes. Let the chicken rest for 5 minutes before slicing each breast and serving.

GRILLED WHOLE CHICKEN UNDER A BRICK

This method for preparing chicken results in quick, even cooking and a crispy skin.

Serves 4

8 cloves garlic, peeled and minced

1 small onion, peeled and grated

2¼ teaspoons salt, divided

2 tablespoons fresh lemon juice

2 bay leaves, crushed

2 teaspoons sweet paprika

¼ cup Metaxa brandy or any other brandy

2 teaspoons chopped fresh rosemary leaves

2 tablespoons extra-virgin olive oil

1 (4-pound) whole chicken, rinsed, dried, and spatchcocked

1. In a medium bowl, whisk the garlic, onion, ¼ teaspoon of salt, lemon juice, bay leaves, paprika, brandy, rosemary, and oil.

2. Pierce the chicken several times with a sharp knife to help the marinade penetrate the chicken. Place the chicken in a glass baking dish just big enough to contain it. Pour the marinade over the chicken and rub it in. Cover the baking dish with plastic wrap and refrigerate the chicken for 3–4 hours. Take the chicken out of the marinade and season it with the remaining salt.

3. Preheat a gas or charcoal grill (with a lid) to medium-high. Wrap 2 heavy bricks individually in aluminum foil. Place the chicken breast-side down on the grill. Place the bricks on the chicken to weigh down the chicken as it grills. Grill the chicken for 10 minutes. Carefully remove the bricks with thick oven mitts. Flip the chicken over and place it on a side of the grill that has indirect heat. Close the grill lid and roast the chicken for 30–40 minutes or until the internal temperature reaches 180°F.

4. Let the chicken rest 10 minutes before serving.

How to Spatchcock a Chicken

Place a whole chicken, breast-side down, on a clean work surface. Using a pair of sharp kitchen scissors, remove the chicken's backbone; starting on the left side of the backbone, cut from the tail to the neck, and then repeat on the right side. Turn the chicken over and press down on the breastbone to flatten it.

SKILLET CHICKEN PARMESAN

This is a great weeknight meal that is easy to prepare in one skillet. Serve it with a green salad.

Serves 4

⅔ cup cornmeal

⅓ cup all-purpose flour

1 teaspoon dried oregano

1 teaspoon finely chopped and 1 cup chopped fresh basil, divided

1 teaspoon finely chopped fresh rosemary

4 boneless, skinless chicken breasts or thighs

½ cup plus 3 tablespoons extra-virgin olive oil, divided

1 teaspoon salt, divided

½ teaspoon pepper, divided

1 medium onion, peeled and diced

5 or 6 cloves garlic, peeled and minced

3 cups canned whole tomatoes, hand crushed

¼ cup dry white wine

2 cups grated mozzarella cheese

1. In a large bowl, combine the cornmeal, flour, oregano, 1 teaspoon of finely chopped basil, and rosemary. Reserve.

2. Using a heavy pot or kitchen mallet, pound the chicken to ½-inch thickness. Cut the chicken pieces in half. Brush the pieces with 3 tablespoons of oil and season with ½ teaspoon of salt and ¼ teaspoon of pepper. Dredge the chicken in the reserved cornmeal and flour mixture.

3. Heat ¼ cup oil in a large skillet over medium-high heat for 30 seconds. Add the chicken (in batches) and fry for 2–3 minutes a side or until browned. Place the chicken on a tray lined with paper towels to soak up excess oil. Discard the oil used for frying and wipe the skillet clean.

4. Heat the remaining oil in the skillet over medium heat for 30 seconds. Add the onions and garlic and cook for 5–6 minutes. Add the tomatoes and wine. Increase the heat to medium-high and bring the sauce to a boil; then reduce the heat to medium-low. Season with the remaining salt and pepper. Nestle the chicken into the sauce. Cover the skillet, and cook for 30 minutes or until the sauce has thickened and chicken is tender.

5. Stir in the remaining basil and top the sauce with cheese. Cover the skillet and let the cheese melt for 2 minutes. Serve warm.

CHIANTI CHICKEN

If you can't find lemon verbena, use lemon thyme or a combination of lemon zest and regular thyme. Serve this dish with some couscous and mushrooms.

Serves 4

3 cloves garlic, peeled and minced

2 tablespoons finely chopped lemon verbena or lemon thyme

2 tablespoons finely chopped fresh parsley

2¼ teaspoons salt, divided

⅓ cup and 2 tablespoons extra-virgin olive oil, divided

4 chicken quarters (legs and thighs), rinsed and dried

¾ teaspoon pepper

4 tablespoons unsalted butter, divided

2 cups red grapes (in clusters)

1 medium red onion, peeled and sliced

1 cup Chianti red wine

1 cup Chicken or Turkey Stock or Basic Vegetable Stock (see recipes in Chapter 2)

1. Preheat the oven to 400°F. In a small bowl, whisk the garlic, lemon verbena, parsley, ¼ teaspoon of salt, and 2 tablespoons of oil.

2. Season the chicken with the remaining salt and pepper. Place your finger between the skin and meat of the chicken thigh and loosen it by moving your finger back and forth to create a pocket. Spread one quarter of the garlic-herb mixture into the pocket. Repeat the process with the remaining chicken quarters.

3. Heat the remaining oil and 2 tablespoons of butter in a large oven-safe pot over medium-high heat for 30 seconds. Add the chicken quarters and brown them for 3–4 minutes per side.

4. Top the chicken with the grapes. Roast the chicken on the middle rack of the oven for 20–30 minutes or until the chicken's internal temperature reaches 180°F. Remove the chicken and grapes from the pot and keep them warm. Remove any excess fat from the pot.

5. Return the pot to the stovetop over medium heat; add the onions and cook for 3–4 minutes. Add the wine and stock, and increase the heat to medium-high. Bring the mixture to a boil, and then reduce the heat to medium-low. Cook the sauce until it thickens. Take the pot off the heat and stir in the remaining butter.

6. To serve, put some of the sauce on the bottom of a plate and top with the chicken and grapes. Serve this dish with extra sauce on the side.

Chianti

Chianti is a wine-growing region in Tuscany (near Florence, Italy). Its gentle, rolling hills contain a mix of olive groves and vineyards.

CHICKEN BREASTS WITH SPINACH AND FETA

Spinach and feta is a classic Greek combination that pairs well with chicken, wine, and cream.

Serves 4

½ cup frozen spinach, thawed, excess water squeezed out

4 tablespoons chopped fresh chives

4 tablespoons chopped fresh dill

½ cup crumbled feta cheese

⅓ cup ricotta cheese

4 boneless, skinless chicken breasts

1½ teaspoons salt

½ teaspoon pepper

½ teaspoon sweet paprika

2 tablespoons extra-virgin olive oil

2 tablespoons unsalted butter

½ cup dry white wine

2 tablespoons minced red onions

1 clove garlic, peeled and smashed

2 tablespoons all-purpose flour

1 cup Chicken or Turkey Stock (see recipe in Chapter 2)

⅓ cup heavy cream

1. In a medium bowl, combine the spinach, chives, dill, feta, and ricotta. Reserve.

2. Using a sharp knife, cut a 3-inch slit into the middle of the thickest part of the chicken breast. The slit should penetrate two-thirds of the way into the chicken breast to create a pocket. Stuff one-quarter of the spinach-cheese filling into the pocket. Secure the opening with toothpicks. Repeat with the remaining chicken. Then season the chicken with salt, pepper, and paprika.

3. Heat the oil and butter in a large skillet over medium-high heat for 30 seconds. Brown the chicken for 3–4 minutes per side. Set the chicken aside and keep it warm. Add the wine to the skillet, and deglaze the pan. Cook for 2 minutes, or until most of the wine has evaporated. Reduce the heat to medium, and stir in the onions, garlic, and flour. Cook for 2 minutes.

4. Add the stock, increase the heat to medium-high, and bring the sauce to a boil. Reduce the heat to medium and return the chicken to the skillet. Cover the skillet and cook for 25 minutes. Remove the chicken again and keep it warm. Add the cream and cook until the sauce thickens. Adjust the seasoning with more salt and pepper, if necessary.

5. Slice the chicken and put it on the plates. Pour the sauce over the chicken and serve the extra sauce on the side.

CHICKEN TAGINE WITH PRESERVED LEMONS AND OLIVES

A tagine is a piece of conical ceramic or clay cookware commonly used in North Africa. If you don't have a tagine, a Dutch oven works just as well.

Serves 4

3 cloves garlic, chopped

1 tablespoon chopped fresh ginger

1½ preserved lemons, divided

4 medium onions (2 peeled and chopped, 2 peeled and sliced), divided

1 small chili pepper

1 tablespoon sweet paprika

½ teaspoon ground cumin

2 teaspoons salt, divided

2 tablespoons plus 1 cup chopped fresh cilantro

2 tablespoons chopped fresh parsley

¼ teaspoon saffron threads, soaked in ½ cup hot water

½ cup extra-virgin olive oil

3 bay leaves

4 chicken quarters (legs and thighs), rinsed and dried

2 ripe tomatoes (1 chopped and 1 sliced), divided

2 large potatoes, peeled and cut into wedges

1 cup water

½ cup pitted green olives

1. To a food processor, add the garlic, ginger, ½ preserved lemon, chopped onions, chili, paprika, cumin, 1 teaspoon salt, 2 tablespoons cilantro, parsley, saffron soaked in water, oil, and bay leaves. Process until everything is chopped and well incorporated. Set the marinade aside.

2. In a large bowl, combine the chicken and half of the marinade. Toss the chicken to coat it well in the marinade. Season the chicken with the remaining salt.

3. In the tagine base (or Dutch oven), put the chopped tomatoes, potatoes, sliced onions, and remaining marinade. Toss to combine and coat the vegetables in the marinade. Add the water to the vegetables and stir. Place the chicken on top of the vegetables. Top the chicken with the tomato slices. Sprinkle with the olives and 1 cup cilantro. Cut the remaining lemon into six wedges and arrange them in the tagine.

4. Cover the tagine and place it on the stove over medium-low heat. Cook for 45–50 minutes. Do not stir or uncover the tagine while it is cooking.

5. Remove the bay leaves; serve the dish in the tagine at the table.

Preserved Lemons

The practice of preserving lemons came from North Africa, but it has gained popularity in Mediterranean kitchens. Lemons are preserved in salt and spices for up to a month before they are ready to use. You can find preserved lemons at Middle Eastern or African grocery stores.

POMEGRANATE-GLAZED CHICKEN

Make sure you use pure pomegranate juice in this recipe. Mastiha can be found at Greek or Middle Eastern grocery stores.

Serves 4

4 bone-in skinless chicken breasts, rinsed and dried

1 teaspoon salt

½ teaspoon pepper

2 cups pomegranate juice

⅛ teaspoon ground mastiha

2 teaspoons grated orange zest

3 cloves garlic, peeled and smashed

1 teaspoon dried rosemary

1. Preheat the oven to 375°F. Season the chicken with the salt and pepper. Place the chicken on a baking sheet lined with parchment paper. Bake the chicken on the middle rack in the oven for 25–30 minutes or until the chicken's internal temperature is 180°F.

2. In a small pan over medium-high heat, combine the pomegranate juice, mastiha, orange zest, garlic, and rosemary. Bring the mixture to a boil, reduce the heat to medium-low, and cook until the sauce reduces to ¼ cup and has a syrup-like consistency. Remove the garlic and take the sauce off the heat.

3. Brush the chicken with the reserved sauce and serve the remaining sauce on the side.

Fresh Pomegranate Juice

You can make your own pomegranate juice. Slice three or four pomegranates in half. With the seed side over a bowl, tap each pomegranate bottom with a wooden spoon to release the seeds. You'll need to tap several times to release all the seeds. Remove any white pith from the bowl. Put the seeds in a food processor, and process for 5 minutes. Strain the juice with a fine-mesh sieve to remove the pits. Refrigerate the juice.

CHICKEN MASKOULI

This chicken dish is a specialty of the northern Greek city Kastoria. The sauce is thickened with ground walnuts. Serve it on a bed of egg noodles.

Serves 4

4 chicken quarters (legs and thighs), rinsed and dried

2 teaspoons salt, divided

1 teaspoon pepper, divided

½ cup extra-virgin olive oil, divided

2 large onions, peeled and sliced

4 or 5 cloves garlic, minced

2 cups sliced cremini mushrooms

3 bay leaves

2 teaspoons thyme leaves

1 cup Riesling wine or other sweet white wine

2 cups Basic Vegetable Stock or Chicken or Turkey Stock (see recipes in Chapter 2)

1 teaspoon sweet paprika

¾ cup chopped walnuts or almonds

¼ cup chopped fresh parsley

1. Season the chicken with 1 teaspoon of salt and ½ teaspoon of pepper. Heat ¼ cup of oil in a large skillet over medium-high heat for 30 seconds. Add the chicken quarters, and brown them for 3–4 minutes per side. Remove the chicken and keep warm.

2. Reduce the heat to medium and add the onions, garlic, mushrooms, bay leaves, and thyme. Cook for 5 minutes, and season the vegetables with the remaining salt and pepper. Cover the skillet and cook for 5 minutes. Remove the cover and cook for another 5 minutes or until almost all of the water has evaporated.

3. Add the wine, stock, and paprika. Increase the heat to medium-high and bring the sauce to a boil. Reduce the heat to medium-low. Add the chicken back to the skillet. Cook for 35–40 minutes. The sauce will reduce and thicken.

4. Put the walnuts and remaining oil in a food processor. Process until the walnuts are ground. When the chicken has finished cooking, remove it and place it on a serving platter. Add the walnut mixture to the sauce, and cook for another 5 minutes. Adjust the seasoning with more salt and pepper, if necessary. Stir in the parsley. Remove the bay leaves.

5. Spoon the sauce over the chicken and serve the remaining sauce on the side.

PESTO-BAKED CHICKEN WITH CHEESE

To keep the pesto from burning, cover it loosely with foil.

Serves 6

6 skinless chicken quarters (legs and thighs), rinsed and dried

¼ cup all-purpose flour

½ cup Basil and Pine Nut Pesto (see recipe in Chapter 2)

1 teaspoon salt

½ teaspoon pepper

1 cup grated mozzarella cheese

1. Preheat the oven to 375°F. Dredge the chicken in flour. In a large bowl, combine the chicken and Basil and Pine Nut Pesto, and toss the chicken to coat it completely.

2. Place the chicken on a baking sheet lined with parchment paper. Season chicken with salt and pepper, and cover loosely with foil. Bake for 45–55 minutes or until the chicken's internal temperature is 180°F.

3. Remove the foil and top the chicken with the cheese. Turn the oven to broil and broil the chicken until the cheese is melted. Serve warm.

ROSEMARY CHICKEN THIGHS AND LEGS WITH POTATOES

Serve this fragrant dish with a side of buttered noodles or a green salad.

Serves 6

2 pounds chicken thighs and legs, rinsed and dried

1 leek, ends trimmed, thoroughly cleaned, cut lengthwise, and sliced

8 cloves garlic, peeled and minced

2 tablespoons chopped fresh rosemary

6 small red potatoes, halved

1 tablespoon extra-virgin olive oil

2 teaspoons salt

¾ teaspoon pepper

¼ cup capers

1. Preheat the oven to 375°F.

2. In a large baking dish, combine all the ingredients except for the capers. Toss well to combine the marinade and coat the chicken and potatoes.

3. Bake in the middle rack of the oven for 1 hour or until the chicken's internal temperature is 180°F.

4. Sprinkle with capers and serve.

ROAST TURKEY

Brining the bird creates a turkey that is always tender and juicy!

Serves 10

1 (12-pound) turkey, cavity and neck empty, rinsed and dried

3 bay leaves

12 peppercorns

3 cloves garlic, peeled and smashed

6 sprigs fresh thyme plus ½ teaspoon thyme leaves

½ cup chopped fresh parsley

½ cup Moscato wine or other fortified wine

10 allspice berries

½ cup orange juice

1 cup plus 2 teaspoons salt, divided

¼ cup extra-virgin olive oil

1 teaspoon pepper

½ teaspoon sweet paprika

1 teaspoon garlic powder

1 teaspoon chopped fresh rosemary

1. In a pot or pail just large enough to hold the turkey, add the turkey and just enough cold water to cover the turkey. Take the turkey out and set it aside.

2. To the water, add the bay leaves, peppercorns, garlic, thyme sprigs, parsley, wine, allspice, orange juice, and 1 cup of salt. Stir the brine until all the salt dissolves, which could take a few minutes. Place the turkey in the brine and cover it. Put the turkey and the brine in the refrigerator for 24 hours.

3. Preheat the oven to 325°F. Remove the turkey from the brine, discard the brine, and let the turkey come to room temperature for 1 hour. Rinse the turkey and pat it dry with paper towels. Place the turkey on the rack of a large roaster. Rub the oil all over the turkey and then season it evenly with the remaining salt, pepper, paprika, and garlic powder. Sprinkle the turkey with the thyme leaves and rosemary.

4. Roast the turkey on the middle rack for 3½ hours. If the skin is getting too brown, cover the bird with aluminum foil. The internal temperature of the turkey should be 180°F (check using a meat thermometer inserted into its thigh without touching the bone).

5. Remove the turkey from the oven and tent it with aluminum foil. Allow the turkey to rest for 45 minutes before serving.

TURKEY BREAST PICCATA

Try this lighter version of the Italian classic that traditionally uses veal or chicken.

Serves 6

1½ pounds whole boneless, skinless turkey breast

¼ cup all-purpose flour

¼ cup extra-virgin olive oil

¼ cup dry white wine

3 tablespoons fresh lemon juice

½ cup turkey or Chicken or Turkey Stock (see recipe in Chapter 2)

½ tablespoon capers

¼ cup chopped fresh parsley

1. Slice the turkey breast into thin scallopine-size portions and dredge in the flour.

2. Heat the oil in a large skillet over medium-high heat for 30 seconds. Add the turkey and brown the slices for 2 minutes on each side.

3. Add the wine and lemon juice, and let the liquid reduce by half. Add the stock and cook for 5–6 minutes or until the sauce thickens.

4. To serve, sprinkle the sliced turkey with the capers and parsley, and then drizzle the sauce over the slices.

BACON-WRAPPED QUAIL

Although delicious, quail are little game birds that are very lean. Adding bacon fattens them up a bit.

Serves 4

½ cup extra-virgin olive oil, divided

3 or 4 cloves garlic, peeled and minced

½ tablespoon grated lemon zest

2 tablespoons fresh lemon juice

1 tablespoon grated orange zest

1 teaspoon sweet paprika

½ teaspoon ground cinnamon

2 teaspoons fresh thyme leaves

1 teaspoon salt

½ teaspoon pepper

4 (7-ounce) whole quail, rinsed and dried

8 strips bacon

1 large lemon, cut into wedges

1. In a large baking dish, combine ¼ cup of oil, garlic, lemon zest, lemon juice, orange zest, paprika, cinnamon, thyme, salt, and pepper. Mix to combine the ingredients well. Add the quail and toss to coat them in the marinade. Cover the quail with plastic wrap and refrigerate them for 6 hours.

2. Let the quail come to room temperature. To help the quail roast evenly, tuck each quail's wingtips back under the bird and tie the legs together with butcher's twine.

3. Preheat the oven to 400°F. Wrap each quail with two strips of bacon, and tuck the ends of the bacon underneath the bird. Heat the remaining oil in a large cast-iron pan for 1 minute. Add the quail and brown them on all sides.

4. Roast the quail in the cast-iron pan on the middle rack for 20 minutes. Let them rest for 5 minutes before serving with lemon wedges.

ROASTED CORNISH HENS STUFFED WITH GOAT CHEESE AND FIGS

Here's another Sunday roast or a holiday dinner offering. The filling is tart and sweet with figs and goat cheese.

Serves 4

4 Cornish hens, rinsed and dried

1 cup plus 1 teaspoon salt, divided

½ cup plus 2 tablespoons extra-virgin olive oil, divided

¼ cup dry white wine

4 cloves garlic, peeled and minced

1 teaspoon ground fennel seeds

1 tablespoon sweet paprika

1½ tablespoons grated lemon zest, divided

3 tablespoons fresh lemon juice

3 tablespoons plus 1 teaspoon fresh thyme leaves, divided

1 teaspoon pepper

¾ cup goat cheese, crumbled

10 dried figs, roughly chopped

1 large egg, beaten

1. In a pot or pail large enough to hold the hens, add the hens and just enough cold water to cover them. Take the hens out and set them aside. Add 1 cup of salt to the water, stirring until all the salt dissolves. This could take a few minutes. Place the hens in the brine and cover them. Put the hens and brine in the refrigerator overnight.

2. In a large baking dish, combine the hens, ¼ cup of oil, wine, garlic, fennel, paprika, 1 tablespoon of lemon zest, lemon juice, 3 tablespoons thyme, remaining salt, and pepper. Toss to combine and coat the hens in the marinade. Refrigerate the hens for 3 hours. Let the hens come to room temperature for 30 minutes in the marinade then discard marinade. Preheat the oven to 400°F.

3. In a bowl, combine the goat cheese, remaining oil, remaining thyme, figs, remaining lemon zest, and egg. Stir well to combine the filling. Stuff each hen with one-quarter of the cheese stuffing. Tie the legs together with butcher's twine.

4. Place the hens in a roasting pan (raised on a rack) and pour the excess marinade over them. Roast the hens on the middle rack for 1 hour or until their internal temperature is 180°F.

5. Tent the hens with aluminum foil and let them rest for 10 minutes before serving them.

ROAST LEMON CHICKEN

You can add potato wedges to the pan in this recipe, just make sure to add enough water to almost cover the potatoes, along with the juice of one more lemon and 2 more tablespoonfuls of olive oil.

Serves 4

1 whole chicken

Salt and pepper to taste

Juice of 2 lemons, shells retained

2 tablespoons extra-virgin olive oil

1 tablespoon prepared mustard

1 teaspoon dried oregano

1. Preheat the oven to 400°F.

2. Wash the chicken well inside and out and pat dry. Sprinkle inside and out with salt and pepper, and stuff the squeezed-out lemon halves into the cavity. Place chicken breast down on a rack in a shallow roasting dish. Combine lemon juice, olive oil, mustard, and oregano; brush/pour over entire chicken.

3. Bake for 60–70 minutes, making sure to turn chicken over at halfway point and basting it regularly with juices from pan.

4. To test if it's done, prick with a fork and see if juices run clear, or test with a meat thermometer for 165°F. When done, turn off the oven and cover chicken in aluminum foil. Let rest in a warm oven for 10 minutes.

5. Serve hot with pan juices.

Lemon History

The lemon is not native to the Mediterranean region. It is conjectured to have been brought from Asia sometime around the first or second centuries A. D. A first-century A. D. wall painting in Pompeii is the earliest available evidence of the lemon in Europe.

CHICKEN WITH YOGURT

You don't need to use a whole chicken for this recipe; drumsticks, thighs, and breasts can all be used exclusively or in combination.

Serves 4

1 whole chicken

2 lemons, halved

Salt and pepper

2 cups strained yogurt

2 tablespoons milk

2 tablespoons fresh mint, chopped

2 cups dry bread crumbs

½ cup salted butter

1. Preheat the oven to 350°F.

2. Wash chicken well inside and out and pat dry with a paper towel. Cut chicken into sections; rub vigorously with lemon halves and sprinkle with salt and pepper. Place pieces in a colander; let stand for 1 hour.

3. Place yogurt in a mixing bowl. Add milk and mint; mix well with a whisk until smooth.

4. Dip each piece of chicken into yogurt mix, then cover entirely with a good sprinkling of bread crumbs. Place on a greased roasting pan; drizzle melted butter over the top.

5. Bake for about 1 hour, until the chicken pieces are golden brown.

6. Serve with a side of rice or fried potatoes.

CHICKEN WITH EGG NOODLES AND WALNUTS

If you have a nut allergy, the walnuts are really an optional element and not necessary for the success of this dish.

Serves 4–6

1 whole chicken

½ cup extra-virgin olive oil

1 onion, diced

¼ cup butter

2 cups tomato pulp, minced and sieved

4 cups boiling water

1 tablespoon fresh mint, chopped

Salt and pepper

1 pound square egg noodles (Greek hilopites)

½ cup crushed walnuts

Grated myzithra or Parmesan cheese for garnish (optional)

1. Wash chicken well inside and out and pat dry with a paper towel. Cut into sections.

2. Heat oil. Sauté onion slightly; add butter and chicken and sauté thoroughly on all sides.

3. Add tomatoes, boiling water, mint, salt, and pepper. Bring to a boil; cover and simmer over medium-low heat for 30 minutes.

4. Add egg noodles and crushed walnuts; give a good stir. Cover and continue to simmer for another 30 minutes.

5. Stir before serving hot with some grated myzithra or Parmesan cheese over each helping.

STUFFED GRILLED CHICKEN BREASTS

Make sure to pin the open end of the breasts closed tightly so the stuffing does not drip out into your barbecue and cause flare-ups.

Serves 6

6 large boneless, skinless chicken breasts

1 cup crumbled Greek feta cheese

½ cup finely minced sun-dried tomatoes

1 teaspoon dried oregano

2 tablespoons extra-virgin olive oil

Salt and pepper

1. Wash chicken breasts well and pat dry with a paper towel.

2. In a bowl, mix feta with sun-dried tomatoes and oregano; combine thoroughly.

3. Place each chicken breast on a flat surface; using a sharp paring knife, carefully slit the top edge of each breast and make a deep incision that runs within the length of each breast. Be careful not to pierce any holes that would allow stuffing to seep out while grilling.

4. Use a small spoon to stuff an equal portion of cheese mixture into each breast; use poultry pins or toothpicks to close openings.

5. Sear breasts in a heated frying pan with olive oil, approximately 2–3 minutes per side.

6. Sprinkle with salt and pepper; cook on a prepared grill over high heat for about 15 minutes, approximately 8 minutes per side. Serve immediately.

CHICKEN LIVERS IN RED WINE

For a nice (and sweet!) variation on this recipe, you can try using a fortified wine.

Serves 4

1 pound chicken livers

1 cup chicken broth

½ cup butter

1 small onion, diced

1 tablespoon all-purpose flour

½ cup red wine

Salt and pepper

2 tablespoons fresh parsley, finely chopped

1. Wash chicken livers thoroughly and drain well before using. Bring broth to a boil in a small pan and let simmer over low heat.

2. Melt butter in another frying pan. Slightly sauté onion; add chicken livers and cook over high heat for 3–5 minutes, stirring constantly to avoid browning.

3. Sprinkle flour over top of livers and butter; continue to stir well to form a sauce in the bottom of the pan. Stir constantly to avoid clumping.

4. Slowly add hot broth to the pan with the livers, stirring constantly. Turn heat to high and slowly add wine; continue to simmer and stir several minutes. Reduce heat to low; cook for another 5–10 minutes to thicken sauce.

5. Season with salt and pepper and serve hot with chopped parsley as a garnish over a bed of mashed potatoes.

CHICKEN GALANTINE

You can encase the ground chicken mixture in roasted eggplant instead of using skin. This will add additional flavor to the chicken.

Serves 6

1 small whole chicken

1 shallot

2 cloves garlic

¼ cup pistachio nuts

8 dates

½ pound ground chicken

1 egg white

1 teaspoon dried oregano

1 teaspoon dried marjoram

Fresh-cracked black pepper, to taste

Kosher salt, to taste

1. Preheat the oven to 325°F.

2. Carefully remove all the skin from the chicken by making a slit down the back and loosening the skin with your fingers (keep the skin intact as much as possible); set aside the chicken and the skin. Remove the breast from bone. Chop the shallot and mince the garlic. Chop the nuts and dates.

3. Mix together the ground chicken, egg white, nuts, dates, shallots, garlic, oregano, marjoram, pepper, and salt.

4. Lay out the skin, then lay the breast lengthwise at the center. Spoon the ground chicken mixture on top, and fold over the rest of skin. Place in a loaf pan and bake for 1½–2 hours (when the internal temperature of the loaf reaches 170° F, it's done). Let cool, then slice.

SPICY TURKEY BREAST WITH FRUIT CHUTNEY

There are several types of pears to choose from, but first try either Bosc or Anjou (if available) with this recipe.

Serves 6

2 jalapeño chili peppers

2 cloves garlic

1 tablespoon olive oil

2 teaspoons all-purpose flour

Fresh-cracked black pepper, to taste

Cooking spray

1½ pounds whole boneless turkey breast

1 shallot

1 lemon

2 pears

1 tablespoon honey

1. Preheat the oven to 350°F.

2. Stem, seed, and mince the peppers. Mince the garlic. In a blender, purée the chili peppers, garlic, and oil. Mix together the flour and black pepper.

3. Spray a rack with cooking spray. Dredge the turkey in the flour mixture, then dip it in the pepper mixture, and place on rack. Cover loosely with foil and roast for 1 hour. Remove foil and brown for 10 minutes.

4. While the turkey cooks, prepare the chutney: Finely dice the shallots. Juice the lemon and grate the rind for zest. Dice the pears. Mix together the pears, shallot, lemon juice, zest, and honey.

5. Thinly slice the turkey, and serve with chutney.

GRILLED DUCK BREAST WITH FRUIT SALSA

Duck breast has the best flavor when cooked rare to medium-rare. For this recipe, try using Moulard duck breast.

Serves 6

1 plum

1 peach

1 nectarine

1 red onion

3 sprigs mint

Fresh-cracked black pepper, to taste

1 tablespoon olive oil

1 teaspoon chili powder

1½ pounds boneless duck breast

1. Preheat the grill. Dice the plum, peach, nectarine, and onion. Mince the mint. Toss together the fruit, onion, mint, and pepper.

2. Mix together the oil and chili powder. Dip the duck breast in the oil, and cook to desired doneness on grill.

3. Slice duck on the bias and serve with a spoonful of salsa.

QUAIL WITH PLUM SAUCE

Plums, with their rich summer flavor, complement all forms of poultry. Try them in your favorite recipes.

Serves 6

6 quail

12 plums

2 yellow onions

1 stalk celery

1 carrot

¼ cup olive oil

2 bay leaves

1 cup dry red wine

1 quart Hearty Red Wine Brown Stock (see recipe in Chapter 2)

2 sprigs thyme, leaves only

½ bunch parsley stems

Kosher salt, to taste

Fresh-cracked black pepper, to taste

1. Cut the quail in half and remove breast and back bones (reserve bones). Peel, pit, and chop the plums. Chop the onions and celery. Peel and chop the carrot.

2. Heat the oil to medium-high temperature in a large stockpot. Brown the quail bones, then add the onions, carrots, and celery, and brown slightly. Add the plums and wine, and let reduce by half.

3. Add the stock and herbs; simmer for 6 hours, then strain, removing bay leaves.

4. Preheat grill.

5. Season the quail meat with the salt and pepper; grill on each side until golden brown. Serve with stock.

Where to Get Quail

Most of the quail available to you will have been raised on farms, unless of course you have a hunter in your family. The average local supermarket is not likely to carry fresh quail. However, there are some specialty markets that offer both fresh and frozen quail.

SLOW-COOKED DUCK

You'll need a day's head start on this recipe. Slow-cooking makes any ingredient extremely tender.

Serves 6

3-pound duck

6 bay leaves

1 bunch parsley stems, chopped

2 tablespoons coarse salt

1 teaspoon black pepper

½ bunch sage

½ bunch thyme

½ cup olive oil

1. Remove and discard all the skin and visible fat from the duck. Cut the duck into serving portions.

2. Place the duck in a single layer on a baking sheet. Cover the duck with the herbs and spices. Wrap with plastic wrap. Refrigerate overnight. Rinse and dry thoroughly before baking.

3. Preheat the oven to 250°F.

4. Place the oil in a baking dish. Add the duck, cover, and bake for 8–12 hours. Allow the duck to cool for approximately 1 hour.

5. Thoroughly drain off and discard the oil from the duck; remove bay leaves. Transfer the duck to a broiler pan; flash under the broiler to brown before serving.

GOOSE BRAISED WITH CITRUS

Goose typically has a very heavy flavor, but the citrus in this dish cuts the flavor of the goose.

Serves 6

2 yellow onions

1 carrot

1 stalk celery

1 grapefruit

2 oranges

1 lemon

1 lime

1 tablespoon olive oil

3-pound goose

½ cup port wine

¼ cup honey

2 cups Hearty Red Wine Brown Stock (see recipe in Chapter 2)

1. Preheat the oven to 350°F.

2. Cut the onions into wedges. Peel and cut the carrot into quarters. Roughly chop the celery. Quarter the grapefruit, oranges, lemon, and lime (leave the peels on).

3. Heat the oil to medium-high temperature in a large Dutch oven. Sear the goose on all sides. Add the vegetables and fruit; cook for 5 minutes, stirring constantly. Add the wine and reduce by half, then add the honey and stock. When the liquid begins to boil, cover and braise in the oven for 3–4 hours.

4. Serve the cooking liquid (which will thicken as it cooks) as a sauce accompanying the goose.

SAGE-RICOTTA CHICKEN BREASTS

If you have difficulty spreading the cheese mixture under the chicken skin, you can lift the skin completely off, spoon on the cheese mixture, and replace the skin.

Serves 6

6 chicken breast halves with bone and skin on

6 fresh sage leaves

½ cup part-skim ricotta cheese

1 egg white

¼ cup niçoise olives

Fresh-cracked black pepper, to taste

1. Preheat the oven to 375°F.

2. Rinse the chicken in cold water. Using your finger, make an opening in the skin where the wing was joined and loosen the skin away from the breast. Slice the sage.

3. Mix together the sage, cheese, and egg, and place this mixture in a pastry bag. Pipe the mixture under the skin through the opening you made. Place the chicken on a rack in a baking dish; roast for approximately 30–45 minutes, until the internal temperature of the chicken reaches 165°F and the outside is browned.

4. Remove pits and chop olives. After you remove the chicken from the rack, sprinkle with olives and pepper, and serve.

TURKEY TETRAZZINI

This is best when served over pasta, noodles, or in a puff pastry shell.

Serves 6

1 pound boneless, skinless turkey

1 leek (white part only)

3 cloves garlic

3 cups mushrooms

¼ cup olive oil, divided

⅛ cup bread crumbs

¼ cup all-purpose flour

1 cup skim milk

2 ounces Parmesan, grated

2 ounces Romano, grated

Fresh-cracked black pepper, to taste

1. Preheat the oven to 375°F.

2. Cut the turkey into bite-size portions. Slice the leek and mince the garlic. Clean the mushrooms with a damp paper towel, then slice them. Mix half of the oil with the bread crumbs.

3. Heat the remaining oil over medium heat in a medium-size saucepan; brown the turkey, then remove and keep warm. Add the leeks, garlic, and mushrooms to the pan that you cooked the turkey in; cook thoroughly, then add the flour.

4. Whisk in the milk, stirring constantly to avoid lumping. Remove from heat and add the cheeses. Spoon the mixture into a casserole pan and top with bread crumb mixture; bake for 30 minutes. Season with pepper before serving.

CHAPTER 10

FISH AND SEAFOOD ENTRÉES

BIANKO FROM CORFU

This dish comes from the Ionian island of Corfu. Although the island is Greek, its dishes have an Italian flair.

Serves 4

½ cup extra-virgin olive oil, divided

2 large onions, peeled and sliced

6 cloves garlic, peeled and minced

2 medium carrots, peeled and sliced

1 cup chopped celery

1½ teaspoons salt, divided

1 teaspoon pepper, divided

4 large potatoes, peeled and cut into
   ½-inch slices

4 whitefish fillets (cod or grouper), skinned

3–5 tablespoons fresh lemon juice

¼ cup chopped fresh parsley

1. Heat ¼ cup of oil in a heavy-bottomed pot over medium heat for 30 seconds. Add the onions, garlic, carrots, and celery. Cook the vegetables for 5–7 minutes or until the onions soften. Then season them with ½ teaspoon of salt and ¼ teaspoon of pepper.

2. Add the potatoes and the remaining salt and pepper. Add just enough hot water to cover the potatoes. Increase the heat to medium-high and bring the water to a boil. Reduce the heat to medium-low, cover the pot, leaving the lid slightly ajar, and cook for 12 minutes.

3. Place the fillets over the potatoes and top with the remaining oil. Cover the fish and cook for another 12–15 minutes or until the whitefish is opaque and flaky.

4. Uncover the pot and add the lemon juice. Don't stir it; shake the pot back and forth to allow the juice to penetrate the layers. Adjust the seasoning with more salt and pepper, if necessary.

5. Place the fish and potatoes on a large platter and top with the parsley. Serve immediately.

Whitefish

Whitefish have a light, white, flaky flesh. They are low in fat and a healthy option for a meal. Halibut, cod, sea bass, pollock, tilapia, and hake are all considered whitefish.

GRILLED SALMON WITH LEMON AND LIME

With a clean grill top and a little patience, anyone can grill fish without it sticking. Serve this salmon with Tzatziki (see recipe in Chapter 2).

Serves 4

4 (6-ounce) salmon fillets, skins on

¼ cup extra-virgin olive oil

1 tablespoon grated lemon zest

1½ teaspoons grated lime zest

1½ teaspoons salt

½ teaspoon pepper

3 tablespoons vegetable oil

1 large lemon, cut into wedges

1. Preheat a gas or charcoal grill to medium-high. Brush the grill surface to make sure it is thoroughly clean. Rinse the fillets and pat them dry with a paper towel. Rub the fillets with the olive oil on both sides.

2. Sprinkle both sides of the fillets with the lemon zest, lime zest, salt, and pepper.

3. When the grill is ready, dip a clean tea towel in the vegetable oil and wipe the grill surface with the oil.

4. Place the salmon on the grill, skin-side down, and grill for 6–7 minutes. Don't touch the fillets, just let them grill. Flip the salmon over and grill for another 2–3 minutes.

5. Serve the salmon with lemon wedges.

Salmon

Salmon is one of the healthiest fish and one of the tastiest. It helps with heart health, is high in protein, and is rich in omega-3 fatty acids.

SEA BASS BAKED WITH COARSE SEA SALT

For this recipe, the fish is encased in a salt-herb mixture and baked at a high temperature. The result is a showstopper presentation and a perfectly seasoned fish.

Serves 2

1 pound whole sea bass, cleaned, gutted, and scaled

3 or 4 sprigs fresh thyme

½ cup chopped fresh parsley

1 large lemon, sliced

2 cups coarse sea salt

⅓ cup all-purpose flour

3 egg whites, beaten

1 tablespoon grated lemon zest

½ cup cold water

½ cup Ladolemono (see recipe in Chapter 2)

1. Preheat the oven to 450°F. Rinse fish and pat dry with a paper towel. Place thyme, parsley, and lemon slices in the cavity of the fish. Reserve the sea bass.

2. In a medium bowl, combine the salt, flour, eggs, and zest. Gradually stir in the water until the mixture comes together and resembles a paste. You may not need all the water; the paste should not be too runny.

3. On a baking sheet lined with parchment paper, place a layer of the salt mixture just large enough to set the entire fish on (about ⅓ of the salt mixture). Place the fish on top of the salt and encase it (leave the head and tail exposed) with the remaining salt mixture. Pack the salt around the sea bass so it adheres. Place the sheet on the middle rack and bake for 30 minutes. Let the fish cool for 10 minutes.

4. Using a hammer or the flat side of a meat tenderizer, carefully crack the salt crust to reveal the fish. With the back of a knife, remove the salty skin and carefully flip the fish onto a serving platter and remove the skin from the other side.

5. Spoon a little of the Ladolemono sauce over the fish and serve the rest of the sauce on the side.

BEER-BATTER FISH

Every country in the Mediterranean has its own version of a beer-battered fish. Greeks use cod, but you can try whatever is fresh at your fishmonger or supermarket. Serve this fish with a garlicky Almond-Potato Skordalia (see recipe in Chapter 2).

Serves 4

¾ cup all-purpose flour

¾ cup cornstarch

1 teaspoon baking powder

1¼ teaspoons salt, divided

1–1½ cups cold dark beer

4 (6-ounce) haddock or cod fillets, skins removed and cut into 3 or 4 pieces

Sunflower oil for frying

1. In a large bowl, combine the flour, cornstarch, baking powder, and ½ teaspoon of salt. Slowly stir in the beer to reach the consistency of a thin pancake batter (you might not need all the beer, so drink what's left). Place the batter in the refrigerator for an hour.

2. Rinse the fish and pat it dry with a paper towel. Season the fish with ½ teaspoon of salt.

3. Fill a deep frying pan with 3 inches of the oil. Over medium-high heat, bring the oil temperature to 365°F. Adjust the heat to keep the temperature at 365°F while frying. Fry the fish (in batches) for 3–4 minutes or until just golden. Transfer the fish to a tray lined with paper towels to soak up excess oil.

4. Season the fish with the remaining salt and serve it immediately.

GRILLED SARDINES

Serve these delicious sardines with some boiled greens, such as kale or spinach.

Serves 4

2 pounds fresh sardines, heads removed, cleaned, gutted, and scaled

½ cup extra-virgin olive oil, divided

2 teaspoons salt

¾ teaspoon pepper

3 tablespoons vegetable oil

3 tablespoons fresh lemon juice

1½ teaspoons dried oregano

1. Preheat a gas or charcoal grill to medium-high. Brush the grill surface to make sure it is thoroughly clean. Rinse the sardines and pat them dry with a paper towel.

2. Rub the sardines on both sides with ¼ cup of olive oil. Sprinkle both sides with salt and pepper.

3. When the grill is ready, dip a clean tea towel in the vegetable oil and wipe the grill surface with the oil.

4. Place the sardines on the grill and grill them for 2–3 minutes on each side.

5. Drizzle the sardines with remaining olive oil and lemon juice. Sprinkle them with the oregano and serve.

Sardines

If you were to visit any Mediterranean country, you'd notice the locals eating these small fish in restaurants. This little powerhouse fish is high in calcium, rich in B and D vitamins, and high in omega-3 fatty acids.

GRILLED WHOLE FISH

One of the finest dining experiences in the Mediterranean region is to eat a whole grilled fish as you sit by the sea. As any good fishmonger will tell you, the best fish is the freshest fish.

Serves 4

4 (½-pound) whole fish (sea bream or red snapper), cleaned, gutted, and scaled

½ cup extra-virgin olive oil

4 teaspoons salt

1½ teaspoons pepper

1 large lemon, thinly sliced

2 tablespoons chopped fresh oregano

2 tablespoons fresh thyme leaves

2 tablespoons chopped fresh rosemary

2 tablespoons chopped fresh tarragon

3 tablespoons vegetable oil

½ cup Ladolemono (see recipe in Chapter 2)

1. Rinse the fish and pat them dry with a paper towel. Rub the fish on both sides with the olive oil. Then sprinkle both sides and the cavity with the salt and pepper. Refrigerate the fish for 30 minutes and then return them to room temperature. Fill the cavity of each fish with equal amounts of the lemon slices and herbs.

2. Preheat a gas or charcoal grill to medium-high. Brush the grill surface to make sure it is thoroughly clean. When the grill is ready, dip a clean tea towel in the vegetable oil and wipe the grill surface with the oil.

3. Place the fish on the grill and grill for 5–6 minutes per side.

4. Serve the fish with Ladolemono sauce. Serve immediately.

How to Pick the Freshest Fish

First, smell the fish; it should smell only of the sea. Next, look at its eyes; they should be bright and shiny, not sunken. Open the gills with your finger; they should be bright red. Finally, press your finger into the body; the flesh should be firm and the scales should be firmly attached to the body.

OLIVE OIL–POACHED COD

Poaching cod in olive oil produces a succulent, delicate fish that will wow your family or guests.

Serves 4

4 (6-ounce) fresh cod fillets, skins removed

2½–3 cups extra-virgin olive oil

1 teaspoon salt

2 tablespoons fresh lemon juice

1 tablespoon grated lemon zest

1. Rinse the fillets and pat them dry with a paper towel.

2. Choose a pot that will just fit the fillets and fill it with the oil. Bring the oil to a temperature of 210°F. Adjust the heat to keep the temperature at 210°F while poaching the fish.

3. Carefully place the fillets in the oil and poach them for 6 minutes or until the fish is opaque in color. Carefully remove the fish from the oil and put it on a plate. Sprinkle the fish with salt.

4. Spoon some of the warm oil over the fish and then drizzle it with lemon juice. Sprinkle the zest over the fish and serve it immediately.

PLAKI-STYLE BAKED FISH

In Greece, plaki *refers to something baked with tomatoes and oil. In this case, it's a whole fish. Use a large red snapper, trout, cod, or grouper for this dish.*

Serves 4

1 (2-pound) whole fish, cleaned, scaled, and gutted

2 teaspoons salt, divided

1¼ teaspoons pepper, divided

1½ cups chopped fresh parsley

4 medium potatoes, peeled and cut into wedges

2 large cubanelle peppers, stemmed, seeded, and sliced

5 cloves garlic, peeled and roughly chopped

2 large tomatoes (1 diced and 1 halved and sliced), divided

4 tablespoons chopped fresh oregano or 2 teaspoons dried oregano

½ cup extra-virgin olive oil

5 tablespoons flour

1 teaspoon sweet paprika

1 cup hot water

1. Preheat the oven to 350°F. Rinse the fish and pat it dry with a paper towel. Season the fish on both sides and in the cavity with 1½ teaspoons of salt and ¾ teaspoon of pepper.

2. Sprinkle the parsley on the bottom of a large baking dish. Top the parsley with the potatoes, peppers, garlic, tomatoes, and oregano. Place the fish on top of the vegetables.

3. In a medium bowl, whisk the oil, flour, and paprika. Pour the oil mixture over the fish. Pour the hot water over the surrounding vegetables. Season with the remaining salt and pepper.

4. Bake on the middle rack of the oven for 40–45 minutes.

5. Serve the fish over a bed of the vegetables. Spoon some of the sauce over the fish. Serve immediately.

PISTACHIO-CRUSTED HALIBUT

This elegant dish is easy enough to make on a weekday or as a dish for company. All you need is a food processor and an oven. Serve this fish with rice pilaf or roasted potatoes.

Serves 4

½ cup shelled unsalted pistachios, roughly chopped

2 teaspoons grated lemon zest

1 teaspoon grated lime zest

2 teaspoons grated orange zest

4 teaspoons chopped fresh parsley

1 cup bread crumbs

¼ cup extra-virgin olive oil

4 (6-ounce) halibut fillets, skins removed

1½ teaspoons salt

½ teaspoon pepper

4 teaspoons Dijon mustard

1. Preheat the oven to 400°F. Put the pistachios, zests, parsley, and bread crumbs into the food processor and pulse to combine the ingredients. With the processor running, add the oil until it is well incorporated.

2. Rinse the fish and pat it dry with a paper towel. Season the fish with the salt and pepper.

3. Brush the tops of the fish with the mustard. Divide the pistachio mixture evenly and place some on the top of each fish. Press down on the mixture to help the crust adhere.

4. Line a baking sheet with parchment paper and carefully place the crusted fish on the baking sheet. Bake it in the upper middle rack of the oven for 20 minutes or until the crust is golden brown.

5. Let the fish cool for 5 minutes, and serve it immediately.

Pistachios

Pistachios are grown all over Italy, Greece, and Turkey. These Mediterranean favorites are high in fiber and rich in B vitamins.

ROASTED SEA BASS WITH POTATOES AND FENNEL

Serve this one-pot meal with a dry white wine and lots of bread to soak up the sauce.

Serves 2

4 medium potatoes, peeled and halved

1 small onion, peeled and sliced

2 tablespoons chopped fresh parsley

1 cup thinly sliced fennel

1½ teaspoons grated lemon zest

1 tablespoon fresh lemon juice

⅓ cup plus 2 tablespoons extra-virgin olive oil, divided

2 teaspoons salt, divided

1 teaspoon pepper, divided

½ cup Basic Vegetable Stock (see recipe in Chapter 2)

2 ripe medium tomatoes, sliced

2 (½-pound) whole European sea bass, cleaned, gutted, and scaled

6 tablespoons chopped fennel fronds, divided

4 scallions, softened in boiling water for 10 seconds

8 kalamata olives, pitted

4 caper berries, rinsed

¼ cup dry white wine

1 large lemon, cut into wedges

1. Preheat the oven to 450°F. Place the potatoes, onions, parsley, fennel, lemon zest, and lemon juice in a medium baking dish. Add ⅓ cup of oil and toss to combine the ingredients. Season with 1 teaspoon of salt and ½ teaspoon of pepper. Stir in the stock.

2. Top the potatoes and fennel with the tomatoes. Bake in the middle rack of the oven for 25 minutes.

3. In the meantime, rinse the fish and pat it dry with a paper towel. Rub both sides of each fish with the remaining oil, and then season both sides and the cavity with the remaining salt and pepper. Place 2 tablespoons of fennel fronds in each cavity. Wrap 2 scallions around each fish.

4. Take the baking dish out of the oven; place the fish on top of the vegetables. Sprinkle with the olives and caper berries. Pour the wine over the fish and vegetables. Bake the dish on the middle rack of the oven for 20–25 minutes or until the potatoes are tender and the fish is golden.

5. Place each fish over a bed of the cooked vegetables. Garnish with the remaining fennel fronds and serve with the lemon wedges.

Mediterranean Versus Chilean

Don't confuse the sea bass from the Mediterranean with the endangered Chilean sea bass. The European variety is abundant, widely available, and wonderful when grilled or baked in the oven.

RED MULLET SAVORO STYLE

A visit to the Mediterranean wouldn't be complete without tasting red mullet. This small fish is prized for its sweet, delicate meat. Fry red mullet and finish it with a tangy savoro sauce made with red wine vinegar.

Serves 4

4 (½-pound) whole red mullet, cleaned, gutted, and scaled

2 teaspoons salt

1 cup all-purpose flour

⅔ cup extra-virgin olive oil, divided

6 or 7 sprigs fresh rosemary

8 cloves garlic, peeled and coarsely chopped

⅔ cup red wine vinegar

1. Rinse the fish and pat them dry with a paper towel. Season both sides and the cavity of the fish with salt. Let them sit for 20 minutes. Dredge the fish in flour and set aside.

2. Heat ⅓ cup of oil in a frying pan over medium-high heat for 1 minute or until the oil is hot. Fry the fish (in batches) for 4–5 minutes a side or until golden. Place the fish on a serving platter. Discard the frying oil and wipe the pan clean.

3. Add the remaining oil to the pan and heat for 1 minute. Add the rosemary; fry until it crisps and turns an olive color. Remove the rosemary from the oil. Stir the garlic into the oil and keep stirring until the garlic turns golden. Immediately add the vinegar. Stir until the sauce has thickened and becomes a little sweet.

4. Pour the sauce over the fish and serve immediately. Garnish the fish with the fried rosemary.

SPINACH-STUFFED SOLE

This is an impressive dish that is easy to make. Choose any flatfish fillet as a substitute for sole. Serve these fillets on a bed of braised lentils.

Serves 4

¼ cup extra-virgin olive oil, divided

4 scallions, ends trimmed and sliced

1 pound package frozen spinach, thawed and drained

3 tablespoons chopped fennel fronds, or tarragon

1 teaspoon salt, divided

½ teaspoon pepper, divided

4 (6-ounce) sole fillets, skins removed

2 tablespoons plus 1½ teaspoons grated lemon zest, divided

1 teaspoon sweet paprika

1. Preheat the oven to 400°F. Heat 2 tablespoons of oil in a medium skillet over medium heat for 30 seconds. Add the scallions and cook them for 3–4 minutes. Allow the scallions to cool to room temperature.

2. In a bowl, combine the scallions, spinach, and fennel. Season the ingredients with ½ teaspoon of salt and ¼ teaspoon of pepper.

3. Rinse the fish fillets and pat them dry with a paper towel. Rub the fish with the remaining oil and sprinkle them with 2 tablespoons of lemon zest. Season the fillets with remaining salt and pepper, and sprinkle them with the paprika.

4. Divide the spinach filling among the fillets; to ensure that the fillets don't unravel when baking, place the stuffing on the skin side. Roll up each fillet, starting from the widest end. Use two toothpicks to secure each fillet. Place the fillets on a baking sheet lined with parchment paper, and drizzle the remaining oil over them.

5. Bake on the middle rack of the oven for 15–20 minutes. Remove the toothpicks and sprinkle the fillets with the remaining lemon zest. Serve immediately.

GRILLED OCTOPUS

Frozen octopus is perfectly fine to use in this dish. Just thaw it slowly in your fridge overnight. Serve this dish with ouzo on ice.

Serves 4

2½- to 3-pound octopus, cleaned and beak removed

3 bay leaves

¼ cup red wine

3 tablespoons balsamic vinegar, divided

⅔ cup extra-virgin olive oil, divided

1 teaspoon dried oregano

1 teaspoon salt

1 teaspoon pepper

1 large lemon, cut into wedges

1. Put the octopus and bay leaves in a large pot over medium-high heat. Cover the pot and cook the octopus for 5–8 minutes. Uncover the pot to see whether the octopus has released some liquid (about a cup). If the octopus hasn't released its liquid, just cover and continue cooking for another 5 minutes or until it has released its liquid. Reduce the heat to medium-low and cook for 45 minutes or until the octopus is tender.

2. Add the wine and 2 tablespoons of vinegar. Remove the pot from the heat and allow the octopus to cool to room temperature in the liquid.

3. Preheat a gas or charcoal grill to medium-high. Remove the octopus from the liquid and cut it into pieces, leaving each tentacle whole. In a large bowl, combine the octopus, ⅓ cup of oil, the oregano, and the remaining vinegar. Season it with the salt and pepper.

4. Place the octopus on the grill and cook for 2–3 minutes a side.

5. Drizzle the grilled octopus with the remaining oil and serve it with the lemon wedges.

Tenderizing Octopus

Greek fishermen tenderized octopus by pounding it against a large rock up to 100 times. That would tenderize just about anything! It's easier to tenderize an octopus by braising it in its own juices, wine, and olive oil.

SCALLOPS SAGANAKI

If you want to tone down the heat in this dish, just use half a chili pepper. Be sure to have plenty of crusty bread to soak up the sauce.

Serves 4

16 medium scallops, rinsed and patted dry

1 teaspoon salt

½ teaspoon pepper

½ cup extra-virgin olive oil

⅓ cup dry white wine

2 ounces ouzo

2 tablespoons fresh lemon juice

6 cloves garlic, peeled and thinly sliced

1 small red chili pepper, stemmed and thinly sliced

½ teaspoon sweet paprika

1 small leek, ends trimmed, thoroughly cleaned, cut lengthwise, and julienned into matchsticks

⅔ cup bread crumbs

2 tablespoons chopped fresh parsley

1 large lemon, cut into wedges

1. Preheat the oven to 450°F. Season both sides of the scallops with the salt and pepper. Place the scallops in a medium baking dish (or divide them among four small baking dishes or ramekins). Set aside.

2. In a medium bowl, whisk the oil, wine, ouzo, lemon juice, garlic, chili, and sweet paprika. Pour the sauce over the scallops; top with the leeks and then the bread crumbs.

3. Bake on the middle rack for 8–10 minutes. Set the oven to broil and bake for another 2–3 minutes or until the bread crumbs are golden.

4. Let the scallops cool for 5 minutes and top them with parsley. Serve the scallops with the lemon wedges.

GRILLED GROUPER STEAKS

Grouper has a firm meat that doesn't dry out easily and holds up well on the grill. Serve this fish with a heaping spoonful of Mediterranean Saltsa (see recipe in Chapter 2) and Greek roasted potatoes.

Serves 4

¼ cup extra-virgin olive oil

1 tablespoon grated lemon zest

½ cup dry white wine

½ teaspoon chopped fresh rosemary

4 (½-pound) grouper steaks, rinsed and dried

3 tablespoons vegetable oil

1½ teaspoons salt

1. In a medium baking dish, whisk the oil, zest, wine, and rosemary. Add the fish and toss. Cover with plastic and refrigerate for 1 hour. Allow the fish to return to room temperature for 30 minutes before grilling.

2. Preheat a gas or charcoal grill to medium-high. Dip a clean tea towel in the vegetable oil and wipe the grill surface with the oil.

3. Season the fish on both sides with the salt. Place fish on the grill and grill for 5–6 minutes per side. Serve.

GRILLED CALAMARI

Serve this delicious and tender calamari with a seasonal salad and some wine. It's a wonderful summer meal.

Serves 4

4 (5-inch-long) squid, cleaned

¼ cup extra-virgin olive oil

1 clove garlic, peeled and minced

1 teaspoon salt

½ teaspoon pepper

3 tablespoons vegetable oil

2 tablespoons fresh lemon juice

½ teaspoon dried oregano

1. Preheat a gas or charcoal grill to medium-high heat. In a medium bowl, combine the squid, olive oil, garlic, salt, and pepper.

2. Dip a clean tea towel in the vegetable oil and wipe the grill surface with the oil. Place the squid on the grill and cook for 2–3 minutes per side.

3. Drizzle lemon juice on the squid, sprinkle it with oregano, and serve it warm.

GRILLED LOBSTER

An underappreciated way to prepare lobster is to grill it. Always make sure you use live, whole lobsters the day you buy them.

Serves 4

4 (1¼–1½ pound) live lobsters, split lengthwise

⅔ cup plus ¼ cup extra-virgin olive oil, divided

1½ teaspoons salt, divided

½ teaspoon pepper

¾ teaspoon sweet paprika

1 clove garlic, peeled and minced

2 tablespoons fresh lemon juice

1½ tablespoons Dijon mustard

1 scallion, ends trimmed and finely chopped

1 tablespoon chopped fresh parsley

1 tablespoon dried oregano

3 tablespoons vegetable oil

1. Preheat a gas or charcoal grill to medium-high. Brush the grill surface to make sure it is thoroughly clean. Brush the flesh side of the lobster with ¼ cup olive oil and season it with 1 teaspoon of salt, pepper, and paprika. Break off the claws and reserve them.

2. In a medium bowl, whisk the remaining oil, garlic, lemon juice, mustard, scallion, parsley, oregano, and remaining salt. Set the sauce aside.

3. When the grill is ready (medium-high heat), dip a clean tea towel in the vegetable oil and wipe the grill surface with the oil.

4. Place the lobster claws on the grill first because they need longer to grill. A minute later, place the lobster bodies on the grill, flesh-side down. Grill for 3–4 minutes and then flip the bodies and claws. Grill for another 2–3 minutes or until the shells have turned red and the meat is cooked.

5. Drizzle the sauce over the lobsters and serve the remaining sauce on the side.

GRILLED JUMBO SHRIMP

Jumbo shrimp are plump, juicy, and perfect for grilling. Serve the grilled shrimp with rice pilaf or couscous.

Serves 4

¼ cup extra-virgin olive oil

¾ teaspoon salt

¼ teaspoon pepper

½ teaspoon sweet paprika

12 large jumbo shrimp, deveined but shells on

½ cup butter

2 tablespoons fresh lemon juice

1 clove garlic, peeled and minced

⅛ teaspoon red pepper flakes

1 teaspoon minced fresh ginger

1 tablespoon chopped fresh parsley

1 tablespoon chopped fresh chives

3 tablespoons vegetable oil

1. Preheat a gas or charcoal grill to medium-high. Brush the grill surface to make sure it is thoroughly clean. In a medium bowl, whisk together olive oil, salt, pepper, and paprika. Add the shrimp and marinate for 10 minutes.

2. In a small pot over medium heat, cook the butter, lemon juice, garlic, red pepper flakes, and ginger until the butter melts. Add the parsley and chives. Keep the sauce warm.

3. When the grill is ready (medium-high heat), dip a clean tea towel in the vegetable oil and wipe the grill surface with the oil. Place the shrimp on the grill and grill for 2 minutes per side or until they turn pink.

4. Drizzle the shrimp with the butter sauce and serve the remaining sauce on the side.

OCTOPUS STIFADO

Here's an octopus dish that you can enjoy during the winter when it's too cold to grill. The octopus is braised with wine, pearl onions, tomato, herbs, and spices in a stew called stifado.

Serves 4

1 (2-pound) octopus, cleaned and beak removed

½ cup extra-virgin olive oil

1½ cups pearl onions, blanched and skins removed

½ cup dry white wine

¼ cup red wine vinegar

2 tablespoons tomato paste

3 bay leaves

6 or 7 whole allspice berries

½ teaspoon grated orange zest

1 teaspoon salt

½ teaspoon pepper

⅛ teaspoon ground cinnamon

⅓ cup chopped fresh dill

1. Put the octopus in a large oven-safe pot over medium-high heat, cover the pot, and cook for 10 minutes. Take the pot off the heat, remove the octopus from the liquid, reserve the liquid, and let the octopus cool.

2. Preheat the oven to 350°F. To the pot with the reserved octopus cooking liquid, add the oil, onions, wine, vinegar, tomato paste, bay leaves, allspice, and zest. Season the sauce with salt and pepper.

3. Cut up the octopus; separate the tentacles from the head and roughly chop up the head. Return the octopus to the pot, and cover it.

4. Bake the octopus in the oven on the middle rack for 90 minutes or until the octopus is fork-tender. Uncover it, and bake for another 10 minutes to thicken the sauce.

5. Remove the bay leaves, and stir in the cinnamon and dill. Serve the octopus hot.

Serve these oysters with hot sauce or with Mediterranean Mignonette Sauce (see recipe in Chapter 2).

Serves 4

16 live fresh oysters

4 cups crushed ice

1 large lemon, cut into wedges

1. Place an oyster on a steady work surface with the hinged end facing up. Using a tea towel to help you hold the oyster, grip it with one hand. With the other hand, carefully stick a knife or oyster shucker into the hinge. Dig the knife into the hinge, wiggling the knife until the shell begins to open.

2. Slide the knife across the top shell to disconnect the muscle from the shell.

3. You should be able to open the oyster. Discard the top shell. Slip the knife underneath the oyster and disconnect it from the bottom shell. Remove any pieces of dirt or broken shell. Smell the oyster; it should smell like the sea. If it doesn't, discard it.

4. Repeat this process with the remaining oysters.

5. Serve the oysters (in their bottom shells) on a bed of crushed ice with the lemon wedges.

COD WITH RAISINS

In ancient Greece, raisins were used as a seasoning. They are the only ingredients used to flavor this dish today.

Serves 4

1½ pounds salted cod, fresh or frozen

3–4 tablespoons extra-virgin olive oil

2 cooking onions, chopped, but not too finely

1 tablespoon tomato paste, diluted in ¾ cup water

¾ cup black raisins

1 cup water

1. If using salted cod, make sure to soak in water at least 24 hours, changing water several times to remove salt.

2. Heat olive oil in a cooking pot over medium heat. Add onions; sauté lightly for a few minutes. Make sure to stir constantly to avoid browning the onion; it should be tender but not burned.

3. Add tomato paste to onions; bring to boil and simmer for 10 minutes.

4. Add raisins and continue to cook for 3 more minutes.

5. Add water; bring to boil and simmer for 30 minutes, until raisins have expanded.

6. Add cod; simmer for 15 minutes, until the sauce has reduced. Serve with raisin-onion sauce spooned over top.

Fresh or Cured

Throughout the Mediterranean, fresh fish that is not for immediate consumption is often salt-cured for easy storage and later use.

EGEAN BAKED SOLE

Turbot, halibut, or flounder can also be used as substitutes for the sole in this recipe.

Serves 4

8 sole fillets

Salt and pepper to taste

2 lemons

4 tablespoons extra-virgin olive oil, divided

1 teaspoon dried oregano

¼ cup capers

4 tablespoons chopped fresh dill

2 tablespoons chopped fresh green onion (or celery leaves or parsley)

1. Preheat the oven to 250°F.

2. Wash fish well under cold water and pat dry with a paper towel. Season fillets with salt and pepper and set aside.

3. Slice 1 lemon into thin slices, then cut slices in half.

4. Pour 2 tablespoons olive oil into a baking dish; layer fish and lemon slices alternately.

5. Sprinkle oregano, capers, dill, and onion over fish and lemon slices.

6. Drizzle remaining olive oil and squeeze juice of remaining lemon over everything.

7. Cover and bake for 30 minutes.

BAKED SEA BREAM WITH FETA AND TOMATO

If you have trouble finding sea bream, this fish is also sometimes referred to as porgy.

Serves 4

4 small whole sea bream

½ cup extra-virgin olive oil

6 ripe tomatoes, peeled and minced

1 teaspoon dried marjoram

Salt and pepper

½ cup water

½ cup fresh parsley, finely chopped

½ pound Greek feta cheese

1. Preheat the oven to 400°F.

2. Wash and clean fish well; set aside to drain.

3. In a saucepan, heat olive oil; add tomatoes, marjoram, salt, pepper, and water. Bring to a boil; simmer for 15 minutes.

4. Place fish side by side in the baking dish; pour sauce over top and sprinkle with parsley. Bake for 30 minutes.

5. Crumble feta cheese; remove baking dish from oven and sprinkle feta over fish. Return to oven to bake for another 5–7 minutes, until cheese starts to melt. Remove and serve immediately.

BAKED TUNA

Archaeologists have discovered evidence of extensive tuna fishing operations in Argolis, Greece, as early as 6000 B.C.

Serves 4

4 center-cut tuna fillets, 6–8 ounces each (2 pounds total)

¼ cup extra-virgin olive oil, divided

1 large yellow onion, sliced

1 large green pepper, diced

2 cloves garlic, minced or pressed

2 tablespoons chopped parsley

1 teaspoon dried marjoram (or ½ teaspoon dried oregano)

Salt and fresh-ground pepper to taste

2 cups peeled tomatoes, finely minced (canned tomatoes are fine)

½ cup water

1. Preheat the oven to 400°F.

2. Wash tuna steaks well and set aside.

3. In a large frying pan, heat 2 tablespoons olive oil on medium-high. Sauté onion and green pepper until soft.

4. Add garlic, parsley, marjoram, salt, and pepper; stir over heat for another minute or so.

5. Add tomatoes and water; bring to a boil. Lower heat to medium-low and simmer for 15–20 minutes.

6. Place tuna steaks in a baking dish along with the remaining olive oil, making sure to coat the tuna with the oil; pour the sauce over the top. Bake uncovered for 45 minutes. Serve immediately, spooning some sauce over each portion.

BRAISED CUTTLEFISH

The tentacles, eyes, skin, and beak of the cuttlefish need to be removed along with the ink sac and central bony cartilage. Most fish markets will do this for you.

Serves 4–6

2 pounds cuttlefish, cleaned and cut into strips

⅓ cup extra-virgin olive oil

2 large onions, diced

3 cloves garlic, pressed or finely chopped

1 cup red wine

2 cups minced tomatoes

2 tablespoons fresh parsley, finely chopped

1 teaspoon dried marjoram

1 bay leaf

Salt and pepper to taste

1. Clean cuttlefish and cut into strips; set aside to drain well. Make sure to pat strips dry with a paper towel before using in order to avoid hot oil pops.

2. Heat olive oil in a pan; sauté onions until soft.

3. Add garlic and sauté for another 30 seconds or so before adding (drained) cuttlefish. Continue to sauté and stir continuously until cuttlefish starts to turn a yellowish color, approximately 6–8 minutes.

4. Add wine and continue to cook for another 10 minutes, stirring regularly.

5. Add tomatoes, parsley, marjoram, bay leaf, salt, and pepper; cover and simmer over medium-low heat for approximately 90 minutes, until sauce has thickened and cuttlefish is tender. Add ½–1 cup water to pan should liquid thicken before cuttlefish has softened sufficiently.

6. Serve warm with fresh bread.

Clever Fish

Since ancient times the cuttlefish has been renowned for its cleverness. Modern studies have concluded that cuttlefish are indeed among the most intelligent of invertebrates.

STOVETOP FISH

Due to the heat of the summer months in Mediterranean countries, dishes like this are common, as you do not have to use an oven that will add to the heat in the kitchen.

Serves 4

2 pounds whitefish fillets

3 tablespoons extra-virgin olive oil

4 or 5 cloves garlic, minced

1 pound ripe tomatoes, peeled and minced

6–8 fresh mint leaves, finely chopped

Salt and pepper

1 tablespoon dried oregano

½ cup water

1 small bunch fresh parsley

1. Wash fish fillets and pat with a paper towel to dry.

2. Heat olive oil in a large frying pan and quickly sauté the garlic.

3. Add the tomatoes, mint, salt, pepper, and oregano. Bring to a boil and let simmer for 10 minutes, until thickened.

4. Add the water and continue to simmer for another 3–4 minutes.

5. Place the fish in the pan and allow to simmer for 15 minutes. Do not stir; simply shake pan gently from time to time to avoid sticking.

6. Garnish with chopped parsley and serve immediately with rice.

RILLED SEA BASS

he secret to successfully grilling sea bass is to not overcook it, so make sure to check the fish on the grill for flakiness and remove it quickly when it is done.

Serves 4

4 whole sea bass (1½ pounds each), gutted and scaled

Salt and pepper

4 lemons

¼ cup extra-virgin olive oil

1 teaspoon dried oregano

1 cup fresh parsley, finely chopped

1. Wash the fish well inside and out. Using a sharp knife, cut several diagonal slits on both sides of each fish. Sprinkle with salt and pepper, including inside cavity, and set aside.

2. Squeeze juice from 2 lemons and mix with olive oil and oregano.

3. Slice remaining 2 lemons into thin slices and stuff each fish with chopped parsley and several lemon slices.

4. Brush both sides of each fish liberally with olive oil and lemon mixture and set aside for 10 minutes.

5. Heat grill to medium heat; brush grilling rack with oil. Place fish on hot rack and close grill cover.

6. Cook for 15 minutes, until fish flakes easily. Brush with remaining olive oil and lemon mixture and serve hot.

OCTOPUS IN WINE

When braising the octopus you do not need to use much water, as it will release a good deal of its own liquid into the pan. Also, be sure to remove the beak, eyes, and ink sac before cooking.

Serves 4

1 large octopus

1 tablespoon white vinegar

½ cup extra-virgin olive oil

3 onions, sliced

4 tomatoes, diced and sieved (fresh or canned)

1 cup white wine

2 bay leaves

1 teaspoon whole peppercorns

Salt and pepper

½ cup drained capers

¼ cup water

1. Place octopus in a saucepan with vinegar; cover and simmer over low heat until soft, approximately 15–20 minutes. Remove and cut into small pieces.

2. Heat olive oil in a frying pan and sauté onions until soft.

3. Add tomatoes, wine, bay leaves, peppercorns, salt, and pepper; simmer for 15 minutes.

4. Add octopus, capers, and water; simmer until sauce has thickened. Remove the bay leaves; serve hot.

OPPINO

is dish is so delicious, your family will ask for it every week!

Serves 6

6 clams

6 mussels

6 ounces skinless, boneless cod fillet

1 shallot

1 yellow onion

2 cloves garlic

2 stalks celery

2 carrots

3 plum tomatoes

1 cup dry white wine

3 cups Fish Stock (see recipe in Chapter 2)

½ teaspoon saffron threads

¼ teaspoon dried red pepper flakes

½ teaspoon extra-virgin olive oil

¼ teaspoon capers

1. Rinse the clams in ice-cold water. Thoroughly clean the mussels. Cut the cod into chunks. Small-dice the shallot, onion, garlic, and celery. Peel and small-dice the carrots and tomatoes (see Tomato Fritters recipe in Chapter 4 for tomato peeling instructions).

2. Place the cod, vegetables, wine, stock, saffron, and pepper flakes into a large stockpot; simmer over medium heat for approximately 1 hour.

3. Add the shellfish and cook until the shells open. (Discard any clams or mussels that do not open!)

4. Ladle the Cioppino into bowls. Drizzle with the oil and sprinkle with the capers before serving.

STEAMED SNOW CRAB LEGS

Serve with chopped vegetables and broth. Steam some rice as a nice accompaniment.

Serves 6

6 snow crab claw clusters

2 pounds parsnips

6 celery stalks

1 yellow onion

½ bunch fresh parsley

½ cup white wine (Pinot Grigio or Sauvignon Blanc)

Juice of 1 lemon

1 cup Fish Stock (see recipe in Chapter 2)

3 bay leaves

Fresh-cracked black pepper, to taste

1. Clean the crab legs thoroughly in ice-cold water. Peel and roughly chop the parsnips. Roughly chop the celery and onion. Chop the parsley.

2. Combine all the ingredients except the snow crab in a medium-size saucepot and bring to a boil; reduce to a simmer and cook uncovered for approximately 20–30 minutes.

3. Add the crab legs, and cook for 10–15 minutes, until the crab is cooked. Remove the bay leaves, then serve.

EAMED SEAFOOD DINNER

el free to alter the seafood to your preferences. It is easy to substitute lobster for scallops, for example.

Serves 6

1 pound lobster

½ dozen clams

½ dozen oysters

½ dozen mussels

½ dozen large shrimp

½ dozen sea scallops

3 large potatoes

½ dozen carrots

½ bunch fresh parsley

½ dozen celery stalks

6 shallots

6 small sprigs thyme

½ cup white wine (Pinot Grigio or Sauvignon Blanc)

Juice of 1 lemon

1 cup Seafood Stock (see recipe in Chapter 2)

3 bay leaves

½ teaspoon Old Bay Seasoning

Fresh-cracked black pepper, to taste

1. Clean the shellfish thoroughly in ice-cold water. Cut the potatoes in half. Peel the carrots (leave whole). Chop the parsley. (Leave the celery and shallots whole.)

2. In a medium-size saucepot, bring the wine, lemon juice, and stock to a boil. Add the potatoes, carrots, celery, shallots, herbs, and spices; let simmer for 45 minutes. Add the rest of the ingredients and reduce to a simmer; cook for 10–15 more minutes. Remove the thyme sprigs, then serve.

GRILLED FISH WITH POLENTA

Try out different types of fish with this recipe. Also, you can substitute Romano or Parmesan for the manchego.

Serves 6

½ serrano chili pepper

2 teaspoons olive oil

1 quart Fish Stock (see recipe in Chapter 2)

1½ cups cornmeal

1 teaspoon extra-virgin olive oil

1½ pounds red snapper

Pinch of coarse sea salt

Fresh-cracked black pepper, to taste

3 ounces manchego cheese

1 tablespoon cider vinegar

1. Preheat grill to medium heat. Stem, seed, and dice the serrano chili pepper.

2. Heat the olive oil in a stockpot over medium heat. Lightly sauté the chili, then add the stock and bring to a boil.

3. Whisk in the cornmeal slowly; cook for approximately 20–30 minutes, stirring frequently (add more broth if necessary).

4. While the polenta cooks, lightly dip the fish in the extra-virgin olive oil and place on a rack to drain. Season with salt and pepper.

5. When the polenta is done cooking, remove it from the heat and add the manchego; keep warm.

6. Grill the fish for 3–5 minutes on each side, depending on the thickness of the fish.

7. To serve, spoon out a generous dollop of polenta on each serving plate and arrange the fish on top. Drizzle with the vinegar.

CCALÁ

...calá is a traditional Italian Christmas Eve dish. Perhaps you can add it to your own Christmas Eve ...dition.

Serves 6

1½ pounds baccalá (salted cod)

3 cloves garlic

2 plum tomatoes

1 stalk celery

½ bunch fresh parsley

1 tablespoon olive oil

¼ cup dry white wine

½ cup Fish Stock (see recipe in Chapter 2)

Fresh-cracked black pepper, to taste

1. Soak the baccalá for 24 hours in water.

2. Mince the garlic. Medium-dice the tomatoes and celery. Mince the parsley.

3. Heat the oil in a large sauté pan over medium-high heat. Add the baccalá, garlic, tomatoes, and celery; sauté the baccalá on each side for approximately 1 minute. Add the wine and let it reduce by half. Add the stock and pepper; simmer, covered, for 10 minutes.

4. Serve with the cooking liquid and sprinkle with parsley.

Salted Cod

Baccalá is the Italian name for dried, salted cod. It must be soaked in ice water for a minimum of 24 hours before using, with the water being changed and discarded several times throughout the day.

FLOUNDER WITH BALSAMIC REDUCTION

To make the most of the delicate texture of flounder, try to purchase fresh fish. Be sure to keep the flounder ice cold until you are ready to prepare it. If fresh is not available to you, don't despair: Frozen fish can work very nicely as well.

Serves 6

¼ cup all-purpose flour

1 tablespoon cornmeal

1½ pounds flounder

1 tablespoon olive oil

½ cup Balsamic Reduction (see recipe in Chapter 2)

Fresh-cracked black pepper, to taste

3 sprigs dill

1. Mix together the flour and cornmeal; coat the flounder in the mixture.

2. Heat the oil over medium heat in a large sauté pan. Cook the flounder for approximately 7 minutes on each side.

3. While the flounder cooks, heat the Balsamic Reduction sauce. Serve the fish drizzled with the sauce and sprinkled with pepper; garnish each serving with half a sprig of dill.

LIBUT ROULADE

illing doesn't suit you, try baking the fillet.

Serves 6

1-pound halibut fillet

½ pound shrimp

3 limes

¼ bunch cilantro

3 cloves garlic

½ leek

1 tablespoon olive oil

Fresh-cracked black pepper, to taste

1 cup seafood Demi-Glace Reduction Sauce (see recipe in Chapter 2)

1. Soak 12 wooden skewers in water for at least 2 hours.

2. Preheat grill.

3. Clean the halibut and keep chilled. Completely remove the shells and tails from the shrimp (save for future use in stock). Slice the shrimp in half lengthwise and remove the veins. Juice 2 of the limes and grate the rinds for zest. Cut the remaining lime into 6 wedges. Reserve 6 whole leaves of cilantro for garnish and chop the rest. Mince the garlic and finely slice the leek.

4. Butterfly the halibut fillet lengthwise to make a ½- to ¾-inch-thick fillet. Lay the fillet out, then layer the shrimp, half of the lime zest, half of the chopped cilantro, the garlic, and leek. Gently roll up the stuffed fillet, then cut into 6 pinwheels. Insert 2 skewers into each pinwheel, forming an *X*, which will hold the pinwheels together. Brush with some of the oil, and grill for 4 minutes on each side.

5. To serve, sprinkle each with pepper and the remaining zest and cilantro. Drizzle with the remaining oil and Demi-Glace Reduction Sauce.

PARCHMENT SALMON

Try this method with any fish except bluefish. If you would like to use bluefish, increase the onions and decrease the butter since the fish is already oily.

Serves 6

¼ cup Compound Butter (see recipe in Chapter 2)

½ pound fresh forest mushrooms

1 tablespoon minced shallot

2 bunches green onions, chopped

2 teaspoons chopped fresh marjoram

1½ pounds salmon fillet

¼ cup dry white wine

1. Combine the butter, mushrooms, shallot, green onions, and marjoram. Roll in parchment paper and chill for a minimum of 6 hours, until firm.

2. Preheat the oven to 400°F.

3. Cut the salmon into 4 portions and place each on a folded sheet of parchment paper. Top each with 2 ample slices of the butter. Sprinkle each with about 1 tablespoon of the white wine. Fold up each, folding the parchment over the top and continuing to fold until well sealed.

4. Roast for 7–10 minutes, until the paper is slightly brown. Slit open paper and serve immediately.

Forest Mushrooms

Forest mushrooms encompass a wide variety of choices. Feel free to use your favorites. However, if you choose to hunt down your own wild mushrooms, be careful not to pick any that may be poisonous. Poisonous mushrooms can make you very sick, and some can even be fatal.

BARBECUED MARINATED TUNA

If you just can't bring yourself to eat anchovies, try kalamata olives instead!

Serves 6

1½ pounds fresh tuna

¼ cup apple juice

¼ cup dry red wine

1 tablespoon olive oil

½ tablespoon honey

¼ cup minced serrano chili pepper

Zest of 1 lemon

2 anchovies, chopped

Fresh-cracked black pepper, to taste

1. Rinse the fish in ice water and pat dry.

2. Blend together the juice, wine, oil, honey, chili, and zest. Pour the mixture over the tuna and let marinate for 30 minutes.

3. Preheat grill.

4. Place the fish on the grill (reserve the marinade) and cook for 2–4 minutes on each side, depending on the thickness of the fish and desired doneness.

5. While the tuna cooks, place the marinade in a small saucepan over medium heat and reduce by half.

6. To serve, plate the tuna and drizzle with marinade syrup, then sprinkle with anchovies and pepper.

FISH CHILI WITH BEANS

If you enjoy this dish, branch out and experiment with different types of fish and beans.

Serves 6

1¼ pounds fresh fish (sea bass, halibut, or red snapper)

1 leek

1 medium yellow onion

12 fresh plum tomatoes

4 ounces firm tofu

1 fresh jalapeño

1 fresh serrano

1 teaspoon curry powder

1 teaspoon chili powder

¼ teaspoon cayenne pepper

Fresh-cracked black pepper, to taste

2 tablespoons olive oil

2 cups cooked beans (pintos, cannellini, or red kidney)

½ cup dry red wine

1 cup Seafood Stock (see recipe in Chapter 2)

½ cup brewed strong coffee

1 teaspoon brown sugar

1 tablespoon honey

1. Rinse the fish in ice water and pat dry. Slice the leek and medium-dice the onion. Dice the tomatoes. Cut the tofu into large dice. Mince the jalapeño and serrano. Mix together the curry and chili powders, the cayenne, and black pepper.

2. Heat most of the oil over medium heat in a large saucepan. Add the leeks, onions, tomatoes, and tofu; cook for 2 minutes. Sprinkle with some of the seasoning mixture, then add all the remaining ingredients except the fish; stew for approximately 60 minutes.

3. Preheat grill to medium temperature.

4. Brush the fish with the remaining olive oil and seasoning mixture; grill on each side until cooked through (the cooking time will vary depending on the type of fish and thickness), about 5–15 minutes.

5. To serve, ladle the stew into bowls and top with grilled fish.

SAUTÉED RED SNAPPER

You'll love the flavor of this extremely rich fish.

Serves 6

1½ pounds fresh red snapper

¼ teaspoon turmeric

1 teaspoon curry powder

¼ teaspoon garam masala

Fresh-cracked black pepper, to taste

1 cup all-purpose unbleached flour

¼ cup plain nonfat yogurt

¼ cup buttermilk

2 tablespoons olive oil

1. Rinse the fish in ice water and pat dry. Cut the fish into 6 serving pieces. Sift together the turmeric, curry powder, garam masala, black pepper, and flour. In a separate bowl, mix together the yogurt and buttermilk.

2. Dust the fish with the flour mixture, then dip into the yogurt mix, and back into the flour mixture.

3. Heat the oil over medium-high heat in a large sauté pan; sauté the fish on each side until crispy, golden brown, and flaky. Drain on rack lined with paper towels and serve.

SALMON AND HADDOCK TERRINE

Start a day in advance for this recipe, which creates a beautiful plate for presentation. You can also use a chutney or salsa with this.

Serves 6

1 tablespoon olive oil

¾ pound fresh salmon fillet

¾ pound haddock fillet

3 cloves garlic

1 medium eggplant

Fresh-cracked black pepper, to taste

Kosher salt, to taste

1 head arugula

2 Roasted Red Peppers (see recipe in Chapter 4)

1. Preheat the oven to 375°F. Grease a loaf pan with the olive oil.

2. Rinse the fish in ice water and pat dry. Thinly slice the garlic. Cut eggplant in half lengthwise; roast for 20 minutes.

3. Season the fish with black pepper and salt. In the prepared pan, layer the salmon, cooled eggplant, arugula, haddock, cooled red peppers, garlic, then more arugula, and top with eggplant.

4. Wrap tightly with foil and bake for 20 minutes. Unwrap and press down on the layered ingredients; rewrap tightly and bake for 10–20 minutes longer, until thoroughly cooked. Remove from oven and let cool in the refrigerator overnight.

5. To serve, unmold from loaf pan. Slice and serve.

TILAPIA WITH SMOKED GOUDA

The smoky flavor of the Gouda cheese nicely complements the crisp flavor of the tilapia.

Serves 6

1¼ pounds fresh tilapia fillets

6 fresh plum tomatoes

2 turnips

1 leek

1 shallot

3 cloves garlic

¼ bunch parsley

3 ounces smoked Gouda

1 tablespoon olive oil

1 cup Fish Stock (see recipe in Chapter 2)

¼ cup dry red wine

Fresh-cracked black pepper, to taste

1. Preheat the oven to 375°F.

2. Rinse the fish in ice water and pat dry. Medium-dice the tomatoes. Peel and thinly slice the turnips. Finely slice the leek. Mince the shallot and garlic. Chop the parsley. Grate the cheese.

3. Paint a medium-size baking dish with olive oil, then layer the leek, turnips, shallot, garlic, and fish. Pour in the stock and wine; bake, covered, for 30–40 minutes.

4. Uncover and sprinkle with tomatoes and cheese. Return to oven until cheese is completely melted. Serve hot, sprinkled with parsley and pepper.

Using Wine with Fish

Use a nice dry wine to stand up to the smoky flavor of the cheese. Generally speaking, a light, nonrobust, drinking red wine works well in fish dishes.

CHAPTER 11

DESSERTS AND DRINKS

DESSERTS

GREEK MESS

If you can't find Greek almond cookies, use the classic Italian amaretti. Mastiha can be found at Greek or Middle Eastern grocery stores.

Serves 10

2 cups whipping cream

1 cup confectioners' sugar, divided

1 teaspoon ground mastiha

2 pints raspberries or other seasonal berry, divided

12 Greek almond cookies, crumbled, divided

½ cup chopped almonds

4 tablespoons chopped mint leaves

1. In a medium bowl, beat the whipping cream until soft peaks form. Add ½ cup of sugar and the mastiha. Continuing whipping the mixture until stiff peaks form. Keep the mixture cool.

2. In another medium bowl, combine ⅔ of the berries and the remaining sugar. Stir until the sugar is melted. Coarsely mash the berries into the consistency of a chunky jam.

3. Gently fold the berry mixture into the whipped cream. Fold half of the crumbled cookies into the berry–whipped cream mixture.

4. Divide the mixture into individual serving bowls or glasses, and top with the remaining crumbled cookies, remaining berries, almonds, and mint.

5. Serve immediately or cover and refrigerate for up to 1 day.

CRÈME CARAMEL

Serve these individual creamy desserts with Greek coffee. You'll be working with hot sugar, so be very careful when making the caramel for this dish.

Serves 12

5 cups whole milk

2 teaspoons vanilla extract

8 large egg yolks

4 large eggs

2 cups sugar, divided

¼ cup water

1. Preheat the oven to 350°F. Heat milk in a medium pot over medium-high heat to scalding (just below the boiling point). Remove from heat and add vanilla.

2. Whisk eggs and 1 cup of sugar in a large bowl. Slowly whisk a ladle of milk into the eggs. Keep ladling milk, until all the milk is incorporated into the eggs. Let cool.

3. Have twelve (3-inch) ramekins ready to fill. Bring remaining sugar and water to a boil in a small nonstick saucepan over medium-high heat. Reduce the heat to medium. Do not stir the sugar; gently swirl the pan instead. The water will evaporate and the sugar will darken and turn to caramel. Don't walk away from the pan because the sugar will burn quickly. When the sugar turns a dark golden caramel, remove the pan from the heat and divide the caramel evenly among the ramekins. Let the caramel harden.

4. Distribute the custard evenly among the ramekins. Set ramekins in a large baking pan. Add hot water to pan until it reaches halfway up the side of the ramekins.

5. Bake the custards for 25–30 minutes or until the custard is set. Carefully remove the ramekins from the water. Let the ramekins cool completely, and then refrigerate them for 8 hours or overnight.

6. To serve the Crème Caramel, run a small knife around the edge of each ramekin and unmold it by inverting the ramekin over a dessert plate.

DAD'S RICE PUDDING

This recipe uses long-grain rice, but you can also use Arborio, jasmine, or basmati rice.

Serves 12

2½ cups long-grain rice, rinsed

9 cups whole milk, divided

1 large cinnamon stick, broken in two

¾ teaspoon salt

1 tablespoon vanilla extract

3 (2-inch) strips lemon peel, pith removed

3 (2-inch) strips orange peel, pith removed

1 cup sugar

2 large egg yolks

½ cup raisins, soaked in 1 cup warm water

1 teaspoon ground cinnamon

1. In a large pot over medium-high heat, combine the rice, 8 cups of milk, the cinnamon stick, salt, vanilla, lemon peel, orange peel, and sugar. Stir the mixture until the milk is scalding (just before boiling). Immediately reduce the temperature to medium-low. Cook the rice for 60–90 minutes or until the rice is cooked and the pudding has a creamy consistency. Stir occasionally to keep the rice from sticking to the bottom of the pot.

2. Remove the cinnamon stick, lemon peel, and orange peel.

3. Cook the remaining milk in a small pan over medium-high heat until scalded (just before boiling). In a small bowl, whisk the eggs thoroughly. Then slowly whisk a ladle of milk into the eggs. Keep ladling milk, one ladle at a time, until all the milk is incorporated into the eggs.

4. Drain the raisins. Add the egg mixture and raisins to the rice pudding and stir to combine. Pour the pudding into a casserole dish and let it cool to room temperature. Cover and chill in the refrigerator for 8 hours or overnight.

5. Serve the rice pudding at room temperature topped with a sprinkle of cinnamon.

Scalded Milk

Milk that is scalded has been heated, over medium-high heat, to just before the boiling point. You can tell the milk is scalding when you see tiny bubbles form around the perimeter of the pot.

BAKLAVA

Organization is the key to assembling this dish. Make sure the phyllo is at room temperature, the syrup is ready, and the filling is made before you start.

Serves 16

2¼ cups sugar, divided

1 cup water

½ cup honey

1 tablespoon fresh lemon juice

2 cups walnuts

2 cups blanched almonds

½ teaspoon ground cloves

2 teaspoons ground cinnamon

¾ cup white bread crumbs or ground melba toast

1 cup unsalted butter, melted

1 package phyllo, thawed, at room temperature

1. Put 2 cups of sugar, water, and honey into a medium pot over medium-high heat. Bring the mixture to a boil, and then reduce the heat to medium-low and cook for 10 minutes. Add the lemon juice and cook for another 10 minutes. Allow the syrup to cool to room temperature.

2. In a food processor, pulse the walnuts and almonds until they are finely crumbled. Transfer the nuts to a bowl and add the cloves, cinnamon, remaining sugar, and bread crumbs. Stir to combine and set it aside.

3. Preheat the oven to 300°F. Brush the bottom and sides of a 9" × 13" baking pan with the melted butter.

4. Cover the phyllo sheets with a damp towel so they don't dry out. Take a sheet, brush one side with butter, and lay it in the pan with a quarter of it hanging off the top edge. Repeat for the bottom, left, and right edges of the pan. Place a fifth buttered sheet directly into the pan, so the entire bottom of the pan is covered.

5. Sprinkle a third of the filling over the phyllo. Place four buttered sheets over the filling. Sprinkle another third of the filling over the sheets. Top the filling with another four buttered sheets. Sprinkle the remaining filling over the sheets. Top with four more buttered sheets. Fold in the hanging edges from the first four sheets and brush the entire surface with butter.

6. With a sharp knife, score the top layers of phyllo, about ¼-inch deep, into serving squares. The scoring will make the baklava easier to cut after it is baked. Bake the baklava for 90 minutes or until the phyllo is golden.

7. Immediately after baking, ladle the syrup over the entire surface of the baklava. Use all the syrup. Let the baklava absorb the syrup as it comes to room temperature.

8. Cut the baklava and serve at room temperature. Store uncovered at room temperature.

LEMON HALVA

Semolina flour looks like Cream of Wheat and comes in fine, medium, and coarse textures. Look for it at Greek and Middle Eastern grocers.

Serves 10

4 cups water

2 cups sugar

8 (2-inch) strips lemon peel, pith removed

⅛ teaspoon ground cinnamon

1 cup plus 1 tablespoon unsalted butter, divided

2 cups coarse semolina flour

½ cup plus 2 tablespoons chopped blanched almonds, divided

½ cup plus 2 tablespoons pine nuts, divided

½ teaspoon vanilla

2 tablespoons grated lemon zest

2 tablespoons lemon juice

1. Put the water, sugar, and lemon peels in a medium pot over medium-high heat. Bring the water to a boil, and then reduce the heat to medium-low and cook for 5 minutes. Add the cinnamon. Allow syrup to cool to room temperature. Remove the lemon peels and discard them. Set the syrup aside and reserve.

2. Melt 1 cup of butter in a large pot over medium heat. Stir in the semolina with a wooden spoon and continue stirring for 5–6 minutes until the semolina is lightly toasted. Add ½ cup of almonds and ½ cup of pine nuts, and stir for 2 more minutes.

3. To the pot, add the syrup and the vanilla, and reduce the heat to medium-low. Keep stirring for 2–3 minutes or until the semolina absorbs the liquid and starts to come away from the sides of the pan. Take the pot off the heat. Add the lemon zest and juice. Place a tea towel over the pan, and then cover the pan with a lid to prevent a crust from forming on the halva. Cool for 10 minutes.

4. Grease a bundt pan with the remaining butter. Spoon the halva into the pan and smooth out the top. Let the halva cool completely before unmolding it.

5. Top the halva with the remaining almonds and pine nuts. Serve the halva at room temperature or cold.

Halva

Halva originated in the Arab world but is a popular Mediterranean dessert. It is a molded and firm dessert that is like a pudding but shouldn't be confused with a cake.

TIRAMISU

Tiramisu means "pick me up" in Italian, no doubt referring to the caffeine kick from the coffee in the dessert.

Serves 10

3 large eggs, separated

⅛ teaspoon nutmeg

¼ cup sugar, divided

1 cup mascarpone cheese

½ cup strong black coffee, freshly made

6 tablespoon Marsala or coffee liqueur

16 ladyfinger cookies, divided

2 tablespoons cocoa powder

1. In a medium bowl, whisk egg yolks, nutmeg, and 2 tablespoons of sugar until the mixture has thickened. Stir in the mascarpone. In another medium bowl, beat the egg whites until they form stiff peaks. Gently fold the mascarpone-egg mixture into the egg whites. Set it aside.

2. In a medium bowl, add the remaining sugar, coffee, and Marsala. Stir the mixture until the sugar is dissolved. Dip eight ladyfingers (one at a time) into the coffee mixture for 1 second, and then place it on a small baking dish. Don't leave the ladyfingers in the coffee for more than a second or they will be mushy.

3. Spread half of the mascarpone filling over the ladyfingers. Dip the remaining ladyfingers (one at a time) in the coffee mixture for 1 second, and then place them in the dish over the filling. Spread the remaining mascarpone filling over the ladyfingers. Cover the tiramisu and refrigerate it for 8 hours or overnight.

4. Sprinkle the dessert with cocoa powder before serving. Serve it cool or at room temperature.

EKMEK KATAIFI

Kataifi pastry comes in long strands that need to be untangled before using to separate any large clumps.

Serves 10

1 cup sugar

1 cup water

2 (2-inch) strips lemon peel, pith removed

1 tablespoon fresh lemon juice

½ cup plus 1 tablespoon unsalted butter, melted and divided

½ pound frozen kataifi pastry, thawed, at room temperature

2½ cups whole milk

½ teaspoon ground mastiha

2 large eggs

¼ cup fine semolina

1 teaspoon of cornstarch

¼ cup sugar

½ cup sweetened coconut flakes

1 cup whipping cream

1 teaspoon vanilla extract

1 teaspoon powdered milk

3 tablespoons confectioners' sugar

½ cup chopped unsalted pistachios

1. Put the sugar, water, lemon peel, and lemon juice in a medium pot over medium-high heat. Bring the mixture to a boil, and then reduce the heat to medium-low and cook for 10 minutes. Allow the syrup to cool to room temperature and reserve.

2. Preheat the oven to 350°F. Grease a 9" × 5" loaf pan with 1 tablespoon of butter. In a large bowl, add the kataifi (untangle first) and pour the remaining butter over it. Toss the kataifi in the butter to coat it and then add it to the pan. Bake the pastry on the middle rack of the oven for 30 minutes or until golden. Remove the pan from the oven and immediately ladle the reserved syrup over the kataifi. Allow the kataifi to cool to room temperature.

3. Heat the milk and mastiha in a medium pot over medium-high heat until the milk is scalded (just before boiling). Immediately reduce the temperature to medium-low to keep milk warm. In a large bowl, whisk the eggs, semolina, cornstarch, and sugar. Slowly whisk a ladle of the milk mixture into the eggs. Add two more ladles, one at a time.

4. Transfer the egg mixture into the pot with the milk, on medium heat. Stir until it thickens and has the consistency of custard. Stir in the coconut. Remove pot from the heat, and cover the surface with plastic wrap so it doesn't forma crust. Cool to room temperature.

5. Spread the custard over the kataifi. Refrigerate for 8 hours or overnight to set. Unmold the kataifi by running a knife around the edges of the pan and flipping the pan over a serving plate. Invert the kataifi on the plate so the custard is facing up.

6. In a large bowl, whip the cream until it forms soft peaks. Add the vanilla, powdered milk, and confectioners' sugar. Resume whipping the cream until it forms stiff peaks. Spread the whipped cream over the custard, and top with the pistachios. Serve immediately.

PORTOKALOPITA (ORANGE PHYLLO PIE)

Instead of raisins, try dried cranberries in this dish.

Serves 16

2 cups sugar, divided

2 cups water

2 large oranges, sliced

½ cup plus 1 tablespoon unsalted butter, melted and divided

1 package phyllo, thawed, at room temperature

2 teaspoons ground cinnamon

5 large eggs

2 tablespoons grated orange zest

1 teaspoon vanilla extract

1 tablespoon orange liqueur

⅛ teaspoon salt

1½ teaspoons baking powder

1½ cups extra-virgin olive oil

1 cup plain yogurt

½ cup raisins

1. Heat 1 cup of sugar and the water in a medium pot over medium-high heat until it boils, and then reduce the heat to medium-low. Add the orange slices, and cook for 30–40 minutes or until the oranges soften and begin to look translucent. Remove the orange slices and discard them. Allow the syrup to cool to room temperature and reserve it.

2. Preheat the oven to 350°F. Brush the bottom and sides of a 13" × 9" baking pan with 1 tablespoon of butter. Open the phyllo package, and cover sheets with a slightly damp tea towel so they don't dry out. In a small bowl, combine ½ cup of sugar and the cinnamon.

3. Brush a phyllo sheet with melted butter, and sprinkle the surface with some of the cinnamon-sugar. Loosely fold about 1 inch of phyllo from the bottom over the cinnamon sugar and lightly pinch the right and left ends. Continue to loosely fold, over and under so it looks like ruffled curtains, and lightly pinch the ends together. Set the folded phyllo sheet on the baking pan, ruffles facing up. Repeat the process with seven or eight more sheets. Set them on the pan leaning against each other until the pan is full. Keep the remaining phyllo sheets covered. Bake for 10–12 minutes. Let the phyllo cool to room temperature. Leave the oven on.

4. In a large bowl, whisk the eggs and the remaining sugar (not the cinnamon sugar). Whisk in the orange zest, vanilla, and orange liqueur. Whisk in the salt, baking powder, oil, and yogurt. Stir in the raisins. Shred the remaining phyllo sheets with your hands. Stir them into the yogurt mixture. Spread the mixture over the baked phyllo.

5. Bake the pie on the middle rack for 35–40 minutes or until golden. Immediately ladle the reserved syrup over the portokalopita. Allow the phyllo pie to cool before serving.

LOUKOUMADES (FRIED HONEY BALLS)

Switch up the nuts by using almonds. Try serving these little doughnuts with melted Nutella or chocolate sauce.

Serves 10

2 cups sugar

1 cup water

1 cup honey

1½ cups tepid water

1 tablespoon brown sugar

¼ cup vegetable oil

1 tablespoon active dry yeast

1½ cups all-purpose flour

½ cup cornstarch

⅛ teaspoon salt

Vegetable oil for frying

1½ cups chopped walnuts

¼ cup ground cinnamon

1. Bring the sugar and 1 cup water to a boil in a medium pot over medium-high heat. Then reduce the heat to medium and let it cook for 10 minutes. Add the honey, and allow the syrup to cool to room temperature and reserve it.

2. In a large bowl, combine the tepid water, brown sugar, oil, and yeast. Set the mixture aside for 7–10 minutes to allow the yeast to activate. In another large bowl, combine the flour, cornstarch, and salt. Using a large wooden spoon or your hands, stir the flour mixture into the yeast to form wet dough. Cover the dough and let it rise in a warm place for 2 hours. The dough will be spongy.

3. Set up a frying station: a glass of water, a teaspoon, and a deep frying pan. Heat 3 inches of oil in a deep frying pan over medium-high heat until the oil's temperature reaches 350°F. Adjust the heat to keep the temperature at 350°F while frying. Take a handful of dough in your palm, squeeze a small amount of dough onto the teaspoon (dunk the teaspoon in the water every so often), and drop the dough into the oil. Repeat with remaining dough. Fry for 3–4 minutes.

4. Immediately after frying each batch, drop the loukoumades in the reserved syrup. Allow them to soak up the syrup for 3–4 minutes, and then place them on a rack over a baking pan to drain. Catch the excess syrup in the pan, and then add it back to the syrup bowl.

5. Serve the loukoumades topped with the walnuts and cinnamon. Serve them warm or at room temperature.

Loukoumades

These are Greece's answer to doughnuts. These fried balls of dough are always found at Greek outdoor festivals.

REVANI SYRUP CAKE

This simple cake is finished with syrup that soaks into the cake. Serve it with a scoop of ice cream.

Serves 24

1 tablespoon unsalted butter

2 tablespoons all-purpose flour

1 cup ground rusk or bread crumbs

1 cup fine semolina flour

¾ cup ground toasted almonds

3 teaspoons baking powder

16 large eggs

2 tablespoons vanilla extract

3 cups sugar, divided

3 cups water

5 (2-inch) strips lemon peel, pith removed

3 tablespoons fresh lemon juice

1 ounce brandy

1. Preheat the oven to 350°F. Grease a 13" × 9" baking pan with the butter and then coat it with the flour.

2. In a medium bowl, combine the rusk, semolina flour, almonds, and baking powder. In another medium bowl, whisk the eggs, vanilla, and 1 cup of sugar using an electric mixer on medium for 5 minutes or until the eggs turn a light yellow. Stir the semolina mixture into the eggs in three batches.

3. Pour the batter into the baking pan, and bake it on the middle rack for 30–35 minutes or until a toothpick inserted into the middle of the cake comes out clean. While the cake is baking, make the syrup. Bring the remaining sugar, water, and lemon peel to a boil in a medium pot over medium-high heat. Reduce the heat to medium-low and cook for 6 minutes. Add the lemon juice and cook for 3 minutes. Take the syrup off the heat and add the brandy. Let the syrup cool. Remove the lemon peel and reserve the syrup.

4. When the cake is finished, ladle the syrup over it and let the cake soak up the syrup.

5. Cut the cake into squares or diamond shapes. Serve the cake at room temperature; you can store leftovers in the refrigerator for up to one week.

CINNAMON ROLLS WITH TAHINI AND HONEY

Tahini and honey give classic cinnamon rolls a Mediterranean twist. Tahini is made from sesame seeds and adds a nutty taste.

Serves 16

1 cup whole milk, warm

2¼ teaspoons active dry yeast

3 tablespoons vegetable oil

3¼ cups unbleached all-purpose flour, divided

½ cup sugar

1 large egg

1 teaspoon salt

¾ cup (packed) golden brown sugar

2 tablespoons ground cinnamon

¾ cup tahini

¾ cup honey

1 teaspoon lemon zest

2 tablespoons lemon juice

¼ cup plus 1 tablespoon unsalted butter, at room temperature, divided

1. In a large bowl, combine the warm milk and yeast. Set the mixture aside for 7–10 minutes to allow the yeast to activate. Stir in the oil, 1 cup of flour, sugar, egg, and salt. Using your hands, mix in 2 cups flour to form a soft dough that is not too sticky. Cover the dough with plastic wrap and let it rise for 2 hours or until it doubles in size.

2. In a small bowl, thoroughly combine the brown sugar and cinnamon, and reserve it. In another small bowl, combine the tahini, honey, lemon zest, and lemon juice. Stir to thoroughly combine and reserve.

3. Grease a 13" × 9" baking pan with 1 tablespoon of butter. Spread the remaining flour on the work surface. After the dough rises, punch it down with your fist and place it on the floured surface. Roll the dough to a 9" × 14" rectangle. Spread the remaining butter over the surface of the dough, leaving a ½-inch border around the dough. Sprinkle the brown sugar mixture over the butter.

4. Beginning at the longest end of the dough, roll the dough to form a tight cylinder. Cut the dough into sixteen equal slices. Place the slices in the pan leaving some space between them to allow them to rise. Cover the rolls with a tea towel and let them rise in a warm place for 3 hours or until they fill the pan. Preheat the oven to 375°F.

5. Bake the rolls on the middle rack for 20–25 minutes or until they turn golden. Let the rolls cool for 5 minutes, and then smear the tahini topping over each one. Pull the rolls apart, and serve them warm or at room temperature.

PEAR CROUSTADE

Serve with a scoop of French vanilla ice cream. Try this with Granny Smith apples as an alternative to pears.

Serves 8

1 cup plus 1 tablespoon all-purpose flour, divided

4½ tablespoons sugar, divided

⅛ teaspoon salt

6 tablespoons unsalted butter, chilled, cut into ½-inch cubes

1 large egg, separated

1½ tablespoons ice-cold water

3 firm ripe pears (Bosc), peeled, cored, sliced into ¼-inch slices

1 tablespoon fresh lemon juice

⅓ teaspoon ground allspice

1 teaspoon anise seeds

1. Put 1 cup flour, 1½ tablespoons sugar, and salt into a food processor, and pulse to combine the ingredients. Add the butter and pulse until the mixture resembles coarse crumbs. Transfer the ingredients to a bowl.

2. In another small bowl, whisk the egg yolk and ice water. Add the egg mixture to the flour-butter mixture, and stir to combine. Form a dough ball, and then flatten it into a disc. Wrap the dough in plastic wrap, and chill it for an hour.

3. Preheat the oven to 400°F. Place the dough on parchment paper and roll it until it is 10 inches around. Transfer the dough and the parchment to a baking sheet.

4. In a large bowl, add the pears, remaining sugar, remaining flour, lemon juice, allspice, and anise, and toss to combine the ingredients.

5. Place the filling in the center of the dough and spread it out evenly, leaving a 2-inch border around the edges. Fold the dough border over the fruit to form a rustic edge. Pinch any dough that has cracked to seal it. In a small bowl, whisk the egg white and brush it over the dough.

6. Place the baking sheet on the middle rack of the oven, and bake for 40 minutes or until the croustade is golden and bubbling. Let it cool for 15 minutes before serving. Serve the croustade warm or at room temperature.

GALAKTOBOUREKO

Patisseries throughout Greece serve this classic dessert. Galaktoboureko is semolina custard baked in buttered phyllo pastry and topped with lemon syrup.

Serves 12

4 cups sugar, divided

1 cup water

1 tablespoon fresh lemon juice

1 tablespoon plus 1½ teaspoons grated lemon zest, divided

10 cups whole milk, at room temperature

1 cup plus 2 tablespoons unsalted butter, melted and divided

2 tablespoons vanilla extract

7 large eggs, at room temperature

1 cup fine semolina

1 package phyllo, thawed and at room temperature

1. In a medium pot over medium-high heat, bring 2 cups of sugar, water, lemon juice, and 1½ teaspoons lemon zest to a boil. Reduce the heat to medium-low and cook for 10 minutes. Remove the pot from the heat, let syrup come to room temperature, and set it aside.

2. Put the milk, 2 tablespoons of butter, the remaining sugar, and vanilla in a large pot over medium-high heat. Cook the mixture until the milk is scalded and take it off the heat.

3. In another bowl, whisk the eggs and semolina. Slowly whisk a ladle of milk into the egg mixture. Add four more ladles of milk, one at a time. Transfer the egg mixture into the milk mixture and place the pot over medium heat. Stir the mixture until it thickens to a consistency like custard. Add the remaining zest and take off the heat. Place a tea towel over the pan, and cover the pan with a lid to prevent a crust from forming. Set it aside.

4. Preheat the oven to 350°F. Remove the phyllo from package and divide the sheets into two equal piles (tops and bottoms). Cover each pile with a damp tea towel so the phyllo doesn't dry out. Brush the bottom and sides of a 13" × 9" baking pan with butter.

5. Take one sheet of phyllo from the bottom pile, and brush with butter. Place the phyllo sheet in the bottom of the pan with a quarter of the sheet hanging over the sides. Continue buttering and laying the bottom-layer sheets in the pan until the entire bottom and edges are covered with phyllo. Add the custard, spread it evenly over the bottom sheets, then wrap the overhanging phyllo over the custard.

6. Take one sheet from the top pile and brush the surface with butter. Place the sheet on top of the filling and repeat the process with the remaining sheets to cover the entire surface of the pan. If excess phyllo is hanging from the edges of the pan, tuck the excess into the sides of the pan. Score the top layers of the phyllo, about ¼-inch deep, into serving squares.

7. Bake the pie on the middle rack of the oven for 35–40 minutes or until the top is golden. As soon as the pie is removed from the oven, ladle the reserved syrup over the entire surface. Use all the syrup. Let the galaktoboureko absorb the syrup as it comes to room temperature. Cut it and serve it at room temperature or cold.

LEMON MERINGUE PHYLLO TARTS

Ready-made phyllo cups are convenient, but making your own is easy, too. Add a splash of lemon liqueur to your curd if you like.

Serves 6

⅔ cup plus ¼ cup sugar, divided

¼ cup ground almonds

11 tablespoons unsalted butter (5 tablespoons melted, 6 tablespoons cold and cut into cubes), divided

4 sheets phyllo pastry, thawed

6 large eggs, separated (refrigerate egg whites until needed)

⅛ teaspoon salt

⅓ cup fresh lemon juice

2 teaspoons grated lemon zest

¾ teaspoon cream of tartar

¼ cup confectioners' sugar

1. Preheat the oven to 325°F. In a small bowl combine ¼ cup sugar and ¼ cup almonds. Brush six cups in a muffin tin with 1 tablespoon of melted butter. Work quickly so the phyllo doesn't dry out: Place a phyllo sheet on a work surface and brush it with the melted butter. Sprinkle ⅓ of the sugar-almond mixture over the butter. Repeat with a second sheet and place it over the first sheet. Repeat with a third sheet and place it over the second sheet. Brush the fourth sheet with butter and place it on the third sheet, butter side up.

2. Cut the stack into 4" × 4" squares. Press the squares into the buttered muffin tin cups and bake them for 10 minutes or until they are lightly golden. Allow the phyllo cups to cool for 5 minutes, then remove them from the muffin tin, and let them cool on a rack. The phyllo cups can be made one or two days before using and left uncovered at room temperature.

3. Have an ice bath ready for the curd. Pour 2 inches of water into a medium pan over medium-low heat. In a medium metal bowl, whisk the egg yolks and remaining sugar until smooth. Whisk in the salt, lemon juice, and zest. Place the bowl over the pan of simmering water. Whisking continuously, add the 6 tablespoons of cold butter, one cube at a time. Whisk until the curd has thickened. Immediately place the metal bowl in the ice bath to cool the curd. Stir the curd occasionally as it cools to room temperature, and then refrigerate it overnight.

4. Pour the egg whites into a clean bowl. Using an electric beater, beat the eggs until soft peaks form. Start at a low and gradually increase the speed until you get soft peaks. Add the cream of tartar and confectioners' sugar, and continue to beat the whites until they are glossy, smooth, and form stiff peaks. Place the meringue in a piping bag with a large tip at the end.

5. Assemble the tarts by placing a phyllo cup on a work surface and filling it with a portion of the chilled lemon curd. Pipe a mound of meringue on top of the curd. Using a kitchen blowtorch, lightly toast the meringue. Repeat with the remaining cups, curd, and meringue.

6. Serve the tarts immediately or refrigerate them until they are needed. Serve the tarts at room temperature.

KOURABIEDES (ALMOND COOKIES)

These cookies are traditionally served at Christmas, but they are great any time.

Serves 20

1½ cups unsalted butter, clarified, at room temperature

2 cups confectioners' sugar, divided

1 large egg yolk

2 tablespoons brandy

1½ teaspoons baking powder

1 teaspoon vanilla extract

5½ cups all-purpose flour, sifted

1 cup roasted almonds, chopped

1. In a large bowl, cream the butter and ½ cup of sugar. Add the egg and continue to beat the mixture for 2 minutes. In a small bowl, combine the brandy and baking powder, stirring until the baking powder is absorbed. Add the brandy mixture and the vanilla to the egg mixture, and continue to beat until the ingredients are combined.

2. Using a large wooden spoon, slowly add the flour to the egg mixture to create dough. Add the almonds, and knead the dough to incorporate all the flour and almonds.

3. Preheat the oven to 350°F. Divide the dough into forty pieces. Take each piece, roll it into a ball, and then form it into a crescent shape. Place the formed cookie on a baking sheet lined with parchment paper. Repeat the process with the remaining dough.

4. Bake the cookies in batches on the middle rack of the oven for 25 minutes. Put the remaining sugar in a medium bowl. Allow the cookies to cool for 5 minutes or until they are cool enough to handle. Add the cookies, one at a time, to the confectioners' sugar to coat them. Let the cookies cool completely.

5. Sprinkle additional confectioners' sugar over the cookies before serving. Store the cookies in a sealed container.

Clarified Butter

Clarified butter is melted butter without the milk solids. To make clarified butter, place a stick of butter in a pan over low heat. The butter will begin to separate as it melts, and white foam will form on the surface. Remove the pan from the heat and carefully remove the white foam with a spoon. The clarified butter is what is left.

MELOMAKARONA (WALNUT COOKIES)

Try using a combination of almonds and walnuts in these cookies.

Serves 20

4 cups sugar, divided

4 cups water

1 cup plus 1 tablespoon honey, divided

1 (2-inch) strip orange peel, pith removed

1 cinnamon stick

½ cup extra-virgin olive oil

¼ cup unsalted butter, room temperature

¼ cup Metaxa brandy or any other brandy

1 tablespoon grated orange zest

¾ cup orange juice

¼ teaspoon baking soda

3 cups pastry flour

¾ cup fine semolina flour

1½ teaspoons baking powder

4 teaspoons ground cinnamon, divided

1 teaspoon ground cloves, divided

1½ cups finely chopped walnuts

⅓ cup brown sugar

1. Heat 3½ cups sugar, water, 1 cup honey, orange peel, and cinnamon stick in a medium pot over medium-high heat until it boils. Reduce heat to medium-low and cook for 10 minutes. Allow to cool to room temperature.

2. Using a stand mixer with a dough hook attachment, mix the remaining sugar, oil, and butter for 5 minutes. Mix in the brandy, remaining honey, and orange zest. In a small bowl, combine the orange juice and baking soda. Add to the mixer. Mix for another minute.

3. In a large bowl, combine pastry flour, semolina flour, baking powder, 2 teaspoons cinnamon, and ½ teaspoon cloves. Slowly add the dry ingredients to the mixer (1 cup at a time). Run the mixer until the ingredients combine into a soft pliable dough that is not too sticky. Cover dough and let it rest for 30 minutes.

4. Preheat the oven to 350°F. Divide the dough into forty balls. Take a ball and form it into an oval. Lightly press the top of the cookie onto the finest side of a box grater to imprint a pattern on the cookie. Place the cookie on a baking sheet lined with parchment paper. Repeat the process with the remaining balls.

5. Bake the cookies for 30 minutes. Drop the hot cookies into the reserved syrup a few at a time. Allow them to soak in the syrup for 10 minutes, turn them over, and leave them in the syrup for another 3 minutes. Transfer the cookies to a cooling rack.

6. In a small bowl, combine the walnuts, brown sugar, remaining cinnamon, and remaining cloves. Brush the tops of the cookies with the leftover syrup and top with the walnut mixture. Store the cookies in a sealed container.

LEMON-COCONUT ICE CREAM

For an adult treat, add a shot of lemon or coconut liqueur to the cream just before chilling it.

Serves 4

16 ounces coconut milk

10 ounces condensed milk

¼ cup honey

1 tablespoon vanilla extract

½ teaspoon salt

2 tablespoons grated lemon zest

5 tablespoons fresh lemon juice

1½ cups full-fat Greek yogurt

1 cup sweetened coconut flakes, toasted

1. In a large bowl, combine the coconut milk, condensed milk, honey, vanilla, salt, zest, lemon juice, and yogurt.

2. Cover the mixture with plastic wrap, and refrigerate it for 8 hours or overnight.

3. Add the cream mixture to an ice-cream maker, and process according to the manufacturer's instructions.

4. Transfer the ice cream to a plastic container and place it in the freezer to harden.

5. Serve the ice cream with a sprinkle of toasted coconut.

LENTEN CAKE

This is a delicious vegan cake that will delight everyone.

Serves 16

1 tablespoon vegetable oil

3½ cups plus 1 tablespoon all-purpose flour, divided

½ teaspoon salt

1 tablespoon grated lemon zest

2 tablespoons grated orange zest

1 tablespoon ground cinnamon

¼ teaspoon ground cloves

½ cup ground almonds

1 teaspoon baking powder

1½ cups orange juice

1 teaspoon baking soda

1 cup extra-virgin olive oil, warm

1 cup sugar

1 ounce ouzo or brandy

½ teaspoon rose water

¼ cup chopped walnuts

¼ cup chopped dried cranberries

¼ cup chopped dried cherries

¼ cup raisins

¼ cup toasted sesame seeds

¼ cup confectioners' sugar

1. Preheat the oven to 350°F. Lightly grease a bundt pan with the vegetable oil, and then coat with 1 tablespoon of flour.

2. In a large bowl, mix the remaining flour, salt, lemon zest, orange zest, cinnamon, cloves, and almonds. In a small bowl, combine the baking powder and orange juice until the baking powder is absorbed. Reserve the mixture.

3. In a medium bowl, combine the olive oil and sugar. Add the mixture to the flour bowl, and stir to combine the ingredients. Pour in the reserved orange juice mixture, ouzo, and rose water. Add the walnuts, cranberries, cherries, raisins, and sesame seeds. Mix well.

4. Add the batter to the prepared pan and bake it on the middle rack of the oven for 45 minutes or until a toothpick inserted into the cake comes out clean. Allow the cake to cool for 5 minutes before removing it from the pan. Cool the cake completely.

5. Dust the cake with the confectioners' sugar and serve.

SESAME SNAPS

Replace the orange zest with lemon zest if you prefer a lemon flavor.

Serves 16

1 tablespoon unsalted butter

2 cups granulated sugar

⅓ cup water

⅓ cup honey

1 teaspoon fresh lemon juice

¼ teaspoon sea salt

1⅓ cups toasted sesame seeds

1 tablespoon grated orange zest

1. Grease a medium baking sheet with 1 tablespoon of butter.

2. Bring the sugar, water, honey, lemon juice, and salt to a boil in a medium-size, heavy-bottomed pan over medium-high heat. Continue cooking the syrup for 10 minutes or until the sugar turns a deep amber color.

3. Stir the sesame seeds and orange zest into the syrup. Remove the pan from the heat. Immediately add the syrup to the baking sheet. Quickly spread the syrup evenly around the pan with a greased spatula.

4. Before the syrup cools completely, score the top into serving pieces (squares or diamond shapes) with a greased knife. Scoring will make the snaps easier to cut when the syrup cools. When the syrup has cooled completely, use a spatula to remove it from the pan, and then cut it into serving pieces.

5. Store the Sesame Snaps in an airtight container.

Toasting Sesame Seeds

Toasting sesame seeds is easy, but it requires some patience. Put the sesame seeds in a dry frying pan over medium heat. Stir them constantly with a wooden spoon until they are toasted to your liking. Toasting can take up to 10 minutes, so be patient. Don't walk away from the pan because the seeds burn very quickly.

TOULOUMBES

For safety and accuracy, always use a candy thermometer when frying.

Serves 16

4½ cups water, divided

2 cups sugar

4 whole cloves

¼ cup honey

2½ cups all-purpose flour

⅓ cup sunflower oil plus extra for frying

1 teaspoon vanilla extract

5 large eggs

2–3 tablespoons ground cinnamon

1. Bring 2 cups of water, the sugar, and cloves to a boil in a medium pot over medium-high heat. Reduce the heat to medium-low and add the honey. Cook the mixture for 10 minutes and then let the syrup cool to room temperature. Set it aside.

2. Pour the flour into a large bowl and make a small well in the middle of the flour. Bring the remaining water and the oil to a boil in a medium pot over medium-high heat. Pour the hot water into the middle of the flour. Using an electric mixer, beat the mixture to incorporate the flour and hot water. Add the vanilla and the eggs, one at a time, and beat the batter to blend it. Set the batter aside.

3. Heat 2 inches of oil in a deep frying pan over medium-high heat until the temperature of the oil reaches 315°F. Adjust the heat to keep the temperature at 315°F while frying.

4. Fill a piping bag (fitted with a #6 star tip) with the batter. You might need to fry the batter in batches. When the oil is ready, carefully squeeze the batter out of the bag; using scissors, cut 3-inch pieces of batter into the oil. Fry five or six pieces at a time until they are golden. Remove them from the oil and place them in the reserved syrup for 5–6 minutes. Remove the touloumbes from the syrup and place them on a wire rack to cool. Repeat the process with the remaining batter.

5. Serve with a sprinkle of cinnamon on top.

FETA CHEESECAKE

You can top this cheesecake with your favorite fruit sauce or try Shortcut Sour Cherry Spoon Sweet (see recipe in Chapter 2) or Sesame Snaps (see recipe in this chapter).

Serves 10–12

2 cups graham cracker crumbs (about 30 crackers)

½ teaspoon ground cinnamon

6 tablespoons unsalted butter, melted

½ cup sesame seeds, toasted

12 ounces cream cheese, softened

1 cup crumbled feta cheese

3 large eggs

1 cup sugar

2 cups plain yogurt

2 tablespoons grated lemon zest

1 teaspoon vanilla

1. Preheat the oven to 350°F. Lightly grease an 8-inch springform pan with cooking spray. Wrap the exterior of the pan in heavy foil so that water cannot enter from the bottom or the sides. In a medium bowl, toss graham cracker crumbs, cinnamon, butter, and sesame seeds with a fork until it comes together. Empty mixture into the springform pan and gently spread and press down the mixture evenly over the base. Refrigerate until needed.

2. In another medium bowl, combine cream cheese and feta. Using an electric mixer on low, beat the cheeses together until they are smooth. Add eggs one at a time and beat after each addition. Add sugar and continue beating mixture until incorporated and creamy. Stir in yogurt, lemon zest, and vanilla.

3. Remove the springform pan from the refrigerator and pour the batter over the crust. Place the pan in a baking pan large enough to hold it and fill the baking pan with enough very hot water to reach halfway up the side of the pan.

4. Bake for 45–50 minutes or until the cheesecake is set and the center still jiggles a little. Remove the cheesecake from the water in the baking pan and discard the foil. Allow the cheesecake to cool on a wire rack in the springform pan, then refrigerate it for 4 hours or overnight to set completely.

5. Remove the cheesecake from the refrigerator and run a knife around the edge to loosen it from the pan. Unfasten the pan and carefully transfer the cheesecake to a serving platter. Serve cool or at room temperature.

ALMOND TANGERINE BITES

This Greek almond treat originates from the island of Kerkyra (or Corfu), one of the Ionian Islands off the west coast of Greece.

Yields approximately 20–25 pieces

2 cups raw almonds

5 tangerines

1 cup brown sugar

Icing sugar

1. Blanch almonds by boiling them in water; when they start floating to the top they can be removed from the water, drained, and easily peeled. Boil 3 tangerines in a generous amount of water for 5 minutes to remove the bitterness from the rind.

2. Squeeze juice from remaining 2 tangerines and set aside; discard skins.

3. Peel 3 boiled tangerines and put skins along with blanched almonds into a blender; purée until very finely ground.

4. Remove puréed almond mix from blender; in large bowl, mix with brown sugar.

5. Slowly add tangerine juice while continuing to mix well.

6. Roll small pieces of mixture into walnut-size balls using the palms of your hands; set aside on a sheet of wax paper to dry.

7. Dust balls lightly with icing sugar before serving.

The Greek Nut

The ancient Romans referred to the almond as the "Greek nut" because the almond tree had its origins in Asia Minor (modern-day Turkey).

AMYGDALOTA (ALMOND BISCUITS)

Amygdalota biscuits are a staple product in any Greek bakery, and they are wildly popular in Greece.

Yields approximately 25–30 pieces

1 pound blanched almonds

1 tablespoon fine semolina

3 eggs, separated

1½ cups sugar

1 tablespoon orange blossom water

1. Preheat the oven to 350°F.

2. Purée blanched almonds and semolina in a food processor until very fine.

3. Beat 2 egg yolks and 1 egg white well with a mixer in a large bowl; add sugar, almond purée, and orange blossom water. Mix well with a dough hook (stand mixer) or a wooden spoon.

4. In a mixing bowl, whip 2 egg whites until nice and stiff with peaks; incorporate thoroughly into the almond purée mixture.

5. Take up small pieces of dough and roll into balls between your palms. Place balls on a cookie sheet and press an almond into the center of each, flattening lower hemisphere of biscuit.

6. Bake for 20–30 minutes, or until cookies are starting to turn slightly golden. Remove from the oven and leave to cool for at least 1 hour. Important: To maintain the inner chewiness of these biscuits, it is a good idea to store them in sealed, airtight containers or wrapped in cellophane/plastic.

CYPRIOT LOUKOUMIA

You can use any type of marmalade, jam, or preserved fruit for the filling of these cookies.

Yields approximately 20 pieces

½ cup butter

2 cups flour

1½ cups milk

½ cup sugar

1 egg, beaten

1 teaspoon baking powder

½ cup orange marmalade

1 cup finely chopped almonds

2 tablespoons orange blossom water

½ teaspoon cinnamon

½ teaspoon nutmeg

Confectioners' sugar

1. Preheat the oven to 350°F.

2. Melt butter in a pot over medium-high heat. Slowly add flour, stirring constantly with a wooden spoon to avoid clumping.

3. Lower heat to medium-low and slowly add milk, making sure to stir continuously as the mixture thickens and starts clumping.

4. When all the milk has been added, remove from heat and add sugar, egg, and baking powder; mix well until the dough is uniformly smooth.

5. Prepare the filling by mixing the marmalade, almonds, orange blossom water, cinnamon, and nutmeg.

6. Using a rolling pin, spread pieces of dough on a floured surface to uniform thickness of a banana peel.

7. Place a small amount of filling mixture in the center of each disc. Fold each disc in half over the filling into a half-moon shape; tightly pinch together edges to ensure a good seal.

8. Place cookies on a buttered pan and bake for 20 minutes. Let stand for 30 minutes. Sprinkle cookies with confectioners' sugar before serving.

GALATOPITA (MILK PIE)

The fat content of the milk you use for this recipe is irrelevant, but use 2% or higher for a fuller flavor.

Serves 6

5 cups milk

½ cup butter

1 cup sugar

1 cup fine semolina

3 eggs

Ground cinnamon or icing sugar for sprinkling

1. Preheat the oven to 350°F.

2. On the stovetop, bring milk almost to a boil in a saucepan. Add butter, sugar, and semolina, making sure to stir continuously until thick crème is formed. Turn off the heat and let stand a couple of minutes to cool slightly.

3. Beat eggs and add to thickened mixture; whisk well.

4. Butter or oil the sides and bottom of a pie dish or other high-walled oven pan. Pour in mixture; bake for approximately 1 hour, until the top has browned. Turn off the oven but do not remove the pie for another 15 minutes.

5. Once the pie is removed from the oven, let it stand for a couple of hours. Serve topped with cinnamon or icing sugar. Can also be topped with fruit preserve or jam of your choosing.

MILOPITA (APPLE CAKE)

The Granny Smith variety of apple works best in this cake.

Serves 6

3 medium-sized apples

1½ cups self-rising flour (regular flour with 1½ teaspoons baking powder will do in a pinch)

Pinch of salt

¾ cup butter

1 cup white sugar

2 eggs, separated

⅓ cup milk

1 tablespoon vanilla extract

1 tablespoon grated lemon rind

¼ cup brown sugar

1 teaspoon ground cinnamon

1. Preheat the oven to 350°F.

2. Peel and core apples and slice into sixteenths. Set aside in a bowl of water with some lemon juice squeezed into it to keep from browning.

3. Sift flour with salt (and baking powder, if required).

4. Using a mixer, cream ½ cup of butter and all of the white sugar until smooth. While continually mixing, add egg yolks one at a time, alternating with 1 tablespoon of flour to achieve a smooth and creamy consistency. Add the rest of the flour in stages, alternating with the milk.

5. Add vanilla and lemon rind; mix until batter is smooth.

6. In a separate mixing bowl, whip egg whites into stiff peaks; using a spatula, carefully fold into batter.

7. Butter the sides of a pie dish and pour in the batter. Arrange apple slices in a perpendicular fashion over the top of the batter in a circular pattern to form an outer ring of apple slices. Fill center of ring with any remaining slices.

8. Melt remaining ¼ cup butter; mix with brown sugar and cinnamon.

9. Pour over apple slices in circular fashion, making sure to distribute evenly in long stream.

10. Bake for 60 minutes. Let stand at least a couple of hours before serving.

PASTELI (SESAME BRICKLE)

You can also toast the sesame seeds and almonds in the oven before using them in this recipe. Simply spread them on a baking sheet and place them in a preheated oven at 350°F for about 5 minutes or so. Make sure not to burn them.

Yields approximately 24 pieces

1½ cups Greek thyme honey

2½ cups sesame seeds

½ cup raw almonds (or pistachios or walnuts)

Orange blossom water

1. In a saucepan over medium-low heat, heat honey until it starts to bubble. Add sesame seeds and almonds; mix well. Stir continuously with a wooden spoon until mixture reaches a rich golden-brown color, about 10 minutes or so.

2. Prepare a marble or glass cutting board surface by sprinkling with the orange blossom water and spreading to cover the working surface.

3. Pour the hot honey-sesame mixture onto the working surface; spread with a spatula to a uniform thickness of a ½ inch or so. Take a sufficiently large piece of parchment paper and cover the outspread mixture. Use a rolling pin to further thin and spread mix into a rough rectangle of uniform thickness, about ¼ inch or so. Remove parchment paper (do not throw it out); square edges with a spatula or icing tool and let stand to cool.

4. Equally divide and cut outspread pasteli into full-length rectangles using a large sharp knife. Further divide and cut rectangles into squares, then cut squares at a 45-degree angle to achieve triangular pieces.

5. Use a metal spatula to remove pasteli triangles from the working surface and place in an airtight container lined with the saved parchment paper. Do not refrigerate, simply store in cupboard or pantry and serve wafers as a snack or dessert.

Pasteli, AKA Itrion

The combination of honey and sesame seeds to form wafers of chewy wholesome goodness is one Greek food concoction that has been around—quite literally—for ages. In the Archaic age and later in the Classical and Hellenistic periods this confection was known as *itrion*. Subsequently, it became known as *pasteli* among the Byzantines and remains a very popular sweet in Modern Greece.

STUFFED DRIED FIGS

Purchase kalamata dried string figs if you can find them, as they are larger and sweeter than most other commercially available varieties.

Serves 4

12 dried figs

24 walnut halves

2 tablespoons thyme honey

2 tablespoons sesame seeds

1. Snip the tough stalk ends off the figs. For each fig, slice a side and open with your fingers.

2. Stuff 2 walnut halves inside each fig and fold closed.

3. Arrange figs on a platter. Drizzle with honey and sprinkle with sesame seeds to serve.

Need Calcium and Fiber?

Fresh or dried, figs are an excellent source of calcium and fiber, as well as many other nutrients. They are also rich in antioxidants and polyphenols.

BYZANTINE FRUIT MEDLEY

Feel free to experiment with the fruits you use in this recipe.

Serves 4

2 apples, peeled and cubed

2 pears, peeled and cubed

Seeds from 1 pomegranate

3 mandarins, peeled and sectioned

½ cup red wine

½ cup Greek anthomelo (blossom honey)

1. Prepare fruits and mix together in a medium-size bowl.

2. Bring the wine and blossom honey to a boil and let it boil for a few minutes to burn off most of the alcohol. Allow to cool for 20 minutes.

3. Pour over mixed fruit and refrigerate for at least 1 hour. Be sure to stir the fruit a few times to ensure the sauce covers everything. Serve anytime as a snack or dessert.

ACORN SQUASH BAKE

This can be used as a side dish for a starch as well as a dessert.

Serves 6

6 acorn squashes

2 cups apple juice

6 teaspoons fresh-grated orange zest

6 teaspoons rolled oats

6 teaspoons raisins

3 teaspoons ground cinnamon

1 teaspoon ground nutmeg

1. Preheat the oven to 375°F.

2. Cut the acorn squashes in half and remove the seeds. Place halves cut-side down in a small roasting pan. Pour the apple juice over the top and cover tightly.

3. Bake for approximately 40 minutes. Turn squashes over and sprinkle each with 1 teaspoon zest, oats, and raisins. Sprinkle each with ½ teaspoon of cinnamon and a dash of nutmeg.

4. Baste with reduced apple juice. Cover and bake for 10 minutes longer. Then uncover and bake 10 minutes longer. Serve in individual bowls.

Acorn Squash

Acorn squash has a flavor similar to pumpkin and sweet potato. If you enjoy the taste of these two traditional favorites, you'll love the Acorn Squash Bake.

FIGS WITH BRIE AND PORT WINE REDUCTION

A tiny piece of dark chocolate is a nice addition to the cheese and figs.

Serves 6

2 cups port wine

1 tablespoon cold unsalted butter

12 ounces Brie cheese

6 fresh figs

¼ cup confectioners' sugar

1. Heat the wine on medium in a medium-size saucepan, and let reduce by half. Remove from heat and add the cold butter.

2. Cut the Brie into 2-ounce portions. Cut the figs in half.

3. To serve, drizzle wine reduction on plates, sprinkle with confectioners' sugar, and arrange figs and Brie on top.

Chocolate and Cheese

Though it may not sound all too appealing at first, chocolate and cheese go extremely well together. A bit of fruit rounds off the combination.

DATE-ALMOND TART

For an added kick, use flavored yogurt with this recipe.

Serves 6

1 cup flour

2 teaspoons olive oil

1 teaspoon ice water

1 cup chopped dried dates

½ cup chopped almonds

½ cup honey

1 cup plain nonfat yogurt

¼ cup confectioners' sugar

1. Preheat the oven to 375°F.

2. Mix together the flour, olive oil, and ice water to form a dough. Roll out the dough into a pie shell. Place in a quiche or pie pan.

3. Mix together the dates, almonds, and honey. Place the date mixture in the center of the dough and loosely fold over pastry edges.

4. Bake for 20 minutes. Let cool and serve with yogurt and sprinkled confectioners' sugar.

FRESH FRUIT CHOWDER

For best results, use seasonal and local fruit when available.

Serves 6

2 peaches

2 plums

½ cup strawberries

½ cup blackberries

3 sprigs mint

1 cup canned cubed pineapple

½ cup blueberries

3 ounces nonfat plain yogurt

¼ cup cocoa powder (optional)

1. Cut the peaches and plums into wedges. Slice the strawberries. Slice the blackberries in half. Remove the bottom leaves from the mint sprigs and save the tops for garnish.

2. Purée the pineapple in a blender or food processor until smooth.

3. Mix the puréed pineapple with the other fruit and place in a shallow bowl. Dollop with yogurt and sprinkle with mint leaves and cocoa.

ROASTED PEARS

Try any favorite light wine with this recipe. Or, you can try pear cider or eau de vie.

Serves 6

6 pears

6 sprigs fresh mint

1 cup sweet white wine

1 tablespoon lemon zest

1 teaspoon honey

3 ounces low-fat vanilla yogurt

1. Preheat the oven to 375°F.

2. Peel the pears and cut in half from top to bottom. Chop the mint, saving the tops for garnish. Place the pears cut-side down in a small roasting pan and pour the wine over them. Sprinkle with zest and drizzle with honey.

3. Cover tightly and roast for approximately 40 minutes. Then uncover and roast for 10 minutes longer.

4. To serve, place ½-ounce dollops of yogurt on each plate. Prop half a pear on the dollop and sprinkle with chopped mint. Place mint sprig tops on sides for garnish.

APRICOT PASTRY

Any type of jam can be used. Also, try other kinds of nuts, such as almonds or pecans, for different flavors.

Serves 6

1 cup flour

2 teaspoons olive oil

1 teaspoon ice water

2 cups chopped apricots

½ cup chopped walnuts

½ cup currants

¼ cup apricot jam

¼ cup light brown sugar

1. Preheat the oven to 375°F.

2. Mix together the flour, olive oil, and ice water to form a dough. Roll out the dough into a large square and place on a baking sheet.

3. Arrange the apricots, nuts, currants, jam, and sugar in the center and pinch together the edges up to 1 or 2 inches from center. Fold back the corners to leave a small opening in the center. Bake for 30 minutes.

LIME TART

Try using key limes for a richer lime flavor. Also, add some zest to the crust!

Serves 6

Tart Crust

¼ cup unsalted butter

¼ cup olive oil

¼ cup whole-wheat flour

½ cup all-purpose flour

1 tablespoon water

Lime Filling

3 limes

3 eggs, beaten

2 tablespoons cornstarch

½ cup granulated sugar

1 cup water

1. Preheat the oven to 375°F.

2. To make the crust: Blend the butter and oil; sift together the flours; then combine the two mixtures with a dough hook at low speed (or by hand), adding the water 1 spoonful at a time. Roll out the dough on a floured surface, then place in a pie pan; bake for 10 minutes.

3. To make the lime filling: Juice the limes and grate the rinds for zest. Mix together all the filling ingredients; bring to a slow simmer in a medium-size saucepan, stirring constantly until it becomes thick. Pour the lime mixture into the parbaked pie shell and bake for 15 minutes longer.

BLUEBERRY RAVIOLI

You can bake the ravioli after boiling, but be sure to spray them with cooking spray first to prevent sticking.

Serves 6

½ cup all-purpose flour

¼ cup whole-wheat flour

¼ cup semolina

¼ cup granulated sugar

1 whole egg

1 egg white

2 tablespoons olive oil

1 tablespoon water

1 pint blueberries

¼ cup confectioners' sugar

1 teaspoon fresh-grated lemon zest

1. Mix together the flours, granulated sugar, eggs, oil, and water on low speed until fully incorporated. Let the dough rest for 1 hour in the refrigerator.

2. Roll out the dough on a floured surface. Cut into 4-inch squares and put a spoonful of blueberries into each square. Fold to form a triangle, and seal.

3. Bring 2 gallons of water to a boil. Cook the ravioli for approximately 6–8 minutes. Then strain, place on plates, and sprinkle with confectioners' sugar and zest before serving.

SAUTÉED STRAWBERRIES IN YOGURT SOUP

To make the most of this delectable dessert, serve with a dollop of nonfat vanilla yogurt.

Serves 6

1 cup skim milk

1 vanilla bean

2 tablespoons granulated sugar

2 cups nonfat plain yogurt

1 pint strawberries

1 tablespoon unsalted butter

¼ cup brown sugar

1. Heat the milk with the vanilla bean and granulated sugar in a small saucepan; let cool and remove vanilla bean. When the milk is completely cooled, whisk in the yogurt.

2. Slice the strawberries. Melt the butter and toss with the strawberries.

3. Serve the yogurt soup in a shallow bowl. Dollop with the strawberry mixture and sprinkle with brown sugar.

RICE PUDDING WITH CHERRIES IN WINE

Move over ordinary rice pudding, this rice pudding is sure to become your favorite!

Serves 6

1 cup port wine

¾ cup granulated sugar

1 pint Bing cherries, pitted

1 quart whole milk

1 cup basmati or jasmine rice

1 cinnamon stick

Zest of 1 lemon

4 tablespoons granulated sugar

1. In a saucepan, heat the wine and ¾ cup sugar over medium heat until the sugar dissolves. Add the cherries, and sauté for 2 minutes. Remove cherries and reduce sauce to the consistency of a dry, light jelly (also known as sec). Then mix the cherries back in and let cool.

2. In a pan, heat at low-medium temperature the milk, rice, cinnamon stick, and zest. Cook for about 1 hour, stirring frequently.

3. Add the sugar and stir until dissolved. Remove the cinnamon stick, and spoon the pudding into serving dishes. Let the pudding cool. When ready to serve, crown with cherries and wine mixture.

CITRUS SHERBET

Sherbet can be made with any fruit, as long as you have the right ratio of liquid, egg whites, and sugar.

Serves 8

4 Valencia oranges

2 Ruby Red grapefruits

1 key lime

1¼ cups granulated sugar

⅓ cup water

3 egg whites

¼ teaspoon cream of tartar

¼ teaspoon salt

Edible orchid or mint leaves, for garnish

1. Juice the oranges, grapefruits, and lime, then measure out 3 cups of unfiltered juice and set aside.

2. In a saucepan, combine the sugar and water. Bring to a boil, stirring until the sugar dissolves. Cook to 238°F (soft ball on a candy thermometer).

3. While this is cooking, beat the egg whites with the cream of tartar and salt until stiff. Slowly pour the hot syrup into the mixing bowl with the egg whites, continuing to beat at high speed. Continue to beat until the mixture is stiff and glossy (approximately 5 minutes).

4. Stir in the juices, then pour into a shallow pan. Freeze until almost firm, then return to the bowl. Beat again until blended. Return to the container for scooping or smaller serving dish and freeze.

5. To serve, remove from freezer, allowing 15 minutes before serving. Scoop and garnish.

ORANGE CREPES

Other citrus zest and juices can be substituted to suit your taste.

Serves 6

½ cup flour

2 whole eggs

2 egg whites

½ cup skim milk

1½ cups fresh orange juice, divided

1 teaspoon fresh orange zest, divided

½ teaspoon melted butter

1 teaspoon cold unsalted butter

¼ cup confectioners' sugar

1. In a bowl, mix together the flour, eggs, milk, ¼ cup of the orange juice, and ½ teaspoon of the orange zest.

2. Heat a griddle or sauté pan over medium heat. Brush with melted butter and pour in the batter. When the batter begins to bubble and the bottom of the crepe is a light golden brown, flip over and cook for just a few seconds. Remove and keep warm.

3. Prepare the orange syrup by boiling the remaining juice in a small pot. Continue boiling until the juice is reduced by half, then add the 1 teaspoon of cold butter.

4. To serve, place the crepe on a plate (fold if desired), drizzle with the reduced juice, and sprinkle with the remaining zest and sugar.

Whole Butter

Cold whole butter serves to slightly thicken sauces. Try it with this recipe to get a thicker orange syrup. Also, use it in other recipes where a thicker sauce appeals to you.

CLAFOUTIS WITH FRUIT

Clafoutis originated as a dessert made with cherries, but you can use any fruits you love. You can also try serving it chilled.

Serves 2

2 teaspoons unsalted butter, divided

2 cups seasonal fruit (cherries, raspberries, blueberries, blackberries, etc.)

½ cup granulated sugar, divided

2 eggs

1½ cups milk

6 teaspoons all-purpose flour

Confectioners' sugar

1. Preheat the oven to 400°F.

2. Butter individual ovenproof dishes using 1 teaspoon of butter. Sprinkle the fruit with ¼ cup of the granulated sugar and arrange in the bottom of each dish.

3. Mix together the eggs, milk, remaining butter and granulated sugar, and the flour 1 teaspoon at a time until a smooth batter is formed.

4. Pour this mixture over the fruit and bake for approximately 20 minutes, then reduce heat to 325°F and bake 10 minutes more. Insert a knife in the custard to test doneness. If the custard sticks to the knife, it isn't done yet. When the knife comes out clean, then it is done.

5. Sprinkle with confectioners' sugar and serve.

FRESH FRUIT AND MERINGUE

This recipe works well with soft fruits, such as blackberries, blueberries, and raspberries. A perfect ending to a picnic, this meringue provides a sweet, light finish to any summer lunch.

Serves 12

6 egg whites

½ cup granulated sugar

¼ teaspoon cream of tartar

2 cups chopped fresh fruit

¼ teaspoon fresh-grated lemon zest

½ pound chopped almonds

3 tablespoons honey

1. Preheat the oven to 200°F.

2. Line a baking sheet with parchment paper or spray with cooking spray.

3. In a copper or stainless steel bowl, beat the egg whites, sugar, and cream of tartar until stiff. Drop by the spoonful on baking sheet and bake in the oven for 5–6 hours, until dry, crispy, and lightly golden.

4. Serve with fresh seasonal fruit. Sprinkle with lemon zest, almonds, and honey.

POACHED APPLES

To make the most of this dessert, give it a beautiful presentation by dusting the plate with cocoa powder.

Serves 6

6 Granny Smith apples

1 lemon

1 cup apple cider

¼ cup sweet white wine

3 whole cloves or ¼ teaspoon ground cloves

2 cinnamon sticks or ½ teaspoon ground cinnamon

¼ cup golden raisins or confectionery sugar

1. Peel the apples (coring optional). Zest and juice the lemon.

2. Place the apples in a large saucepan with the cider, wine, lemon juice, zest, cloves, and cinnamon; simmer, covered, on medium heat for 30–45 minutes, until the apples are fork tender. Remove apples and keep warm.

3. Reduce the cooking liquid. Serve apples sprinkled with raisins.

CINNAMON ALMOND CAKE

This traditional cake is always a favorite. Add it to your next Thanksgiving meal for a striking touch of variety to the usual string of desserts.

Serves 12

1 cup sugar

¼ teaspoon grated lemon rind

6 egg yolks

½ pound finely ground almonds

½ teaspoon cinnamon

6 egg whites

½ cup heavy cream

¼ teaspoon granulated sugar

1 teaspoon brandy

Chopped almonds, for garnish

1. Preheat oven to 350°F.

2. Cream the sugar, rind, and yolks until light and fluffy. Stir in finely ground almonds and cinnamon.

3. Whip the egg whites until stiff. Stir a few tablespoons of whites into the almond mixture and then fold in the rest.

4. Pour into 2 greased 8-inch pans; bake for 45 minutes. Let cool briefly and remove from pans.

5. Whip the cream with the sugar and brandy. Spread between cake layers and then on top and sides. Garnish with chopped almonds.

DRINKS

GREEK MOUNTAIN TEA

Most Greek households have this tea on hand. You can buy some at any Greek grocery store.

Serves 4

6–8 branches Greek mountain tea

5 cups water

4 tablespoons honey

½ large lemon, cut into 4 wedges

1. Heat the tea and water in a medium pot until it boils. Reduce the heat to medium, and simmer for 5 minutes. Remove the pot from the heat, and allow the tea to steep for 5 minutes.

2. Pour the tea through a strainer into cups, and add 1 tablespoon of honey per cup.

3. Serve the tea hot with lemon wedges.

Greek Mountain Tea

Greek mountain tea is made from the leaves and flowers of *Sideritis* plants, also known as ironwort. These plants grow on the Greek mountainsides and are used by most Greek households. This tea is also known as "shepherd's tea" because shepherds would use the plants to brew tea while tending to their flocks in the mountains.

CAFÉ FRAPPÉ

Frappé is among the most popular drinks in Greece and is available at virtually all Greek cafés. Add a shot of ouzo to your afternoon frappé!

Serves 1

1 tablespoon instant coffee

1 teaspoon sugar

1 tablespoon water

Ice cubes

2 tablespoons evaporated milk

1. Put the coffee, sugar, and water into a cocktail shaker. Put the lid on and shake vigorously for 30 seconds.

2. Pour the creamy mixture into a tall glass with a few ice cubes. Add enough cold water to almost fill the glass.

3. Add milk and serve immediately with a straw.

Instant Coffee

Instant coffee became very popular in Europe when it was brought over by U.S. troops who demanded it in their ration kits. Once Europeans began using it, they were hooked. Now instant coffee is common in places like Greece, Portugal, and Spain.

CHAMOMILE TEA

This soothing and delicious tea will help you relax and can soothe an upset stomach.

Serves 1

1 teaspoon dried chamomile

1½ cups water

1 tablespoon honey

1 wedge lemon

1. Heat the chamomile and water in a medium pot until it boils. Reduce the heat to medium, and simmer for 30 seconds. Take the pot off the heat, and allow the tea to steep for 5 minutes.

2. Pour the tea through a strainer into a cup. Add the honey and serve it hot with a wedge of lemon.

Chamomile

The word *chamomile* is derived from the Greek word meaning "earth apple." When chamomile is in bloom, it looks like a daisy and is gathered and dried to make tea. Greeks drink it to help alleviate anxiety, reduce stress, and induce sleep.

GREEK COFFEE

Serve Greek coffee with koulouraki or sweets. A briki is a special one-handled pot used for making Greek coffees. It comes in various sizes and can be found in Greek or Middle Eastern shops. The grounds will remain at the bottom of the cup. Sip only until you detect a bit of the grounds.

Serves 1

Cold water

1 tablespoon Greek coffee

½ teaspoon sugar

1. Using a demitasse cup, measure the amount of cold water needed to make a serving of coffee. Put the water, coffee, and sugar in a briki.

2. Place the briki over medium heat. Swirl the briki until the coffee and sugar dissolve. As soon as the coffee foams, remove from the heat and pour into the demitasse.

3. Before drinking the coffee, allow the grounds to settle to the bottom of the cup; it will take about 1 minute.

Greek Coffee

Greek coffee is made by roasting a special blend of coffee beans and then grinding them into a fine powder. Visit a Greek specialty store or a Turkish or Middle Eastern shop for similar coffee.

OUZO ON ICE

You need to serve ouzo over ice to bring out its cloudy color and heighten the anise flavor.

Serves 1

1½ ounces ouzo

Ice

1. Pour the ouzo into a highball glass with as much ice as you desire. Remember the ice will melt and dilute the ouzo.

2. Swirl the glass and as soon as the mixture becomes cloudy, begin sipping.

Ouzo and Mezedes

Greeks eat when they drink, and they drink when they eat. Greece's national drink, ouzo, is meant to be sipped cold and always with food. Greeks do not drink shots of ouzo, rather they savor this anise-flavored aperitif with appetizers or, as Greeks call them, *mezedes*.

LEMON VERBENA TEA

Lemon verbena has a mint-lemon aroma that is very soothing. The lemon verbena plant was brought to Europe by Columbus as a gift for Spain's Queen Luisa.

Serves 4

½ cup loose lemon verbena leaves (dried or fresh)

5 cups water

4 tablespoons honey

½ large lemon, cut into 4 wedges

1. Heat the leaves and water in a medium pot until it boils. Reduce the heat to medium, and simmer the tea for 5 minutes. Remove the pot from the heat. Allow the tea to steep for 5 minutes.

2. Pour the tea through a strainer into cups; add 1 tablespoon of honey per cup.

3. Serve the tea hot with lemon wedges.

MASTIHA ON THE ROCKS

Mastiha liqueur is served as a digestive after a big meal.

Serves 1

3 or 4 ice cubes

1½ ounces Skinos Mastiha liqueur

Lemon wedge

1. Fill a rocks or cocktail glass with ice. Pour the mastiha over the ice.

2. Squeeze a lemon wedge over the glass and stir. Allow some of the ice to melt and sip away.

RAKOMELO

Rakomelo is popular in the westernmost part of Crete, in Hania. This after-dinner digestive is made of raki (what many Cretans call tsikoudia). Rakomelo is served cold, and it is a golden color with obvious notes of cinnamon.

Serves 4

4 cups raki or tsipouro or grappa

¼ cup honey

2 cinnamon sticks

2 whole cloves

1. Heat all the ingredients in a large pot over medium-low heat to a slow boil. Stir occasionally. Once the mixture boils, remove it from the heat.

2. Allow the rakomelo to cool, and pour it into a glass bottle with a lid. Serve rakomelo chilled as a digestive after dinner.

METAXA MINT JULEP

This drink is inspired by the classic Mint Julep, which consists of Kentucky bourbon poured into a glass of muddled mint, lime, and sugar. Metaxa brandy replaces the bourbon in this Mediterranean recipe.

Serves 1

1 teaspoon coarse brown sugar

¼ large lime

4 or 5 fresh mint leaves

1½ ounces Metaxa brandy

Ice

1. Put the brown sugar, lime, and mint into a rocks or cocktail glass and muddle for a minute.

2. Add the brandy to the glass and fill it with ice.

3. Allow the ice to melt for a couple of minutes before sipping.

Muddling

Muddling is a bartending term that refers to crushing herbs and fruit to release their oils and flavors into a drink. Muddlers are usually made of wood and come in all sizes. If you don't have one, use the opposite end of a wooden spoon.

MASTIHA COCKTAIL

This is the perfect summer cocktail for a Greek dinner or cocktail party.

Serves 1

¼ cup peeled, seeded, and chopped English cucumber

¼ large lime

⅛ teaspoon salt

½ teaspoon sugar

1½ ounces mastiha liqueur

1 ounce gin

3 or 4 ice cubes

2 ounces club soda, tonic water, or lemon-lime soda

1 lime wedge

1. Add the cucumber, lime, salt, and sugar to a rocks glass. Muddle the ingredients to mash the cucumber and release the oils from the lime.

2. Stir in the mastiha and gin. Add ice, and top with the club soda. Serve the cocktail with a lime wedge.

GREEK SUMMER SANGRIA

This sangria is infused with cinnamon and cloves and has just enough sweetness to be refreshing. This recipe can easily be doubled and tripled.

Serves 10

1 cup water

½ cup sugar

2 strips lemon or orange peel, pith removed

½ cinnamon stick

3 whole cloves

¼ cup honey

1 (25-ounce) bottle red wine

½ cup Metaxa brandy or any other brandy

1 ripe medium peach, sliced

1 medium orange, sliced

24 ounces ginger ale

1. Bring the water, sugar, lemon or orange peel, cinnamon, and cloves to a boil in a small pot over medium-high heat. Lower the heat to medium-low, and cook for another 5 minutes. Remove the pot from the heat, and add the honey. Allow the mixture to cool completely. Remove peel, cinnamon, and cloves. Reserve.

2. Pour the remaining ingredients into a large pitcher. Add the reserved syrup in increments. Keep tasting after each addition of syrup until the sangria reaches your desired level of sweetness. Any remaining syrup can be used in another sangria.

3. Cover and refrigerate the sangria overnight. Serve it cold over ice.

WINDEX COCKTAIL

The American romantic comedy My Big Fat Greek Wedding *brought the Greek immigrant experience into the mainstream. The father in the movie was convinced that Windex cured all. This cocktail offers a fun version you can make at parties.*

Serves 4

5 ounces ouzo

4 ounces blue curaçao liqueur

1⅓ cups lemonade

Ice cubes

1. Pour the ouzo, blue curaçao, and lemonade into a large cocktail shaker with ice, and shake to mix.

2. Pour the cocktail into chilled martini glasses or martini glasses filled with ice and serve.

TSIPOURO

Tsipouro is a spirit enjoyed throughout Greece, although it may have a different name in other parts of the country. In Crete, it is tsikoudia; in other places, it's raki.

Serves 1

1½ ounces tsipouro

Ice

1. Pour the tsipouro into a highball glass with as much ice as you desire. Remember, the ice will melt and dilute the tsipouro.

2. Swirl the glass and as soon as the mixture becomes cloudy, begin sipping.

Tsipouro

Tsipouro is made by distilling grapes. Often it is double-distilled for a cleaner, purer product. Tsipouro is available unflavored, where the flavor of the grapes comes through in the finish. It is also flavored with anise, which makes it taste similar to ouzo but not as sweet. Although tsipouro is meant to be served after dinner as a digestive, it is gaining popularity with Greeks who prefer it to ouzo. It is now also acceptable to sip tsipouro with appetizers, or *mezedes*.

STANDARD U.S./METRIC MEASUREMENT CONVERSIONS

VOLUME CONVERSIONS

U.S. Volume Measure	Metric Equivalent
⅛ teaspoon	0.5 milliliter
¼ teaspoon	1 milliliter
½ teaspoon	2 milliliters
1 teaspoon	5 milliliters
½ tablespoon	7 milliliters
1 tablespoon (3 teaspoons)	15 milliliters
2 tablespoons (1 fluid ounce)	30 milliliters
¼ cup (4 tablespoons)	60 milliliters
⅓ cup	90 milliliters
½ cup (4 fluid ounces)	125 milliliters
⅔ cup	160 milliliters
¾ cup (6 fluid ounces)	180 milliliters
1 cup (16 tablespoons)	250 milliliters
1 pint (2 cups)	500 milliliters
1 quart (4 cups)	1 liter (about)

WEIGHT CONVERSIONS

U.S. Weight Measure	Metric Equivalent
½ ounce	15 grams
1 ounce	30 grams
2 ounces	60 grams
3 ounces	85 grams
¼ pound (4 ounces)	115 grams
½ pound (8 ounces)	225 grams
¾ pound (12 ounces)	340 grams
1 pound (16 ounces)	454 grams

OVEN TEMPERATURE CONVERSIONS

Degrees Fahrenheit	Degrees Celsius
200 degrees F	95 degrees C
250 degrees F	120 degrees C
275 degrees F	135 degrees C
300 degrees F	150 degrees C
325 degrees F	160 degrees C
350 degrees F	180 degrees C
375 degrees F	190 degrees C
400 degrees F	205 degrees C
425 degrees F	220 degrees C
450 degrees F	230 degrees C

BAKING PAN SIZES

U.S.	Metric
8 × 1½ inch round baking pan	20 × 4 cm cake tin
9 × 1½ inch round baking pan	23 × 3.5 cm cake tin
11 × 7 × 1½ inch baking pan	28 × 18 × 4 cm baking tin
13 × 9 × 2 inch baking pan	30 × 20 × 5 cm baking tin
2 quart rectangular baking dish	30 × 20 × 3 cm baking tin
15 × 10 × 2 inch baking pan	30 × 25 × 2 cm baking tin (Swiss roll tin)
9 inch pie plate	22 × 4 or 23 × 4 cm pie plate
7 or 8 inch springform pan	18 or 20 cm springform or loose bottom cake tin
9 × 5 × 3 inch loaf pan	23 × 13 × 7 cm or 2 lb narrow loaf or pâté tin
1½ quart casserole	1.5 liter casserole
2 quart casserole	2 liter casserole

INDEX

ABOUT THE AUTHOR

PETER MINAKI is the creator of the popular *Kalofagas—Greek Food & Beyond* food blog. (*Kalofagas* is the Greek word for "gourmet.") Known for adding twists to his recipes, Peter balances his posts between traditional favorites, modernized takes on classics, and his own unique recipes. Peter is a frequent contributor to Greece's Free Press gastronomy website and has appeared on TV cooking segments in Greece and in Canada. His recipes have been featured in *Canadian Living Magazine* (Canada), *OPA* magazine (Australia), *National Herald* (United States), *Stahl* magazine (Hungary), and *Ensemble Vacations* magazine (Canada).